Landmarks of the Western Heritage

VOLUME II

Landmarks of the

Western Heritage

VOLUME TWO

1715 to the Present

SECOND EDITION

Edited by

C. Warren Hollister

University of California, Santa Barbara

JOHN WILEY & SONS

New York · Chichester · Brisbane · Toronto · Singapore

Library of Congress Cataloging in Publication Data:

Hollister, Charles Warren, comp.
  Landmarks of the Western Heritage.

   CONTENTS: v. 1. The Ancient Near East to 1789.—
v. 2. 1715 to the Present.
   1. Civilization, Occidental—Addresses, essays,
lectures. I. Title.

CB245.H6 1973 910'.03'1821 72–7315
ISBN 0–471–40704–6 (v. 2)

Printed in the United States of America

10

To Nancy

PREFACE

This new, revised edition has a simplified organizational scheme as well as improvements in the format and headnotes. I have also deleted some material that proved to be unclear or redundant and have included a number of new selections, many of them at the suggestion of professors and students who used the first edition. I thank these individuals for their good advice, particularly, Professors Gloria Aronson, Gerald Owen, Theodore G. Corbett, David C. Riede, John W. Osborne, Melvyn Berens, Stan Claussen, Edward Pessen, and Joseph W. Ink. I am grateful to my editorial assistants in Santa Barbara, Mrs. Randi Johnson and Carole Moore, for their labors, their erudition, and their perceptive judgment.

C. Warren Hollister

PREFACE TO THE FIRST EDITION

This book of readings is intended primarily for students in Western Civilization courses. It was prepared in the belief that exposure to a substantial body of original sources provides an essential supplement to the reading of textbooks and modern interpretive studies. Original sources provide a direct encounter with the past that is obtainable in no other way, besides exploring historic sites or examining in museums the cultural products of past ages. Textbooks and lectures enable students to learn about the past; the reading of sources deepens this learning process by enabling students, in some small degree, to *experience* the past. This experience is apt to leave the student with the feeling that history is by no means so neat, simple, and "well-organized" as many textbooks would suggest. The sources raise questions that are yet unsolved or are highly controversial. They illustrate trends and climates of opinion, while at the same time making explicit the exceptions and loose ends that defy the structured categories of the historian. Hence, encounter with the sources is likely to make a Western Civilization course at once more difficult and more authentic.

The selection of sources to be included in a book such as this is necessarily a very difficult process, circumscribed by the limitations of space and dependent on the inclinations and judgments of the individual editor. This book was prepared with certain fundamental ideas in mind. First of all, Western Civilization is far more than a mere sequence of political events. Politics cannot be ignored but must be balanced against social and economic developments and the products of mind and spirit. No proper course in Western Civilization can exclude philosophy or science, economic or political thought, literature or the arts. Painting, sculpture, architecture, and poetry, for example, are almost invariably overlooked in the typical source book, yet they are historical documents of immense significance. Literary and artistic sources will be found here along with the more normal political texts and intellectual treatises, because all are necessary to convey a comprehensive picture of an historical epoch or a cultural milieu.

Finally, in the conviction that a source book should neither substitute for a textbook nor harness the student to the interpretations of the editor, introductory material and editorial comment have been kept to a minimum. By and large, the sources have been left to stand on their own, to challenge the student's judgment and imagination, to supplement lectures in any way that the instructor might devise, and to evoke wide-ranging discussion.

A number of people have given generously of their labors and talents in the preparation of these volumes. I am particularly grateful to Mrs. Barbara Walker and Miss Nancy Unger for their wise and devoted editorial assistance, as well as to Mrs. Betty Fervolino for her patience with detail. Mrs. Mary Ellington and Professor Thomas Reeves contributed their time and perceptive judgment. William L. Gum, editor and friend, shared with me the initial conception of the project and supported it firmly and sympathetically. All of these people made important intellectual contributions to the work. It was, for example, Gum's provocative idea to break with tradition and exclude Woodrow Wilson's often quoted Fourteen Points.

C. Warren Hollister
Santa Barbara, California

CONTENTS

PART ONE

The Age of Reason

c. 1715–1789

THE seven and a half decades between the death of Louis XIV and the advent of the French Revolution constituted an era of relative peace, security, and optimism. The age was marked by dynastic power politics and wars in both Europe and her New World colonies, but the military struggles were less severe than the wars of the sixteenth and seventeenth centuries or the subsequent French Revolution and the wars of the Napoleonic era. The grandiosity and tortured fluidity of Baroque art gradually gave way to a strict Neo-Classicism—simple, elegant, and restrained. The emotionalism of Baroque poetry was replaced by the balanced verses and optimistic humanism of Alexander Pope and his contemporaries. This was an age of mature, confident synthesis—a new Augustan Age—a relatively peaceful intermission between the religious struggles of the past and the national and social upheavals of the future.

This was, above all, the age of Enlightenment, less original perhaps than the age of genius that preceded it, but imbued with the thought of John Locke and Isaac Newton that nature was orderly and harmonious and that the universe was fundamentally rational. Newton was the patron saint of the Enlightenment, and eighteenth-century thought was beguiled by the vision of the Newtonian world-machine. It was the elusive goal of many Enlightenment thinkers to apply the principles of reason and the harmony of nature to the problems of man and society exactly as Newton had applied them with such spectacular success to the operations of the physical universe. Philosophers such as Voltaire endeavored to rationalize religion, stripping it of superstition and reducing it to its essentials. Voltaire was a deist—he believed in God as the creator of the world-machine but rejected prayer, miracles, holy water, and all the myriad trappings of organized religion. Others, such as David Hume, rejected deism itself as rationally unverifiable, and took a completely skeptical position with regard to God and his works.

The *philosophes* of the Enlightenment sought also to rationalize government and society—to purge the state of inefficient customs and archaic institutions, and to create a rational political order. Voltaire and others endorsed enlightened despotism, giving their blessing to "enlightened" monarchs such as Frederick the Great of Prussia. Enlightenment ideals had at least a superficial effect on the policies of a number of contemporary rulers. Other intellectuals of the day, following Locke, advocated limited, constitutional monarchy and even republicanism, cast within the framework of a carefully ordered constitution. The political ideas of Jean Jacques Rousseau, which transcend in many ways the intellectual categories of the Enlightenment, tended toward a version of popular government based on the rather vague concept of the "general will" which was all-powerful and could not err. Rousseau's state, despite its more-or-less popular basis, was so limitless in its power that some scholars have regarded it as a precursor of modern totalitarianism.

The prevailing concept of natural order and harmony expressed itself in the realm of economic thought in the works of the French Physiocrats and the Englishman Adam Smith. These men were deeply hostile to the widespread policies of government regulation, protective tariffs, state bounties, and navigation laws that constituted the machinery of mercantilism. They argued that economic life was governed by natural laws which were no less orderly, dependable, or beneficent than the laws of physics. The economic system should be left to function without interference; the state should keep its hands off—should follow a policy of strict *laissez-faire*.

In these and other ways, the core concepts of reason and natural order dominated eighteenth-century thought. They were often accompanied by a fundamental optimism with regard to man's future. Reason, many *philosophes* believed, would open the way to a far better world, more prosperous, more peaceful, and more just than anything that Europe had theretofore experienced.

CHAPTER 1

THE RATIONALIZATION
OF NATURE

a. ROGER COTES, FROM HIS "PREFACE" TO THE SECOND EDITION OF NEWTON'S *PRINCIPIA*, 1713

NEWTON HIMSELF was a devoted Christian, as were many of his followers. The excerpt from Roger Cotes' "Preface" to the second edition of Newton's Principia *(1713), demonstrates how the Newtonian world-machine might be regarded as the handiwork of the Christian God. It also illustrates the profound reverence of eighteenth-century writers toward Newton and his thought. The vision of a mechanical universe may have seemed to some to be consistent with Christianity; to others it drained the cosmos of its mystery and transformed God from a loving, compassionate Father to a remote watchmaker who, in creating the ordered universe, had performed his essential task and was no longer needed.*

Without all doubt, this world, so diversified with that variety of forms and motions we find in it, could arise from nothing but the perfectly free will of God directing and presiding over all.

From this Fountain it is that those laws, which we call the laws of Nature, have flowed; in which there appear many traces, indeed, of the most wise contrivance, but not the least shadow of necessity. These, therefore, we must not seek from uncertain conjectures, but learn them from observations and experiments. He who thinks to find the true principles of physics and the laws of natural things by the force alone of his own mind, and the internal light of his reason, must either suppose that the world exists by necessity, and by the same necessity follows the laws proposed; or, if the order of Nature was established by the will of God, that himself, a miserable reptile, can tell what was fittest to be done. All sound and true philosophy is founded on the appearances of things, which, if they draw us ever so much against our wills to such principles as most clearly manifest to us the most excellent counsel and supreme dominion of the Allwise and Almighty Being, those principles are not therefore to be laid aside, because some men may perhaps dislike them. They may call them, if they please, miracles or occult qualities; but names maliciously given ought not to be a disadvantage to the

5

things themselves; unless they will say, at last, that all philosophy ought to be founded in atheism. Philosophy must not be corrupted in complaisance to these men; for the order of things will not be changed.

Fair and equal judges will therefore give sentence in favour of this most excellent method of philosophy, which is founded on experiments and observations. To this method it is hardly to be said or imagined what light, what splendor, hath accrued from this admirable work of our illustrious author, whose happy and sublime genius, resolving the most difficult problems, and reaching to discoveries of which the mind of man was thought incapable before, is deservedly admired by all those who are somewhat more than superficially versed in these matters. The gates are now set open; and by his means we may freely enter into the knowledge of the hidden secrets and wonders of natural things. He has so clearly laid open and set before our eyes the most beautiful frame of the System of the World, that, if King Alphonsus were now alive, he would not complain for want of the graces either of simplicity or of harmony in it. Therefore we may now more nearly behold the beauties of Nature, and entertain ourselves with the delightful contemplation; and, which is the best and most valuable fruit of philosophy, be thence incited the more profoundly to reverence and adore the great Maker and Lord of all. He must be blind, who, from the most wise and excellent contrivances of things, cannot see the infinite wisdom and goodness of their Almighty Creator; and he must be mad and senseless who refuses to acknowledge them.

b. ALEXANDER POPE ON THE HARMONY OF NATURE, FROM HIS "ESSAY ON MAN," 1734

REVERENCE FOR REASON and the harmony of nature, which was so basic to the thought of the Enlightenment, expressed itself in countless ways. We have included here two celebrations of the Newtonian natural order. The first of these is Alexander Pope's Neo-Classical poem "Essay on Man" (1734)—written in the form of epistles to the English deist, Henry St. John, Lord Bolingbroke.

Epistle I

Awake, my St. John! leave all meaner things
To low ambition, and the pride of Kings.

Let us (since Life can little more supply
Than just to look about us and to die)
Expatiate free o'er all this scene of Man;
A mighty maze! but not without a plan;
A Wild, where weeds and flow'rs promiscuous shoot;
Or Garden, tempting with forbidden fruit.
Together let us beat this ample field,
Try what the open, what the covert yield;
The latent tracts, the giddy heights, explore
Of all who blindly creep, or sightless soar;
Eye Nature's walks, shoot Folly as it flies,
And catch the Manners living as they rise;
Laugh where we must, be candid where we can;
But vindicate the ways of God to Man.

    I. Say first, of God above, or Man below,
What can we reason, but from what we know?
Of Man, what see we but his station here,
From which to reason, or to which refer?
Thro' worlds unnumber'd tho' the God be known,
'T is ours to trace him only in our own.
He, who thro' vast immensity can pierce,
See worlds on worlds compose one universe,
Observe how system into system runs,
What other planets circle other suns,
What vary'd Being peoples ev'ry star,
May tell why Heav'n has made us as we are.
But of this frame the bearings, and the ties,
The strong connexion, nice dependencies,
Gradations just, has thy pervading soul
Look'd thro'? or can a part contain the whole?
    Is the great chain, that draws all to agree,
And drawn supports, upheld by God, or thee?

    II. Presumptuous Man! the reason wouldst thou find,
Why form'd so weak, so little, and so blind?
First, if thou canst, the harder reason guess,
Why form'd no weaker, blinder, and no less?

    VII. Far as Creation's ample range extends,
The scale of sensual, mental pow'rs ascends:
Mark how it mounts, to Man's imperial race,
From the green myriads in the peopled grass:
What modes of sight betwixt each wide extreme,
The mole's dim curtain, and the lynx's beam:
Of smell, the headlong lioness between,
And hound sagacious on the tainted green:

Of hearing, from the life that fills the Flood,
To that which warbles thro' the vernal wood:
The spider's touch, how exquisitely fine!
Feels at each thread, and lives along the line:
In the nice bee, what sense so subtly true
From pois'nous herbs extracts the healing dew?
How Instinct varies in the grov'ling swine,
Compar'd, half-reas'ning elephant, with thine!
'Twixt that, and Reason, what a nice barrier,
For ever sep'rate, yet for ever near!
Remembrance and Reflection how ally'd;
What thin partitions Sense from Thought divide:
And Middle natures, how they long to join,
Yet never pass th' insuperable line!
Without this just gradation, could they be
Subjected, these to those, or all to thee?
The pow'rs of all subdu'd by thee alone,
Is not thy Reason all these pow'rs in one?

    VIII. See, thro' this air, this ocean, and this earth,
All matter quick, and bursting into birth.
Above, how high, progressive life may go!
Around, how wide! how deep extend below!
Vast chain of Being! which from God began,
Natures ethereal, human, angel, man,
Beast, bird, fish, insect, what no eye can see,
No glass can reach; from Infinite to thee,
From thee to Nothing.—On superior pow'rs
Were we to press, inferior might on ours:
Or in the full creation leave a void,
Where, one step broken, the great scale's destroy'd:
From Nature's chain whatever link you strike,
Tenth or ten thousandth, breaks the chain alike.
    And, if each system in gradation roll
Alike essential to th' amazing Whole,
The least confusion but in one, not all
That system only, but the Whole must fall.
Let Earth unbalanc'd from her orbit fly,
Planets and Suns run lawless thro' the sky;
Let ruling angels from their spheres be hurl'd,
Being on Being wreck'd, and world on world;
Heav'n's whole foundations to their centre nod,
And Nature tremble to the throne of God.
All this dread Order break—for whom? for thee?
Vile worm!—Oh Madness! Pride! Impiety!

IX. What if the foot, ordain'd the dust to tread,
Or hand, to toil, aspir'd to be the head?
What if the head, the eye, or ear repin'd
To serve mere engines to the ruling Mind?
Just as absurd for any part to claim
To be another, in this gen'ral frame:
Just as absurd, to mourn the tasks or pains,
The great directing Mind of All ordains.
    All are but parts of one stupendous whole,
Whose body Nature is, and God the soul;
That, chang'd thro' all, and yet in all the same;
Great in the earth, as in th' ethereal frame;
Warms in the sun, refreshes in the breeze,
Glows in the stars, and blossoms in the trees,
Lives thro' all life, extends thro' all extent,
Spreads undivided, operates unspent;
Breathes in our soul, informs our mortal part,
As full, as perfect, in a hair as heart:
As full, as perfect, in vile Man that mourns,
As the rapt Seraph that adores and burns:
To him no high, no low, no great, no small;
He fills, he bounds, connects, and equals all.

    X. Cease then, nor Order Imperfection name:
Our proper bliss depends on what we blame.
Know thy own point: This kind, this due degree
Of blindness, weakness, Heav'n bestows on thee.
Submit.—In this, or any other sphere,
Secure to be as blest as thou canst bear:
Safe in the hand of one disposing Pow'r,
Or in the natal, or the mortal hour.
All Nature is but Art, unknown to thee;
All Chance, Direction, which thou canst not see;
All Discord, Harmony not understood;
All partial Evil, universal Good:
And, spite of Pride, in erring Reason's spite,
One truth is clear, WHATEVER IS, IS RIGHT.

SOURCE. *Poetical Works of Alexander Pope,* Boston: Little, Brown & Co., 1854, II, pp. 36–48.

c. BARON D'HOLBACH, PRAYER TO NATURE, 1770

THE CHRISTIAN GOD is forthrightly rejected in this "prayer," taken from the comprehensive work, The System of Nature, *by the important eighteenth-century physicist, Baron d'Holbach.*

O Nautre, sovereign of all beings! and ye, her adorable daughters, Virtue, Reason, and Truth! remain forever our revered protectors! it is to you that belong the praises of the human race; to you appertains the homage of the earth. Show us then, O Nature! that which man ought to do, in order to obtain the happiness which thou makest him desire. Virtue! animate him with thy beneficent fire. Reason! conduct his uncertain steps through the paths of life. Truth! let thy torch illumine his intellect, dissipate the darkness of his road. Unite, O assisting deities! your powers, in order to submit the hearts of mankind to your dominion. Banish error from our mind; wickedness from our hearts; confusion from our footsteps; cause knowledge to extend its salubrious reign; goodness to occupy our souls; serenity to occupy our bosoms.

SOURCE. John Herman Randall, *The Making of the Modern Mind,* rev. ed., Boston: Houghton Mifflin Co., 1940, p. 279. Reprinted by permission of Houghton Mifflin Co.

Chapter 2

THE RATIONALIZATION OF RELIGION AND SOCIETY

a. CATHOLICISM AND DEISM: VOLTAIRE, FROM THE *PHILOSOPHICAL DICTIONARY*

VOLTAIRE'S HOSTILITY to the Church and his advocacy of deism emerge clearly from the passages included here from his Philosophical Dictionary *(which began to appear in 1764). The first two are witty attacks on organized religion; the last—"Theist"—is a statement in support of the deist position, a belief in God stripped of "superstitious" accretions Voltaire treated "deist" and "theist" as synonyms.*

Abbé

The word *abbé*, let it be remembered, signifies father. If you become one you render a service to the state; you doubtless perform the best work that a man can perform; you give birth to a thinking being. In this action there is something divine. But if you are *Monsieur l' Abbé* only because you have had your head shaved, wear a clerical collar, and a short cloak, and are waiting for a fat benefice, you do not deserve the name of *abbé*.

The ancient monks gave this name to the superior whom they elected; the *abbé* was their spiritual father. What different things do the same words signify at different times! The spiritual father was a poor man at the head of others equally poor; but the poor spiritual fathers have since had incomes of two hundred or four hundred thousand livres, and there are poor spiritual fathers in Germany who have regiments of guards.

A poor man, making a vow of poverty, and in consequence becoming a sovereign? It has been said before, but it must be said a thousand times: this is intolerable. The laws protest such an abuse; religion is shocked by it, and the really poor, who want food and clothing, appeal to heaven at the door of *Monsieur l'Abbé.*

But I hear the *abbés* of Italy, Germany, Flanders, and Burgundy ask: "Why are not we to accumulate wealth and honors? Why are we not to become princes? The bishops, who were originally poor, are like us; they have enriched and elevated themselves; one of them has become superior even to kings; let us imitate them as far as we are able."

Gentleman, you are right. Invade the land; it belongs to him whose strength or skill obtains possession of it. You have made ample use of the times of ignorance, superstition, and infatuation, to strip us of our inheritances, and trample us under your feet, that you might fatten on the substance of the unfortunate. But tremble for fear that the day of reason will arrive! . . .

Religion

Tonight I was in a meditative mood. I was absorbed in the contemplation of nature; I admired the immensity, the movements, the harmony of those infinite globes which the vulgar do not know how to admire.

I admired still more the intelligence which directs these vast forces. I said to myself: "One must be blind not to be dazzled by this spectacle; one must be stupid not to recognize the author of it; one must be mad not to worship Him. What tribute of worship should I render Him? Should not this tribute be the same in the whole of space, since it is the same supreme power which reigns equally in all space? Should not a thinking being who dwells in a star in the Milky Way offer Him the same homage as the thinking being on this little globe where we are? Light is uniform for the star Sirius and for us; moral philosophy must be uniform. If a sentient, thinking animal in Sirius is born of a tender father and mother who have been occupied with his happiness, he owes them as much love and care as we owe to our parents. If someone in the Milky Way sees a needy cripple, if he can help him, and if he does not do so, he is guilty in the sight of all globes. Everywhere the heart has the same duties: on the steps of the throne of God, if He has a throne; and in the depth of the abyss, if He is an abyss."

I was plunged in these ideas when one of those genii who throng the interplanetary spaces came down to me. I recognized this aerial creature as one who had appeared to me on another occasion, to teach me how different God's judgments were from our own, and how a good action is preferable to an argument.

He transported me into a desert, covered with piles of bones; and between these heaps of dead men there were walks of evergreen trees, and at the end of each walk there was a tall man of august mien, who regarded these sad remains with pity.

"Alas! my archangel," said I, "where have you brought me?"

"To desolation," he answered.

"And who are these fine patriarchs whom I see sad and motionless at the end of these green walks? They seem to be weeping over this countless crowd of dead."

"You shall know, poor human creature," answered the genie from the interplanetary spaces. "But first of all you must weep."

He began with the first pile. "These," he said, "are the twenty-three thousand Jews who danced before a calf, with the twenty-four thousand who were killed while lying with Midianitish women. The number of those massacred for such errors and offenses amounts to nearly three hundred thousand.

"In the other walks are the bones of the Christians slaughtered by each other in metaphysical quarrels. They are divided into several heaps of four centuries each. One heap would have mounted right to the sky, so they had to be divided."

"What!" I cried. "Brothers have treated their brothers like this, and I have the misfortune to be of this brotherhood!"

"Here," said the spirit, "are the twelve million Americans killed in their native land because they had not been baptized."

"My God! why did you not leave these frightful bones to dry in the hemisphere where their bodies were born, and where they were consigned to so many different deaths? Why assemble here all these abominable monuments to barbarism and fanaticism?"

"To instruct you."

"Since you wish to instruct me," I said to the genie, "tell me if there have been peoples other than the Christians and the Jews in whom zeal and religion wretchedly transformed into fanaticism have inspired so many horrible cruelties."

"Yes," he said. "The Mohammedans were sullied with the same inhumanities, but rarely; and when one asked *amman,* pity, of them and offered them tribute, they were merciful. As for the other nations, there has not been a single one, from the beginning of the world, which has ever made a purely religious war. Follow me now." I followed him.

A little beyond these piles of dead men, we found other piles; they were composed of sacks of gold and silver, and each had its label: "Substance of the heretics massacred in the eighteenth century, the seventeenth, and the sixteenth." And so on in going back: "Gold and silver of Americans slaughtered," etc., etc. And all these piles were surmounted with crosses, mitres, croziers, and triple crowns studded with precious stones.

"What, my genie! Do you mean that these dead were piled up for the sake of their wealth?"

"Yes, my son."

I wept. And when, by my grief, I was worthy of being led to the end of the green walks, he led me there.

"Contemplate," he said, "the heroes of humanity who were the world's benefactors, and who were all united in banishing from the world, as far as they were able, violence and rapine. Question them."

I ran to the first of the band. He had a crown on his head, and a little censer in his hand. I humbly asked him his name. "I am Numa Pompilius," he said to me. "I succeeded a brigand, and I had to govern brigands. I taught them virtue and the worship of God, but after me they forgot both more than once. I forbade that there should be any image in the temples, because the Deity which animates nature cannot be represented. During my reign the Romans had neither wars nor seditions, and my religion did nothing but good. All the neighboring peoples came to honor me at my funeral; and a unique honor it was."

I kissed his hand, and I went to the second. He was a fine old man about a hundred years old, clad in a white robe. He put his middle finger on his mouth, and with the other hand he cast some beans behind him. I recognized Pythagoras. He assured me he had never had a golden thigh, and that he had never been a cock; but that he had governed the Crotoniates with as much justice as Numa governed the Romans, almost at the same time; and that this justice was the rarest and most necessary thing in the world. I learned that the Pythagoreans examined their consciences twice a day. The honest people! How far we are from them! But we, who have been nothing but assassins for thirteen hundred years, we call these wise men arrogant.

In order to please Pythagoras, I did not say a word to him, and I passed on to Zoroaster, who was occupied in concentrating the celestial fire in the focus of a concave mirror, in the middle of a hall with a hundred doors which all led to wisdom. (Zoroaster's precepts are called *doors,* and are a hundred in number.) Over the principal door I read these words which are the sum of all moral philosophy, and which cut short all the disputes of the casuists: "When in doubt if an action is good or bad, refrain."

"Certainly," I said to my genie, "the barbarians who immolated all these victims had never read these beautiful words."

We then saw Zaleucus, Thales, Anaximander, and all the sages who had sought truth and practiced virtue.

When we came to Socrates, I recognized him very quickly by his flat nose. "Well," I said to him, "so you are one of the Almighty's confidants! All the inhabitants of Europe, except the Turks and the Tartars of the Crimea, who know nothing, pronounce your name with respect. It is revered, loved, this great name, to the point that people have wanted to know those of your persecutors. Melitus and Anitus are known because of you, just as Ravaillac is known because of Henry IV; but I know only this name of Anitus. I do not know precisely who was the scoundrel who culumniated you, and who succeeded in having you condemned to drink hemlock."

"Since my adventure," replied Socrates, "I have never thought about that man, but seeing that you make me remember it, I pity him. He was a wicked priest who secretly conducted a business in hides, a trade reputed shameful among us. He sent his two children to my school. The other disciples taunted them with having a father who was a currier, and they were obliged to leave. The irritated father did not rest until he had stirred up all the priests and all the sophists against me. They persuaded the council of five hundred that I was an impious fellow who did not believe that the Moon, Mercury, and Mars were gods. Indeed, I used to think, as I think now, that there is only one God, master of all nature. The judges handed me over to the poisoner of the republic. He cut short my life by a few days: I died peacefully at the age of seventy, and since that time I have led a happy life with all these great men whom you see, and of whom I am the least.''

After enjoying some time in conversation with Socrates, I went forward with my guide into a grove situated above the thickets where all the sages of antiquity seemed to be tasting sweet repose.

I saw a man of gentle, simple countenance, who seemed to me to be about thirty-five years old. From afar he cast compassionate glances on these piles of whitened bones, across which I had had to pass to reach the sages' abode. I was astonished to find his feet swollen and bleeding, his hands likewise, his side pierced, and his ribs flayed with whip cuts. "Good Heavens!" I said to him, "is it possible for a just man, a sage, to be in this state? I have just seen one who was treated in a very hateful way, but there is no comparison between his torture and yours. Wicked priests and wicked judges poisoned him. Were priests and judges your torturers?''

He answered with much courtesy: "Yes.''

"And who were these monsters?''

"They were hypocrites.''

"Ah! that says everything. I understand by this single word that they must have condemned you to death. Had you proved to them then, as Socrates did, that the Moon was not a goddess, and that Mercury was not a god?''

"No, these planets were not in question. My compatriots did not know what a planet is; they were all errant ignoramuses. Their superstitions were quite different from those of the Greeks.''

"You wanted to teach them a new religion, then?''

"Not at all. I said to them simply: 'Love God with all your heart and your fellow creature as yourself, for that is man's whole duty.' Judge if this precept is not as old as the universe; judge if I brought them a new religion. I did not stop telling them that I had come not to destroy the law but to fulfill it. I observed all their rites; circumcized as they all were, baptized as were the most zealous among them. Like them I paid the Corban; I observed the Passover as they did, eating, standing up, a lamb cooked with lettuce. I and my friends went to pray in the temple; my friends even frequented this temple after my death. In a word, I fulfilled all their laws without a single exception.''

"What! these wretches could not even reproach you with swerving from their laws?"

"Not, not possibly."

"Why then did they reduce you to the condition in which I now see you?"

"What do you expect me to say! They were very arrogant and selfish. They saw that I knew them for what they were; they knew that I was making the citizens acquainted with them; they were the stronger; they took away my life: and people like them will always do as much, if they can, to anyone who does them too much justice."

"But did you say nothing, do nothing that could serve them as a pretext?"

"To the wicked everything serves as pretext."

"Did you not say once that you were come not to bring peace, but a sword?"

"It is a copyist's error. I told them that I brought peace and not a sword. I never wrote anything; what I said may have been changed without evil intention."

"You therefore contributed in no way by your speeches, badly reported, badly interpreted, to these frightful piles of bones which I saw on my road in coming to consult you?"

"It is with horror only that I have seen those who have made themselves guilty of these murders."

"And these monuments of power and wealth, of pride and avarice, these treasures, these ornaments, these signs of grandeur, which I have seen piled up on the road while I was seeking wisdom, do they come from you?"

"That is impossible. I and my followers lived in poverty and meanness: my grandeur was in virtue only."

I was about to beg him to be so good as to tell me just who he was. My guide warned me to do nothing of the sort. He told me that I was not made to understand these sublime mysteries. But I did implore him to tell me in what true religion consisted.

"Have I not already told you? Love God and your fellow creature as yourself."

"What! If one loves God, one can eat meat on Friday?"

"I always ate what was given me, for I was too poor to give anyone food."

"In loving God, in being just, should one not be rather cautious not to confide all the adventures of one's life to an unknown being?"

"That was always my practice."

"Can I not, by doing good, dispense with making a pilgrimage to St. James of Compostella?"

"I have never been in that region."

"Is it necessary for me to imprison myself in a retreat with fools?"

"As for me, I was always making little journeys from town to town."

"Is it necessary for me to take sides either for the Greek Church or the Latin?"

"When I was in the world, I never differentiated between the Jew and the Samaritan."

"Well, if that is so, I take you for my only master." Then he made me a sign with his head which filled me with consolation. The vision disappeared, and a clear conscience stayed with me. . . .

Theist

The theist is a man firmly persuaded of the existence of a Supreme Being, as good as He is powerful, who has created all beings that are extensive, vegetative, sentient, and reflective; who perpetuates their species, who punishes crimes without cruelty, and rewards virtuous actions with kindness.

The theist does not know how God punishes, how he protects, how he pardons, for he is not bold enough to flatter himself that he knows how God acts, but he knows that God acts and that He is just. Arguments against Providence do not shake him in his faith, because they are merely great arguments, and not proofs. He submits to this Providence, although he perceives only a few effects and a few signs of this Providence: and—judging of the things he does not see by the things he does see—he considers that this Providence extends to all time and space.

United by this principle with the rest of the universe, he does not embrace any of the sects, all of which contradict one another. His religion is the most ancient and the most widespread, for the simple worship of a God has preceded all the systems of the world. He speaks a language that all peoples understand, while they do not understand one another. He has brothers from Pekin to Cayenne, and he counts all wise men as his brethren. He believes that religion does not consist either in the opinions of an unintelligible metaphysic, or in vain display, but in worship and justice. The doing of good, there is his service; being submissive to God, there is his doctrine. The Mohammedan cries to him: "Have a care if you do not make the pilgrimage to Mecca!" "Woe unto you," says a Recollet, "if you do not make a journey to Our Lady of Loretto!" He laughs at Loretto and at Mecca; but he succors the needy and he defends the oppressed.

SOURCE. B. R. Redman, ed., *The Portable Voltaire*, H. I. Wolf, tr., New York: The Viking Press, 1959, pp. 53–54, 88–90, 187–195, 200–202, 207–208. Reprinted by permission of The Viking Press, Inc.

b. RELIGIOUS SKEPTICISM: HUME, FROM
AN ENQUIRY CONCERNING HUMAN UNDERSTANDING

DAVID HUME (1711–1776), in his Enquiry Concerning Human Understanding, *undertook a ruthless criticism of the rational verifiability of God.
His criticism eroded the logical foundations of Christianity, but Christians
had long been willing to base their beliefs on faith. The real victim of
Hume's analysis was deism—the "religion of reason"—which was not shown
to be itself irrational. The main thrust of Hume's argument here is against
the traditional demonstration of God's existence from the apparently intelligent design of the universe (see Thomas Aquinas, above, Vol. I, Chapter 17,
c, fifth argument).*

What must a philosopher think of those vain reasoners, who, instead of
regarding the present scene of things as the sole object of their contemplation, so far reverse the whole course of nature, as to render this life merely
a passage to something farther; a porch, which leads to a greater, and vastly
different building; a prologue, which serves only to introduce the piece, and
give it more grace and propriety? Whence, do you think, can such philosophers derive their idea of the gods? From their own conceit and imagination
surely. For if they derived it from the present phenomena, it would never
point to anything farther, but must be exactly adjusted to them. That the divinity may *possibly* be endowed with attributes, which we have never seen
exerted; may be governed by principles of action, which we cannot discover
to be satisfied: all this will freely be allowed. But still this is mere *possibility* and hypothesis. We never can have reason to *infer* any attributes, or
any principles of action in him, but as far as we know them to have been
exerted and satisfied.

Are there any marks of a distributive justice in the world? If you answer
in the affirmative, I conclude, that, since justice here exerts itself, it is satisfied. If you reply in the negative, I conclude, that you have then no reason
to ascribe justice, in our sense of it, to the gods. If you hold a medium between affirmation and negation, by saying, that the justice of the gods, at
present, exerts itself in part, but not in its full extent; I answer, that you
have no reason to give it any particular extent, but only so far as you see it,
at present, exert itself. . . .

[Hume now presents what he regards as a specious argument for God's
existence:] If you saw . . . a half-finished building, surrounded with
heaps of brick and stone and mortar, and all the instruments of masonry,
could you not *infer* from the effect, that it was a work of design and
contrivance? And could you not return again, from this inferred cause, to

infer new additions to the effect, and conclude, that the building would soon be finished, and receive all the further improvements, which art could bestow upon it? If you saw upon the sea-shore the print of one human foot, you would conclude, that a man had passed that way, and that he had also left the traces of the other foot, though effaced by the rolling of the sands or inundation of the waters. Why then do you refuse to admit the same method of reasoning with regard to the order of nature? Consider the world and the present life only as an imperfect building, from which you can infer a superior intelligence; and arguing from that superior intelligence, which can leave nothing imperfect; why may you not infer a more finished scheme or plan, which will receive its completion in some distant point of space or time? Are not these methods of reasoning exactly similar? And under what pretence can you embrace the one, while you reject the other?

[Hume's reply:] The infinite difference of the subjects . . . is a sufficient foundation for this difference in my conclusions. In works of *human* art and contrivance, it is allowable to advance from the effect to the cause, and returning back from the cause, to form new inferences concerning the effect, and examine the alterations, which it has probably undergone, or may still undergo. But what is the foundation of this method of reasoning? Plainly this; that man is a being, whom we know by experience, whose motives and designs we are acquainted with, and whose projects and inclinations have a certain connexion and coherence, according to the laws which nature has established for the government of such a creature. When, therefore, we find, that any work has proceeded from the skill and industry of man; as we are otherwise acquainted with the nature of the animal, we can draw a hundred inferences concerning what may be expected from him; and these inferences will all be founded in experience and observation. But did we know man only from the single work or production which we examine, it were impossible for us to argue in this manner; because our knowledge of all the qualities, which we ascribe to him, being in that case derived from the production, it is impossible they could point to anything farther, or be the foundation of any new inference. The print of a foot in the sand can only prove, when considered alone, that there was some figure adapted to it, by which it was produced: but the print of a human foot proves likewise, from our other experience, that there was probably another foot, which also left its impression, though effaced by time or other accidents. Here we mount from the effect to the cause; and descending again from the cause, infer alterations in the effect; but this is not a continuation of the same simple chain of reasoning. We comprehend in this case a hundred other experiences and observations, concerning the *usual* figure and members of that species of animal, without which this method of argument must be considered as fallacious and sophistical.

The case is not the same with our reasonings from the works of nature. The Deity is known to us only by his productions, and is a single being in the universe, not comprehended under any species or genus, from whose experienced attributes or qualities, we can, by analogy, infer any attribute or quality in him. As the universe shews wisdom and goodness, we infer wisdom and goodness. As it shews a particular degree of these perfections, we infer a particular degree of them, precisely adapted to the effect which we examine. But farther attributes or farther degrees of the same attributes, we can never be authorised to infer or suppose, by any rules of just reasoning. Now, without some such licence of supposition, it is impossible for us to argue from the cause, or infer any alteration in the effect, beyond what has immediately fallen under our observation. Greater good produced by this Being must still prove a greater degree of goodness: a more impartial distribution of rewards and punishments must proceed from a greater regard to justice and equity. Every supposed addition to the works of nature makes an addition to the attributes of the Author of nature; and consequently, being entirely unsupported by any reason or argument, can never be admitted but as mere conjecture and hypothesis.

The great source of our mistake in this subject, and of the unbounded licence of conjecture, which we indulge, is, that we tacitly consider ourselves, as in the place of the Supreme Being, and conclude, that he will, on every occasion, observe the same conduct, which we ourselves, in his situation, would have embraced as reasonable and eligible. But, besides [the fact] that the ordinary course of nature may convince us, that almost everything is regulated by principles and maxims very different from ours; besides this, I say, it must evidently appear contrary to all rules of analogy to reason, from the intentions and projects of men, to those of a Being so different, and so much superior. In human nature, there is a certain experienced coherence of designs and inclinations; so that when, from any fact, we have discovered one intention of any man, it may often be reasonable, from experience, to infer another, and draw a long chain of conclusions concerning his past or future conduct. But this method of reasoning can never have place with regard to a Being, so remote and incomprehensible, who bears much less analogy to any other being in the universe than the sun to a waxen taper, and who discovers himself only by some faint traces or outlines, beyond which we have no authority to ascribe to him any attribute or perfection. What we imagine to be a superior perfection, may really be a defect. Or were it ever so much a perfection, the ascribing of it to the Supreme Being, where it appears not to have been really exerted, to the full, in his works, savours more of flattery and panegyric, than of just reasoning and sound philosophy. All the philosophy, therefore, in the world, and all the religion, which is nothing but a species of philosophy, will never be able to carry us beyond the usual course of experience, or give us measures of conduct and behaviour different from those which are furnished by reflections on common life. No new fact can ever be inferred from the religious hypothesis; no event foreseen or foretold; no reward or punishment expected or dreaded, beyond what is already known by practice and observation.

SOURCE. David Hume, *An Enquiry Concerning Human Understanding*, Chicago (La Salle): The Open Court Publishing Co., 1924, pp. 149–150, 151–155. Reprinted by permission of The Open Court Publishing Co., La Salle, Illinois.

c. POLITICAL ORGANIZATION: MONTESQUIEU, FROM *THE SPIRIT OF THE LAWS*

CHARLES-LOUIS DE MONTESQUIEU, one of the keenest minds of the French Enlightenment, presented in his Spirit of the Laws *(1748) a rational analysis of society and political institutions. He rejected any single blueprint for political and social organization, arguing that the system best suited to particular human groups depended on their geographical location and natural environment. He believed, nevertheless, that a successful political system should include a division of authority among various branches of government. His notion of checks and balances found expression some decades later in the American Constitution.*

As soon as mankind enter into a state of society they lose the sense of their weakness; equality ceases, and then commences the state of war.

Each particular society begins to feel its strength, whence arises a state of war betwixt different nations. The individuals likewise of each society become sensible of their force; hence the principal advantages of this society they endeavour to convert to their own emolument, which constitutes a state of war betwixt individuals.

These two different kinds of states give rise to human laws. Considered as inhabitants of so great a planet, which necessarily contains a variety of nations, they have laws relative to their mutual intercourse, which is what we call the *law of nations*. As members of a society that must be properly supported, they have laws relative to the governors and the governed, and this we distinguish by the name of *politic law*. They have also another sort of laws, as they stand in relation to each other; by which is understood the *civil law*.

The law of nations is naturally founded on this principle, that different nations ought in time of peace to do one another all the good they can, and in time of war as little injury as possible, without prejudicing their real interests.

The object of war is victory; that of victory is conquest; and that of conquest, preservation. From this and the preceding principle all those rules are derived which constitute the *law of nations*.

All countries have a law of nations, not excepting the Iroquois themselves, though they devour their prisoners; for they send and receive ambassadors, and understand the rights of war and peace. The mischief is, that their law of nations is not founded on true principles.

Besides the law of nations relating to all societies, there is a polity or civil constitution for each particularly considered. No society can subsist without a form of government. "The united strength of individuals," as Gravina[1] well observes, "constitutes what we call the body politic." . . .

The government most conformable to nature, is that which best agrees with the humour and disposition of the people in whose favour it is established.

The strength of individuals cannot be united without a conjunction of all their wills. "The conjunction of those wills," as Gravina again very justly observes, "is what we call the *civil state.*"

Law in general is human reason, inasmuch as it governs all the inhabitants of the earth; the political and civil laws of each nation ought to be only the particular cases in which human reason is applied. . . .

They should be relative to the climate of each country, to the quality of its soil, to its situation and extent, to the principal occupation of the natives, whether husbandmen, huntsmen, or shepherds; they should have a relation to the degree of liberty which the constitution will bear; to the religion of the inhabitants, to their inclinations, riches, numbers, commerce, manners, and customs. In fine, they have relations to each other, as also to their origin, to the intent of the legislator, and to the order of things on which they are established; in all which different lights they ought to be considered.

This is what I have undertaken to perform in the following work. These relations I shall examine, since all these together constitute what I call the *Spirit of Laws.* . . .

When the body of the people is possessed of the supreme power, this is called a *democracy*. When the supreme power is lodged in the hands of a part of the people, it is then an *aristocracy*.

In a democracy the people are in some respects the sovereign, and in others the subject.

There can be no exercise of sovereignty but by their suffrages, which are their own will; now the sovereign's will is the sovereign himself. The laws

[1] Giovanni Vincenzo Gravina (1664–1718), whose important work, *The Origins of Civil Law,* was published in 1713.

therefore which establish the right of suffrage are fundamental to this government. And indeed it is as important to regulate in a republic, in what manner, by whom, to whom, and concerning what, suffrages are to be given, as it is in a monarchy to know who is the prince, and after what manner he ought to govern. . . .

It is an essential point to fix the number of citizens who are to form the public assemblies; otherwise it would be uncertain whether the whole, or only a part of the people, had given their votes. At Sparta the number was fixed to ten thousand. But Rome . . . never fixed the number; and this was one of the principal causes of her ruin.

The people, in whom the supreme power resides, ought to have the management of everything within their reach: what exceeds their abilities, must be conducted by their ministers.

But they can not properly be said to have their ministers without the power of nominating them: it is, therefore, a fundamental maxim in this government that the people should choose their ministers, that is, their magistrates.

They have occasion, as well as monarchs, and even more so, to be directed by a council or senate. But to have a proper confidence in these, they should have the choosing of the members; whether the election be made by themselves, as at Athens; or by some magistrate deputed for that purpose, as on certain occasions was customary at Rome.

The people are extremely well qualified for choosing those whom they are to intrust with part of their authority. They have only to be determined by things to which they cannot be strangers, and by facts that are obvious to sense. They can tell when a person has fought many battles, and been crowned with success; they are, therefore, very capable of electing a general. They can tell when a judge is assiduous in his office, gives general satisfaction, and has never been charged with bribery: this is sufficient for choosing a praetor. They are struck with the magnificence or riches of a fellow-citizen; no more is requisite for electing an edile.[2] These are facts of which they can have better information in a public forum, than a monarch in his palace. But are they capable of conducting an intricate affair, of seizing and improving the opportunity and critical amount of action? No; this surpasses their abilities. . . .

As most citizens have sufficient abilities to choose, though unqualified to be chosen; so the people, though capable of calling others to an account for their administration, are incapable of conducting the administration themselves.

The public business must be carried on with a certain motion, neither too quick nor too slow. But the motion of the people is always either too remiss or too violent. Sometimes with a hundred thousand arms they overturn all

[2] A magistrate of ancient Rome.

before them; and sometimes with a hundred thousand feet they creep like insects.

In every government there are three sorts of power: the legislative; the executive, in respect to things dependent on the laws of nations; and the executive, in regard to matters that depend on the civil law.

By virtue of the first, the prince or magistrate enacts temporary or perpetual laws, and amends or abrogates those that have been already enacted. By the second, he makes peace or war, sends or receives embassies, establishes the public security, and provides against invasions. By the third, he punishes criminals, or determines the disputes that arise between individuals. The latter we shall call the judiciary power, and the other simply the executive power of the state.

The political liberty of the subject is a tranquillity of mind arising from the opinion each person has of his safety. In order to have this liberty, it is requisite the government be so constituted as one man needs not be afraid of another.

When the legislative and executive powers are united in the same person, or in the same body of magistrates, there can be no liberty; because apprehensions may arise, lest the same monarch or senate should enact tyrannical laws, to execute them in a tyrannical manner.

Again there is no liberty, if the judiciary power be not separated from the legislative and executive. Were it joined with the legislative, the life and liberty of the subject would be exposed to arbitrary control; for the judge would be then the legislator. Were it joined to the executive power, the judge might behave with violence and oppression.

There would be an end of everything, were the same man, or the same body, whether of the nobles or of the people, to exercise those three powers, that of enacting laws, that of executing the public resolutions, and of trying the causes of individuals.

Most kingdoms in Europe enjoy a moderate government, because the prince who is invested with the two first powers, leaves the third to his subjects. In Turkey, where these three powers are united in the Sultan's person, the subjects groan under the most dreadful oppression.

SOURCE. Charles-Louis de Montesquieu, *The Spirit of the Laws,* rev. ed., Thomas Nugent, tr., 1873.

d. ENLIGHTENED DESPOTISM: VOLTAIRE, LETTER TO FREDERICK THE GREAT, 1736

ENLIGHTENED DESPOTISM was, to a number of contemporary thinkers, a valuable means of rationalizing government. For one thing, an autocratic king could act quickly and, if properly disposed, could institute reforms that would require much time in a parliamentary commonwealth. For another, most Continental states were, in fact, dominated by all-powerful kings and princes, and enlightened despotism was a way of achieving reform without revolution. In a letter of 26 August, 1736 to Frederick the Great (who acceded to the Prussian throne four years later), Voltaire expresses his confidence in enlightened despotism.

Paris, 26th August, 1736.

My Lord,

I should indeed be insensitive were I not infinitely touched by the letter with which your Royal Highness has been graciously pleased to honor me. My self-love was but too flattered; but that love of the human race which has always existed in my heart and which I dare to say determines my character, gave me a pleasure a thousand times purer when I saw that the world holds a prince who thinks like a man, a philosophical prince who will make men happy.

Suffer me to tell you that there is no man on the earth who should not return thanks for the care you take in cultivating by sane philosophy a soul born to command. Be certain there have been no truly good kings except those who began like you, by educating themselves, by learning to know men, by loving the truth, by detesting persecution and superstition. Any prince who thinks in this way can bring back the golden age to his dominions. Why do so few kings seek out this advantage? You perceive the reason, My Lord; it is because almost all of them think more of royalty than of humanity: you do precisely the opposite. If the tumult of affairs and the malignancy of men do not in time alter so divine a character, you will be adored by your people and admired by the whole world. Philosophers worthy of that name will fly to your dominions; and, as celebrated artists crowd to that country where their art is most favored, men who think will press forward to surround your throne.

The illustrious Queen Christina left her kingdom to seek the arts; reign, My Lord, and let the arts come to seek you.

May you never be disgusted from the sciences by the quarrels of learned men! From those circumstances which you were graciously pleased to inform me of, My Lord, you see that most of them are men like courtiers themselves.

They are sometimes as greedy, as intriguing, as treacherous, as cruel; and the only difference between the pests of the court and the pests of the school is that the latter are the more ridiculous.

It is very sad for humanity that those who term themselves the messengers of Heaven's command, the interpreters of the Divinity, in a word theologians, are sometimes the most dangerous of all; that some of them are as pernicious to society as they are obscure in their ideas and that their souls are inflated with bitterness and pride in proportion as they are empty of truths. For the sake of a sophism they would trouble the earth and would persuade all kings to avenge with fire and steel the honor of an argument. . . .

Every thinking being not of their opinion is an atheist; and every king who does not favor them will be damned. You know, My Lord, that the best one can do is to leave to themselves these pretended teachers and real enemies of the human race. Their words, when unheeded, are lost in the air like wind; but if the weight of authority is lent them, this wind acquires a force which sometimes overthrows the throne itself.

I see, My Lord, with the joy of a heart filled with love of the public weal, the immense distance you set between men who seek the truth in peace and those who would make war for words they do not understand. I see that Newton, Leibnitz, Bayle, Locke, those elevated minds, so enlightened, so gentle, have nourished your spirit and that you reject other pretended nourishment which you find poisoned or without substance. . . .

You have the kindness, My Lord, to promise that you will send me the *Treatise on God, the Soul and the World.* What a present, My Lord, and what an interchange! The heir of a monarchy designs to send instruction from the heart of his palace to a solitary! Be graciously pleased to send me this present, My Lord; my extreme love of truth is the one thing which makes me worthy of it. Most princes fear to listen to the truth, but you will teach it.

As to the verses you speak of—you think as wisely of this art as in everything else. Verses which do not teach men new and moving truths do not deserve to be read. You perceive that there is nothing more contemptible than for a man to spend his life in rhyming worn-out commonplaces which do not deserve the name of thoughts. If there is anything viler it is to be nothing but satirical poet and to write only to decry others. Such poets are to Parnassus what those doctors, who know nothing but words and intrigue against those who write things, are to the schools.

If *La Henriade* did not displease your Royal Highness I must thank that love of truth, that horror which my poem inspires for the factious, for persecutors, for the superstitious, for tyrants and for rebels. 'Tis the work of an honest man; and should find grace in the eyes of a philosophic prince.

You command me to send you my other work; I shall obey you, My Lord, you shall be my judge, you shall stand to me in lieu of the public. I will submit to you what I have attempted in philosophy; your instruction shall be my reward: 'tis a prize which few sovereigns can give. I am certain of your secrecy; your virtue must be equal to your knowledge.

I should consider it a most valuable privilege to wait upon your Royal Highness. We go to Rome to see churches, pictures, ruins, and bas-reliefs. A prince like yourself is far more deserving of a journey; 'tis a more marvelous rarity. But friendship, which holds me in my retreat, does not permit me to leave it. Doubtless you think like Julian, that calumniated great man, who said that friends should always be preferred to kings.

In whatever corner of the world I end my life, be certain, My Lord, that I shall constantly wish you well, and in doing so wish the happiness of a nation. My heart will be among your subjects; your fame will ever be dear to me. I shall wish that you may always be like yourself and that other kings may be like you. I am with deep respect, your Royal Highness's most humble, etc.

SOURCE. B. R. Redman, ed., *The Portable Voltaire*, Richard Aldington, tr., New York: The Viking Press, 1959, pp. 439–444. Reprinted by permission of The Viking Press, Inc. and the Ann Elmo Agency, Inc.

e. THE RATIONAL SOCIETY: ROUSSEAU, FROM *THE SOCIAL CONTRACT*

JEAN JACQUES ROUSSEAU (1712–1778) was a man of broad but eccentric vision and deep sensitivity who, in his profound love of nature, went beyond the Enlightenment to foreshadow the subsequent rise of Romanticism. He was, nevertheless, a devotee of reason who, in his Social Contract, subjected the problems of political authority to logical analysis. He derived from Locke and his predecessors the notion of the state of nature, the social contract, and the popular basis of political authority (see Chapter 27, a, b), and in his use of the idea of the general will he developed a concept of unlimited sovereign power that anticipated the extreme nationalism of later generations.

Man is born free, and everywhere he is in chains. Many a man believes himself to be the master of others who is, no less than they, a slave. How did this change take place? I do not know. What can make it legitimate? To this question I hope to be able to furnish an answer.

Were I considering only force and the effects of force, I should say: 'So long as a People is constrained to obey, and does, in fact, obey, it does well. So soon as it can shake off its yoke, and succeeds in doing so, it does better. The fact that it has recovered its liberty by virtue of that same right by which it was stolen, means either that it is entitled to resume it, or that its theft by others was, in the first place, without justification.' But the social order is a sacred right which serves as a foundation for all other rights. This right, however, since it comes not by nature, must have been built upon conventions. To discover what these conventions are is the matter of our inquiry. But, before proceeding further, I must establish the truth of what I have so far advanced. . . .

'Some form of association must be found as a result of which the whole strength of the community will be enlisted for the protection of the person and property of each constituent member, in such a way that each, when united to his fellows, renders obedience to his own will, and remains as free as he was before.' That is the basic problem of which the Social Contract provides the solution.

The clauses of this Contract are determined by the Act of Association in such a way that the least modification must render them null and void. Even though they may never have been formally enunciated, they must be everywhere the same, and everywhere tacitly admitted and recognized. So completely must this be the case that, should the social compact be violated, each associated individual would at once resume all the rights which once were his, and regain his natural liberty, by the mere fact of losing the agreed liberty for which he renounced it.

It must be clearly understood that the clauses in question can be reduced, in the last analysis, to one only, to wit, the complete alienation by each associate member to the community of *all his rights*. For, in the first place, since each has made surrender of himself without reservation, the resultant conditions are the same for all: and, because they are the same for all, it is in the interest of none to make them onerous to his fellows.

Furthermore, this alienation having been made unreservedly, the union of individuals is as perfect as it well can be, none of the associated members having any claim against the community. For should there be any rights left to individuals, and no common authority be empowered to pronounce as between them and the public, then each, being in some things his own judge, would soon claim to be so in all. Were that so, a state of Nature would still remain in being, the conditions of association becoming either despotic or ineffective.

In short, whoso gives himself to all gives himself to none. And, since there is no member of the social group over whom we do not acquire precisely the same rights as those over ourselves which we have surrendered to him, it follows that we gain the exact equivalent of what we lose, as well as an added power to conserve what we already have.

If, then, we take from the social pact all that is not essential to it, we shall find it to be reduced to the following terms: 'each of us contributes to the group his person and the powers which he wields as a person under the supreme direction of the general will and we receive into the body politic each individual as forming an indivisible part of the whole.'

As soon as the act of association becomes a reality, it substitutes for the person of each of the contracting parties a moral and collective body made up of as many members as the constituting assembly has votes, which body receives from this very act of constitution its unity, its dispersed *self*, and its will. The public person thus formed by the union of individuals was known in the old days as a *City*, but now as the *Republic* or *Body Politic*. This, when it fulfils a passive role, is known by its members as *The State*, when an active one, as *The Sovereign People*, and, in contrast to other similar bodies, as a *Power*. In respect of the constituent associates, it enjoys the collective name of *The People*, the individuals who compose it being known as *Citizens*, in so far as they share in the soverign authority, as *Subjects* in so far as they owe obedience to the laws of the State. But these different terms frequently overlap, and are used indiscriminately one for the other. It is enough that we should realize the difference between them when they are employed in a precise sense. . . .

. . . the body politic, or Sovereign, in that it derives its being simply and solely from the sanctity of the said Contract, can never bind itself, even in its relations with a foreign Power, by any decision which might derogate from the validity of the original art. It may not, for instance, alienate any portion of itself, nor make submission to any other sovereign. To violate the act by reason of which it exists would be tantamount to destroying itself, and that which is nothing can produce nothing.

As soon as a mob has become united into a body politic, any attack upon one of its members is an attack upon itself. Still more important is the fact that, should any offence be committed against the body politic as a whole, the effect must be felt by each of its members. Both duty and interest, therefore, oblige the two contracting parties to render one another mutual assistance. The same individuals should seek to unite under this double aspect all the advantages which flow from it.

Now, the Sovereign People, having no existence outside that of the individuals who compose it, has, and can have, no interest at variance with theirs.

Consequently, the sovereign power need give no guarantee to its subjects, since it is impossible that the body should wish to injure all its members, nor, as we shall see later, can it injure any single individual. The Sovereign, by merely existing, is always what it should be. But the same does not hold true of the relation of subject to sovereign. In spite of common interest, there can be no guarantee that the subject will observe his duty to the sovereign unless means are found to ensure his loyalty.

Each individual, indeed, may, as a man, exercise a will at variance with, or different from, that general will to which, as citizen, he contributes. His personal interest may dictate a line of action quite other than that demanded by the interest of all. The fact that his own existence as an individual has an absolute value, and that he is, by nature, an independent being, may lead him to conclude that what he owes to the common cause is something that he renders of his own free will; and he may decide that by leaving the debt unpaid he does less harm to his fellows than he would to himself should he make the necessary surrender. Regarding the moral entity constituting the State as a rational abstraction because it is not a man, he might enjoy his rights as a citizen without, at the same time, fulfilling his duties as a subject, and the resultant injustice might grow until it brought ruin upon the whole body politic.

In order, then, that the social compact may not be but a vain formula, it must contain, though unexpressed, the single undertaking which can alone give force to the whole, namely, that whoever shall refuse to obey the general will must be constrained by the whole body of his fellow citizens to do so: which is no more than to say that it may be necessary to compel a man to be free—freedom being that condition which, by giving each citizen to his country, guarantees him from all personal dependence and is the foundation upon which the whole political machine rests, and supplies the power which works it. Only the recognition by the individual of the rights of the community can give legal force to undertakings entered into between citizens, which, otherwise, would become absurd, tyrannical, and exposed to vast abuses. . . .

It follows from what has been said above that the general will is always right and ever tends to the public advantage. But it does not follow that the deliberations of the People are always equally beyond question. It is ever the way of men to wish their own good, but they do not at all times see where that good lies. The People are never corrupted though often deceived, and it is only when they are deceived that they appear to will what is evil.

There is often considerable difference between the will of all and the general will. The latter is concerned only with the common interest, the former with interests that are partial, being itself but the sum of individual wills. But take from the expression of these separate wills the pluses and minuses—which cancel out, the sum of the differences is left, and that is the general will.

If the People, engaged in deliberation, were adequately informed, and if no means existed by which the citizens could communicate one with another, from the great number of small differences the general will would result, and the decisions reached would always be good. But when intriguing groups and partial associations are formed to the disadvantage of the whole, then the will of each of such groups is general only in respect of its own members, but partial in respect of the State. When such a situation arises it may be said that there are no longer as many votes as men, but only as many votes as there are groups. Differences of interest are fewer in number, and the result is less general. Finally, when one of these groups becomes so large as to swamp all the others, the result is not the sum of small differences, but one single difference. The general will does not then come into play at all, and the prevailing opinion has no more validity than that of an individual man.

If, then, the general will is to be truly expressed, it is essential that there be no subsidiary groups within the State, and that each citizen voice his own opinion and nothing but his own opinion. It was the magnificent achievement of Lycurgus to have established the only State of this kind ever seen. But where subsidiary groups do exist their numbers should be made as large as possible, and none should be more powerful than its fellows. This precaution was taken by Solon, Numa, and Servius. Only if it is present will it be possible to ascertain the general will, and to make sure that the People are not led into error. . . .

From which it becomes clear that the sovereign power, albeit absolute, sacrosanct, and inviolable, does not, and cannot, trespass beyond the limits laid down by general agreement, and that every man has full title to enjoy whatever of property and freedom is left to him by that agreement. The sovereign is never entitled to lay a heavier burden on any one of its subjects than on others, for, should it do so, the matter would at once become particular rather than general, and, consequently, the sovereign power would no longer be competent to deal with it.

These distinctions once admitted, it becomes abundantly clear that to say that the individual, by entering into the social contract, makes an act of renunciation is utterly false. So far from that being the case, his situation within the contract is definitely preferable to what it was before. Instead of giving anything away, he makes a profitable bargain, exchanging peril and uncertainty for security, natural independence for true liberty, the power of injuring others for his own safety, the strength of his own right arm—which others might always overcome—for a right which corporate solidity renders invincible. The life which he devotes to the State is, by the State continually protected, and, when he offers it in the State's defence, what else is he doing than giving back the very boon which he has received at its hands? What, in such circumstances, does he do that he has not done more often and more perilously in a state of nature when, inevitably involved in mortal combat, he defended at the risk of his life what served him to maintain it? All citizens, it is true, may, should the need arise, have to fight for their country, but no one of them has ever to fight singly for himself. Is it not preferable, in the interest of what makes for our security, to run some part of the risks which we should have to face in our own defence, were the boon of forming one of a society taken from us? . . .

The principle of political life is in the sovereign authority. The Legislative Power is the heart of the State, the Executive is its brain, and gives movement to all its parts. The brain may be struck with paralysis and the patient yet live. A man may be an imbecile and yet not die. But once the heart ceases to function, it is all over with the animal.

It is not by the laws that a State exists, but by the Legislative Power. Yesterday's law has no authority to-day, but silence is held to imply consent, and the sovereign is deemed to confirm all laws that it does not abrogate—the assumption being that it has power to do so. When once it has declared its will on some specific issue, that will is perpetually valid, unless it be revoked.

SOURCE. Jean Jacques Rousseau, *The Social Contract,* Sir Ernest Barker, ed., Gerard Hopkins, tr., London: Oxford University Press, 1946, pp. 240, 253–258, 260–262, 274–276, 281–282, and 364. Reprinted by permission of Oxford University Press.

f. THE NATURAL ECONOMY: ADAM SMITH, FROM *THE WEALTH OF NATIONS*

THE EIGHTEENTH-CENTURY RATIONALIST ATTACK on mercantilism found its most eloquent and comprehensive expression in The Wealth of Nations *(1776) of the Scottish economist Adam Smith (1723–1790). The* Wealth of Nations *was a learned and systematic appeal to the national states of the day to allow the natural economic processes to function without interference. The economic system, like the Newtonian universe, would operate smoothly and to the advantage of all, if left alone.*

Every individual is continually exerting himself to find out the most advantageous employment for whatever capital he can command. It is his own advantage, indeed, and not that of the society, which he has in view. But the study of his own advantage naturally, or rather necessarily leads him to prefer that employment which is most advantageous to the society. . . . .

Every individual who employs his capital in the support of domestic industry, necessarily endeavours so to direct that industry, that its produce may be of the greatest possible value.

The produce of industry is what it adds to the subject or materials upon which it is employed. In proportion as the value of this produce is great or small, so will likewise be the profits of the employer. But it is only for the sake of profit that any man employs a capital in the support of industry; and he will always, therefore, endeavour to employ it in the support of that industry of which the produce is likely to be of the greatest value, or to exchange for the greatest quantity either of money or of other goods.

But the annual revenue of every society is always precisely equal to the exchangeable value of the whole annual produce of its industry, or rather is precisely the same thing with that exchangeable value. As every individual, therefore, endeavours as much as he can both to employ his capital in the support of domestic industry, and so to direct that industry that its produce may be of the greatest value; every individual necessarily labours to render the annual revenue of the society as great as he can. He generally, indeed, neither intends to promote the public interest, nor knows how much he is promoting it. By preferring the support of domestic to that of foreign industry, he intends only his own security, and by directing that industry in such a manner as its produce may be of the greatest value, he intends only his own gain, and he is in this, as in many other cases, led by an invisible hand to promote an end which was no part of his intention. Nor is it always the worse for the society that it was no part of it. By pursuing his own interest he frequently promotes that of the society more effectually than when he really intends to promote it. I have never known much good done by those who affected to trade for the public good. It is an affectation, indeed, not very common among merchants, and very few words need be employed in dissuading them from it.

What is the species of domestic industry which his capital can employ, and of which the produce is likely to be of the greatest value, every individual, it is evident, can, in his local situation, judge much better than any statesman or lawgiver can do for him. The statesman, who should attempt to direct private people in what manner they ought to employ their capitals, would not only load himself with a most unnecessary attention, but assume an authority which could safely be trusted, not only to no single person, but to council or senate whatever, and which would nowhere be so dangerous as in the hands of a man who had folly and presumption enough to fancy himself fit to exercise it.

To give the monopoly of the home-market to the produce of domestic industry, in any particular art or manufacture, is in some measure to direct private people in what manner they ought to employ their capitals, and must, in almost all cases, be either a useless or a hurtful regulation. If the produce of domestic can be brought there as cheap as that of foreign industry, the regulation is evidently useless. If it cannot, it must generally be hurtful. It is the maxim of every prudent master of a family, never to attempt to make at home what it will cost him more to make than to buy. The taylor does not attempt to make his own shoes, but buys them of the shoemaker. The shoemaker does not attempt to make his own clothes, but employs a tailor. The farmer attempts to make neither the one nor the other, but employs those different artificers. All of them find it for their interest to employ their whole industry in a way in which they have some advantage over their neighbours, and to purchase with a part of its produce, or what is the same thing, with the price of a part of it, whatever else they have occasion for.

What is prudence in the conduct of every private family, can scarce be folly in that of a great kingdom. If a foreign country can supply us with a commodity cheaper than we ourselves can make it, better buy it of them with some part of the produce of our own industry, employed in a way in which we have some advantage. The general industry of the country, being always in proportion to the capital which employs it, will not thereby be diminished, no more than that of the above-mentioned artificers; but only left to find out the way in which it can be employed with the greatest advantage. It is certainly not employed to the greatest advantage, when it is thus directed towards an object which it can buy cheaper than it can make. The value of its annual produce is certainly more or less diminished, when it is thus turned away from producing commodities evidently of more value than the commodity which it is directed to produce. According to the supposition, that commodity could be purchased from foreign countries cheaper than it can be made at home. It could, therefore, have been purchased with a part only of the commodities, or, what is the same thing, with a part only of the price of the commodities, which the industry employed by an equal capital would have produced at home, had it been left to follow its natural course. The industry of the country, therefore, is thus turned away from a more, to a less advantageous employment, and the exchangeable value of its annual produce, instead of being increased, according to the intention of the lawgiver, must necessarily be diminished by every such regulation.

Consumption is the sole end and purpose of all production; and the interest of the producer ought to be attended to, only so far as it may be necessary for promoting that of the consumer. The maxim is so perfectly self-evident, that it would be absurd to attempt to prove it. But in the mercantile system, the interest of the consumer is almost constantly sacrificed to that of the producer; and it seems to consider production, and not consumption, as the ultimate end and object of all industry and commerce.

In the restraints upon the importation of all foreign commodities which can come into competition with those of our own growth, or manufacture, the interest of the home-consumer is evidently sacrificed to that of the producer. It is altogether for the benefit of the latter, that the former is obliged to pay that enhancement of price which this monopoly almost always occasions.

It is altogether for the benefit of the producer that bounties are granted upon the exportation of some of his productions. The home-consumer is obliged to pay, first, the tax which is necessary for paying the bounty, and secondly, the still greater tax which necessarily arises from the enhancement of the price of the commodity in the home market. . . .

In the system of laws which has been established for the management of our American and West Indian colonies, the interest of the home-consumer has been sacrificed to that of the producer with a more extravagant profusion than in all our other commercial regulations. A great empire has been established for the sole purpose of raising up a nation of customers who should be obliged to buy from the shops of our different producers, all the goods with which these could supply them. For the sake of that little enhancement of price which this monopoly might afford our producers, the home-consumers have been burdened with the whole expence of maintaining and defending that empire. For this purpose, and for this purpose only, in the two last wars, more than two hundred millions have been spent, and a new debt of more than a hundred and seventy millions has been contracted over and above all that had been expended for the same purpose in former wars. The interest of this debt alone is not only greater than the whole extraordinary profit, which, it ever could be pretended, was made by the monopoly of the colony trade, but than the whole value of that trade, or than the whole value of the goods, which at an average have been annually exported to the colonies.

It cannot be very difficult to determine who have been the contrivers of this whole mercantile system; not the consumers, we may believe, whose interest has been entirely neglected; but the producers, who interest has been so carefully attended to; and among this latter class our merchants and manufacturers have been by far the principal architects.

SOURCE. Adam Smith, *The Wealth of Nations,* Edwin Cannan, ed., New York: Modern Library, 1937, pp. 420–21, 422–24, 625–626. Reprinted by permission of Random House, Inc.

g. HUMAN PROGRESS THROUGH REASON: CONDORCET, FROM *THE PROGRESS OF THE HUMAN MIND*

THE MARQUIS DE CONDORCET'S VIEWS ON PROGRESS, so ironic in retrospect, are expressions not only of an optimism rooted in Enlightenment rationalism but also of the intoxicating hopes that arose from the early successes of the French Revolution. The Progress of the Human Mind *was published in 1795; Condorcet was completing it at about the time of the Reign of Terror.*

Our hopes, as to the future condition of the human species, may be reduced to three points: the destruction of inequality between different nations; the progress of equality in one and the same nation; and lastly, the real improvement of man.

Will not every nation one day arrive at the state of civilization attained by those people who are most enlightened, most free, most exempt from prejudices, as the French, for instance, and the Anglo-Americans? Will not slavery of countries subjected to kings, the barbarity of African tribes, and the ignorance of savages gradually vanish? Is there upon the face of the globe a single spot the inhabitants of which are condemned by nature never to enjoy liberty, never to exercise their reason?

Does the difference of knowledge, of means, and of wealth, observable hitherto in all civilized nations, between the classes into which the people constituting those nations are divided; does that inequality which the earliest progress of society has augmented, or, to speak more properly, produced, belong to civilization itself, or to the imperfections of the social order? Must it not continually weaken, in order to give place to that actual equality, the chief end of the social art, which diminishing even the effects of the natural difference of the faculties, leaves no other inequality subsisting but what is useful to the interest of all, because it will favour civilization, instruction, and industry, without drawing after it either dependence, humiliation or poverty? In a word, will not men be continually verging towards that state in which all will possess the requisite knowledge for conducting themselves in the common affairs of life by their own reason, and of maintaining that reason uncontaminated by prejudices; in which they will understand their rights and exercise them according to their opinion and their conscience; in which all will be able, by the developement of their faculties, to procure the certain means of providing for their wants; lastly, in which folly and wretchedness will be accidents, happening only now and then, and not the habitual lot of a considerable portion of society?

In fine, may it not be expected that the human race will be meliorated by new discoveries in the sciences and the arts, and, as an unavoidable consequence, in the means of individual and general prosperity; by farther progress in the principles of conduct and in moral practice; and lastly, by the real improvement of our faculties, moral, intellectual and physical, which may be the result either of the improvement of the instruments which increase the power and direct the exercise of those faculties, or of the improvement of our natural organization itself?

In examining the three questions we have enumerated, we shall find the strongest reasons to believe, from past experience, from observation of the progress which the sciences and civilization have hitherto made, and from the analysis of the march of the human understanding, and the development of its faculties, that nature has fixed no limits to our hopes. . . .

The progress of the sciences secures the progress of the art of instruction, which again accelerates in its turn that of the sciences; and this reciprocal influence, the action of which is incessantly increased, must be ranked in the number of the most prolific and powerful causes of the improvement of the human race. At present, a young man, upon finishing his studies and quitting our schools, may know more of the principles of mathematics than Newton acquired by profound study, or discovered by the force of his genius, and may exercise the instrument of calculation with a readiness which at that period was unknown. The same observation, with certain restrictions, may be applied to all the sciences. In proportion as each shall advance, the means of compressing, within a smaller circle, the proofs of a greater number of truths, and of facilitating their comprehension, will equally advance. Thus, notwithstanding future degrees of progress, not only will men of equal genius find themselves, at the same period of life, upon a level with the actual state of science, but, respecting every generation, what may be acquired in a given space of time, by the same strength of intellect and the same degree of attention, will necessarily increase, and the elementary part of each science, that part which every man may attain, becoming more and more extended, will include, in a manner more complete, the knowledge necessary for the direction of every man in the common occurrences of life, and for the free and independent exercise of his reason. . . .

. . . It cannot be doubted that the progress of the sanative art, that the use of more wholesome food and more comfortable habitations, that a mode of life which shall develope the physical powers by exercise, without at the same time impairing them by excess; in fine, that the destruction of the two most active causes of deterioration, penury and wretchedness on the one hand, and enormous wealth on the other, must necessarily tend to prolong the common duration of man's existence, and secure him a more constant health and a more robust constitution. It is manifest that the improvement of the practice of medicine, become more efficacious in consequence of the progress of reason and the social order, must in the end put a period to transmissible or contagious disorders, as well to those general maladies resulting from climate, aliments, and the nature of certain occupations. Nor would it be difficult to prove that this hope might be extended to almost every other malady, of which it is probable we shall hereafter discover the most remote causes. Would it even be absurd to suppose this quality of melioration in the human species as susceptible of an indefinite advancement; to suppose that a period must one day arrive when death will be nothing more than the effect either of extraordinary accidents, or of the slow and gradual decay of the vital powers; and that the duration of the middle space, of the interval between the birth of man and this decay, will itself have no assignable limit? . . .

Lastly, may we not include in the same circle the intellectual and moral faculties? May not our parents, who transmit to us the advantages or defects of their conformation, and from whom we receive our features and shape, as well as our propensities to certain physical affections, transmit to us also that part of organization upon which intellect, strength of understanding, energy of soul or moral sensibility depend? Is it not probable that education, by improving these qualities, will at the same time have an influence upon, will modify and improve this organization itself? . . .

. . . How admirably calculated is this view of the human race, emancipated from its chains, released alike from the dominion of chance, as well as from that of the enemies of its progress, and advancing with a firm and indeviate step in the paths of truth, to console the philosopher lamenting the errors, the flagrant acts of injustice, the crimes with which the earth is still polluted? It is the contemplation of this prospect that rewards him for all his efforts to assist the progress of reason and the establishment of liberty. He dares to regard these efforts as a part of the eternal chain of the destiny of mankind; and in this persuasion he finds the true delight of virtue. . . .

He unites himself in imagination with man restored to his rights, delivered from oppression, and proceeding with rapid strides in the path of happiness; he forgets his own misfortunes while his thoughts are thus employed; he lives no longer to adversity, calumny and malice, but becomes the associate of these wiser and more fortunate beings whose enviable condition he so earnestly contributed to produce.

SOURCE: Marquis de Condorcet, *Outlines of an Historical View of the Progress of the Human Mind*, translated from the French, Philadelphia, 1796.

Chapter 3

NEO-CLASSICISM

a. ARCHITECTURE AND SCULPTURE

THE RATIONALISM of eighteenth-century thought was paralleled by the classical balance and restraint of eighteenth-century art in a style called Neo-Classicism which continued on well into the nineteenth century. Architects, sculptors, and painters joined in rejecting the ornate and flowing Baroque style in favor of a purer, more elegant form of expression. In Barthélemy Vignon's La Madeleine in Paris (completed 1824), one encounters an unblemished Classicism purged of Baroque exuberance.

BARTHÉLEMY VIGNON, LA MADELEINE, PARIS, COMPLETED 1824

THE PERSEUS (1797) of the sculptor Antonio Canova, although not entirely successful as a work of art, is an excellent example of Neo-Classical purity and simplicity (compare Bernini's Triton Fountain, p. 86).

ANTONIO CANOVA, *PERSEUS*, 1797

b. PAINTING

ONE FINDS the same qualities of purity and simplicity in the paintings of artists such as Jacques Louis David (1748–1825) and the late Neo-Classicist Jean-Auguste Ingres (1780–1867). In their works Baroque fluidity gives way to immobility, severity, and understatement. David's Oath of the Horatii *also expresses the stern commitment of French reformers on the eve of the Revolution. See, by contrast, the radically different approach of romantic painters such as Delacroix and Turner (Chapter 5, f.)*

JACQUES LOUIS DAVID, *OATH OF THE HORATII*, 1785

JEAN-AUGUSTE INGRES, *MADEMOISELLE RIVIERE*

PART TWO

Revolution, Romanticism, and Counter-Revolution

1789–1848

THE course of eighteenth-century European history changed abruptly in 1789 with the outbreak of the French Revolution. Plagued by severe financial problems, King Louis XVI was obliged to summon the French Estates General for the first time in 175 years. Grievances had long been building up against the archaic, privilege-ridden *ancien régime,* which offered nothing to the peasantry and very little to the middle class. To the *philosophes* it appeared as a model of unenlightened despotism. Immediately upon the assembling of the Estates General, the Third Estate (representatives of the people in general and the middle class in particular) demanded a greater voice than the First and Second Estates (clergy and nobility), arguing that its authority should be appropriate to the vast numbers that it represented. Organizing themselves into a "National Assembly," the representatives of the Third Estate invited the delegates of the other estates to join them, and thereupon proceeded to direct the course of the Revolution.

Thenceforth the Revolution followed a progressively leftward course. The delegates to the National Assembly prepared a constitution designed to create a constitutional monarchy, but with the abortive flight and subsequent execution of Louis XVI, France became a republic. The radical Jacobin Party rose to power, the Reign of Terror ensued, and after a period of conservative reaction under the Directory government (1795–1799) Napoleon became the master of France. His far-ranging armies spread French influence and the Revolutionary ideology across the length and breadth of Europe. The era of the Napoleonic wars came to an end with the Congress of Vienna (1815) at which the victorious great powers—Austria, Prussia, Russia, and Great Britain—reconstructed the political system of Europe on a conservative, royalist basis. France was given a new Bourbon king, Louis XVIII.

Europe responded to the French Revolution in a variety of ways. The two potent Revolutionary concepts of liberalism and nationalism extended across Europe and played a significant role in the politics of the nineteenth century. It was these two concepts, above all, that underlay the revolutions of 1830 and 1848, both of which began in France and quickly expanded to the rest of Europe. To many people, however, the French Revolution was simply a bloody catastrophe. Statesmen such as the Austrian Prince Metternich who dominated the Vienna settlement, and writers such as the Englishman Edmund Burke, were bitter opponents of the Revolutionary ideology. They cautioned against the dangers of overturning the social order and preached a philosophy of conservatism and reverence for the past.

The frame of mind that produced Enlightenment rationalism and Neo-Classical art gave way to the radically different mood of Romanticism. The

Romantics protested against the bloodless intellectualism and Classical formalism of the past, replacing them with a new emphasis on personal, emotional values. Their works are sometimes tender, sometimes moody, sometimes imaginatively descriptive, and always infused with rich, exotic imagery. They drew their inspiration not so much from Classical Greece and Rome as from the colorful, mystical ethos of the Middle Ages which they idealized and romanticized. Among Romantics, the passions of the heart took priority over the abstractions of the mind, and form bowed before feeling.

Chapter 4

THE FRENCH REVOLUTION AND NAPOLEON

a. ABBÉ SIEYES, FROM "WHAT IS THE THIRD ESTATE?"

THE CLAIMS OF THE THIRD ESTATE, which resulted in the transformation of the Estates General into the National Assembly, are set forth boldly in Abbé Sieyes' pamphlet "What Is the Third Estate?," which appeared in January, 1789, on the eve of the Revolution, just as the election of delegates was beginning.

The plan of this pamphlet is very simple. We have three questions to ask:
1st. What is the third estate? Everything.
2nd. What has it been heretofore in the political order? Nothing.
3rd. What does it demand? To become something therein.
We shall see if the answers are correct. Then we shall examine the measures that have been tried and those which must be taken in order that the third estate may in fact become *something*. Thus we shall state:
4th. What the ministers have *attempted*, and what the privileged classes themselves *propose* in its favor.
5th. What *ought* to have been done.
6th. Finally, what *remains* to be done in order that the third estate may take its rightful place.

Chapter I   The Third Estate is a Complete Nation

What are the essentials of national existence and prosperity? *Private* enterprise and *public* functions.

Private enterprise may be divided into four classes: 1st. Since earth and water furnish the raw material for man's needs, the first class will comprise all families engaged in agricultural pursuits. 2nd. Between the original sale of materials and their consumption or use, further workmanship, more or less manifold, adds to these materials a second value, more or less compounded. Human industry thus succeeds in perfecting the benefits of nature and in increasing the gross produce twofold, tenfold, onehundredfold in value. Such is the work of the second class. 3rd. Between production and consumption, as well as among the different degrees of production, a group of intermediate agents, useful to producers as well as to consumers, comes into being; these are the dealers and merchants. . . . 4th. In addition to these three classes of industrious and useful citizens concerned with goods for consumption and use, a society needs many private undertakings and endeavors which are *directly* useful or agreeable to the *individual*. This fourth class includes from the most distinguished scientific and liberal professions to the least esteemed domestic services. Such are the labors which sustain society. Who performs them? The third estate.

Public functions likewise under present circumstances may be classified under four well known headings: the Sword, the Robe, the Church, and the Administration. It is unnecessary to discuss them in detail in order to demonstrate that the third estate everywhere constitutes nineteen-twentieths of them, except that it is burdened with all that is really arduous, with all the tasks that the privileged order refuses to perform. Only the lucrative and honorary positions are held by members of the privileged order. . . . nevertheless they have dared lay the order of the third estate under an interdict. They have said to it: "Whatever be your services, whatever your talents, you shall go thus far and no farther. It is not fitting that you be honored." . . .

It suffices here to have revealed that the alleged utility of a privileged order to public service is only a chimera; that without it, all that is arduous in such service is performed by the third estate; that without it, the higher positions would be infinitely better filled; that they naturally ought to be the lot of and reward for talents and recognized services; and that if the privileged classes have succeeded in usurping all the lucrative and honorary positions, it is both an odious injustice to the majority of citizens and a treason to the commonwealth.

Who, then, would dare to say that the third estate has not within itself all that is necessary to constitute a complete nation? It is the strong and robust man whose one arm remains enchained. If the privileged order were abolished, the nation would be not something less but something more. Thus, what is the third estate? Everything; but an everything shackled and oppressed. What would it be without the privileged order? Everything; but an everything free and flourishing. Nothing can progress without it; everything would proceed infinitely better without the others. It is not sufficient to have demonstrated that the privileged classes, far from being useful to the nation, can only enfeeble and injure it; it is necessary, moreover, to prove that the nobility does not belong to the social organization at all; that, indeed, it may be a *burden* upon the nation, but that it would not know how to constitute a part thereof. . . .

What is a nation? a body of associates living under a *common* law and represented by the same *legislature*.

Is it not exceedingly clear that the noble order has privileges, exemptions, even rights separate from the rights of the majority of citizens? Thus it deviates from the common order, from the common law. Thus its civil rights already render it a people apart in a great nation. It is indeed *imperium in imperio*.

Also, it enjoys its political rights separately. It has its own representatives, who are by no means charged with representing the people. Its deputation sits apart; and when it is assembled in the same room with the deputies of ordinary citizens, it is equally true that its representation is essentially distinct and separate; it is foreign to the nation in principle, since its mandate does not emanate from the people, and in aim, since its purpose is to defend not the general but a special interest.

The third estate, then, comprises everything appertaining to the nation; and whatever is not the third estate may not be regarded as being of the nation. What is the third estate? Everything!

Chapter II   *What has the Third Estate been Heretofore? Nothing*

We shall examine neither the state of servitude in which the people has suffered so long, nor that of constraint and humiliation in which it is still confined. Its civil status has changed; it must change still more; it is indeed impossible that the nation as a whole, or that even any order in particular, may become free if the third estate is not. Freedom is not the consequence of privileges, but of the rights appertaining to all. . . .

. . . the third estate must be understood to mean the mass of the citizens belonging to the common order. Legalized privilege in any form deviates from the common order, constitutes an exception to the common law, and, consequently, does not appertain to the third estate at all. We repeat, a common law and a common representation are what constitutes *one* nation. It is only too true that one is *nothing* in France when one has only the protection of the common law; if one does not possess some privilege, one must resign oneself to enduring contempt, injury, and vexations of every sort. . . .

But here we have to consider the order of the third estate less in its civil status than in its relation with the constitution. Let us examine its position in the Estates General.

Who have been its so-called representatives? The ennobled or those privileged for a period of years. These false deputies have not even been always freely elected by the people. Sometimes in the Estates General, and almost always in the provincial Estates, the representation of the people has been regarded as a perquisite of certain posts or offices. . . .

Add to this appalling truth that, in one manner or another, all branches of the executive power also have fallen to the caste which furnishes the Church, the Robe, and the Sword. A sort of spirit of brotherhood causes the nobles to prefer themselves . . . to the rest of the nation. Usurpation is complete; in truth, they reign.

. . . it is a great error to believe that France is subject to a monarchical régime.

. . . it is the court, and not the monarch, that has reigned. It is the court that makes and unmakes, appoints and discharges ministers, creates and dispenses positions, etc. And what is the court if not the head of this immense aristocracy which overruns all parts of France; which through its members attains all and everywhere does whatever is essential in all parts of the commonwealth? . . .

Let us sum up: the third estate has not heretofore had real representatives in the Estates General. Thus its political rights are null.

Chapter III   What does the Third Estate Demand? To be Something

. . . The true petitions of this order may be appreciated only through the authentic claims directed to the government by the large municipalities of the kingdom. What is indicated therein? That the people wishes to be *something,* and, in truth, the very least that is possible. It wishes to have real representatives in the Estates General, that is to say, deputies *drawn from its order,* who are competent to be interpreters of its will and defenders of its interests. But what will it avail it to be present at the Estates General if the predominating interest there is contrary to its own! Its presence would only consecrate the oppression of which it would be the eternal victim. Thus, it is indeed certain that it cannot come to vote at the Estates General unless it is to have in that body *an influence at least equal to that of the privileged classes;* and it demands a number of representatives equal to that of the first two orders together. Finally, this equality of represenatation would become completely illusory if every chamber voted separately. The third estate demands, then, that votes be taken *by head and not by order.* This is the essence of those claims so alarming to the privileged classes, because they believed that thereby the reform of abuses would become inevitable. The real intention of the third estate is to have an influence in the Estates General equal to that of the privileged classes. I repeat, can it ask less? And is it not clear that if its influence therein is less than equality, it cannot be expected to emerge from its political nullity and become *something?* . . .

. . . Obviously there are abuses in France; these abuses are profitable to someone; they are scarcely advantageous to the third estate—indeed, they are injurious to it in particular. Now I ask if, in this state of affairs, it is possible to destroy any abuse so long as those who profit therefrom control the *veto?* All justice would be powerless; it would be necessary to rely entirely on the sheer generosity of the privileged classes. Would that be your idea of what constitutes the social order?

SOURCE. J. H. Stewart, ed., *A Documentary History of the French Revolution,* New York: Macmillan, 1951, pp. 42–47. Copyright 1951 by The Macmillan Company. Reprinted by permission of The Macmillan Company.

b. THE TENNIS COURT OATH, 1789

THE DELEGATES OF THE THIRD ESTATE, insisting on the principle set forth by Abbé Sieyes "that votes be taken by head and not by order," constituted themselves a National Assembly and invited delegates of the First and Second Estates to join their body. (Few responded.) Finding themselves locked out of their meeting place (apparently by accident), they met in an indoor tennis court and swore never to separate until a constitution had been enacted.

The National Assembly, considering that it has been summoned to determine the Constitution of the kingdom, to effect the regeneration of public order, to maintain the true principles of the monarchy; that nothing can prevent it from continuing its deliberations in whatever place it may be forced to establish itself, and lastly, that wherever its members meet together, there is the National Assembly.

Decrees that all the members of this Assembly shall immediately take a solemn oath never to separate, and to reassemble wherever circumstances shall require, until the Constitution of the kingdom shall be established and consolidated upon firm foundations; and that, the said oath being taken, all the members and each of them individually shall ratify by their signatures this steadfast resolution.

SOURCE. F. M. Anderson, ed., *The Constitutions and Other Select Documents Illustrative of the History of France,* Minneapolis: H. W. Wilson Co., 1904, p. 3. Reprinted by permission of Dr. Gaylord W. Anderson.

c. THE ABOLITION OF FEUDALISM, AUGUST 4, 1789

THE FOURTH OF AUGUST DECREES, in which the National Assembly, in an outburst of enthusiasm, transformed the privilege-ridden social order of the ancient *régime by abolishing French feudalism and manorialism, were prompted by the violence in the countryside that followed the storming of the Bastille on July 14. These Decrees were promulgated in slightly revised form on August 11, 1789. Their effect was revolutionary, not only in reforming the social order but also in ending the age-old system of magnates and churchmen sharing with the royal government the power to tax, to judge, and to command. Thenceforth all sovereign power was centralized in the state.*

1. The National Assembly hereby completely abolishes the feudal system. It decrees that, among the existing rights and dues, both feudal and *censuel,* all those originating in or representing real or personal serfdom *(main morte)* or personal servitude, shall be abolished without indemnification. All other dues are declared redeemable, the terms and mode of redemption to be fixed by the National Assembly. Those of the said dues which are not extinguished by this decree shall continue to be collected until indemnification shall take place. . . .

3. The exclusive right to hunt and to maintain unenclosed warrens is likewise abolished, and every land owner shall have the right to kill or to have destroyed on his own land all kinds of game, observing, however, such police regulations as may be established with a view to the safety of the public. . . .

The president of the assembly shall be commissioned to ask of the King the recall of those sent to the galleys or exiled, simply for violations of the hunting regulations, as well as for the release of those at present imprisoned for offences of this kind, and the dismissal of such cases as are now pending.

4. All manorial courts are hereby suppressed without indemnification. But the magistrates of these courts shall continue to perform their functions until such time as the National Assembly shall provide for the establishment of a new judicial system.

5. Tithes of every description, as well as the dues which have been substituted for them, under whatever denomination they are known or collected (even when compounded for), possessed by secular or regular congregations, by holders of benefices, members of corporations (including the Order of Malta and other religious and military orders), as well as those devoted to the maintenance of churches, those impropriated to lay persons and those substituted for the *portion congrue,* are abolished, on condition, however, that some other method be devised to provide for the expenses of divine worship, the

support of the officiating clergy, for the assistance of the poor, for repairs and rebuilding of churches and parsonages, and for the maintenance of all institutions, seminaries, schools, academies, asylums, and organizations to which the present funds are devoted. Until such provision shall be made and the former possessors shall enter upon the enjoyment of an income on the new system, the National Assembly decrees that the said tithes shall continue to be collected according to law and in the customary manner.

Other tithes, of whatever nature they may be, shall be redeemable in such manner as the Assembly shall determine. Until such regulation shall be issued, the National Assembly decrees that these, too, shall continue to be collected.

6. All perpetual ground rents, payable either in money or in kind, of whatever nature they may be, whatever their origin and to whomsoever they may be due, as to members of corporations, holders of the domain or appanages or to the Order of Malta, shall be redeemable. . . .

7. The sale of judicial and municipal offices shall be suppressed forthwith. Justice shall be dispensed *gratis*. Nevertheless, the magistrates at present holding such offices shall continue to exercise their functions and to receive their emoluments until the Assembly shall have made provision for indemnifying them.

8. The fees of the country priests are abolished, and shall be discontinued so soon as provision shall be made for increasing the minimum salary of the parish priests and the payment to the curates. A regulation shall be drawn up to determine the status of the priests in the towns.

9. Pecuniary privileges, personal or real, in the payment of taxes are abolished forever. Taxes shall be collected from all the citizens, and from all property, in the same manner and in the same form. Plans shall be considered by which the taxes shall be paid proportionally by all, even for the last six months of the current year.

10. Inasmuch as a national constitution and public liberty are of more advantage to the provinces than the privileges which some of these enjoy, and inasmuch as the surrender of such privileges is essential to the intimate union of all parts of the realm, it is decreed that all the peculiar privileges, pecuniary or otherwise, of the provinces, principalities, districts, cantons, cities and communes, are once for all abolished and are absorbed into the law common to all Frenchmen.

11. All citizens, without distinction of birth, are eligible to any office or dignity, whether ecclesiastical, civil or military; and no profession shall imply any derogation. . . .

15. The National Assembly shall consider, in conjunction with the King, the report which is to be submitted to it relating to pensions, favors and salaries, with a view to suppressing all such as are not deserved and reducing

those which shall prove excessive; and the amount shall be fixed which the King may in the future disburse for this purpose.

16. The National Assembly decrees that a medal shall be struck in memory of the recent grave and important deliberations for the welfare of France, and that a *Te Deum*[1] shall be chanted in gratitude in all the parishes and the churches of France.

17. The National Assembly solemnly proclaims the King, Louis XVI, the *Restorer of French Liberty*.

18. The National Assembly shall present itself in a body before the King, in order to submit to him the decrees which have just been passed, to tender to him the tokens of its most respectful gratitude and to pray him to permit the *Te Deum* to be chanted in his chapel, and to be present himself at this service.

19. The National Assembly shall consider, immediately after the constitution, the drawing up of the laws necessary for the development of the principles which it has laid down in the present decree. The latter shall be transmitted without delay by the deputies to all the provinces, together with the decree of the tenth of this month, in order that it may be printed, published, announced from the parish pulpits, and posted up wherever it shall be deemed necessary.

SOURCE. F. M. Anderson, ed., *The Constitutions and Other Select Documents Illustrative of the History of France,* Minneapolis: H. W. Wilson Co., 1904, pp. 11–15. Reprinted by permission of Dr. Gaylord W. Anderson.

d. DECLARATION OF THE RIGHTS OF MAN AND CITIZEN, 1789

ON AUGUST 27 the National Assembly issued a general statement of principles, the Declaration of the Rights of Man and Citizen, which reflects the optimistic psychology and political ideology of the Enlightenment and seems to have been modeled on the bills of rights of certain American states.

The representatives of the French people, organized in National Assembly, considering that ignorance, forgetfulness or contempt of the rights of man are the sole causes of the public miseries and of the corruption of governments,

---

[1] A Catholic chant of thanksgiving, traditionally performed on the occasion of great military victories.

have resolved to set forth in a solemn declaration the natural, inalienable, and sacred rights of man, in order that this declaration, being ever present to all the members of the social body, may unceasingly remind them of their rights and their duties: in order that the acts of the legislative power and those of the executive power may be each moment compared with the aim of every political institution and thereby may be more respected; and in order that the demands of the citizens, grounded henceforth upon simple and incontestable principles, may always take the direction of maintaining the constitution and the welfare of all.

In consequence, the National Assembly recognizes and declares, in the presence and under the auspices of the Supreme Being,[2] the following rights of man and citizen.

1. Men are born and remain free and equal in rights. Social distinctions can be based only upon public utility.

2. The aim of every political association is the preservation of the natural and imprescriptible rights of man. These rights are liberty, property, security, and resistance to oppression.

3. The source of all sovereignty is essentially in the nation; no body, no individual can exercise authority that does not proceed from it in plain terms.

4. Liberty consists in the power to do anything that does not injure others; accordingly, the exercise of the natural rights of each man has for its only limits those that secure to the other members of society the enjoyment of these same rights. These limits can be determined only by law.

5. The law has the right to forbid only such actions as are injurious to society. Nothing can be forbidden that is not interdicted by the law and no one can be constrained to do that which it does not order.

6. Law is the expression of the general will. All citizens have the right to take part personally or by their representatives in its formation. It must be the same for all, whether it protects or punishes. All citizens being equal in its eyes, are equally eligible to all public dignities, places, and employments, according to their capacities, and without other distinction than that of their virtues and their talents.

7. No man can be accused, arrested, or detained except in the cases determined by the law and according to the forms that it has prescribed. Those who procure, expedite, execute, or cause to be executed arbitrary orders ought to be punished: but every citizen summoned or seized in virtue of the law ought to render instant obedience; he makes himself guilty by resistance.

8. The law ought to establish only penalties that are strictly and obviously necessary and no one can be punished except in virtue of a law established and promulgated prior to the offence and legally applied.

[2] An echo of enlightenment deism. See Voltaire; above, Chapter 2, a.

9. Every man being presumed innocent until he has been pronounced guilty, if it is thought indispensable to arrest him, all severity that may not be necessary to secure his person ought to be strictly suppressed by law.

10. No one ought to be disturbed on account of his opinions, even religious, provided their manifestation does not derange the public order established by law.

11. The free communication of ideas and opinions is one of the most precious of the rights of man; every citizen then can freely speak, write, and print, subject to responsibility for the abuse of this freedom in the cases determined by law.

12. The guarantee of the rights of man and citizen requires a public force; this force then is instituted for the advantage of all and not for the personal benefit of those to whom it is entrusted.

13. For the maintenance of the public force and for the expenses of adminisration a general tax is indispensable; it ought to be equally apportioned among all the citizens according to their means.

14. All the citizens have the right to ascertain, by themselves or by their representatives, the necessity of the public tax, to consent to it freely, to follow the employment of it, and to determine the quota, the assessment, the collection, and the duration of it.

15. Society has the right to call for an account from every public agent of its administration.

16. Any society in which the guarantee of the rights is not secured or the separation of powers not determined has no constitution at all.

17. Property being a sacred and inviolable right, no one can be deprived of it unless a legally established public necessity evidently demands it, under the condition of a just and prior indemnity.

SOURCE. F. M. Anderson, ed., *The Constitutions and Other Select Documents Illustrative of the History of France,* Minneapolis: H. W. Wilson Co., 1904, pp. 58–60. Reprinted by permission of Dr. Gaylord W. Anderson.

e. THE KING'S DECLARATION, JUNE 20, 1791

IN JUNE, 1791, King Louis XVI and his family attempted to flee France secretly and join an Austrian army that was gathered on the northeastern frontier. The King left a declaration explaining his actions to be read after he had left Paris. Although obviously self-serving, it is a valuable statement of the King's reaction to two years of revolutionary change.

As long as the King was able to hope to see order and well-being rise again through the means employed by the National Assembly and by his residence near that Assembly, no sacrifice was too expensive; he would not have even drawn any inference from the lack of liberty, of which he has been deprived since the month of October, 1789; but today when the result of all the operations is to see the monarchy destroyed, property violated, the security of persons compromised, in all parts of the empire a complete anarchy, without any appearance of authority sufficient to arrest it, the King, after having protested against all the acts emanating from him during his captivity, believes that he ought to put before the eyes of the French a representation of his conduct.

In the month of July, 1789, the King, secure in his conscience, did not fear to come among the Parisians. In the month of October of the same year, warned by the movements of the factious, he feared that they would make a pretence of his departure to stir up civil war. Everybody is aware of the impunity with which crimes were then committed. The King, yielding to the view expressed by the army of the Parisians, came to establish himself at the chateau of the Tuileries. Nothing was ready to receive him; and the King, very far from finding the accommodations to which he was accustomed in his other residences, did not even meet with the comforts which persons in easy circumstances procure for themselves.

Despite all the constraints, he believed that he ought from the morrow of his arrival to reassure the provinces about his sojourn at Paris. A more painful sacrifice was reserved for him: he was required to send away his body guards, whose fidelity he had proven. Two had been massacred, several had been wounded in carrying out the order not to fire which they had received. Every art of the factious was employed to cause to be considered in a bad light a faithful wife who was about to fill up the measure of her good conduct: it is likewise evident that all the machinations were directed against the King himself. It was to the soldiers of the French guards and to the Parisian National Guard that the protection of the King was confided, under the orders of the municipality of Paris, from which the commanding general took his place.

The King is thus seen a prisoner in his own dominions, for how could one be called otherwise who saw himself forcibly surrounded by persons whom he suspects; it is not in order to inculpate the Parisian National Guard that I recall these details, but in order to relate the exact truth; on the contrary, I render justice to its attachment when it has not been led astray by the factious. The King ordered the convocation of the States-General, he granted to the Third Estate a double representation; the union of the orders, the sacrifices of the twenty-third of June, all that was his work; but his services have been misunderstood and misconstrued. The moment when the States-General gave itself the name of National Assembly, recalls the maneuvers of the factious in several provinces; it recalls the movements which have been effected in order to nullify the provision of the *cahiers*, which provided that the drawing up of the laws should be done in concert with the King. The Assembly has put the King outside of the constitution, in refusing to him the right to sanction the constitutional acts, in arranging in that class those which it was pleased to arrange there, and in limiting to the third legislature in any case refusal of sanction. They gave him 25,000,000 which are entirely consumed by the expense that the pomp necessary for his household requires. They left to him the use of certain domains with embarrassing restrictions, thus depriving him of the patrimony of his ancestors; they took care not to include in his expenses the services rendered to the King, as if they were not inseparable from those rendered to the State. Let one examine the different points of the administration and he will see that the King is removed from it: he has no part in the making of the laws; he can only pray the Assembly to occupy itself with such and such things. As to the administration of justice, he only causes the decrees of the judges to be forwarded and appoints the commissioners of the King, whose functions are indeed less considerable than those of the former *procureurs-generaux*. The public prosecution has been devolved upon new officers. There remained one last prerogative, the most attractive of all, that of pardon and of commuting penalties; you have taken it away from the King, it is now the jurors who have it, applying according to their will the sense of the law. This diminishes the royal majesty; the people were accustomed to have recourse there as to a common centre of bounty and beneficence. The internal administration within the departments is embarrassed by wheels which clog the movement of the machine; the supervision of the ministers is reduced to nothing. . . .

The King has been declared the supreme head of the administration of the kingdom, yet he can change nothing without the decision of the Assembly. The leaders of the dominant party have exhibited such a defiance to the agents of the King, and the penalties inflicted upon the disobedient have given birth to so much uneasiness, that these agents have remained without authority. The form of government is especially vicious for two reasons: the Assembly exceeds the limit of its powers, in occupying itself with the administration of justice and internal administration; it exercises through its investigating committees the most barbarous of all despotisms. There have been established associations known under the name of the Friends of the Constitution, which are corporations infinitely more dangerous than the former ones; they deliberate upon all the concerns of the government, exercise a power so preponderant that all the bodies, not even excepting the National Assembly itself, do nothing except by their order. The King does not think that it would be possible to preserve such a government; the more they see approaching the end of the labors of the Assembly, the more wise men lose of their confidence in it. The new regulations, instead of applying balm to the wounds, on the contrary aggravate the discontent; the thousand newspapers and calumniating pamphlets, which are only the echoes of the clubs, perpetuate the disorder and the Assembly has never dared to remedy it; they tend only to a government metaphysical and impossible in the execution.

Frenchmen, is it this that you designed in sending your representatives? Do you desire that the despotism of the clubs should replace the monarchy under which the kingdom has prospered during fourteen hundred years? The love of Frenchmen for their King is reckoned among their virtues. I have had too many touching tokens of it to be able to forget it: the King would not offer the accompanying picture except to trace for his faithful subjects the spirit of the factious. . . . A proposal was even made to carry him off and to put the Queen in a convent, and this proposal was at the moment applauded. . . .

Frenchmen, and you who may be called inhabitants of the good city of Paris, distrust the suggestion of the factious, return to your King, he will always be your friend, when your holy religion shall be respected, when the government shall be laid upon a firm footing, and liberty established upon an enduring foundation.

Signed, Louis.

Paris, June 20, 1791.

SOURCE. F. M. Anderson, ed., *The Constitutions and Other Select Documents Illustrative of the History of France*, Minneapolis: H. W. Wilson Co., 1904, pp. 45–50. Reprinted by permission of Dr. Gaylord W. Anderson.

f. THE REIGN OF TERROR: A PARISIAN NEWSPAPER SUPPORTS IT

CAPTURED AT VARENNES, the royal family was returned to Paris, its prestige decisively compromised. The abortive flight doomed the National Assembly's attempt to establish a constitutional monarchy. Nevertheless, the Assembly's Constitution was completed and promulgated later in the year (it took effect in September, 1791), and elections were held for delegates to the new assembly. This newly elected body, known as the National Convention (1792–1795) was radical and anti-royalist in its composition. It repudiated the Constitution of 1791, declared France a republic, and sent the King and Queen to the guillotine. The leftward drift of the National Convention culminated in the rise of Robespierre and the "Committee of Public Safe-

ty" in the summer of 1793 which brought on the Reign of Terror. Threatened by hostile armies on France's frontiers, and fearful of internal conservatism and reaction, the Revolutionary leaders adopted a policy of massive executions in which at least 15,000 people lost their lives. The Terror found support in many quarters, as a contemporary article from a Paris newspaper makes clear.

Yes, terror is the order of the day, and ought to be for the selfish, for the federalists, for the heartless rich, for dishonest opportunists, for shameless intriguers, for unpatriotic cowards, for all who do not feel the dignity of being free men and pure republicans. Rivers of blood have been shed for the gold of Peru and the diamonds of Golconda. Well! Does not liberty, that inestimable blessing which one would surely not tarnish by comparing it with the vile metals of the Indies, have the same right to sacrifice lives, fortunes, and even, for a time, individual liberties? In the thick of battle is there any foolish wailing over the soldiers fallen from the ranks? They are promptly replaced by others, and with the perfidious aggressor repulsed, one is free to weep over the unfortunate victims mowed down on the field of battle. Is not the French Revolution just such a deadly combat, a war to the death between those who want to be free and those content to be slaves? This is the situation, and the French people have gone too far to retreat with honor and safety. These is no middle ground; France must be entirely free or perish in the attempt, and any means are justifiable in fighting for so fine a cause. But our resources are being exhausted, say some. Well, when the Revolution is finished, they will be replenished by peace. A free people, as long as they have weapons and hands, can fight their enemies and plow their fields. . . .

SOURCE. E. L. Higgins, ed., *The French Revolution as Told by Contemporaries,* Boston: Houghton Mifflin Co., 1939, pp. 306–307. Reprinted by permission of Houghton Mifflin Co.

g. THE REIGN OF TERROR: THE LAW OF SUSPECTS

THE REPRESSIVE political atmosphere of the period is illustrated by the Law of Suspects (September 17, 1793). Compare the Declaration of the Rights of Man and Citizen (above, d).

1. Immediately after the publication of the present decree, all suspected persons within the territory of the Republic and still at liberty shall be placed in custody.

2. The following are deemed suspected persons: 1st, those who, by their conduct, associations, talk, or writings have shown themselves partisans of tyranny or federalism and enemies of liberty; 2nd, those who are unable to justify, in the manner prescribed by the decree of 21 March last, their means of existence and the performance of their civic duties; 3rd, those to whom certificates of patriotism have been refused; 4th, public functionaries suspended or dismissed from their positions by the National Convention or by its commissioners, and not reinstated, especially those who have been or are to be dismissed by virtue of the decree of 14 August last; 5th, those former nobles, husbands, wives, fathers, mothers, sons or daughters, brothers or sisters, and agents of the *émigrés*, who have not steadily manfested their devotion to the Revolution; 6th, those who have emigrated during the interval between 1 July, 1789, and the publication of the decree of 30 March—8 April, 1792, even though they may have returned to France within the period established by said decree or prior thereto.

3. The Watch Committees established according to the decree of 21 March last, or those substituted therefor, either by orders of the representatives of the people dispatched to the armies and the departments, or by virtue of particular decrees of the National Convention, are charged with drafting, each in its own *arrondissement,* a list of suspected persons, with issuing warrants of arrest against them, and with having seals placed on their papers. Commanders of the public force to whom such warrants are remitted shall be required to put them into effect immediately, under penalty of dismissal. . . .

SOURCE. E. L. Higgins, ed., *The French Revolution as Told by Contemporaries,* Boston: Houghton Mifflin Co., 1939, pp. 477–479. Reprinted by permission of Houghton Mifflin Co.

h. THE FIRST PROCLAMATION OF THE CONSULS, 1799

THE NATIONAL CONVENTION soon gave way to a more conservative regime dominated by five executive Directors (1795–1799) and the leftward swing of the Revolution was reversed. On November 9, 1799, Napoleon Bonaparte, one of the most successful of the Revolutionary generals, engineered a coup d'état which had the effect of overthrowing the Directory and establishing in its place a three-man executive Consulate with Napoleon as

First Consul. In the first proclamation of the new government (December 15, 1799), Napoleon announced the consummation and end of the Revolution. In 1804, he assumed direct power as Emperor of the French.

Frenchmen!

A Constitution is presented to you.

It ends the uncertainties which the provisional government introduced into foreign relations, into the internal and military situation of the Republic.

It places in the institutions which it establishes first magistrates whose devotion has appeared necessary for its success.

The Constitution is founded on the true principles of representative government, on the sacred rights of property, equality, and liberty.

The powers which it institutes will be strong and stable, as they must be in order to guarantee the rights of citizens and the interests of the State.

Citizens, the Revolution is established upon the principles which began it: It is ended.

SOURCE. J. H. Stewart, ed., *A Documentary History of the French Revolution,*New York: Macmillan, 1951, p. 780. Copyright 1951 by The Macmillan Company. Reprinted by permission of The Macmillan Company.

i. THE NAPOLEONIC DREAM, 1816

AFTER NAPOLEON'S FALL from power, during his exile on the Island of St. Helena, he expressed himself freely to the Count de Las Cases on the subject of his own dreams of transforming Europe. It should not be surprising that he interpreted his actions in the best possible light.

"Peace, concluded at Moscow, would have fulfilled and wound up my hostile expeditions. It would have been, with respect to the grand cause, the term of casualties and the commencement of security. A new horizon, new undertakings, would have unfolded themselves, adapted, in every respect, to the well-being and prosperity of all. The foundation of the European system would have been laid, and my only remaining task would have been its organization.

"Satisfied on these grand points, and everywhere at peace, I should have also had my [peace] congress and my holy alliance. These are plans which were stolen from me. In that assembly of all the sovereigns, we should have discussed our interest in a family way, and settled our accounts with the people, as a clerk does with his master.

"The cause of the age was victorious, the Revolution accomplished; the only point in question was to reconcile it with what it had not destroyed. . . . I became the arch of the old and new alliance, the natural mediator between the ancient and modern order of things. I maintained the principles and possessed the confidence of the one; I had identified myself with the other. I belonged to them both; I should have acted conscientiously in favor of each:

"My glory would have consisted in my equity."

And, after having enumerated what he would have proposed between sovereign and sovereign, and between sovereigns and their people, he continued: "Powerful as we were, all that we might have conceded would have appeared grand. It would have gained us the gratitude of the people. At present, what they may extort will never seem enough to them, and they will be uniformly distrustful and discontented."

He next took a review of what he would have proposed for the prosperity, the interests, the enjoyments and the well-being of the European confederacy. He wished to establish the same principles, the same system everywhere. A European code; a court of European appeal, with full powers to redress all wrong decisions, as ours redresses at home those of our tribunals. Money of the same value but with different coins; the same weights, the same measures, the same laws, etc.

"Europe would soon in that manner," he said, "have really been but the same people, and everyone who traveled would have everywhere found himself in one common country."

He would have required, that all the rivers should be navigable in common; that the seas should be thrown open; that the great standing armies should, in future, be reduced to the single establishment of a guard for the sovereign, etc.

. . . "On my return to France, in the bosom of my country, at once great, powerful, magnificent, at peace and glorious, I would have proclaimed the immutability of boundaries, all future wars, purely *defensive;* all new aggrandizement, *anti-national.* I would have associated my son with the empire; my dictatorship would have terminated, and his constitutional reign commenced. . . . Paris would have been the capital of the world, and the French the envy of nations! . . . These also, my dear Las Cases, were among my dreams!!!"

SOURCE. David L. Dowd, *Napoleon: Was He the Heir of the Revolution?*, New York: Holt, Rinehart and Winston, 1957, pp. 15–16. Copyright 1957 by David L. Dowd. Used by permission of Holt, Rinehart and Winston, Inc. All rights reserved. From E. A. D. M. J. Count de Las Cases, *Memorial de Sainte Helene, Journal of the Private Life and Conversations of the Emperor Napoleon at St. Hélèna,* London: 1823, V, pp. 265–267.

j. NATIONALISM SPREADS: WILLIAM III OF PRUSSIA CALLS HIS PEOPLE TO ARMS

NAPOLEON'S ARMIES, as they marched across Europe, spread the doctrines of liberalism and fervent devotion to country which the French Revolution had nourished. King William III of Prussia was obviously playing on this new sense of nationalism when on March 17, 1813, he called his people to arms against Napoleonic France.

There is no need of explaining to my loyal subjects, or to any German, the reasons for the war which is about to begin. They lie plainly before the eyes of awakened Europe. We succumbed to the superior force of France. The peace which followed deprived me of my people and, far from bringing us blessings, it inflicted upon us deeper wounds than the war itself, sucking out the very marrow of the country. Our principal fortresses remained in the hand of the enemy, and agriculture, as well as the highly developed industries of our towns, was crippled. The freedom of trade was hampered and thereby the sources of commerce and prosperity cut off. The country was left a prey to the ravages of destitution.

I hoped, by the punctilious fulfillment of the engagements I had entered into, to lighten the burdens of my people, and even to convince the French emperor that it would be to his advantage to leave Prussia her independence. But the purest and best of intentions on my part were of no avail against insolence and faithlessness, and it became only too plain that the emperor's treaties would gradually ruin us even more surely than his wars. The moment is come when we can no longer harbor the slightest illusion as to our situation.

Brandenburgers, Prussians, Silesians, Pomeranians, Lithuanians! You know what you have borne for the past seven years; you know the sad fate that awaits you if we·do not bring this war to an honorable end. Think of the times gone by,—of the Great Elector, the great Frederick! Remember the blessings for which your forefathers fought under their leadership and which they paid for with their blood,—freedom of conscience, national honor, independence, commerce, industry, learning. Look at the great example of our powerful allies, the Russians; look at the Spaniards, the Portuguese. For such objects as these even weaker peoples have gone forth against mightier enemies and returned in triumph. Witness the heroic Swiss and the people of the Netherlands.

Great sacrifices will be demanded from every class of the people, for our undertaking is a great one, and the number and resources of our enemies far from insignificant. But would you not rather make these sacrifices for the fatherland and for your own rightful king than for a foreign ruler, who, as he has shown by many examples, will use you and your sons and your uttermost farthing for ends which are nothing to you?

Faith in God, perseverance, and the powerful aid of our allies will bring us victory as the reward of our honest efforts. Whatever sacrifices may be required of us as individuals, they will be outweighed by the sacred rights for which we make them, and for which we must fight to a victorious end unless we are willing to cease to be Prussians or Germans. This is the final, the decisive struggle; upon it depends our independence, our prosperity, our existence. There are no other alternatives but an honorable peace or a heroic end. You would willingly face even the latter for honor's sake, for without honor no Prussian or German could live.

However, we may confidently await the outcome. God and our own firm purpose will bring victory to our cause and with it an assured and glorious peace and the return of happier times.

FREDERICK WILLIAM.

Breslau, March 17, 1813.

SOURCE. J. H. Robinson, ed., *Readings in European History,* Boston: Ginn and Co., 1906, II, pp. 522–523.

k. CONSERVATIVE MISGIVINGS: EDMUND BURKE, FROM *REFLECTIONS ON THE REVOLUTION IN FRANCE,* 1790

OPPOSED BY MOST of the powers of Europe, Napoleon was crushed in 1814 and exiled to the Island of Elba. He returned to France in 1815 while delegates of the great powers were assembled at Vienna to work out a peace settlement. With Napoleon's subsequent defeat at Waterloo and exile to remote St. Helena, Europe could devote its full attention once again to the problems of reconstructing Europe on conservative principles.

The conservative reaction that accompanied the French Revolution achieved its most perceptive expression in Edmund Burke's Reflections on the Revolution in France (1790). Burkean thought constitutes the fountainhead of modern conservatism; many of his fundamental ideas are present in the passages given below. At the time this work was written the French Revolution was only a year old. The execution of Louis XVI, the Reign of Terror, and the era of Napoleon all lay in the future.

Abstractedly speaking, government, as well as liberty, is good; yet could I, in common sense, ten years ago, have felicitated France on her enjoyment of a government (for she then had a government), without inquiring what the nature of that government was, or how it was administered? Can I now congratulate the same nation upon its freedom? Is it because liberty in the abstract may be classed amongst the blessings of mankind, that I am seriously to felicitate a madman who has escaped from the protecting restraint and wholesome darkness of his cell on his restoration to the enjoyment of light and liberty? Am I to congratulate a highwayman and murderer who has broke prison upon the recovery of his natural rights? . . .

When I see the spirit of liberty in action, I see a strong principle at work; and this, for a while, is all I can possibly know of it. The wild gas, the fixed air, is plainly broke loose: but we ought to suspend our judgment until the first effervescence is a little subsided, till the liquor is cleared, and until we see something deeper than the agitation of a troubled and frothy surface. I must be tolerably sure, before I venture publicly to congratulate men upon a blessing, that they have really received one. Flattery corrupts both the receiver and the giver; and adulation is not of more service to the people than to kings. I should therefore suspend my congratulations on the new liberty of France, until I was informed how it had been combined with government, with public force, with the discipline and obedience of armies, with the collection of an effective and well-distributed revenue, with morality and religion, with solidity and property, with peace and order, with civil and social manners. All these (in their way) are good things, too; and, without them, liberty is not a benefit whilst it lasts, and is not likely to continue long. The effect of liberty to individuals is that they may do what they please: we ought to see what it will please them to do before we risk congratulations, which may be soon turned into complaints. Prudence would dictate this in the case of separate, insulated, private men. But liberty, when men act in bodies, is power. Considerate people, before they declare themselves, will observe the use which is made of power—and particularly of so trying a thing as new power in new persons, of whose principles, tempers, and dispositions they have little or no experience, and in situations where those who appear the most stirring in the scene may possibly not be the real movers . . .

You will observe, that, from Magna Carta to the Declaration of Right, it has been the uniform policy of our Constitution to claim and assert our liberties as an entailed inheritance derived to us from our forefathers, and to be transmitted to our posterity—as an estate especially belonging to the people of this Kingdom, without any reference whatever to any other more general or prior right. By this means our Constitution preserves an unity in so great a diversity of its parts. We have an inheritable Crown, an inheritable Peerage, and a House of Commons and a people inheriting privileges, franchises, and liberties from a long line of ancestors.

This policy appears to me to be the result of profound reflection—or rather the happy effect of following Nature, which is wisdom without reflection, and above it. A spirit of innovation is generally the result of a selfish temper and confined views. People will not look forward to posterity, who never look backward to their ancestors. Besides, the people of England well know that the idea of inheritance furnishes a sure principle of conservation, and a sure principle of transmission, without at all excluding a principle of improvement. It leaves acquisition free; but it secures what it acquires. Whatever advantages are obtained by a state proceeding on these maxims are locked fast as in a sort of family settlement. . . . By a constitutional policy working after the pattern of Nature, we receive, we hold, we transmit our government and our privileges, in the same manner in which we enjoy and transmit our property and our lives. The institutions of policy, the goods of fortune, the gifts of Providence, are handed down to us, and from us, in the same course and order. Our political system is placed in a just correspondence and symmetry with the order of the world, and with the mode of existence decreed to a permanent body composed of transitory parts—wherein, by the disposition of a stupendous wisdom, moulding together the great mysterious incorporation of the human race, the whole, at one time, is never old or middle-aged or young, but, in a condition of unchangeable constancy, moves on through the varied tenor of perpetual decay, fall, renovation, and progression. Thus, by preserving the method of Nature in the conduct of the state, in what we improve we are never wholly new, in what we retain we are never wholly obsolete. . . . In this choice of inheritance we have given to our frame of policy the image of a relation in blood: binding up the Constitution of our country with our dearest domestic ties; adopting our fundamental laws into the bosom of our family affections; keeping inseparable, and cherishing with the warmth of all their combined and mutually reflected charities, our state, our hearths, our sepulchres, and our altars. . . .

Believe me, Sir, those who attempt to level never equalise. In all societies consisting of various descriptions of citizens, some description must be uppermost. The Levellers, therefore, only change and pervert the natural order of things: they load the edifice of society by setting up in the air what the solidity of the structure requires to be on the ground. The associations of tailors and carpenters, of which the republic (of Paris, for instance) is composed, cannot be equal to the situation into which, by the worst of usurpations, an usurpation on the prerogatives of Nature, you attempt to force them.

The Chancellor of France, at the opening of the States, said, in a tone of oratorial flourish, that all occupations were honourable. If he meant only that no honest employment was disgraceful, he would not have gone beyond the truth. But in asserting that anything is honourable, we imply some distinction in its favour. The occupation of a hair-dresser, or a working tallow-chandler, cannot be a matter of honour to any person—to say nothing of a number of other more servile employments. Such descriptions of men ought not to suffer oppression from the state; but the state suffers oppression if such as they, either individually or collectively, are permitted to rule. In this you think you are combating prejudice, but you are at war with Nature. . . .

Do not imagine that I wish to confine power, authority, and distinction to blood and names and titles. No, Sir. There is no qualification for government but virtue and wisdom, actual or presumptive. Wherever they are actually found, they have, in whatever state, condition, profession, or trade, the passport of Heaven to human place and honour. Woe to the country which would madly and impiously reject the service of the talents and virtues, civil, military, or religious, that are given to grace and to serve it. . . . Woe to that country, too, that, passing into the opposite extreme, considers a low education, a mean, contracted view of things, a sordid, mercenary occupation, as a preferable title to command! . . .

Far am I from denying . . . the *real* rights of men. In denying their false claims of right, I do not mean to injure those which are real, and are such as their pretended rights would totally destroy. If civil society be made for the advantage of man, all the advantages for which it is made become his right. It is an institution of beneficence; and law itself is only beneficence acting by a rule. Men have a right to justice, as between their fellows, whether their fellows are in politic function or in ordinary occupation. They have a right to the fruits of their industry, and to the means of making their industry fruitful. They have a right to the acquisitions of their parents, to the nourishment and improvement of their offspring, to instruction in life and to consolation in death. Whatever each man can separately do, without trespassing upon others, he has a right to do for himself; and he has a right to a fair portion of all which society, with all its combinations of skill and force, can do in his favour. In this partnership all men have equal rights; but not to equal things. He that has but five shillings in the partnership has as good a right to it as he that has five hundred pounds has to his larger proportion; but he has not a right to an equal dividend in the product of the joint stock. And as to the share of power, authority, and direction which each individual ought to have in the management of the state, that I must deny to be amongst the direct original rights of man in civil society. . . .

The science of constructing a commonwealth, or renovating it, or reforming it, is like every other experimental science, not to be taught *a priori*. Nor is it a short experience that can instruct us in that practical science; because the real effects of moral causes are not always immediate, but that which, in the first instance, is prejudicial may be excellent in its remoter operation, and its excellence may arise even from the ill effects it produces in the beginning. The reverse also happens; and very plausible schemes, with very pleasing commencements, have often shameful and lamentable conclusions. In states there are often some obscure and almost latent causes, things which appear at first view of little moment, on which a very great part of their prosperity or adversity may most essentially depend. The science of government being, therefore, so practical in itself, and intended for such practical purposes, a matter which requires experience, and even more experience than any person can gain in his whole life, however sagacious and observing he may be, it is with infinite caution that any man ought to venture upon pulling down an edifice which has answered in any tolerable degree for ages the common purposes of society, or on building it up again without having models and patterns of approval utility before his eyes. . . .

I do not know under what description to class the present ruling authority in France. It affects to be a pure democracy, though I think it in a direct train of becoming shortly a mischievous and ignoble oligarchy. But for the present I admit it to be a contrivance of the nature and effect of what it pretends to. I reprobate no form of government merely upon abstract principles. There may be situations in which the purely democratic form will become necessary. There may be some (very few, and very particularly circumstanced) where it would be clearly desirable. This I do not take to be the case of France, or of any other great country. Until now, we have seen no examples of considerable democracies. The ancients were better acquainted with them. Not being wholly unread in the authors who had seen the most of those constitutions, and who best understood them, I cannot help concurring with their opinion, that an absolute democracy no more than absolute monarchy is to be reckoned among the legitimate forms of government. They think it rather the corruption and degeneracy than the sound constitution of a republic. If I recollect rightly, Aristotle observes that a democracy has many striking points of resemblance with a tyranny. Of this I am certain, that in a democracy the majority of the citizens is capable of exercising the most cruel oppressions upon the minority, whenever strong divisions prevail in that kind of policy, as they often must—and that oppression of the minority will extend to far greater numbers, and will be carried on with much greater fury, than can almost ever be apprehended from the dominion of a single sceptre. In such a popular persecution, individual sufferers are in a much more deplorable condition than in any other. . . .

Chapter 5

ROMANTICISM

a. VICOMTE DE CHATEAUBRIAND, FROM
THE GENIUS OF CHRISTIANITY

THE ROMANTIC REVOLT against Neo-Classicism and Enlightenment rationalism was in many respects profoundly conservative. Some Romantics rebelled against the facile anticlericalism of the eighteenth century and asserted their devotion to the Church. To the Vicomte de Chateaubriand (1768–1848), the mystery and majesty of Christianity were far more appealing than the antiseptic rationalism of its eighteenth-century critics.

There is nothing beautiful, pleasing, or grand in life, but that which is more or less mysterious. The most wonderful sentiments are those which produce impressions difficult to be explained. . . .

We perceive at the first glance, that, in regard to mysteries, the Christian religion has a great advantage over the religions of antiquity. The mysteries of the latter bore no relation to man, and afforded, at the utmost, but a subject of reflection to the philosopher or of song to the poet. Our mysteries, on the contrary, speak directly to the heart; they comprehend the secrets of our existence. The question here is not about a futile arrangement of numbers, but concerning the salvation and felicity of the human race. Is it possible for man, whom daily experience so fully convinces of his ignorance and frailty, to reject the mysteries of Jesus Christ? They are the mysteries of the unfortunate!

The Trinity, which is the first mystery presented by the Christian faith, opens an immense field for philosophic study, whether we consider it in the attributes of God, or examine the vestiges of this dogma, which was formerly diffused throughout the East. It is a pitiful mode of reasoning to reject whatever we cannot comprehend.

There is a God. The plants of the valley and the cedars of the mountain bless his name; the insect hums his praise; the elephant salutes him with the rising day; the bird glorifies him among the foliage; the lightning bespeaks his power, and the ocean declares his immensity. Man alone has said, "There is no God."

Has he then in adversity never raised his eyes toward heaven? Has he in prosperity never cast them on the earth? Is Nature so far from him that he has not been able to contemplate its wonders; or does he consider them as the mere result of fortuitous causes? But how could chance have compelled crude and stubborn materials to arrange themselves in such exquisite order?

It might be asserted that man is the *idea of God displayed,* and the universe *his imagination made manifest.* They who have admitted the beauty of nature as a proof of a supreme intelligence, ought to have pointed out a truth which greatly enlarges the sphere of wonders. It is this: motion and rest, darkness and light, the seasons, the revolutions of the heavenly bodies, which give variety to the decorations of the world, are successive only in appearance, and permanent in reality. The scene that fades upon our view is painted in brilliant colors for another people; it is not the spectacle that is changed, but the spectator. Thus God has combined in his work absolute duration and progressive duration. The first is placed in time, the second in space; by means of the former, the beauties of the universe are one, infinite, and invariable; by means of the latter, they are multiplied, finite, and perpetually renewed. Without the one, there would be no grandeur in the creation; without the other, it would exhibit nothing but dull uniformity.

Here time appears to us in a new point of view; the smallest of its fractions becomes a complete whole, which comprehends all things, and in which all things transpire, from the death of an insect to the birth of a world; each minute is in itself a little eternity. Combine, then, at the same moment, in imagination, the most beautiful incidents of nature; represent to yourself at once all the hours of the day and all the seasons of the year, a spring morning and an autumnal morning, a night spangled with stars and a night overcast with clouds, meadows enamelled with flowers, forests stripped by the frosts, and fields glowing with their golden harvests; you will then have a just idea of the prospect of the universe.

SOURCE. Vicomte de Chateaubriand, *The Genius of Christianity,* C. I. White, tr., Baltimore: J. Murphy and Co., 1862, pp. 51, 53–54.

b. WILLIAM WORDSWORTH, "TINTERN ABBEY"

IN GENERAL, the Romantics were deeply attracted to what they conceived to be the spirit of the Middle Ages—violent, colorful, mystical, and otherworldly, its ruined churches mellowed with age and haunted by long-dead dreams. Nature was important to the Romantics, as it had been to the men of the Enlightenment, but the Romantic view of nature was far different from that of the eighteenth century. To most philosophes, *"nature" suggested the ordered system of Newton and the formal gardens of Versailles. To the Romantics, nature was wild, mysterious, and virgin. William Wordsworth (1770–1850), in his "Tintern Abbey," celebrates nature's lonely beauty.*

Lines Composed a Few Miles Above Tintern Abbey, on Revisiting the Banks of the Wye During a Tour. July 13, 1798

Five years have past; five summers, with the length
Of five long winters! and again I hear
These waters, rolling from their mountain-springs
With a soft inland murmur.—Once again
Do I behold these steep and lofty cliffs,
That on a wild, secluded scene impress
Thoughts of more deep seclusion, and connect
The landscape with the quiet of the sky.
The day is come when I again repose
Here, under this dark sycamore, and view
These plots of cottage-ground, these orchard-tufts,
Which at this season, with their unripe fruits,
Are clad in one green hue, and lose themselves
'Mid groves and copses. Once again I see
These hedge-rows, hardly hedge-rows, little lines
Of sportive wood run wild: these pastoral farms,
Green to the very door; and wreaths of smoke
Sent up, in silence, from among the trees!
With some uncertain notice, as might seem
Of vagrant dwellers in the houseless woods,
Or of some Hermit's cave, where by his fire
The Hermit sits alone.

          These beauteous forms,
Through a long absence, have not been to me
As is a landscape to a blind man's eye:
But oft, in lonely rooms, and 'mid the din
Of towns and cities, I have owed to them,
In hours of weariness, sensations sweet,
Felt in the blood, and felt along the heart;
And passing even into my purer mind,
With tranquil restoration:—feelings too
Of unremembered pleasure: such, perhaps,
As have no slight or trivial influence

On that best portion of a good man's life,
His little, nameless, unremembered acts
Of kindness and of love. Nor less, I trust,
To them I may have owed another gift,
Of aspect more sublime: that blessed mood,
In which the burden of the mystery,
In which the heavy and the weary weight
Of all this unintelligible world,
Is lightened:—that serene and blessed mood,
In which the affections gently lead us on,—
Until, the breath of this corporeal frame
And even the motion of our human blood
Almost suspended, we are laid asleep
In body, and become a living soul:
While with an eye made quiet by the power
Of harmony, and the deep power of joy,
We see into the life of things.
                              If this
Be but a vain belief, yet, oh! how oft—
In darkness and amid the many shapes
Of joyless daylight; when the fretful stir
Unprofitable, and the fever of the world,
Have hung upon the beatings of my heart—
How oft, in spirit, have I turned to thee,
O sylvan Wye! thou wanderer through the woods,
How often has my spirit turned to thee!

    And now, with gleams of half-extinguished thought,
With many recognitions dim and faint,
And somewhat of a sad perplexity,
The picture of the mind revives again:
While here I stand, not only with the sense
Of present pleasure, but with pleasing thoughts
That in this moment there is life and food
For future years. And so I dare to hope,
Though changed, no doubt, from what I was when first
I came among these hills; when like a roe
I bounded o'er the mountains, by the sides
Of the deep rivers, and the lonely streams,
Wherever nature led: more like a man
Flying from something that he dreads, than one
Who sought the thing he loved. For nature then
(The coarser pleasures of my boyish days
And their glad animal movenments all gone by)
To me was all in all.—I cannot paint
What then I was. The sounding cataract

Haunted me like a passion: the tall rock,
The mountain, and the deep and gloomy wood,
Their color and their forms, were then to me
An appetite; a feeling and a love,
That had no need of a remoter charm
By thoughts supplied, nor any interest
Unborrowed from the eye.—That time is past,
And all its aching joys are now no more,
And all its dizzy raptures. Not for this
Faint I, nor mourn nor murmur; other gifts
Have followed; for such loss, I would believe,
Abundant recompense. For I have learned
To look on nature, not as in the hour
Of thoughtless youth; but hearing oftentimes
The still, sad music of humanity,
Nor harsh nor grating, though of ample power
To chasten and subdue. And I have felt
A presence that disturbs me with the joy
Of elevated thoughts; a sense sublime
Of something far more deeply interfused,
Whose dwelling is the light of setting suns,
And the round ocean, and the living air,
And the blue sky, and in the mind of man:
A motion and a spirit, that impels
All thinking things, all objects of all thought,
And rolls through all things. Therefore am I still
A lover of the meadows and the woods,
And mountains; and of all that we behold
From this green earth; of all the mighty world
Of eye, and ear,—both what they half create,
And what perceive; well pleased to recognize
In nature and the language of the sense,
The anchor of my purest thoughts, the nurse,
The guide, the guardian of my heart, and soul
Of all my moral being.
                        Nor perchance,
If I were not thus taught, should I the more
Suffer my genial spirits to decay:
For thou art with me here upon the banks
Of this fair river; thou my dearest Friend,
My dear, dear Friend; and in thy voice I catch
The language of my former heart, and read
My former pleasures in the shooting lights
Of thy wild eyes. O yet a little while
May I behold in thee what I was once,

My dear, dear Sister! and this prayer I make,
Knowing that Nature never did betray
The heart that loved her; 'tis her privilege,
Through all the years of this our life, to lead
From joy to joy: for she can so inform
The mind that is within us, so impress
With quietness and beauty, and so feed
With lofty thoughts, that neither evil tongues,
Rash judgments, nor the sneers of selfish men,
Nor greetings where no kindness is, nor all
The dreary intercourse of daily life,
Shall e'er prevail against us, or disturb
Our cheerful faith, that all which we behold
Is full of blessings. Therefore let the moon
Shine on thee in thy solitary walk;
And let the misty mountain-winds be free
To blow against thee: and, in after years,
When these wild ecstasies shall be matured
Into a sober pleasure; when thy mind
Shall be a mansion for all lovely forms,
Thy memory be as a dwelling-place
For all sweet sounds and harmonies; O, then,
If solitude, or fear, or pain, or grief,
Should be thy portion, with what healing thoughts
Of tender joy wilt thou remember me,
And these my exhortations! Nor, perchance,—
If I should be where I no more can hear
Thy voice, nor catch from thy wild eyes these gleams
Of past existence,—wilt thou then forget
That on the banks of this delightful stream
We stood together; and that I, so long
A worshipper of Nature, hither came
Unwearied in that service: rather say
With warmer love,—oh! with far deeper zeal
Of holier love. Nor wilt thou then forget,
That after many wanderings, many years
Of absence, these steep woods and lofty cliffs,
And this green pastoral landscape, were to me
More dear, both for themselves and for thy sake!

c. SHELLEY, "A DIRGE"

ROMANTIC WRITERS also evoked the dark violence of nature, none more movingly than the young Percy Bysshe Shelley (1792–1822).

Rough wind, that moanest loud
  Grief too sad for song;
Wild wind, when sullen cloud
  Knells all the night long;

Sad storm, whose tears are vain,
Bare woods, whose branches strain,
Deep caves and dreary main,—
  Wail, for the world's wrong!

d. KEATS, "WHEN I HAVE FEARS"

THE ROMANTIC VIEW OF NATURE permeates this romantic sonnet by John Keats (1795–1821).

When I have fears that I may cease to be
  Before my pen has glean'd my teeming brain,
Before high-piled books, in charactery,
  Hold like rich garners the full ripen'd grain;
When I behold, upon the night's starr'd face,
  Hugh cloudy symbols of a high romance,
And think that I may never live to trace
  Their shadows, with the magic hand of chance;
And when I feel, fair creature of an hour,
  That I shall never look upon thee more,
Never have relish in the faery power
  Of unreflecting love;—then on the shore
Of the wide world I stand alone, and think
Till love and fame to nothingness do sink.

e. ARCHITECTURE

THE EXUBERANT ANTI-CLASSICISM of some Romantic architects and their willingness to draw inspiration from distant times and places are strikingly exemplified in John Nash's Royal Pavilion at Brighton, England (1815–1818), patterned vaguely after the Indian Taj Mahal.

JOHN NASH, THE ROYAL PAVILION, BRIGHTON, 1815–1818

THE REVIVAL OF INTEREST in the Middle Ages resulted in many structures being built in the Neo-Gothic style. The Houses of Parliament (begun 1836), designed by Sir Charles Berry and A. Welby Pugin, are notable examples.

SIR CHARLES BERRY AND A. WELBY PUGIN, THE HOUSE OF PARLIAMENT

f. PAINTING

BRILLIANT COLOR, mysterious shadows, and an indefatigable quest for exotic subject matter mark the Oriental Tiger Hunt *and* Oriental Lion Hunt *by the French Romantic painter Eugene Delacroix (1798–1863).*

EUGÈNE DELACROIX, *ORIENTAL TIGER HUNT*

EUGÈNE DELACROIX, *ORIENTAL LION HUNT*

THE SLAVE SHIP *of Joseph Mallord William Turner (1775–1851), with its dramatic subject, rich colors, and fantastic details, epitomizes the Romantic movement in a single work of art, yet also prefigures the later impressionist style (below, Chapter II, b.). Compare the radically different style of the slightly earlier Neo-Classical school (above, Chapter 3,b.)*

JOSEPH MALLORD WILLIAM TURNER, *THE SLAVE SHIP*, 1839

PART THREE

Industrialism
and Its Consequences

THE Industrial Revolution, with its radically new organization of the processes of production, began in England in the later eighteenth century. During the nineteenth century it spread to Belgium, France, Germany, the United States, and elsewhere. At the present time it is still continuing to spread. The development of the factory system, and the dramatic population shift from countryside to city, created severe social problems for nineteenth-century Europe and America and, indeed, transformed the social structure. There now emerged two new and often mutually hostile classes—the factory owners and the factory workers—the "capitalists" and the "proletarians," in Marxist terminology. The profound social dislocation and urban poverty wrought by the Industrial Revolution created severe problems to which the political and intellectual leaders of the nineteenth century reacted in a number of ways. As industrialization continues, these problems, and the reactions to them, remain deeply relevant to our own age.

A number of economists in England remained faithful to the *laissez-faire* philosophy of Adam Smith. But influenced also by the pessimistic Malthusian notion that human fecundity outstripped productivity, they tended to take a more somber view of economic reality than did Smith. Poverty to them was unfortunate but inevitable, and any attempt to mitigate it would be not merely pernicious but useless. The works of these *laissez-faire* economists won for their discipline the name "the dismal science."

The unhappy condition of the proletariat evoked a far different response among the Socialist and Communist thinkers of the nineteenth century. These men undertook a direct attack against the concept of private ownership on which the capitalist system was based, argued that the factory owners were unnecessary social parasites, and insisted that the organs of production should be owned by the workers themselves through a proletarian-dominated state. Socialism tended at first to be visionary and utopian, but with the writings of Karl Marx it took on a more scientific, hard-headed character and became rigorously systematic. The European Communist movement, rooted in Marxist thought, made important gains in the later nineteenth and early twentieth centuries. By no means a monolithic force, it was sharply divided as to the best method of achieving the Communist society. Revisionist Marxists argued that the proletariat could rise to power gradually by winning elections and eventually gaining control of national legislatures. Strict Marxists such as Lenin held to the belief that the transition from capitalism to Communism could only take place by violent revolution. All were agreed, however, that the workers were destined to control society and that the replacement of capitalism by Communism was inevitable.

Chapter 6

THE INDUSTRIAL REVOLUTION

a. TESTIMONY BEFORE THE SADLER COMMITTEE ON FACTORY CONDITIONS

THE LIVES OF WORKERS in early-industrial England were wretched indeed. In 1831 to 1832 the British government, succumbing to reformist pressure, conducted an investigation of factory conditions in which the Sadler Committee heard testimony from workers and other employees of the factory owners. The Sadler Committee was predisposed to reform and sought in its hearings to expose the terrible conditions that existed in the factories.

Elizabeth Bentley, called in; and Examined

What age are you?—Twenty-three.

Where do you live?—At Leeds.

What time did you begin to work at a factory?—When I was six years old.

At whose factory did you work?—At Mr. Busk's.

What kind of mill is it?—Flax-mill.

What was your business in that mill?—I was a little doffer.

What were your hours of labour in that mill?—From 5 in the morning till 9 at night, when they were thronged.

For how long a time together have you worked that excessive length of time?—For about half a year.

What were your usual hours of labour when you were not so thronged?—From 6 in the morning till 7 at night.

What time was allowed for your meals?—Forty minutes at noon.

Had you any time to get your breakfast or drinking?—No, we got it as we could.

And when your work was bad, you hardly had anytime to eat at all?—No; we were obliged to leave it or take it home, and when we did not take it, the overlooker took it, and gave it to his pigs.

Do you consider doffing a laborious employment?—Yes.

Explain what it is you had to do?—When the frames are full, they have to stop the frames, and take the flyers off, and take the full bobbins off, and carry them to the roller; and then put empty ones on, and set the frame going again.

Does that keep you constantly on your feet?—Yes, there are so many frames, and they run so quick.

Your labour is very excessive?—Yes; you have not time for anything.

Suppose you flagged a little, or were too late, what would they do?—Strap us.

Are they in the habit of strapping those who are last in doffing?—Yes.

Constantly?—Yes.

Girls as well as boys?—Yes.

Have you ever been strapped?—Yes.

Severely?—Yes.

Is the strap used so as to hurt you excessively?—Yes, it is.

Were you strapped if you were too much fatigued to keep up with the machinery?—Yes; the overlooker I was under was a very severe man, and when we have been fatigued and worn out, and had not baskets to put the bobbins in, we used to put them in the window bottoms, and that broke the panes sometimes, and I broke one one time, and the overlooker strapped me on the arm, and it rose a blister, and I ran home to my mother.

How long did you work at Mr. Busk's?—Three or four years.

Where did you go to then?—Benyon's factory.

That was when you were about 10 years?—Yes.

What were you then?—A weigher in the card-room.

How long did you work there?—From half-past 5 till 8 at night.

Was that the ordinary time?—Till 9 when they were thronged.

What time was allowed for meals at that mill?—Forty minutes at noon.

Any time at breakfast or drinking?—Yes, for the card-rooms, but not for the spinning-rooms, a quarter of an hour to get their breakfast.

And the same for their drinking?—Yes.

So that the spinners in that room worked from half-past 5 till 9 at night?—Yes.

Having only forty minutes' rest?—Yes.

The carding-room is more oppressive than the spinning department?—Yes, it is so dusty they cannot see each other for dust.

It is on that account they are allowed a relaxation of those few minutes?—Yes; the cards get so soon filled up with waste and dirt, they are obliged to stop them, or they would take fire.

There is a convenience in that stoppage?—Yes, it is as much for their benefit as for the working people.

When it was not necessary no such indulgence was allowed?—No.

Never?—No.

Were the children beat up to their labour there?—Yes.

With what?—A strap; I have seen the overlooker go to the top end of the room, where the little girls hug the can to the backminders;[1] he has taken a strap, and a whistle in his mouth, and sometimes he has got a chain and chained them, and strapped them all down the room.

All the children?—No, only those hugging the cans.

What was his reason for that?—He was angry.

Had the children committed any fault?—They were too slow.

Were the children excessively fatigued at that time?—Yes, it was in the afternoon.

Were the girls so struck as to leave marks upon their skin?—Yes, they have had black marks many times, and their parents dare not come to him about it, they were afraid of losing their work.

If the parents were to complain of this excessive ill-usage, the probable consequence would be the loss of the situation of the child?—Yes.

In what part of the mill did you work?—In the card-room.

It was exceedingly dusty?—Yes.

Did it affect your health?— Yes; it was so dusty, the dust got upon my lungs, and the work was so hard; I was middling strong when I went there, but the work was so bad; I got so bad in health, that when I pulled the baskets down, I pulled my bones out of their places.

You dragged the baskets?—Yes; down the rooms to where they are worked.

And as you had been weakened by excessive labour, you could not stand that labour?—No.

It has had the effect of pulling your shoulders out?—Yes; it was a great basket that stood higher than this table a good deal.

How heavy was it?—I cannot say; it was a very large one, that was full of weights up-heaped, and pulling the basket pulled my shoulders out of its place, and my ribs have grown over it.

You continued at that work?—Yes.

You think that work is too much for children?—Yes.

It is woman's work, not fit for children?—Yes.

Is that work generally done by women?—Yes.

How came you to do it?—There was no spinning for me.

Did they give you women's wages?—They gave me 5s. and the women had 6s. 6d.

What wages did you get as a spinner?—Six shillings.

Did you perceive that many other girls were made ill by that long labour?—Yes, a good many of them.

[1] A wooden vehicle that persons were tied to when punishment was administered.

So that you were constantly receiving fresh hands to supply the places of those that could no longer bear their work?—Yes, there were fresh hands every week; they could not keep their hands.

Did they all go away on account of illness?—They were sick and ill with the dust.

Do you know whether any of them died in consequence of it?—No, I cannot speak to that.

You do not know what became of them?—No, we did not know that.

If a person was to take an account of a mill, and the hands in it that were ill, they would know very little of those who had suffered from their labour; they would be elsewhere?—Yes.

But you are sure of this, that they were constantly leaving on account of the excessive labour they had to endure?—Yes.

And the unhealthy nature of their employment?—Yes.

Did you take any means to obviate the bad effects of this dust?—No.

Did it make you very thirsty?—Yes, we drank a deal of water in the room.

Were you heated with your employment at the same time?—No, it was not so very hot as in the summer time; in the winter time they were obliged to have the windows open, it made no matter what the weather was, and sometimes we got very severe colds in frost and snow.

You were constantly exposed to colds, and were made ill by that cause also?—Yes.

Could you eat your food well in that factory?—No, indeed I had not much to eat, and the little I had I could not eat it, my appetite was so poor, and being covered with dust; and it was no use to take it home, I could not eat it, and the overlooker took it, and gave it to the pigs.

You are speaking of the breakfast?—Yes.

How far had you to go for dinner?—We could not go home to dinner.

Where did you dine?—In the mill.

Did you live far from the mill?—Yes, two miles.

Had you a clock?—No, we had not.

Supposing you had not been in time enough in the morning at these mills, what would have been the consequence?—We should have been quartered.

What do you mean by that?—If we were a quarter of an hour too late, they would take off half an hour; we only got a penny an hour, and they would take a halfpenny more.

The fine was much more considerable than the loss of time?—Yes.

Were you also beaten for being late?—No, I was never beaten myself, I have seen the boys beaten for being too late.

Were you generally there in time?—Yes; my mother has been up at 4 o'clock in the morning, and at 2 o'clock in the morning; the colliers used to go to their work about 3 or 4 o'clock, and when she heard them stirring she has got up out of her warm bed, and gone out and asked them the time; and I have sometimes been at Hunslet Car at 2 o'clock in the morning, when it was streaming down with rain, and we have had to stay till the mill was opened. . . .

Supposing your hours of labour had been moderate, could you have awoke regularly?—Yes.

Was it a matter of anxiety and difficulty for you to rouse yourself to be early enough for those hours of labour?—Yes.

You are considerably deformed in your person in consequence of this labour?—Yes, I am.

At what time did it come on?—I was about 13 years old when it began coming, and it has got worse since. . . .

Do you know of any body that has been similarily injured in their health?—Yes, in their health, but not many deformed as I am.

You are deformed in the shoulders?—Yes.

It is very common to have weak ankles and crooked knees?—Yes, very common indeed.

That is brought on by stopping the spindle?—Yes.

Do you know anything of wet-spinning?—Yes, it is very uncomfortable; I have stood before the frame till I have been wet through to my skin; and in winter time, when we have gone home, our clothes have been frozen, and we have nearly caught our death of cold.

Were you permitted to give up your labour at any time to suit your convenience and your health, and resume it again when you were more capable of it?—Yes, we have stopped at home one day or two days, just as we were situated in our health.

If you had stopped away any length of time, should you have found a difficulty to keep your situation?—Yes, we should.

Were the children constantly beaten to their labour, as you have described?—Yes.

Where are you now?—In the poorhouse.

Where?—At Hunslet.

Do any of your former employers come to see you?—No.

Did you ever receive any thing from them when you became afflicted?—When I was at home Mr. Walker made me a present of 1s. or 2s., but since I have left my work and gone to the poorhouse, they have not come nigh me.

You are supported by the parish?—Yes.

You are utterly incapable now of any exertion of that sort?—Yes.

You were very willing to have worked as long as you were able, from your earliest age?—Yes.

And to have supported your widowed mother as long as you could?—Yes.

State what you think as to the circumstances in which you have been placed during all this time of labour, and what you have considered about it as to the hardship and cruelty of it.

[The Witness was too much affected to answer the question.]

SOURCE. *Parliamentary Papers, Reports from Committees*, XV, "Labour of Children in Factories, 1831–1832," London, 1832.

b. THE ENGLISH FACTORY ACT OF 1833

THE INVESTIGATIONS of the Sadler Committee gave rise to the Factory Act of 1833 which mitigated somewhat the worst abuses of child labor.

An act to regulate the labour of children and young persons in the mills and factories of the united kingdom. . . . no person under eighteen years of age shall be allowed to work in the night—that is to say, between the hours half-past eight o'clock in the evening and half-past five o'clock in the morning— . . . in or about any cotton, woolen, worsted, hemp, flax, two, linen, or silk mill or factory. . . .

. . . no person under the age of eighteen years shall be employed in any such mill or factory . . . more than twelve hours in any one day, nor more than sixty-nine hours in any one week. . . . there shall be allowed in the course of every day not less than one and a half hours for meals. . . .

. . . it shall not be lawful for any person whatsoever to employ in any factory or mill as aforesaid, except in mills for the manufacture of silk, any child who shall not have completed his or her ninth year of age.

. . . it shall not be lawful for any person whosoever to employ, keep, or allow to remain in any factory or mill as aforesaid for a longer time than forty-eight hours in any one week, nor for a longer time than nine hours in any one day . . . , any child who shall not have completed his or her eleventh year of age; or, after the expiration of eighteen months from the passing of this act, any child who shall not have completed his or her twelfth year of age; or, after the expiration of thirty months from the passing of this act, any child who shall not have completed his or her thirteenth year of age. Provided, nevertheless, that, in mills for the manufacture of silk, children under the age of thirteen years shall be allowed to work ten hours in any one day.

. . . all children and young persons whose hours of work are regulated and limited by this act shall be entitled to the following holidays, *viz.:*
on Christmas Day and Good Friday, the entire day; and not fewer than
eight half-days besides in every year. . . .

. . . it shall be lawful for his majesty . . . to appoint during his majesty's
pleasure four persons to be inspectors of factories and places where the labour
of children and young persons under eighteen years of age is employed. . . .
And such inspectors or any of them are hereby empowered to enter any
factory or mill, and any school attached or belonging thereto at all times
and seasons, by day or by night, when such mills or factories are at work;
and, having so entered, to examine therein the children and any other person
or persons employed therein, and to make inquiry respecting their condition,
employment, and education. . . .

. . . every child hereinbefore restricted to the performance of forty-
eight hours of labour in any one week shall, so long as such child shall be
within the said restricted age, attend some school. . . .

SOURCE. A. E. Bland, P. A. Brown, and R. H. Tawney, eds., *English Economic History: Select Documents,* London: G. Bell & Sons, 1925, pp. 519–521. Reprinted by permission of G. Bell &
Sons, Ltd., London.

c. THE CONDITION OF MANCHESTER, 1840

*LIFE IN THE NEW INDUSTRIAL CITIES remained grim and dehuman-
ized, as is evident from the surgeon John Robertson's description of sanitary
conditions in Manchester in 1840.*

Until twelve years ago there was no paving and sewering Act in any of the
townships; even in the township of Manchester, containing in the year 1831
upwards of 142,000 inhabitants, this was the case; and the disgraceful condition of the streets and sewers on the invasion of the cholera you have no
doubt learned from Dr. Kay's able and valuable pamphlet. At the present
time the paving of the streets proceeds rapidly in every direction, and great
attention is given to the drains. Upon the whole, it is gratifying to bear testimony to the zeal of the authorities in carrying on the salutary improvements,
especially when it is known that no street can be paved and sewered without
the consent of the owners of property, unless a certain large proportion of
the land on either side is built upon. Owing to this cause several important
streets remain to this hour disgraceful nuisances.

Manchester has no Building Act, and hence, with the exception of certain central streets, over which the Police Act gives the Commissioners power, each proprietor builds as he pleases. New cottages, with or without cellars, huddled together row behind row, may be seen springing up in many parts, but especially in the township of Manchester, where the land is higher in price than the land for cottage sites in other townships is. With such proceedings as these the authorities cannot interfere. A cottage row may be badly drained, the streets may be full of pits, brimful of stagnant water, the receptacle of dead cats and dogs, yet no one may find fault. The number of cellar residences, you have probably learned from the papers published by the Manchester Statistical Society, is very great in all quarters of the town; and even in Hulme, a large portion of which consists of cottages recently erected, the same practice is continued. That it is an evil must be obvious on the slightest consideration, for how can a hole underground of from 12 to 15 feet square admit of ventilation so as to fit it for a human habitation?

We have no authorized inspector of dwellings and streets. If an epidemic disease were to invade, as happened in 1832, the authorities would probably order inspection, as they did on that occasion, but it would be merely by general permission, not of right.

So long as this and other great manufacturing towns were multiplying and extending their branches of manufacture and were prosperous, every fresh addition of operatives found employment, good wages, and plenty of food; and so long as the families of working people are well fed, it is certain they maintain their health in a surprising manner, even in cellars and other close dwellings. Now, however, the case is different. Food is dear, labour scarce, and wagès in many branches very low; consequently, as might be expected, disease and death are making unusual havoc. In the years 1833, 1834, 1835, and 1836 (years of prosperity), the number of fever cases admitted into the Manchester House of Recovery amounted only to 1,685, or 421 per annum; while in the two pinching years, 1838 and 1839, the number admitted was 2,414, or 1,207 per annum. It is in such a depressed state of the manufacturing districts as at present exists that unpaved and badly sewered streets, narrow alleys, close, unventilated courts and cellars, exhibit their malign influence in augmenting the sufferings which that greatest of all physical evils, want of sufficient food, inflicts on young and old in large towns, but especially on the young.

Manchester has no public park or other grounds where the population can walk and breathe the fresh air. New streets are rapidly extending in every direction, and so great already is the expanse of the town, that those who live in the more populous quarters can seldom hope to see the green face of nature. . . . In this respect Manchester is disgracefully defective; more so, perhaps, than any other town in the empire. Every advantage of this nature has been sacrificed to the getting of money in the shape of ground-rents.

d. JEREMY BENTHAM, FROM *A MANUAL OF POLITICAL ECONOMY*

THE GRIMNESS OF LIFE in industrial England was very nearly matched by the grimness of economic thought. In 1789, the opening year of the French Revolution, there appeared two important works in the laissez-faire tradition: A Manual of Political Economy *by the English utilitarian philosopher Jeremy Bentham (1748–1832), and* An Essay on the Principle of Population *by the English economist Thomas Robert Malthus (1766–1834). The Introduction to Bentham's work is a concise statement of the principle of governmental noninterference and an epitome of the viewpoint of the Classical or Liberal school of economics.*

With the view of causing an increase to take place in the mass of national wealth, or with a view to increase of the means either of subsistence or enjoyment, without some special reason, the general rule is, that nothing ought to be done or attempted by government. The motto, or watchword of government, on these occasions, ought to be—*Be quiet.*

For this quietism there are two main reasons:—1. Generally speaking, any interference for this purpose on the part of government is *needless.* The wealth of the whole community is composed of the wealth of the several individuals belonging to it taken together. But to increase his particular portion is, generally speaking, among the constant objects of each individual's exertions and care. Generally speaking, there is no one who knows what is for your interest, so well as yourself—no one who is disposed with so much ardour and constancy to pursue it.

2. Generally speaking, it is moreover likely to be pernicious, viz. by being unconducive, or even obstructive, with reference to the attainment of the end in view. Each individual bestowing more time and attention upon the means of preserving and increasing his portion of wealth, than is or can be bestowed by government, is likely to take a more effectual course than what, in his instance and on his behalf, would be taken by government.

It is, moreover, universally and constantly pernicious in another way, by the restraint or constraint imposed on the free agency of the individual. Pain is the general concomitant of the sense of such restraint, wherever it is experienced.

Without being productive of such coercion, and thereby of such pain—in such a way more or less direct—more or less perceptible, with this or any other view, the interposition of government can hardly take place. If the coercion be not applied to the very individual whose conduct is endeavoured to be made immediately subservient to this purpose, it is at any rate applied to others—indeed, to the whole community taken together.

In coercive measures, so called, it is only to the individual that the coercion is applied. In the case of measures of encouragement, the field of coercion is vastly more extensive. Encouragements are grants of money or money's worth, applied in some shape or other to this purpose. But for this, any more than any other purpose, money is not raised but by taxes, and taxes are the produce of coercive laws appied to the most coercive purpose.

This would not be the less true, though the individual pieces of money thus applied happened to come from a source which had not been fed by any such means. In all communities, by far the greatest share of the money disposed of by government being supplied by taxes, whether this or that particular portion of money so applied, be supplied from that particular source, makes no sort of difference.

To estimate the good expected from the application of any particular mass of government money, compare it always with the mischief produced by the extraction of an equal sum of money by the most burthensome species of tax; since, by forbearing to make application of that sum of money, you might forbear levying the amount of that same sum of money by that tax, and thereby forbear imposing the mass of burthen that results from it.

SOURCE. *The Works of Jeremy Bentham,* Edinburgh: William Tait, 1843, III, pp. 33–34.

e. MALTHUS, FROM *AN ESSAY ON THE PRINCIPLE OF POPULATION AS IT AFFECTS THE FUTURE IMPROVEMENT OF SOCIETY*

THOMAS MALTHUS' ESSAY made a deep impact on subsequent economic thought. It cast a shadow on Enlightenment optimism by arguing that population growth always tended to exceed increases in food production and that general prosperity was a will-o'-the-wisp.

The great and unlooked-for discoveries that have taken place of late years in natural philosophy; the increasing diffusion of general knowledge from the extension of the art of printing; the ardent and unshackled spirit of inquiry that prevails throughout the lettered, and even unlettered, world; the new and extraordinary lights that have been thrown on political subjects, which dazzle and astonish the understanding: and particularly that tremendous phenomenon in the political horizon, the French Revolution, which, like a blazing comet, seems destined either to inspire with fresh life and vigour, or to scorch up and destroy the thinking inhabitants of the earth, have all concurred to lead able men into the opinion, that we are touching upon a period big with the most important changes, changes that would in some measure be decisive of the future fate of mankind.

It has been said, that the great question is now at issue, whether man shall henceforth start forwards with accelerated velocity towards illimitable, and hitherto unconceived improvement; or be condemned to a perpetual oscillation between happiness and misery, and after every effort remain still at an immeasurable distance from the wished-for goal.

Yet, anxiously as every friend of mankind must look forwards to the termination of this painful suspense; and, eagerly as the inquiring mind would hail every ray of light that might assist its view into futurity, it is much to be lamented, that the writers on each side of this momentous question still keep far aloof from each other. Their mutual arguments do not meet with a candid examination. The question is not brought to rest on fewer points; and even in theory scarcely seems to be approaching to a decision.

The advocate for the present order of things, is apt to treat the sect of speculative philosophers, either as a set of artful and designing knaves, who preach up ardent benevolence, and draw captivating pictures of a happier state of society, only the better to enable them to destroy the present establishments, and to forward their own deep-laid schemes of ambition: or, as wild and madheaded enthusiasts, whose silly speculations, and absurd paradoxes, are not worthy the attention of any reasonable man.

The advocate for the perfectibility of man, and of society, retorts on the defender of establishments a more than equal contempt. He brands him as the slave of the most miserable and narrow prejudices; or, as the defender of the abuses of civil society, only because he profits by them. He paints him either as a character who prostitutes his understanding to his interest; or as one whose powers of mind are not of a size to grasp anything great and noble; who cannot see above five yards before him; and who must therefore be utterly unable to take in the views of the enlightened benefactor of mankind.

In this unamicable contest, the cause of truth cannot but suffer. The really good arguments on each side of the question are not allowed to have their proper weight. Each pursues his own theory, little solicitous to correct, or improve it, by an attention to what is advanced by his opponents.

The friend of the present order of things condemns all political speculations in the gross. He will not even condescend to examine the grounds from which the perfectibility of society is inferred. Much less will he give himself the trouble in a fair and candid manner to attempt an exposition of their fallacy.

The speculative philosopher equally offends against the cause of truth. With eyes fixed on a happier state of society, the blessings of which he paints in the most captivating colours, he allows himself to indulge in the most bitter invectives against every present establishment, without applying his talents to consider the best and safest means of removing abuses, and without seeming to be aware of the tremendous obstacles that threaten, even in theory, to oppose the progress of man towards perfection.

It is an acknowledged truth in philosophy, that a just theory will always be confirmed by experiment. Yet so much friction, and so many minute circumstances occur in practice, which it is next to impossible for the most enlarged and penetrating mind to foresee, that on few subjects can any theory be pronounced just, that has not stood the test of experience. But an untried theory cannot be advanced as probable, must less as just, till all the arguments against it have been maturely weighed, and clearly and consistently refuted.

I have read some of the speculations on the perfectibility of man and of society with great pleasure. I have been warmed and delighted with the enchanting picture which they hold forth. I ardently wish for such happy improvements. But I see great, and, to my understanding, unconquerable difficulties in the way to them. These difficulties it is my present purpose to state; declaring, at the same time, that so far from exulting in them, as a cause of triumphing over the friends of innovation, nothing would give me greater pleasure than to see them completely removed.

The most important argument that I shall adduce is certainly not new. The principles on which it depends have been explained in part by Hume, and more at large by Dr. Adam Smith. It has been advanced and applied to the present subject, though not with its proper weight, or in the most forcible point of view, by Mr. Wallace: and it may probably have been stated by many writers that I have never met with. I should certainly, therefore, not think of advancing it again, though I mean to place it in a point of view in some degree different from any that I have hitherto seen, if it had ever been fairly and satisfactorily answered.

The cause of this neglect on the part of the advocates for the perfectibility of mankind is not easily accounted for. I cannot doubt the talents of such men as Godwin and Condorcet. I am unwilling to doubt their candour. To my understanding, and probably to that of most others, the difficulty appears insurmountable. Yet these men of acknowledged ability and penetration, scarcely deign to notice it, and hold on their course in such speculations, with unabated ardour and undiminished confidence. I have certainly no right to say that they purposely shut their eyes to such arguments. I ought rather to doubt the validity of them, when neglected by such men, however forcibly their truth may strike my own mind. Yet in this respect it must be acknowledged that we are all of us too prone to err. If I saw a glass of wine repeatedly presented to a man, and he took no notice of it, I should be apt to think that he was blind or uncivil. A juster philosophy might teach me rather to think that my eyes deceived me, and that the offer was not really what I conceived it to be.

In entering upon the argument I must premise that I put out of the question, at present, all mere conjectures; that is, all suppositions, the probable realization of which cannot be inferred upon any just philosophical grounds. A writer may tell me that he thinks man will ultimately become an ostrich. I cannot properly contradict him. But before he can expect to bring any reasonable person over to his opinion, he ought to show that the necks of mankind have been gradually elongating; that the lips have grown harder, and more prominent; that the legs and feet are daily altering their shape; and that the hair is beginning to change into stubs of feathers. And till the probability of so wonderful a conversion can be shown, it is surely lost time and lost eloquence to expatiate on the happiness of man in such a state; to describe his powers, both of running and flying; to paint him in a condition where all narrow luxuries would be contemned; where he would be employed, only in collecting the necessaries of life; and where, consequently, each man's share of labour would be light, and his portion of leisure ample.

I think I may fairly make two postulata.

First, That food is necessary to the existence of man.

Secondly, That the passion between the sexes is necessary, and will remain nearly in its present state.

These two laws, ever since we have had any knowledge of mankind, appear to have been fixed laws of our nature; and, as we have not hitherto seen any alteration in them, we have no right to conclude that they will ever cease to be what they are now, without an immediate act of power in that Being who first arranged the system of the universe; and for the advantage of his creatures, still executes, according to fixed laws, all its various operations.

I do not know that any writer has supposed that on this earth man will ultimately be able to live without food. But Mr. Godwin has conjectured that the passion between the sexes may in time be extinguished. As, however, he calls this part of his work, a deviation into the land of conjecture, I will not dwell longer upon it at present, than to say, that the best arguments for the perfectibility of man are drawn from a contemplation of the great progress that he has already made from the savage state, and the difficulty of saying where he is to stop. But towards the extinction of the passion between the sexes, no progress whatever has hitherto been made. It appears to exist in as much force at present as it did two thousand, or four thousand years ago. There are individual exceptions now as there always have been. But, as these exceptions do not appear to increase in number, it would surely be a very unphilosophical mode of arguing, to infer merely from the existence of an exception, that the exception would, in time, become the rule, and the rule the exception.

Assuming, then, postulata as granted, I say, that the power of population is indefinitely greater than the power in the earth to produce subsistence for man.

Population, when unchecked, increases in a geometrical ratio. Subsistence only increases in an arithmetical ratio. A slight acquaintance with numbers will show the immensity of the first power in comparison of the second.

By that law our nature which makes food necessary to the life of man, the effects of these two unequal powers must be kept equal.

This implies a strong and constantly operating check on population from the difficulty of subsistence. This difficulty must fall some where; and must necessarily be severely felt by a large portion of mankind.

Through the animal and vegetable kingdoms, nature has scattered the seeds of life abroad with the most profuse and liberal hand. She has been comparatively sparing in the room, and the nourishment necessarily to rear them. The germs of existence contained in this spot of earth, with ample food, and ample room to expand it, would fill millions of worlds in the course of a few thousand years. Necessity, that imperious, all-pervading law of nature, restrains them within the prescribed bounds. The race of plants, and the race of animals shrink under this great restrictive law. And the race of man cannot, by any efforts of reason, escape from it. Among plants and animals its effects are waste of seed, sickness, and premature death. Among mankind, misery and vice. The former, misery, is an absolutely necessary consequence of it. Vice is a highly probable consequence, and we therefore see it abundantly prevail; but it ought not, perhaps, to be called an absolutely necessary consequence. The ordeal of virtue is to resist all temptation to evil.

This natural inequality of the two powers of population, and of production in the earth, and that great law of our nature which must constantly keep their effects equal, form the great difficulty that to me appears insurmountable in the way to perfectibility of society. All other arguments are of slight and subordinate consideration in comparison of this. I see no way by which man can escape from the weight of this law which pervades all animated nature. No fancied equality, no agrarian regulations in their utmost extent, could remove the pressure of it even for a single century. And it appears, therefore to be decisive against the possible existence of a society, all the members of which should live in ease, happiness, and comparative leisure; and feel no anxiety about providing the means of subsistence for themselves and families.

Consequently, if the premises are just, the argument is conclusive against the perfectibility of the mass of mankind.

I have thus sketched the general outline of the argument; but I will examine it more particularly; and I think it will be found that experience, the true source and foundation of all knowledge, invariably confirms its truth.

SOURCE. Thomas Malthus, *An Essay on the Principle of Population as it Affects the Future Improvement of Society,* London: 1798, reprinted 1926, pp. 1–17.

Chapter 7

THE GROWTH
OF SOCIALISM AND COMMUNISM

a. KARL MARX AND FRIEDRICH ENGELS,
FROM *THE COMMUNIST MANIFESTO*

*THE CLASSICAL SUMMARY of Communist doctrine and the call to rev-
olution are to be found in The Communist Manifesto (1848), written in
Paris by Karl Marx and his disciple Friedrich Engels. In the excerpts included here appear the basic Marxist doctrines of dialectical materialism,
class struggle as the key dynamic force in history, and the inevitable victory
of the proletariat. The immense impact of this document on its own and all
subsequent generations goes without saying. It remains today the fundamental statement of the Communist ideology.*

A spectre is haunting Europe—the spectre of Communism. All the powers
of old Europe have entered into a holy alliance to exorcise this spectre; Pope
and Czar, Metternich and Guizot,[1] French Radicals and German police-
spies.

Where is the party in opposition that has not been decried as communistic
by its opponents in power? Where the Opposition that has not hurled back
the branding reproach of Communism, against the more advanced opposition
parties, as well as against its reactionary adversaries?

Two things result from this fact.

1. Communism is already acknowledged by all European Powers to be itself a Power.

2. It is high time that Communists should openly, in the face of the whole
world, publish their views, their aims, their tendencies, and meet this nursery
tale of the Spectre of Communism with a Manifesto of the party itself.

To this end, Communists of various nationalities have assembled in London, and sketched the following manifesto, to be published in the English,
French, German, Italian, Flemish and Danish languages.

The history of all hitherto existing society is the history of class struggles.

Freeman and slave, patrician and plebian, lord and serf, guildmaster and
journeyman, in a word, oppressor and oppressed, stood in constant opposition
to one another, carried on an uninterrupted, now hidden, now open fight, a
fight that each time ended, either in a revolutionary re-constitution of society
at large, or in the common ruin of the contending classes.

[1] Metternich and Guizot were the chief ministers of Austria and France in 1848. Both fell from
power in that year.

In the earlier epochs of history, we find almost everywhere a complicated arrangement of society into various orders, a manifold graduation of social rank. In ancient Rome we have patricians, knights, plebians, slaves; in the Middle Ages, feudal lords, vassals, guildmasters, journeymen, apprentices, serfs; in almost all of these classes, again, subordinate gradations.

The modern bourgeois society that has sprouted from the ruins of feudal society, has not done away with class antagonisms. It has but established new classes, new conditions of oppression, new forms of struggle in place of the old ones.

Our epoch, the epoch of the bourgeoisie, possesses, however, this distinctive feature: it has simplified the class antagonisms. Society as a whole is more and more splitting up into two great hostile camps, into two great classes directly facing each other: Bourgeoisie and Proletariat.

From the serfs of the Middle Ages sprang the chartered burghers of the earliest towns. From these burgesses the first elements of the bourgeoisie were developed.

The discovery of America, the rounding of the Cape, opened up fresh ground for the rising bourgeoisie. The East-Indian and Chinese markets, the colonization of America, trade with the colonies, the increase in the means of exchange and in commodities generally, gave to commerce, to navigation, to industry, an impulse never before known, and thereby, to the revolutionary element in the tottering feudal society, a rapid development.

The feudal system of industry, under which industrial productions was monopolized by close guilds, now no longer sufficed for the growing wants of the new markets. The manufacturing system took its place. The guildmasters were pushed on one side by the manufacturing middle-class; division of labor between the different corporate guilds vanished in the face of division of labor in each single workshop.

Meantime the markets kept growing, the demand, ever rising. Even manufacture no longer sufficed. Thereupon, steam and machinery revolutionized industrial production. The place of manufacture was taken by the giant, Modern Industry, the place of the industrial middle-class, by industrial millionaires, the leaders of whole industrial armies, the modern bourgeois.

Modern industry has established the world-market, for which the discovery of America paved the way. This market has given an immense development to commerce, to navigation, to communication by land. This development has, in its turn, reacted on the extension of industry; and in proportion as industry, commerce, navigation, railways extended, in the same proportion the bourgeoisie developed, increased its capital, and pushed into the background every class handed down from the Middle Ages.

We see, therefore, how the modern bourgeoisie is itself the product of a long course of development, of a series of revolutions in the modes of production and of exchange.

Each step in the development of the bourgeoisie was accompanied by a corresponding political advance of that class. An oppressed class under the sway of the feudal nobility, an armed and self-governing association in the medieval commune, here independent urban republic (as in Italy and Germany), there taxable "third estate" of the monarchy (as in France), afterwards, in the period of manufacture proper, serving either the semi-feudal or the absolute monarchy as a counterpoise against the nobility, and in fact, corner stone of the great monarchies in general, the bourgeoisie has at last, since the establishment of Modern Industry and of the world-market, conquered for itself, in the modern representative State, exclusive political sway. The executive of the modern State is but a committee for managing the common affairs of the whole bourgeoisie.

The bourgeoisie, historically, has played a most revolutionary part.

The bourgeoisie, wherever it has got the upper hand, has put an end to all feudal, patriarchal, idyllic relations. It has pitilessly torn asunder the motley feudal ties that bound man to his "natural superiors," and has left remaining no other nexus between man and man than naked self-interest, than callous "cash payment." It has drowned the most heavenly ecstasies of religious fervor, of chivalrous enthusiasm, of philistine sentimentalism, in the icy water of egotistical calculation. It has resolved personal worth into exchange value, and in place of numberless chartered freedoms, has set up that single, unconscionable freedom—Free Trade. In one word, for exploitation, veiled by religious and political illusions, it has substituted naked, shameless, direct, brutal exploitation.

The bourgeoisie has stripped of its halo every occupation hitherto honored and looked up to with reverent awe. It has converted the physician, the lawyer, the priest, the poet, the man of science, into its paid wage-laborers.

The bourgeoisie has torn away from the family its sentimental veil, and has reduced the family relation to a mere money relation.

The bourgeoisie has disclosed how it came to pass that the brutal display of vigor in the Middle Ages, which reactionaries so much admire, found its fitting complement in the most slothful indolence. It has been the first to show what man's activity can bring about. It has accomplished wonders far surpassing Egyptian pyramids, Roman aqueducts, and Gothic cathedrals; it has conducted expeditions that put in the shade all former Exoduses of nations and crusades.

The bourgeoisie cannot exist without constantly revolutionizing the instruments of production, and thereby the relations of production, and with them the whole relations of society. Conservation of the old modes of production in unaltered form, was, on the contrary, the first condition of existence for all earlier industrial classes. Constant revolutionizing of production, uninterrupted disturbance of all social conditions, everlasting uncertainty and agitation distinguish the bourgeois epoch from all earlier ones. All fixed, fast-frozen relations, with their train of ancient and venerable prejudices and opinions, are swept away, all new-formed ones become antiquated before they can ossify. All that is solid melts into air, all that is holy is profaned, and man is at last compelled to face with sober senses, his real conditions of life, and his relations with his kind.

The need of a constantly expanding market for its products chases the bourgeoisie over the whole surface of the globe. It must nestle everywhere, establish connections everywhere.

The bourgeoisie has through its exploitation of the world-market given a cosmopolitan character to production and consumption in every country. It has drawn from under the feet of industry the national ground on which it stood. All old-established national industries have been destroyed or are daily being destroyed. They are dislodged by new industries, whose introduction becomes a life and death question for all civilized nations, by industries that no longer work up indigenous raw material, but raw material drawn from the remotest zones; industries whose products are consumed, not only at home, but in every quarter of the globe. In place of the old wants, satisfied by the productions of the country, we find new wants, requiring for their satisfaction the products of distant lands and climes. In place of the old local and national seclusion and self-sufficiency, we have intercourse in every direction, universal inter-dependence of nations. And as in material, so also in intellectual production. The intellectual creations of individual nations become common property. National one-sidedness and narrow-mindedness become more and more impossible, and from the numerous national and local literatures there arises a world-literature.

The bourgeoisie, by the rapid improvement of all instruments of production, by the immensely facilitated means of communication, draws all, even the most barbarian, nations into civilization. The cheap prices of its commodities are the heavy artillery with which it batters down all Chinese walls, with which it forces barbarians' intensely obstinate hatred of foreigners to capitulate. It compels all nations, on pain of extinction, to adopt the bourgeois mode of production; it compels them to introduce what it calls civilization into their midst, i.e., to become bourgeois themselves. In a word, it creates a world after its own image.

The bourgeoisie has subjected the country to the rule of the towns. It has created enormous cities, has greatly increased the urban population as compared with the rural, and has thus rescued a considerable part of the population from the idiocy of rural life. Just as it has made the country dependent on the towns, so it has made barbarian and semi-barbarian countries dependent on the civilized ones, nations of peasants on nations of bourgeois, the East on the West.

The bourgeoisie keeps more and more doing away with the scattered state of the population, of the means of production, and of property. It has agglomerated population, centralized means of production, and has concentrated property in a few hands. The necessary consequence of this was political centralization. Independent, or but loosely connected provinces, with separate interests, laws, governments, and systems of taxation, became lumped together in one nation, with one government, one code of laws, one national class-interest, one frontier and one customs-tariff.

The bourgeoisie, during its rule of scarce one hundred years, has created more massive and more colossal productive forces than have all preceding generations together. Subjection of Nature's forces to man, machinery, application of chemistry to industry and agriculture, steam-navigation, railways, electric telegraphs, clearing of whole continents for cultivation, canalization of rivers, whole populations conjured out of the ground—what earlier century had even a presentiment that such productive forces slumbered in the lap of social labor?

We see then: the means of production and of exchange on whose foundation the bourgeoisie built itself up, were generated in feudal society. At a certain stage in the development of these means of production and of exchange, the conditions under which feudal society produced and exchanged the feudual organization of agriculture and manufacturing industry, in one word, the feudal relations of property became no longer compatible with the already developed productive forces; they became so many fetters. They had to burst asunder; they were burst asunder.

Into their places stepped free competition, accompanied by a social and political constitution adapted to it, and by the economical and political sway of the bourgeois class.

A similar movement is going on before our own eyes. Modern bourgeois society with its relations of production, of exchange and of property, a society that has conjured up such gigantic means of production and of exchange, is like the sorcerer, who is no longer able to control the powers of the nether world whom he has called up by his spells. For many a decade past the history of industry and commerce is but the history of the revolt of modern productive forces against modern conditions of production, against the property relations that are the conditions for the existence of the bourgeoisie and of its rule. It is enough to mention the commercial crises that by their periodical return put on its trial, each time more threateningly, the existence of the entire bourgeois society. In these crises a great part not only of the existing products, but also of the previously created productive forces, are periodically destroyed. In these crises there breaks out an epidemic that, in all earlier epochs, would have seemed an absurdity—the epidemic of over-production. Society suddenly finds itself put back into a state of momentary barbarism; it appears as if a famine, a universal war of devastation had cut off the supply of every means of subsistence; industry and commerce seem to be destroyed; and why? Because there is too much civilization, too much means of subsistence, too much industry, too much commerce. The productive forces at the disposal of society no longer tend to further the development of the conditions of bourgeois property; on the contrary, they have become too powerful for these conditions, by which they are fettered, and so soon as they overcome these fetterrs, they bring disorder into the whole of bourgeois society, endanger the existence of bourgeois property. The conditions of bourgeois society are too narrow to comprise the wealth created by them. And how does the bourgeoisie get over these crises? On the one hand by enforced destruction of a mass of productive forces; on the other, by the conquest of new markets, and by the more thorough exploitation of the old ones. That is to say, by paving the way for more extensive and more destructive crises, and by diminishing the means whereby crises are prevented.

The weapons with which the bourgeoisie felled feudalism to the ground are now turned against the bourgeoisie itself.

But not only has the bourgeoisie forged the weapons that bring death to itself; it has also called into existence the men who are to wield those weapons—the modern working-class—the proletarians.

In proportion as the bourgeoisie, i.e., capital, is developed, in the same proportion is the proletariat, the modern working-class, developed, a class of laborers, who live only so long as they find work, and who find work only so long as their labor increases capital. These laborers, who must sell themselves piecemeal, are a commodity, like every other article of commerce, and are consequently exposed to all the vicissitudes of competition, to all the fluctuations of the market.

Owing to the extensive use of machinery and to division of labor, the work of the proletarians has lost all individual character, and, consequently, all charm for the workman. He becomes an appendage of the machine, and it is only the most simple, most monotonous, and most easily acquired knack that is required of him. Hence, the cost of production of a workman is restricted, almost entirely, to the means of subsistence that he requires for his maintenance, and for the propagation of his race. But the price of a commodity, and also of labor, is equal to its cost of production. In proportion, therefore, as the repulsiveness of the work increases, the wage decreases. Nay more, in proportion as the use of machinery and division of labor increases, in the same proportion the burden of toil also increases, whether by prolongation of the working hours, by increase of the work enacted in a given time, or by increased speed of the machinery, etc.

Modern industry has converted the little workshop of the patriarchal master into the great factory of the industrial capitalist. Masses of laborers, crowded into the factory, are organized like soldiers. As privates of the industrial army they are placed under the command of a perfect hierarchy of officers and sergeants. Not only are they the slaves of the bourgeois class, and of the bourgeois State, they are daily and hourly enslaved by the machine, by the over-looker, and, above all, by the individual bourgeois manufacturer himself. The more openly despotism proclaims gain to be its end and aim, the more petty, the more hateful and the more embittering it is.

The less the skill and exertion or strength implied in manual labor, in other words, the more modern industry becomes developed, the more is the labor of men superseded by that of women. Differences of age and sex have no longer any distinctive social validity for the working class. All are instruments of labor, more or less expensive to use, according to their age and sex.

No sooner is the exploitation of the laborer by the manufacturer, so far at an end, that he receives his wages in cash, than he is set upon by the other portions of the bourgeoisie, the landlord, the shopkeeper, the pawnbroker, etc.

The lower strata of the middle class—the small tradespeople, shopkeepers, and retired tradesmen generally, the handicraftsmen and peasants—all these sink gradually into the proletariat, partly because their diminutive capital does not suffice for the scale on which Modern Industry is carried on, and is swamped in the competition with the large capitalists, partly because their specialized skill is rendered worthless by new methods of production. Thus the proletariat is recruited from all classes of the population.

The proletariat goes through various stages of development. With its birth begins its struggle with the bourgeoisie. At first the contest is carried on by individual laborers, then by the workpeople of a factory, then by the operatives of one trade, in one locality, against the individual bourgeois who directly exploits them. They direct their attacks not against the bourgeois conditions of production, but against the instruments of production themselves; they destroy imported wares that compete with their labor, they smash to pieces machinery, they set factories ablaze, they seek to restore by force the vanished status of the workman of the Middle Ages.

At this stage the laborers still form an incoherent mass scattered over the whole country, and broken up by their mutual competition. If anywhere they unite to form more compact bodies, this is not yet the consequence of their own active union, but of the union of the bourgeoisie, which class, in order to attain its own political ends, is compelled to set the whole proletariat in motion, and is moreover yet, for a time, able to do so. At this stage, therefore, the proletarians do not fight their enemies, but the enemies of their enemies, the remnants of absolute monarchy, the landowners, the non-industrial bourgeois, the petty bourgeoisie. Thus the whole historical movement is concentrated in the hands of the bourgeoisie; every victory so obtained is a victory for the bourgeoisie.

But with the development of industry the proletariat not only increases in number, it becomes concentrated in greater masses, its strength grows, and it feels that strength more. The various interests and conditions of life within the ranks of the proletariat are more and more equalized, in proportion as machinery obliterates all distinctions of labor, and nearly everywhere reduces wages to the same low level. The growing competition among the bourgeois, and the resulting commercial crises, make the wages of the workers ever more fluctuating. The unceasing improvement of machinery, ever more rapidly developing, makes their livelihood more and more precarious; the collisions between individual workmen and individual bourgeois take more and more the character of collisions between two classes. Thereupon the workers begin to form combinations (Trades' Unions) against the bourgeois; they club together in order to keep up the rate of wages; they found permanent associations in order to make provision beforehand for these occasional revolts. Here and there the contest breaks out into riots.

Now and then the workers are victorious, but only for a time. The real fruit of their battles lies, not in the immediate result, but in the ever expanding union of the workers. This union is helped on by the improved means of communication that are created by modern industry, and that place the workers of different localities in contact with one another. It was just this contact that was needed to centralize the numerous local struggles, all of the same character, into one national struggle between classes. But every class struggle is a political struggle. And that union, to attain which the burghers of the Middle Ages, with their miserable highways, required centuries, the modern proletarians, thanks to railways, achieve in a few years.

This organization of the proletarians into a class, and consequently into a political party, is continually being upset again by the competition between the workers themselves. But it ever rises up again, stronger, firmer, mightier. It compels legislative recognition of particular interests of the workers, by taking advantage of the divisions among the bourgeoisie itself. Thus the ten-hour bill in England was carried.

Altogether collisions between the classes of the old society further, in many ways, the course of development of the proletariat. The bourgeoisie finds itself involved in a constant battle. At first with the aristocracy; later on, with those portions of the bourgeoisie itself whose interests have become antagonistic to the progess of industry; at all times, with the bourgeoisie of foreign countries. In all these battles it sees itself compelled to appeal to the proletariat, to ask for its help, and thus, to drag it into the political arena.

The bourgeoisie itself, therefore, supplies the proletariat with its own elements of political and general education, in other words, it furnishes the proletariat with weapons for fighting the bourgeoisie.

Further, as we have already seen, entire sections of the ruling classes are, by the advance of industry, precipitated into the proletariat, or are at least threatened in their conditions of existence. These also supply the proletariat with fresh elements of enlightenment and progress.

Finally, in times when the class-struggle nears the decisive hours, the process of dissolution going on within the ruling class, in fact, within the whole range of old society, assumes such a violent, glaring character, that a small section of the ruling class cuts itself adrift, and joins the revolutionary class, the class that holds the future in its hands. Just as, therefore, at an earlier period, a section of the nobility went over to the bourgeoisie, so now a portion of the bourgeoisie goes over to the proletariat, and in particular, a portion of the bourgeois ideologists, who have raised themselves to the level of comprehending theoretically the historical movements as a whole.

Of all the classes that stand face to face with the bourgeoisie today, the proletariat alone is a really revolutionary class. The other classes decay and finally disappear in the face of modern industry; the proletariat is its special and essential product.

The lower middle class, the small manufacturer, the shopkeeper, the artisan, the peasant, all these fight against the bourgeoisie, to save from extinction their existence as fractions of the middle class. They are, therefore, not revolutionary, but conservative. Nay more, they are reactionary, for they try to roll back the wheel of history. If by chance they are revolutionary, they are so, only in view of their inpending transfer into the proletariat, they thus defend not their present, but their future interests, they desert their own standpoint to place themselves at that of the proletariat.

The "dangerous class," the social scum, that passively rotting mass thrown off by the lowest layers of old society, may, here and there, be swept into the movement by a proletarian revolution; its conditions of life, however, prepare it far more for the part of a bribed tool of reactionary intrigue. . . .

All previous historical movements were movements of minorities, or in the interest of minorities. The proletarian movement is the self-conscious, independent movement of the immense majority, in the interest of the immense majority. The proletariat, the lowest stratum of our present society, cannot stir, cannot raise itself up, without the whole superincumbent strata of official society being sprung into the air.

Though not in substance, yet in form, the struggle of the proletariat with the bourgeoisie is at first a national struggle. The proletariat of each country must, of course, first of all settle matters with its own bourgeoisie.

In depicting the most general phases of the development of the proletariat, we traced the more or less veiled civil war, raging within existing society, up to the point where that war breaks out into open revolution, and where the violent overthrow of the bourgeoisie lays the foundation for the sway of the proletariat.

Hitherto, every form of society has been based, as we have already seen, on the antagonism of oppressing and oppressed classes. But in order to oppress a class, certain conditions must be assured to it under which it can, at least, continue its slavish existence. The serf, in the period of serfdom, raised himself to membership in the commune, just as the petty bourgeois, under the yoke of feudal absolutism, managed to develop into a bourgeois. The modern laborer, on the contrary, instead of rising with the progress of industry, sinks deeper and deeper below the conditions of existence of his own class. He becomes a pauper, and pauperism develops more rapidly than population and wealth. And here it becomes evident, that the bourgeoisie is unfit any longer to be the ruling class in society, and to impose its conditions of existence upon society as an overriding law. It is unfit to rule, because it is incompetent to assure an existence to its slave within his slavery, because it cannot help letting him sink into such a state that it has to feed him, instead of being fed by him. Society can no longer live under this bourgeoisie, in other words, its existence is no longer compatible with society.

The essential condition for the existence, and for the sway of the bourgeois class, is the formation and augmentation of capital; the condition for capital is wage-labor. Wage-labor rests exclusively on competition between the laborers. The advance of industry, whose involuntary promoter is the bourgeoisie, replaces the isolation of the laborers, due to competition, by their revolutionary combination, due to association. The development of Modern Industry, therefore, cuts from under its feet the very foundation on which the bourgeoisie produces and appropriates products. What the bourgeoisie therefore produces, above all, are its own gravediggers. Its fall and the victory of the proletariat are equally inevitable.

In what relation do the Communists stand to the proletarians as a whole?

The Communists do not form a separate party opposed to other working class parties.

They have no interests separate and apart from those of the proletariat as a whole.

They do not set up any sectarian principles of their own, by which to shape and mould the proletarian movement.

The Communists are distinguished from the other working class parties by this only: 1. In the national struggles of the proletarians of the different countries, they point out and bring to the front the common interests of the entire proletariat independently of all nationality. 2. In the various stages of development which the struggle of the working class against the bourgeoisie has to pass through, they always and everywhere represent the interests of the movement as a whole.

The Communists, therefore, are on the one hand, practically, the most advanced and resolute section of the working class parties of every country, that section which pushes forward all others; on the other hand, theoretically, they have over the great mass of the proletariat the advantage of clearly understanding the line of march, the conditions, and the ultimate general results of the proletarian movement.

The immediate aim of the Communists is the same as that of all the other proletarian parties: formation of the proletariat into a class, overthrow of the bourgeois supremacy, conquest of political power by the proletariat.

The theoretical conclusions of the Communists are in no way based on ideas or principles that have been invented, or discovered, by this or that would-be universal reformer.

They merely express, in general terms, actual relations springing from an existing class struggle, from a historical movement going on under our very eyes. The abolition of existing property relations is not at all a distinctive feature of Communism.

All property relations in the past have continually been subject to historical change consequent upon the change in historical conditions.

The French Revolution, for example, abolished feudal property in favor of bourgeois property.

The distinguishing feature of Communism is not the abolition of property generally, but the abolition of bourgeois property. But modern bourgeois private property is the final and most complete expression of the system of producing and appropriating products, that is based on class antagonism, on the exploitation of the many by the few.

In this sense, the theory of the Communists may be summed up in the single sentence: Abolition of private property. . . .

You are horrified at our intending to do away with private propery. But in your existing society, private property is already done away with for nine-tenths of the population; its existence for the few is solely due to its non-existence in the hands of those nine-tenths. You reproach us, therefore, with intending to do away with a form of property, the necessary condition for whose existence is, the non-existence of any property for the immense majority of society.

In one word, you reproach us with intending to do away with your property. Precisely so; that is just what we intend.

From the moment when labor can no longer be converted into capital, money, or rent, into a social power capable of being monopolized, i.e., from the moment when individual property can no longer be transformed into bourgeois property, into capital, from that moment, you say, individuality vanishes.

You must, therefore, confess that by "individual" you mean no other person than bourgeois, than the middle-class owner of property. This person must, indeed, be swept out of the way, and made impossible.

Communism deprives no man of the power to appropriate the products of society: all that it does is to deprive him of the power to subjugate the labor of others by means of such appropriation.

It has been objected, that upon the abolition of private property all work will cease, and universal laziness will overtake us.

According to this, bourgeois society ought long ago to have gone to the dogs through sheer idleness; for those of its members who work, acquire nothing, and those who acquire anything, do not work. . . .

Abolition of the family! Even the most radical flare up at this infamous proposal of the Communists.

On what foundation is the present family, the bourgeois family, based? On capital, on private gain. In its completely developed form this family exists only among the bourgeoisie. But this state of things finds its complement in the practical absence of the family among the proletarians, and in public prostitution.

The bourgeois family will vanish as a matter of course when its complement vanishes, and both will vanish with the vanishing of capital.

Do you charge us with wanting to stop the exploitation of children by their parents? To this crime we plead guilty.

But, you will say, we destroy the most hallowed of relations, when we replace home education by social.

And your education! Is not that also social, and determined by the social conditions under which you educate, by the intervention, direct or indirect, of society by means of schools, etc? The Communists have not invented the intervention of society in education; they do but seek to alter the character of that intervention, and to rescue education from the influence of the ruling class.

The bourgeois clap-trap about the family and education, about the hallowed co-relation of parent and child, becomes all the more disgusting, the more, by the action of Modern Industry, all family ties among the proletarians are torn asunder, and their children transformed into simple articles of commerce and instruments of labor.

But you Communists would introduce community of women, screams the whole bourgoisie in chorus.

The bourgeois sees in his wife a mere instrument of production. He hears that the instruments of production are to be exploited in common, and, naturally, can come to no other conclusion, than that the lot of being common to all will likewise fall to the women.

He has not even a suspicion that the real point aimed at is to do away with the status of women as mere instruments of production.

For the rest, nothing is more ridiculous than the virtuous indignation of our bourgeois at the community of women which, they pretend, is to be openly and officially established by the Communists. The Communists have no need to introduce community of women; it has existed almost from time immemorial.

Our bourgeois, not content with having the wives and daughters of their proletarians at their disposal, not to speak of common prostitutes, take the greatest pleasure in seducing each other's wives.

Bourgeois marriage is in reality a system of wives in common and thus, at the most, what the Communists might possibly be reproached with, is that they desire to introduce, in substitution for a hypocritically concealed, an openly legalized community of women. For the rest, it is self-evident, that the abolition of the present system of production must bring with it the abolition of the community of women springing from that system, i.e., of prostitution both public and private. . . .

The charges against Communism made from a religious, a philosophical, and generally, from an ideological standpoint, are not deserving of serious examination.

Does it require deep intuition to comprehend that man's ideas, views, and conceptions, in one word, man's consciousness, changes with every change in the conditions of his material existence, in his social relations and in his social life?

What else does the history of ideas prove, than that intellectual production changes in character in proportion as material production is changed? The ruling ideas of each age have ever been the ideas of its ruling class.

When people speak of ideas that revolutionize society, they do but express the fact that within the old society, the elements of a new one have been created, and that the dissolution of the old ideas keeps even pace with the dissolution of the old conditions of existence.

When the ancient world was in its last throes, the ancient religions were overcome by Christianity. When Christian ideas succumbed in the 18th century to rationalist ideas, feudal society fought its death-battle with the then revolutionary bourgeoisie. The ideas of religious liberty and freedom of conscience, merely gave expression to the sway of free competition within the domain of knowledge. . . .

The Communist revolution is the most radical rupture with traditional property-relations; no wonder that its development involves the most radical rupture with traditional ideas.

But let us have done with the bourgeois objections to Communism.

We have seen above, that the first step in the revolution by the working class, is to raise the proletariat to the position of ruling class, to win the battle of democracy.

The proletariat will use its political supremacy, to wrest, by degrees, all capital from the bourgeoisie, to centralize all instruments of production in the hands of the State, i.e., of the proletariat organized as the ruling class; and to increase the total of productive forces as rapidly as possible.

Of course, in the beginning, this cannot be effected except by means of despotic inroads on the rights of property, and on the conditions of bourgeois production; by means of measures, therefore, which appear economically insufficient and untenable, but which, in the course of the movement, outstrip themselves, necessitate further inroads upon the old social order, and are unavoidable as a means of entirely revolutionizing the mode of production.

These measures will of course be different in different countries.

Nevertheless in the most advanced countries the following will be pretty generally applicable:

1. Abolition of property in land and application of all rents of land to public purposes.

2. A heavy progressive or graduated income tax.

3. Abolition of all rights of inheritance.

4. Confiscation of the property of all emigrants and rebels.

5. Centralization of credit in the hands of the state, by means of a national bank with State capital and an exclusive monopoly.

6. Centralization of the means of communication and transport in the hands of the State.

7. Extension of factories and instruments of production owned by the State; the bringing into cultivation of waste lands, and the improvement of the soil generally in accordance with a common plan.

8. Equal liability of all to labor. Establishment of industrial armies, especially for agriculture.

9. Combination of agriculture with manufacturing industries; gradual abolition of the distinction between town and country, by a more equable distribution of population over the country.

10. Free education for all children in public schools. Abolition of children's factory labor in its present form. Combination of education with industrial production, etc., etc.

When, in the course of development, class distinctions have disappeared, and all production has been concentrated in the hands of a vast association of the whole nation, the public power will lose its political character. Political power, properly so called, is merely the organized power of one class for oppressing another. If the proletariat during its contest with the bourgeoisie is compelled, by the force of circumstances, to organize itself as a class, if, by means of a revolution, it makes itself the ruling class, and, as such, sweeps away by force the old conditions of production, then it will, along with these conditions, have swept away the conditions for the existence of class antagonisms, and of classes generally, and will thereby have abolished its own supremacy as a class.

In place of the old bourgeois society, with its classes and class antagonisms, we shall have an association, in which the free development of each is the condition for the free development of all. . . .

In short, the Communists everywhere support every revolutionary movement against the existing social and political order of things.

In all these movements they bring to the front, as the leading question in each, the property question, no matter what its degree of development at the time.

Finally, they labor everywhere for the union and agreement of the democratic parties of all countries.

The Communists disdain to conceal their views and aims. They openly declare that their ends can be attained only by the forcible overthrow of all existing social conditions. Let the ruling classes tremble at a Communistic revolution. The proletarians have nothing to lose but their chains. They have a world to win.

Workers of the world, unite!

SOURCE. Karl Marx and Friedrich Engels, *The Communist Manifesto*, Samuel Moore, tr., New York: Socialist Labor Party, 1888.

b. REVISIONIST MARXISM:
EDUARD BERNSTEIN, FROM A LETTER
TO THE GERMAN SOCIAL DEMOCRATIC PARTY, 1898

IN THE DECADES following the publication of The Communist Manifesto, *Socialist and Communist theory reflected profoundly the Marxist influence yet remained split into a number of different camps. In general, the differences centered around the question of whether Socialism would be achieved gradually through peaceful constitutional processes or by means of violent revolution. The former position, known as Revisionist Marxism, was summarized and defended by the German evolutionary socialist, Eduard Bernstein, in a letter of October, 1898, to the German Social Democratic Party.*

I set myself against the notion that we have to expect shortly a collapse of the bourgeois economy, and that social democracy should be induced by the prospect of such an imminent, great, social catastrophe to adapt its tactics to that assumption. That I maintain most emphatically.

The adherents of this theory of a catastrophe, base it especially on the conclusions of the *Communist Manifesto*. This is a mistake in every respect.

The theory which the *Communist Manifesto* sets forth of the evolution of modern society was correct as far as it characterised the general tendencies of that evolution. But it was mistaken in several special deductions, above all in the estimate of the *time* the evolution would take. The last has been unreservedly acknowledged by Friedrich Engels, the joint author with Marx of the *Manifesto,* in his preface to the *Class War in France.* But it is evident that if social evolution takes a much greater period of time than was assumed, it must also take upon itself *forms* and lead to forms that were not foreseen and could not be foreseen then.

Social conditions have not developed to such an acute opposition of things and classes as is depicted in the *Manifesto.* It is not only useless, it is the greatest folly to attempt to conceal this from ourselves. The number of members of the possessing classes is to-day not smaller but larger. The enormous increase of social wealth is not accompanied by a decreasing number of large capitalists but by an increasing number of capitalists of all degrees. The middle classes change their character but they do not disappear from the social scale.

The concentration in productive industry is not being accomplished even to-day in all its departments with equal thoroughness and at an equal rate. In a great many branches of production it certainly justifies the forecasts of the socialist critic of society; but in other branches it lags even to-day behind them. The process of concentration in agriculture proceeds still more slowly. Trade statistics shown an extraordinarily elaborated graduation of enterprises in regard to size. No rung of the ladder is disappearing from it. The significant changes in the inner structure of these enterprises and their inter-relationship cannot do away with this fact.

In all advanced countries we see the privileges of the capitalist bourgeoisie yielding step by step to democratic organizations. Under the influence of this, and driven by the movement of the working classes which is daily becoming stronger, a social reaction has set in against the exploiting tendencies of capital, a counteraction which, although it still proceeds timidly and feebly, yet does exist, and is always drawing more departments of economic life under its influence. Factory legislation, the democratising of local government, and the extension of its area of work, the freeing of trade unions and systems of co-operative trading from legal restrictions, the consideration of standard conditions of labour in the work undertaken by public authorities—all these characterise this phase of the evolution.

But the more the political organisations of modern nations are democratised the more the needs and opportunities of great political catastrophes are diminished. He who holds firmly to the catastrophic theory of evolution must, with all his power, withstand and hinder the evolution described above, which, indeed, the logical defenders of that theory formerly did. But is the conquest of political power by the proletariat simply to be by a political catastrophe? Is it to be the appropriation and utilisation of the power of the State by the proletariat exclusively against the whole nonproletarian world?. . .

No one has questioned the necessity for the working classes to gain the control of government. The point at issue is between the theory of a social cataclysm and the question whether with the given social development in Germany and the present advanced state of its working classes in the towns and the country, a sudden catastrophe would be desirable in the interest of the social democracy. I have denied it and deny it again, because in my judgment a greater security for lasting success lies in a steady advance than in the possibilities offered by a catastrophic crash.

And as I am firmly convinced that important periods in the development of nations cannot be leapt over I lay the greatest value on the next tasks of social democracy, on the struggle for the political rights of the working man, on the political activity of working men in town and country for the interests of their class, as well as on the work of the industrial organisation of the workers.

In this sense I wrote the sentence that the movement means everything for me and that what is *usually* called "the final aim of socialism" is nothing; and in this sense I write it down again to-day. Even if the word "usually" had not shown that the proposition was only to be understood conditionally, it was obvious that it *could* not express indifference concerning the final carrying out of socialist principles, but only indifference—or, as it would be better expressed, carelessness—as to the form of the final arrangement of things. I have at no time had an excessive interest in the future, beyond general principles; I have not been able to read to the end any picture of the future. My thoughts and efforts are concerned with the duties of the present and the nearest future, and I only busy myself with the perspectives beyond so far as they give me a line of conduct for suitable action now.

The conquest of political power by the working classes, the expropriation of capitalists, are no ends in themselves but only means for the accomplishment of certain aims and endeavours. As such they are demands in the programme of social democracy and are not attacked by me. Nothing can be said beforehand as to the circumstances of their accomplishment; we can only fight for their realisation. But the conquest of political power necessitates the possession of political *rights;* and the most important problem of tactics which German social democracy has at the present time to solve, appears to me to be to devise the best ways for the extension of the political and economic rights of the German working classes.

SOURCE. Eduard Bernstein, *Evolutionary Socialism*, New York, 1899: Preface.

c. LENIN, FROM *STATE AND REVOLUTION*, 1917

THE EVOLUTIONARY MARXISM of Bernstein and others came under heavy attack by the strict Marxist Vladimir I. Lenin, the architect of the Communist Revolution in Russia. In his State and Revolution (1917), Lenin reasserted the traditional Marxist insistence on violent revolution. Both Bernstein and Lenin appealed to the authority of Marx and Engels in much the way that disputing Christians might cite passages from Scripture against one another.

What is now happening to Marx's doctrine has, in the course of history, often happened to the doctrines of other revolutionary thinkers and leaders of oppressed classes struggling for emancipation. During the lifetime of great revolutionaries, the oppressing classes have visited relentless persecution on them and received their teaching with the most savage hostility, the most furious hatred, the most ruthless campaign of lies and slanders. After their death, attempts are made to turn them into harmless icons, canonise them, and surround their *names* with a certain halo for the "consolation" of the oppressed classes and with the object of duping them, while at the same time emasculating and vulgarising the *real essence* of their revolutionary theories and blunting their revolutionary edge. At the present time, the bourgeoisie and the opportunists within the labour movement are co-operating in this work of adulterating Marxism. They omit, obliterate, and distort the revolutionary side of its teaching, its revolutionary soul. . . .

In such circumstances, the distortion of Marxism being so widespread, it is our first task to *resuscitate* the real teachings of Marx on the state. For this purpose it will be necessary to quote at length from the works of Marx and Engels themselves. . . .

Let us begin with the most popular of Engels' works, *Der Ursprung der Familie, des Privateigentums und des Staats,* the sixth edition of which was published in Stuttgart as far back as 1894. We must translate the quotations from the German originals, as the Russian translations, although very numerous, are for the most part either incomplete or very unsatisfactory.

Summarising his historical analysis Engels says:

> The state is therefore by no means a power imposed on society from the outside; just as little is it "the reality of the moral idea," "the image and reality of reason," as Hegel asserted. Rather, it is a product of society at a certain stage of development; it is the admission that this society has become entangled in an insoluble contradiction with itself, that it is cleft into irreconcilable antagonisms which it is powerless to dispel. But in order that these antagonisms, classes with conflicting economic interests, may not consume themselves and society in sterile struggle, a power apparently standing above society becomes necessary, whose purpose is to moderate the conflict and keep it within the bounds of "order"; and this power arising out of society, but placing itself above it, and increasingly separating itself from it, is the state.

Here we have, expressed in all its clearness, the basic idea of Marxism on the question of the historical rôle and meaning of the state. The state is the product and the manifestation of the *irreconcilability* of class antagonisms. The state arises when, where, and to the extent that the class antagonisms *cannot* be objectively reconciled. And, conversely, the existence of the state proves that the class antagonism *are* irreconcilable.

It is precisely on this most important and fundamental point that distortions of Marxism arise along two main lines.

On the one hand, the bourgeois, and particularly the petty-bourgeois, ideologists, compelled under the pressure of indisputable historical facts to admit that the state only exists where there are class antagonisms and the class struggle, "correct" Marx in such a way as to make it appear that the state is an organ for *reconciling* the classes. According to Marx, the state could neither arise nor maintain itself if a reconciliation of classes were possible. But with the petty-bourgeois and philistine professors and publicists, the state—and this frequently on the strength of benevolent references to Marx!—becomes a conciliator of the classes. According to Marx, the state is an organ of class *domination,* an organ of *oppression* of one class by another; its aim is the creation of "order" which legalises and perpetuates this oppression by moderating the collisions between the classes. But in the opinion of the petty-bourgeois politicians, order means reconciliation of the classes, and not oppression of one class by another; to moderate collisions does not mean, they say, to deprive the oppressed classes of certain definite means and methods of struggle for overthrowing the oppressors, but to practice reconciliation. . . .

Engels develops the conception of that "power" which is termed the state—a power arising from society, but placing itself above it and becoming more and more separated from it. What does this power mainly consist of? It consists of special bodies of armed men who have at their disposal prisons, etc.

We are justified in speaking of special bodies of armed men, because the public power peculiar to every state is not "absolutely identical" with the armed population, with its "self-acting armed organisation." . . .

For the maintenance of a special public force standing above society, taxes and state loans are needed.

Having at their disposal the public force and the right to exact taxes, the officials now stand as organs of society *above* society. The free, voluntary respect which was accorded to the organs of the gentilic form of government does not satisfy them, even if they could have it. . . .

Special laws are enacted regarding the sanctity and the inviolability of the officials. "The shabbiest police servant . . . has more authority" than the representative of the clan, but even the head of the military power of a civilised state "may well envy the least among the chiefs of the clan the unconstrained and uncontested respect which is paid to him." . . .

Engels' words regarding the "withering away" of the state enjoy such popularity, they are so often quoted, and they show so clearly the essence of the usual adulteration by means of which Marxism is made to look like opportunism, that we must dwell on them in detail. Let us quote the whole passage from which they are taken.

The proletariat seizes state power, and then transforms the means of production into state property. But in doing this, it puts an end to itself as the proletariat, it puts an end to all class differences and class antagonisms, it puts an end also to the state as the state. Former society, moving in class antagonisms, had need of the state, that is, or organisation of the exploiting class at each period for the maintenance of its external conditions of production; therefore, in particular, for the forcible holding down of the exploited class in the conditions of oppression (slavery, bondage or serfdom, wage-labour) determined by the existing mode of production. The state was the official representative of society as a whole, its embodiment in a visible corporate body; but it was this only in so far as it was the state of that class which itself, in its epoch, represented society as a whole: in ancient times, the state of the slave-owning citizens; in the Middle Ages, of the feudal nobility; in our epoch, of the bourgeoisie. When ultimately it becomes really representative of society as a whole, it makes itself superfluous. As soon as there is no longer any class of society to be held in subjection; as soon as, along with class domination and the struggle for individual existence based on the former anarchy of production, the collisions and excesses arising from these have also been abolished, there is nothing more to be repressed, and a special repressive force, a state, is no longer necessary. The first act in which the state really comes forward as the representative of society as a whole—the seizure of the means of production in the name of society—is at the same time its last independent act as a state. The interference of a state power in social relations becomes superfluous in one sphere after another, and then becomes dormant of itself. Government over persons is replaced by the administration of things and the direction of the processes of production. The state is not "abolished," *it withers away.* It is from this standpoint that we must appraise the phrase "people's free state"—both its justification at times for agitational purposes, and its ultimate scientific inadequacy—and also the demand of the so-called Anarchists that the state should be abolished overnight.

Without fear of committing an error, it may be said that of this argument by Engels so singularly rich in ideas, only one point has become an integral part of Socialist thought among modern Socialist parties, namely, that, unlike the Anarchist doctrine of the "abolition" of the state, according to Marx the state "withers away." To emasculate Marxism in such a manner is to reduce it to opportunism, for such an "interpretation" only leaves the hazy conception of a slow, even, gradual change, free from leaps and storms, free from revolution. The current popular conception, if one may say so, of the "withering away" of the state undoubtedly means a slurring over, if not a negation, of revolution.

Yet, such an "interpretation" is the crudest distortion of Marxism, which is advantageous only to the bourgeoisie; in point of theory, it is based on a disregard for the most important circumstances and considerations pointed out in the very passage summarising Engels' ideas, which we have just quoted in full.

In the first place, Engels at the very outset of his argument says that, in assuming state power, the proletariat by that very act "puts an end to the state as the state." One is "not accustomed" to reflect on what this really means. Generally, it is either ignored altogether, or it is considered as a piece of "Hegelian weakness" on Engels' part. As a matter of fact, however, these words express succinctly the experience of one of the greatest proletarian revolutions—the Paris Commune of 1871, of which we shall speak in greater detail in its proper place. As a matter of fact, Engels speaks here of the destruction of the bourgeois state by the proletarian revolution, while the words about its withering away refer to the remains of *proletarian* statehood *after* the Socialist revolution. The bourgeois state does not "wither away," according to Engels, but is "put an end to" by the proletariat in the course of the revolution. What withers away after the revolution is the proletarian state or semi-state.

Secondly, the state is a "special repressive force." This splendid and extremely profound definition of Engels' is given by him here with complete lucidity. It follows from this that the "special repressive force" of the bourgeoisie for the suppression of the proletariat, of the millions of workers by a handful of the rich, must be replaced by a "special repressive force" of the proletariat for the suppression of the bourgeoisie (the dictatorship of the proletariat). It is just this that constitutes the "act" of "the seizure of the means of production in the name of society." And it is obvious that such a substitution of one (proletarian) "special repressive force" for another (bourgeois) "special repressive force" can in no way take place in the form of a "withering away."

Thirdly, as to the "withering away" or, more expressively and colourfully, as to the state "becoming dormant," Engels refers quite clearly and definitely to the period *after* "the seizure of the means of production [by the state] in the name of society," that is *after* the Socialist revolution. We all know that the political form of the "state" at that time is complete democracy. . . . The bourgeois state can only be "put an end to" by a revolution. The state in general, *i.e.,* most complete democracy, can only "wither away.". . .

The whole theory of Marx is an application of the theory of evolution—in its most consistent, complete, well considered and fruitful form—to modern capitalism. It was natural for Marx to raise the question of applying this theory both to the *coming* collapse of capitalism and to the *future* evolution of *future* Communism.

On the basis of what *data* can the future evolution of future Communism be considered?

On the basis of the fact that *it has its origin* in capitalism, that it develops historically from capitalism, that it is the result of the action of a social force to which capitalism *has given birth.* There is no shadow of an attempt on Marx's part to conjure up a Utopia, to make idle guesses about that which cannot be known. Marx treats the question of Communism in the same way as a naturalist would treat the question of the evolution of, say, a new biological species, if he knew that such and such was its origin, and such and such the direction in which it changed. . . .

The first fact that has been established with complete exactness by the whole theory of evolution, by science as a whole— a fact which the Utopians forgot, and which is forgotten by the present-day opportunists who are afraid of the Socialist revolution—is that, historically, there must undoubtedly be a special stage or epoch of *transition from capitalism to Communism.*

Between capitalist and Communist society—Marx continues—lies the period of the revolutionary transformation of the former into the latter. To this also corresponds a political transition period, in which the state can be no other than *the revolutionary dictatorship of the proletariat.*

This conclusion Marx bases on an analysis of the rôle played by the proletariat in modern capitalist society, on the data concerning the evolution of this society, and on the irreconciliability of the opposing interests of the proletariat and the bourgeoisie.

Earlier the question was put thus: to attain its emancipation, the proletariat must overthrow the bourgeoisie, conquer political power and establish its own revolutionary dictatorship.

Now the question is put somewhat differently: the transition from capitalist society, developing towards Communism, towards a Communist society, is impossible without a "political transition period," and the state in this period can only be the revolutionary dictatorship of the proletariat.

What, then, is the relation of this dictatorship to democracy?

We have seen that the *Communist Manifesto* simply places side by side the two ideas: the "transformation of the proletariat into the ruling class" and the "establishment of democracy." On the basis of all that has been said above, one can define more exactly how democracy changes in the transition from capitalism to Communism.

In capitalist society, under the conditions most favourable to its development, we have more or less complete democracy in the democratic republic. But this democracy is always bound by the narrow framework of capitalist exploitation, and consequently always remains, in reality, a democracy for the minority, only for the possessing classes, only for the rich. Freedom in capitalist society always remains just about the same as it was in the ancient Greek republics: freedom for the slave-owners. The modern wage-slaves, owing to the conditions of capitalist exploitation, are so much crushed by want and poverty that "democracy is nothing to them," "politics is nothing to them"; that, in the ordinary peaceful course of events, the majority of the population is debarred from participating in social and political life.

The correctness of this statement is perhaps most clearly proved by Germany, just because in this state constitutional legality lasted and remained stable for a remarkably long time—for nearly half a century (1871–1914) —and because Social-Democracy in Germany during that time was able to achieve far more than in other countries in "utilising legality," and was able to organise into a political party a larger proportion of the working class than anywhere else in the world.

What, then, is this largest proportion of politically conscious and active wage-slaves that has so far been observed in capitalist society? One million members of the Social-Democratic Party—out of fifteen million wage-workers! Three million organised in trade unions—out of fifteen millions!

Democracy for an insignificant minority, democracy for the rich—that is the democracy of capitalist society. If we look more closely into the mechanism of capitalist democracy, everywhere, both in the "petty"—so-called petty—details of the suffrage (residential qualification, exclusion of women, etc.), and in the technique of the representative institutions, in the actual obstacles to the right of assembly (public buildings are not for "beggars"!), in the purely capitalist organisation of the daily press, etc., etc.—on all sides we see restriction after restriction upon democracy. These restrictions, exceptions, exclusions, obstacles for the poor, seem slight, especially in the eyes of one who has himself never known want and has never been in close contact with the oppressed classes in their mass life (and nine-tenths, if not ninety-nine hundredths, of the bourgeois publicists and politicians are of this class), but in their sum total these restrictions exclude and squeeze out the poor from politics and from an active share in democracy.

Marx splendidly grasped this *essence* of capitalist democracy, when, in analysing the experience of the Commune, he said that the oppressed were allowed, once every few years, to decide which particular representatives of the oppressing class should be in parliament to represent and repress them!

But from this capitalist democracy—inevitably narrow, subtly rejecting the poor, and therefore hypocritical and false to the core—progress does not march onward, simply, smoothly and directly, to "greater and greater democracy," as the liberal professors and petty-bourgeois opportunists would have us believe. No, progress marches onward, *i.e.,* towards Communism, through the dictatorship of the proletariat; it cannot do otherwise, for there is no one else and no other way to *break the resistance* of the capitalist exploiters.

But the dictatorship of the proletariat—*i.e.,* the organisation of the vanguard of the oppressed as the ruling class for the purpose of crushing the oppressors—cannot produce merely an expansion of democracy. *Together* with an immense expansion of democracy which *for the first time* becomes democracy for the poor, democracy for the people, and not democracy for the rich folk, the dictatorship of the proletariat produces a series of restrictions of liberty in the case of the oppressors, the exploiters, the capitalists. We must crush them in order to free humanity from wage-slavery; their resistance must be broken by force; it is clear that where there is suppression there is also violence, there is no liberty, no democracy.

Engels expressed this splendidly in his letter to Bebel when he said, as the reader will remember, that "as long as the proletariat still *needs* the state, it needs it not in the interests of freedom, but for the purpose of crushing its antagonists; and as soon as it becomes possible to speak of freedom, then the state, as such, ceases to exist."

Democracy for the vast majority of the people, and suppression by force, *i.e.,* exclusion from democracy, of the exploiters and oppressors of the people—this is the modification of democracy during the *transition* from capitalism to Communism.

Only in Communist society, when the resistance of the capitalists has been completely broken, when the capitalists have disappeared, when there are no classes *(i.e.,* there is no difference between the members of society in their relation to the social means of production), *only then* "the state ceases to exist," and *"it becomes possible to speak of freedom."* Only then a really full democracy, a democracy without any exceptions, will be possible and will be realised. And only then will democracy itself begin to *wither away* due to the simple fact that, freed from capitalist slavery, from the untold horrors, savagery, absurdities and infamies of capitalist exploitation, people will gradually *become accustomed* to the observance of the elementary rules of social life that have been known for centuries and repeated for thousands of years in all school books; they will become accustomed to observing them without force, without compulsion, without subordination, without the *special apparatus* for compulsion which is called the state.

The expression "the state *withers away,*" is very well chosen, for it indictates both the gradual and the elemental nature of the process. Only habit can, and undoubtedly will, have such an effect; for we see around us millions of times how readily people get accustomed to observe the necessary rules of life in common, if there is no exploitation, if there is nothing that causes indignation, that calls forth protest and revolt and has to be *suppressed.*

Thus, in capitalist society, we have a democracy that is curtailed, poor, false; a democracy only for the rich, for the minority. The dictatorship of the proletariat, the period of transition to Communism, will, for the first time, produce democracy for the people, for the majority, side by side with the necessary suppression of the minority—the exploiters. Communism alone is capable 'of giving a really complete democracy, and the more complete it is the more quickly will it become unnecessary and wither away of itself.

In other words: under capitalism we have a state in the proper sense of the word, that is, special machinery for the suppression of one class by another, and of the majority by the minority at that. Naturally, for the successful discharge of such a task as the systematic suppression by the exploiting minority of the exploited majority, the greatest ferocity and savagery of suppression are required, seas of blood are required, through which mankind is marching in slavery, serfdom, and wage-labour.

Again, during the *transition* from capitalism to Communism, suppression is *still* necessary; but it is the suppression of the minority of exploiters by the majority of exploited. A special apparatus, special machinery for suppression, the "state," is *still* necessary, but this is now a transitional state, no longer a state in the usual sense, for the suppression of the minority of exploiters, by the majority of the wage slaves of *yesterday,* is a matter comparatively so easy, simple and natural that it will cost far less bloodshed than the suppression of the risings of slaves, serfs or wage labourers, and will cost mankind far less. This is compatible with the diffusion of democracy among such an overwhelming majority of the population, that the need for *special machinery* of suppression will begin to disappear. The exploiters are, naturally, unable to suppress the people without a most complex machinery for performing this task; but *the people* can suppress the exploiters even with very simple "machinery," almost without any "machinery," without any special apparatus, by the simple *organization of the armed masses* (such as the Soviets of Workers' and Soldiers' Deputies, we may remark, anticipating a little).

Finally, only Communism renders the state absolutely unnecessary, for there is *no one* to be suppressed—"no one" in the sense of a *class*, in the sense of a systematic struggle with a definite section of the population. We are not Utopians, and we do not in the least deny the possibility and inevitability of excesses on the part of *individual persons,* nor the need to suppress *such* excesses. But, in the first place, no special machinery, no special apparatus of repression is needed for this; this will be done by the armed people itself, as simply and as readily as any crowd of civilised people, even in modern society, parts a pair of combatants or does not allow a woman to be outraged. And, secondly, we know that the fundamental social cause of excesses which consist in violating the rules of social life is the exploitation of the masses, their want and their poverty. With the removal of this chief cause, excesses will inevitably begin to *"wither away."* We do not know how quickly and in what succession, but we know that they will wither away. With their withering away, the state will also *wither away.*

SOURCE. V. I. Lenin, *State and Revolution,* New York: International Publishers, 1932, pp. 7–10, 12–13, 15–17, 69–75. Reprinted by permission of International Publishers Co., Inc.

d. OROZCO, *VICTIMS*, 1936

THE MARXIST VISION of class struggle and cruel capitalist oppression of the proletariat was powerfully expressed in the art of the Mexican painter José Clemente Orozco (1883–1949). Shown here is his Victims *from a mural cycle painted in 1936 at the University of Guadalajara.*

PART FOUR

Liberalism and Nationalism in the Nineteenth Century

THE forces of liberalism and nationalism, released into Europe in the age of the French Revolution and Napoleon, shaped the politics of the nineteenth century. They expressed themselves in demands for democratic constitutions, widened suffrage, social reform measures and, in Germany, Italy, and the Balkans, movements for national unity and independence. In France, liberal revolutions broke out in 1830 and 1848, followed by an imperial revival in 1852 under Napoleon III which, in turn, gave way to the establishment of a Third Republic (1870's) with a Chamber of Deputies elected on the basis of universal suffrage. In England, the growth of liberalism resulted in the extension of voting privileges in the Reform Acts of 1832, 1867, and 1884. The liberal philosophy was lucidly presented in the writings of John Stuart Mill. Liberalism even made an impact in imperial Russia when, in 1861, Czar Alexander II abolished serfdom.

In Italy liberalism and nationalism worked together toward the goal of national unification. In the 1860's the constitutional monarchy of Piedmont, directed by its astute minister Count Cavour, became the ruling element of a united Italy. Liberalism was also a factor in early efforts to unify Germany, but it gave way to the "blood and iron" nationalism of Bismarck, the conservative Prussian chancellor, who by clever diplomacy and a calculated use of force made Prussia the nucleus of a new German Empire. Once German unification had been achieved, Bismarck sought to consolidate his gains by pursuing a policy of peace in Europe and protecting German security through a complex series of treaties with other powers. The Franco-Prussian War (1870–1871), which had been the final stroke of Bismarck's unification policy, left France defeated and hungering for revenge, and Bismarck sought to isolate France by entering into defensive alliances with Austria, Italy, and Russia.

The nineteenth century closed with republicanism or constitutionl monarchy in the ascendance throughout western and central Europe. But social revolutionary unrest was never far from the surface, and the fierce nationalism that had unified Italy and Germany and secured the independence of several Balkan states tended to intensify national rivalries to an ominous degree. These rivalries, heightened by a sense of unquestioning devotion to the fatherland, led finally to the cataclysmic world wars of the twentieth century.

Chapter 8

THE VICISSITUDES OF LIBERALISM IN FRANCE AND ENGLAND

a. THE REVOLUTION OF 1830:
LOUIS BLANC DESCRIBES EUROPE'S
REACTION TO THE JULY REVOLUTION IN PARIS

THE JULY REVOLUTION of 1830 resulted in the overthrow of the Bourbon monarchy in France which had been resurrected in 1815 by the Congress of Vienna to replace Napoleon. A new "liberal" monarchy was established in 1830 in the person of the Duke of Orleans, Louis-Philippe (1830–1848), and revolutionary violence surged across Europe. The response in other countries to the July Revolution in France is described enthusiastically by Louis Blanc (1811–1882) in his History of Ten Years, 1830–1840. *Louis Blanc, a devoted revolutionary, was to play a major role in the subsequent Revolution of 1848.*

That revolution [in France, of July 1830] sent a universal thrill through the world. The nations that had been enthralled by the treaties of 1815 were aroused. The apparition of the tricolour flag floating over the French consulate in Warsaw made the true hearts of the Poles, our old brethren in arms, beat high with hope. At Brussels, Liege, and Antwerp, men asked themselves at last by what right two millions of Dutchmen commanded four millions of Belgians. The Rhenine provinces, which, though they did not speak our language, wished to retain our laws, desired to belong to us from pride. A formidable fermentation was manifested in the German universities, till then tormented by vague aspirations after liberty. But nothing could compare with the movement that pervaded Italy. Throughout the whole peninsula, including the Roman states, the enthusiasm was boundless. In the streets, the squares, and all public places, the multitude thronged round travellers from France; they made them read aloud the journals of their country; and when they had thus recounted to their eager listeners some of the prodigious events recently enacted on the banks of the Seine, a unanimous burst of applause followed the recital, mingled with cries and sobs. It is almost literally true that for several days the Italians never ceased to look towards the Alps, expecting every hour to see the French descending from them. The revolution of July derived from distance something of a marvellous character; and the people of France sprang up again, in the eyes of wondering Europe, in the gigantic proportions given to it by the Republic, and, after the republic, by the Empire.

SOURCE. Louis Blanc, *The History of Ten Years, 1830–1840,* London: Chapman and Hall, 1844, I, p. 251.

b. THE REVOLUTION OF 1830: DELACROIX, *LIBERTY LEADING THE PEOPLE*

THE HIGH HOPES of French liberals in 1830 are expressed artistically in Eugène Delacroix's painting Liberty Leading the People. *Compare this work of revolutionary romanticism with the Neo-Classical restraint of Ingres'* Mademoiselle Rivière *(above, Chapter 3,b).*

c. DE TOCQUEVILLE ON THE FEBRUARY REVOLUTION, 1848

THE SUPERFICIALITY of Louis-Philippe's liberalism and the continued growth of French republican sentiment resulted in the overthrow of the Orleanist monarchy in the February Revolution of 1848. The keen observer Alexis de Tocqueville described in his Recollections *the popular, lower-class basis of the February Revolution.*

I spent the whole afternoon in walking about Paris. Two things in particular struck me: the first was, I will not say the mainly, but the uniquely and exclusively popular character of the revolution that had just taken place; the omnipotence it had given to the people properly so-called—that is to say, the classes who work with their hands—over all others. The second was the comparative absence of malignant passion, or, as a matter of fact, of any keen passion—an absence which at once made it clear that the lower orders had suddenly become masters of Paris.

Although the working classes had often played the leading part in the events of the First Revolution, they had never been the sole leaders and masters of the State, either *de facto* or *de jure;* it is doubtful whether the Convention contained a single man of the people; it was composed of *bourgeois* and men of letters. The war between the Mountain and the Girondists was conducted on both sides by members of the middle class, and the triumph of the former never brought power down into the hands of the people alone. The Revolution of July was effected by the people, but the middle class had stirred it up and led it, and secured the principal fruits of it. The Revolution of February, on the contrary, seemed to be made entirely outside the *bourgeoisie* and against it.

In this great concussion, the two parties of which the social body in France is mainly composed, had, in a way, been thrown more completely asunder, and the mass of the people, which had stood alone, remained in sole possession of power.

SOURCE. *The Recollections of Alexis de Tocqueville,* J. P. Mayer, ed., Alexander Texeira de Mattos, tr., New York: Columbia University Press, 1949, pp. 73–74. Reprinted by permission of Columbia University Press and Harvill Press Ltd., London.

d. DE TOCQUEVILLE ON THE JUNE DAYS, 1848

THE HOPES of the working classes were disappointed, however, by the bourgeois policies of the republican government that came into power. Later in the year a new wave of popular violence, known as the "June Days," terrorized Paris until suppressed by the army. Tocqueville describes the turbulence of the June Days in vivid terms.

In the evening [June 26] I decided to go myself to the Hôtel de Ville, in order to obtain more certain news of the results of the day. The insurrection, after alarming me by its violence, now alarmed me by its long duration. For who could foresee the effect which the sight of so long and uncertain a conflict might produce in some parts of France, and especially in the great manufacturing towns, such as Lyons? As I went along the Quai de la Ferraille, I met some National Guards from my neighbourhood, carrying on litters several of their comrades and two of their officers wounded. I observed, in talking with them, with what terrible rapidity, even in so civilized a century as our own, the most peaceful minds enter, as it were, into the spirit of civil war, and how quick they are, in these unhappy times, to acquire a taste for violence and a contempt for human life. The men with whom I was talking were peaceful, sober artisans, whose gentle and somewhat sluggish natures were still further removed from cruelty than from heroism. Yet they dreamt of nothing but massacre and destruction. They complained that they were not allowed to use bombs or to sap and mine the streets held by the insurgents, and they were determined to show no more quarter; already that morning I had almost seen a poor devil shot before my eyes on the boulevards, who had been arrested without arms in his hands, but whose mouth and hands were blackened by a substance which they supposed to be, and which no doubt was, powder. I did all I could to calm these rabid sheep. I promised them we should take terrible measures the next day. Lamoricière, in fact, had told me that morning that he had sent for shells to hurl behind the barricades; and I knew that a regiment of sappers was expected from Douai, to pierce the walls and blow up the besieged houses with petards. I added that they must not shoot any of their prisoners, but that they should kill then and there anyone who made as though to defend himself. I left my men a little more contented, and, continuing my road, I could not help examining myself and feeling surprised at the nature of the arguments I had used, and the promptness with which, in two days, I had become familiarized with those ideas of inexorable destruction which were naturally so foreign to my character.

SOURCE. *The Recollections of Alexis de Tocqueville*, J. P. Mayer, ed., Alexander Texeira de Mattos, tr., New York: Columbia University Press 1949, pp. 180–181. Reprinted by permission of Columbia University Press and Harville Press Ltd., London.

e. LOUIS NAPOLEON'S PROCLAMATION TO THE PEOPLE, 1851

AS IN 1830 so in 1848 the revolutionary unrest that began in France spread quickly across Europe. Metternich, the great conservative figure of the Congress of Vienna, was obliged to flee Vienna in disguise, and barricades were thrown up on the streets of Berlin. In general, however, the 1848 revolutions failed. Except in France, the old monarchies managed to retain their lands and powers. In France itself, the Second Republic, established in 1848, was compromised later in the same year by the election of Napoleon's nephew, Louis Napoleon, to the presidency. The republic was demolished in 1852 by Louis Napoleon's coup d'état *and the restoration of the Empire. Dissolving the recalcitrant Assembly, Louis issued on December 2, 1851, a proclamation calling for a plebiscite on his proposal to assume sweeping executive powers. The electorate approved the proposal, and the era of the Second Empire began, with Louis as Emperor Napoleon III.*

Frenchmen!

The present situation cannot last much longer. Each day that passes increases the dangers of the country. The Assembly, which ought to be the firmest support of order, has become a centre of conspiracies. The patriotism of three hundred of its members was not able to arrest its fatal tendencies. Instead of making laws in the general interest, it forges weapons for civil war; it makes an attack upon the authority that I hold directly from the people; it encourages all the evil passions; it puts in jeopardy the repose of France: I have dissolved it, and I make the whole people judge between it and me.

The Constitution, as you know, was made with the purpose of weakening in advance the power that you were about to confer upon me. Six million votes were a striking protest against it, nevertheless I faithfully observed it. Provocations, calumnies, outrages, have found me unmoved. But now that the fundamental compact is no longer respected even by those who incessantly invoke it, and the men who have already destroyed two monarchies wish to bind my hands, in order to overthrow the Republic, it is my duty to defeat their wicked designs and to save the country by invoking the solemn judgment of the only sovereign that I recognize in France, the people.

I make, therefore, a loyal appeal to the whole nation, and I say to you: If you wish to continue this state of uneasiness which degrades us and makes uncertain our future, choose another in my place, for I no longer wish an authority which is powerless to do good, makes me responsible for acts I cannot prevent, and chains me to the helm when I see the vessel speeding toward the abyss.

If, on the contrary, you still have confidence in me, give me the means to accomplish the great mission that I hold from you.

This mission consists in bringing to a close the era of revolutions by satisfying the legitimate wants of the people and by protecting them against subversive passions. It consists, especially, in creating institutions that may survive men and that may be at length foundations upon which something durable can be established.

Persuaded that the instability of authority and the preponderance of a single Assembly are permanent causes of trouble and discord, I submit to you the following fundamental bases of a Constitution which the Assemblies will develop later.

1st. A responsible chief selected for ten years;

2d. Ministers dependent upon the executive power alone;

3d. A Council of State composed of the most distinguished men to prepare the laws and to discuss them before the legislative body;

4th. A legislative body to discuss and vote the laws, elected by universal suffrage without *scrutin de liste* which falsifies the election;

5th. A second assembly, composed of all the illustrious persons of the country, predominant authority, guardian of the fundamental compact and of the public liberties.

This system, created by the First Consul at the beginning of the century, has already given to France repose and prosperity; it will guarantee them to her again.

Such is my profound conviction. If you share it, declare the fact by your votes. If, on the contrary, you prefer a government without force, monarchical or republican, borrowed from I know not what past or from what chimerical future, reply in the negative.

Thus, therefore, for the first time since 1804, you will vote with knowledge of the case, knowing well for whom and for what.

If I do not obtain a majority of your votes I shall then bring about the meeting of a new Assembly, and I shall resign to it the mandate that I have received from you.

But if you believe that the cause of which my name is the symbol, that is, France regenerated by the revolution of '89 and organized by the Emperor, is always yours, proclaim it by sanctioning the powers that I ask of you.

Then France and Europe will be preserved from anarchy, obstacles will be removed, rivalries will have disappeared, for all will respect, in the decision of the people, the decree of Providence.

(signed)   LOUIS NAPOLEON

SOURCE. F. M. Anderson, ed., *The Constitutions and Other Select Documents Illustrative of the History of France*, Minneapolis: H. W. Wilson Co., 1904, pp. 539–540.

f. DECLARATION OF THE PARIS COMMUNE, 1871

FRENCH DEFEATS in the Franco-Prussian War resulted in the fall of Louis Napoleon in 1870. Paris underwent a long and bitter siege by the Prussian army. The provisional French government, located first at Bordeaux and later at Versailles, recognized that the military position was hopeless and entered into an armistice with Prussia. The Parisians, feeling that they had been betrayed by the government, declared their independence and asserted their status as a free commune. At a time when monarchist sentiment was growing in France, the Paris Commune was dominated by republicanism of an increasingly radical sort and, to a degree, by Communism. The political aims of the Communards are set forth in the Declaration of the Paris Commune to the French People, April 19, 1871. In May the Commune was crushed by the military force of the Versailles government, but the deep antagonisms which it caused divided France for years to come.

In the painful and terrible conflict which once again imposes upon Paris the horrors of siege and bombardment, which causes French blood to flow, which causes our brothers, our wives, and our children to perish, sinking before shells and grape shot, it is necessary that public opinion should not be divided and that the national conscience should not be troubled.

It is necessary that Paris and the whole country should know what is the nature, the reason, and the aim of the Revolution which is accomplished. It is necessary, in fine, that the responsibility for the sorrows, the sufferings and the misfortunes of which we are the victims should return upon those who, after having betrayed France and delivered Paris to the foreigner, are seeking with a blind and cruel obstinacy the ruin of the capital, in order to conceal in the disaster to the Republic and to Liberty the double testimony to their treason and their crime.

It is the duty of the Commune to ascertain and assert the aspirations and the views of the population of Paris, to state precisely the character of the movement of March 18, misunderstood, unknown and calumniated by the politicians who sit at Versailles.

Once again Paris labors and suffers for all France, for which by her conflicts and sacrifices she prepares intellectual, moral, adminsitrative and economic regeneration, glory and prosperity.

What does she ask for?

The recognition and consolidation of the Republic, the only form of government compatible with the rights of the people and the regular and free development of society;

The absolute autonomy of the Commune extended to all the localities in France, and insuring to each the integrity of its rights and to every Frenchman the full exercise of his faculties and aptitudes, as man, citizen and worker;

The autonomy of the Commune shall have for its limits only the equal right of autonomy for all the other communes adhering to the contract, the association of which must insure French unity.

The rights inherent in the Commune are:

The voting of the communal budget, receipts and expenditures; the determination and partition of taxation; the management of the local services; the organization of its magistrature, the internal police and education; the administration of the property belonging to the Commune;

The choice by election or competition, with responsibility and the permanent right of control and of removal, of the communal magistrates and functionaries of all sorts;

The absolute guarantee of personal liberty, of liberty of conscience and liberty of labor;

The permanent participation of the citizens in communal affairs by the free expression of their ideas and the free defence of their interests; guarantees to be given for these expressions by the Commune, which alone is to be charged with the supervision and assuring of the free and just exercise of the right of meeting and of publicity;

The organization of urban defence and of the National Guard, which elects its leaders and alone watches over the maintenance of order within the city.

Paris wishes for nothing more in the way of local guarantees, on condition, well understood, of finding in the grand central administration, the delegation of the federated communes, the realization and the practice of the same principles.

But, in favor of its autonomy and profiting from its liberty of action, Paris reserves to herself to effect for herself, as she may think proper, the administrative and economic reforms which her population demand; to create suitable institutions to develop and promote education, production, exchange and credit; to universalize power and property, according to the necessities of the moment and the opinion of those interested and the data furnished by experience.

Our enemies deceive themselves or deceive the country when they accuse Paris of wishing to impose its will or its supremacy upon the remainder of the nation and of designing a dictatorship which would be a veritable attack upon the independence and sovereignty of the other communes.

They deceive themselves or deceive the country when they accuse Paris of seeking the destruction of French unity, established by the Revolution amid the acclamations of our fathers flocking to the Fête of the Federation from all points of old France.

Unity such as has been imposed on us up to this day by the Empire, the Monarchy and Parliamentarism is only despotic, unintelligent, arbitrary and onerous centralization.

Political unity such as Paris wishes is the voluntary association of all the local initiatives, the free and spontaneous cooperation of all the individual energies in view of a common purpose, the welfare, the liberty and the security of all.

The Communal Revolution, begun by the popular initiative of March 18, inaugurates a new political era, experimental, positive, and scientific.

It is the end of the old governmental and clerical world, of militarism, officialism, exploitation, stock jobbing, monopolies, and privileges, to which the proletariate owes its servitude and the fatherland its misfortunes and its disasters.

Let this beloved and splendid fatherland, imposed upon by falsehoods and calumnies, reassure itself then!

The struggle brought on between Paris and Versailles is one of those which cannot be terminated by illusory compromises; the issue of it cannot be doubtful. Victory, pursued with an indomitable energy by the National Guard, will remain with the idea and the right.

We appeal, therefore, to France!

Informed that Paris in arms possesses as much of calmness as of bravery; that it preserves order with as much energy as enthusiasm; that it sacrifices itself with as much reason as heroism; and that it has armed itself only out of devotion to the liberty and glory of all; let France cause this bloody conflict to cease!

It is for France to disarm Versailles by the solemn expression of her irresistible will.

Summoned to profit from our conquests, let her declare herself identified with our efforts; let her be our ally in this conflict which can end only by the triumph of the communal idea or the ruin of Paris!

As for ourselves, citizens of Paris, we have the mission of accomplishing the modern revolution, the greatest and the most fruitful of all those which have illuminated history.

It is our duty to struggle and the conquer!

THE COMMUNE OF PARIS.

Paris, April 19, 1871.

SOURCE. F. M. Anderson, ed., *The Constitutions and Other Select Documents Illustrative of the History of France*, Minneapolis: H. W. Wilson Co., 1904, pp. 609–612.

g. THE THIRD REPUBLIC: LOUIS THIERS ON REPUBLIC AND MONARCHY, 1877

THE THIRD REPUBLIC, which developed in the aftermath of the Franco-Prussian War, took shape gradually in an atmosphere of bitter division between monarchists and republicans. Its first president, Louis Adolphe Thiers, was an elder statesman who had once supported King Louis-Philippe. Thiers had by now become a republican, and his hostility to the monarchist sentiment of the Assembly resulted in his resignation in 1873. In a letter of 1877 he explained his preference for republicanism over monarchism in measured words that contrast strikingly with republican manifestoes of earlier times. His viewpoint prevailed, and the Third Republic, based on liberal statutes and universal suffrage, survived until World War II.

. . . at Bordeaux we, who served the Republic, were formerly monarchists. This, however, was not true of all. But we were demanded; we did not step forward without being called, and we took office purely through goodwill, because our presence re-assured the alarmed nation. And at last we were convinced of the necessity of the Republic. I wish the Republic many similar servitors, and from whatever quarter they may come, they will always be welcomed if they are honestly determined to help on the common cause, which, if it succeed, will be a blessing and not a detriment to France.

The question . . . may be summed up as follows: Is the Republic needed, and, if so, should it be firmly established by men who wish its success? Herein lies the whole question at issue.

Now, I ask every honest man, to whatever party he may belong, if the Count de Chambord[1] could be placed on the throne with the opinions that he professes and with the flag that he unfurls, or if it is hoped that he may some day be acceptable after he has modified his views? We respect him too much to believe it. I will say nothing of the Orleans princes,[2] who wish to be mentioned only after the Count de Chambord, according to their hereditary rank; but I ask if the country is ready to receive the Prince Imperial,[3] who, though innocent of the misfortunes of France, suggests them so keenly, that the nation still shudders at the bare mention of his name? Nobody dare answer me yes; and, in fact, all the friends of these candidates postpone, until a future

---

[1] The Bourbon pretender in the 1870's around whom the monarchists rallied. His insistence on replacing the revolutionary Tricolor flag with the traditional royalist fleur-de-lis lost him much support.

[2] The line of King Louis-Philippe (1830–1848).

[3] Of the Napoleonic line.

time, the day when their claims may be put forward. The truth of this statement is seen in the fact that they make no move, though the greatest indulgence has been shown all the monarchical parties.

Now, until this day—more or less distant—arrives, what will France do? France will wait until her future masters are ready: until one is brought over to other ways of thinking, until another has made an advance in his right of succession, and until a third has finished his education. In the meanwhile everything will be in suspense, commerce, industry, finances, State affairs. How can business men be asked to engage in great industrial enterprises, and financiers to negotiate loans, when the future threatens fresh political troubles? And how can foreign Cabinets be expected to strengthen their relations and form alliances with us, when French policy is liable to be directed by new chiefs and influenced by new ideas? Dare anybody ask such sacrifices of a great nation, that Europe has admired in its prosperity and also in its misfortunes, on seeing it restored once more, on seeing it revive again, displaying a rare wisdom in the midst of provocations, which it endures with such *sang-froid* and calm firmness?

Some men who, because they call themselves monarchists, believe that they know the secrets of the crowned heads, pretend that their reign is desired, and that then France will regain its prestige and alliances. But we would say to these men who think they understand Europe, but who, in reality, know nothing about it, and attribute to it their own ignorance and prejudices, that Europe looks with pity on their pretensions and hopes, and blames them for having got their country into the present trouble, instead of giving it the only form of government possible to-day. This Europe was formerly under absolute princes, but, recognizing the march of time, it is now ruled by constitutional princes, and is satisfied with the change. Europe understands that France, after the fall of three dynasties, has gone over to the Republic, which, during the last six years, has lifted the country out of the abyss into which the monarchists precipitated it. Europe has seen our military prestige destroyed and a new prestige take its place, that of the inexhaustible vitality of a prostrate country, suddenly rising up and furnishing the world an unheard of example of resources of every kind, so that France, even after Wörth, Sedan and Metz, has shown herself to be great still. It was under the Monarchy that she fell, but under the Republic that she arose again. And once more on the road to prosperity, it was the monarchists again that threw obstacles in the way of her reconstruction. If it be the esteem of Europe that is sought, listen to Europe, hearken to its opinion!

For this it is, that we persistently ask if there be any other alternative than the following: Either the Monarchy, which is impossible, because there are three claimants and but one throne; or the Republic, difficult to establish without doubt, not because of itself, but because of the opposition of the monarchical parties, and, nevertheless, possible, for it is supported by an immense majority of the people.

It is the duty, therefore, of this immense majority of the people to consult together, to unite and to vote against those who resist the establishment of the only government possible. The Monarchy to-day, after the three revolutions that have overthrown it, is immediate civil war, if it be established now; and if put off for two years, or three years, the civil war is only postponed until that epoch. The Republic is an equitable participation of all the children of France in the government of their country, according to their abilities, their importance, and their callings.

SOURCE. François le Goff, *The Life of Louis Adolphe Thiers,* T. Stanton, tr.

h. ERNEST RENAN, FROM THE PREFACE TO *RECOLLECTIONS OF MY YOUTH*

THE IMPORTANT SCHOLAR ERNEST RENAN (1823–1892), in his Recollections of My Youth, *expresses a cautiously optimistic view of French liberalism and its effect on science and the intellectual in society.*

The one object in life is the development of the mind, and the first condition for the development of the mind is that it should have liberty. The worst social state from this point of view is the theocratic state, like Islam or the ancient Pontifical state, in which dogma reigns supreme. Nations with an exclusive state religion, like Spain, are not much better off. Nations in which a religion of the majority is recognized are also exposed to serious drawbacks. In behalf of the real or assumed beliefs of the greatest number, the state considers itself bound to impose upon thought terms which thought cannot accept. The belief or the opinion of the one side should not be a fetter upon the other side. As long as the masses were believers, that is to say, as long as the same sentiments were almost universally professed by a people, freedom of research and discussion were impossible. A colossal weight of stupidity pressed down upon the human mind. The terrible catastrophe of the Middle Ages, that break of a thousand years in the history of civilization, is due less to the barbarians than to the triumph of the dogmatic spirit among the masses.

This is a state of things which is coming to an end in our time, and we must not be surprised if some disturbance ensues. There are no longer masses who believe; a great number of the people decline to recognize the supernatural, and the day is not far distant when beliefs of this kind will die out altogether in the masses, just as the belief in familiar spirits and ghosts have disappeared. Even if, as is probable, we are to have a temporary Catholic reaction, the people will not revert to the Church. Religion has become once and for all a matter of personal taste. Now beliefs are only dangerous when they represent something like unanimity or an unquestionable majority. When they are merely individual, there is not a word to be said against them, and it is our duty to treat them with the respect which they do not always exhibit for their adversaries, when they feel that they have force at their back.

There can be no denying that it will take time for the liberty, which is the aim and object of human society, to take root in France as it has in America. French democracy has several essential principles to acquire, before it can become a liberal régime. It will be above all things necessary that we should have laws as to associations, charitable foundations, and the right of legacy, analogous to those which are in force in England and America. Supposing this progress to be effected (if it is utopian to count upon it in France, it is not so for the rest of Europe, in which the aspirations for English liberty become every day more intense), we should really not have much cause to look regretfully upon the favours conferred by the *ancien régime* upon things of the mind.

I quite think that if democratic ideas were to secure a definitive triumph, science and scientific teaching would soon find the modest subsidies now accorded them cut off. This is an eventuality which would have to be accepted as philosophically as may be. The free foundations would take the place of the state institutes, the slight drawbacks being more than compensated for by the advantage of having no longer to make to the supposed prejudices of the majority concessions which the state exacted in return for its pittance. The waste of power in state institutes is enormous. Private foundations would not be exposed to nearly so much waste. It is true that spurious science would, in these conditions, flourish side by side with real science, enjoying the same privileges, and that there would be no official criterion, as there still is to a certain extent now, to distinguish the one from the other. But this criterion becomes every day less reliable. Reason has to submit to the indignity of taking second place behind those who have a loud voice, and who speak with a tone of command. The plaudits and favour of the public will, for a long time to come, be at the service of what is false. But the true has great power, when it is free; the true endures; the false is ever changing and decays. Thus it is that the true, though only understood by a select few, always rises to the surface, and in the end prevails.

In short, it is very possible that the American-like social condition towards which we are advancing, independently of any particular form of government, will not be more intolerable for persons of intelligence than the better guaranteed social conditions which we have already been subject to. We may at least hope that vulgarity will not yet a while persecute freedom of mind. Descartes, living in the brilliant seventeenth century, was nowhere so well off as at Amsterdam, because, as "everyone was engaged in trade there," no one paid any heed to him. It may be that general vulgarity will one day be the condition of happiness, for the worst American vulgarity would not send Giordano Bruno to the stake or persecute Galileo. . . . liberty is like truth; scarcely anyone loves it on its own account, and yet, owing to the impossibility of extremes, one always comes back to it.

SOURCE. Ernest Renan, *Recollections of My Youth,* Mme. Renan, rev., C. B. Pitman, tr., London: Chapman and Hall, 1883, Preface.

i. LORD JOHN RUSSELL INTRODUCES THE ENGLISH REFORM BILL OF 1832 BEFORE PARLIAMENT, 1831

THE ENGLISH REFORM ACT OF 1832, an indirect product of the revolutionary spirit of 1830, was aimed at revising the anachronistic "rotten borough" system and equalizing the suffrage. Its goals were persuasively set forth by Lord John Russell when he introduced the measure to Parliament on March 1, 1831.

It will not be necessary on this occasion that I should go over the arguments which have been so often urged in favour of parliamentary reform; but it is due to the question that I should state shortly the chief points of the general argument on which the reformers rest their claim. Looking at the question then as a question of right, the ancient statutes of Edward I contain the germ and vital principle of our political constitution. . . . The 34th Edward I, commonly called the *Statute de Tallagio Concedendo,* provides "that no tallage or aid shall be taken or levied by us or our heirs in our realm without the good will and assent of archbishops, bishops, earls, barons, knights, burgesses, and other freemen of the land." . . .

To revert again for a moment to ancient times, the assent of the commonalty of the land, thus declared necessary for the grant of any aid or tax, was collected from their representatives consisting of two knights from each country, from each city two citizens, and from every borough two burgesses. For 250 years the constant number of boroughs so sending their representatives was about 120. Some thirty or forty others occasionally exercised or discontinued that practice or privilege, as they rose or fell in wealth and importance. How this construction of the house of commons underwent various changes, till the principle on which it was founded was lost sight of, I will not now detain the house by explaining. There can be no doubt, however, that at the beginning of the period I have alluded to the house of commons did represent the people of England. No man of common sense pretends that this assembly now represents the commonalty or people of England. If it be a question of right, therefore, right is in favour of reform.

Let us now look at the question as one of reason. Allow me to imagine, for a moment, a stranger from some distant country, who should arrive in England to examine our institutions. . . . He would have been told that the proudest boast of this celebrated country was its political freedom. If, in addition to this, he had heard that once in six years this country, so wise, so renowned, so free, chose its representatives to sit in the great council where all the ministerial affairs were discussed and determined, he would not be a little curious to see the process by which so important and solemn an operation was effected. What then would be his surprise if he were taken by his guide, whom he had asked to conduct him to one of the places of election, to a green mound and told that this green mound sent two members to parliament, or to be taken to a stone wall with three niches in it and told that these three niches sent two members to parliament; or, if he were shown a green park with many signs of flourishing vegetable life, but none of human habitation, and told that this green park sent two members to parliament! But his surprise would increase to astonishment if he were carried into the north of England, where he would see large flourishing towns, full of trade and activity, containing vast magazines of wealth and manufactures, and were told that these places had no representatives in the assembly which was said to represent the people. Suppose him, after all, for I will not disguise any part of the case—suppose him to ask for a specimen of popular election, and to be carried for that purpose to Liverpool; his surprise would be turned into disgust at the gross venality and corruption which he would find to pervade the electors. After seeing all this, would he not wonder that a nation which had made such progress in every kind of knowledge, and which valued itself for its freedom, should permit so absurd and defective a system of representation any longer to prevail? But whenever arguments of this kind have been urged, it has been replied—and Mr. Canning placed his opposition to reform on this ground—"We agree that the house of commons is not, in fact, sent here by the people; we agree that, in point of reason, the system by which it is sent is full of anomaly and, absurdity; but government is a matter of experience, and so long as the people are satisified with the actual working of the house of commons, it would be unwise to embark in theoretical change." Of this argument, I confess, I always felt the weight, and so long as the people did not answer the appeals of the friends of reform, it was indeed an argument not to be resisted. But what is the case at this moment? The whole people call loudly for reform. . . .

I arrive at last at the objections which may be made to the plan we propose. I shall be told, in the first place, that we overturn the institutions of our ancestors. I maintain that, in departing from the letter, we preserve the spirit of those institutions. Our opponents say our ancestors gave Old Sarum representatives; therefore we should give Old Sarum representatives. We say our ancestors gave Old Sarum representatives because it *was* a large town; therefore we give representatives to Manchester, which *is* a large town. . . . It has been asserted also, if a reform were to be effected, that many men of great talents, who now get into this house for close boroughs,[4] would not be able to procure seats. I have never entertained any apprehensions of the sort, for I believe that no reform that can be introduced will have the effect of preventing wealth, probity, learning, and wit from having their proper influence upon elections. . . . It may be said, too, that one great and injurious effect of the measures I propose will be to destroy the power and privileges of the aristocracy. This I deny. . . . Wherever the aristocracy reside, receiving large incomes, performing important duties, relieving the poor by charity, and evincing private worth and public virtue, it is not in human nature that they should not possess a great influence upon public opinion and have an equal weight in electing persons to serve their country in parliament. Though such persons may not have the direct nomination of members under this bill, I contend that they will have as much influence as they ought to have. But if by aristocracy those persons are meant who do not live among the people, who know nothing of the people, and who care nothing for them—who seek honours without merit, places without duty, and pensions without service—for such an aristocracy I have no sympathy. . . .

To establish the constitution on a firm basis, you must show that you are determined not to be the representatives of a small class or of a particular interest, but to form a body who, representing the people, springing from the people, and sympathizing with the people, can fairly call on the people to support the future burdens of the country. . . . I conclude, sir, by moving for leave to bring in a bill for amending the state of the representation in England and Wales.

SOURCE. *Parliamentary Debates,* Third Series, II, 1061 f.

[4] Close boroughs were depopulated towns that still sent two representatives to Parliament.

j. DEMANDS OF THE CHARTISTS, 1848

THE REFORM ACT corrected a number of abuses in the English electoral system, in particular the gross underrepresentation of the new industrial cities. But high property qualifications prevented workers themselves from voting, and the suffrage arrangements of 1832 could therefore hardly be described as democratic. A radical workers' movement known as Chartism was inspired by the revolutionary fervor of 1848 to present to Parliament a petition known as the People's Charter. In this document the Chartists proposed a number of democratic reforms including universal suffrage and the secret ballot. Rejected at the time, the Chartists' demands were in later years gradually incorporated into the English constitution in the Reform Acts of 1867 and 1884. By 1884 the election of the House of Commons had been put on a democratic basis.

That the United Kingdom be divided into 200 electoral districts; dividing, as nearly as possible, an equal number of inhabitants; and that each district do send a representative to Parliament.

That every person producing proof of his being 21 years of age, to the clerk of the parish in which he has resided six months, shall be entitled to have his name registered as a voter. That the time for registering in each year be from the 1st of January to the 1st of March.

That a general election do take place on the 24th of June in each year, and that each vacancy be filled up a fortnight after it occurs. That the hours for voting be from six o'clock in the morning till six o'clock in the evening.

That there shall be no property qualification for members; but on a requisition, signed by 200 voters, in favour of any candidate being presented to the clerk of the parish in which they reside, such candidate shall be put in nomination. And the list of all the candidates nominated throughout the district shall be stuck on the church door in every parish, to enable voters to judge of their qualification.

That each voter must vote in the parish in which he resides. That each parish provide as many balloting boxes as there are candidates proposed in the district; and that a temporary place be fitted up in each parish church for the purpose of *secret voting*. And, on the day of election, as each voter passes orderly on to the ballot, he shall have given to him, by the officer in attendance, a balloting ball, which he shall drop into the box of his favourite candidate. At the close of the day the votes shall be counted, by the proper officers, and the numbers stuck on the church doors. The following day the clerk of the district and two examiners shall collect the votes of all the parishes throughout the district, and cause the name of the successful candidate to be posted in every parish of the district.

That the members do take their seats in Parliament on the first Monday in October next after their election, and continue their sittings every day (Sundays excepted) till the business of the sitting is terminated, but not later than the 1st of September. They shall meet every day (during the Session) for business at 10 o'clock in the morning, and adjourn at 4. And every member shall be paid quarterly out of the public treasury £400 a year. That all electoral officers shall be elected by universal suffrage.

k. JOHN STUART MILL, FROM *ON LIBERTY,* 1859

AT THE INTELLECTUAL LEVEL, nineteenth-century English liberalism was cogently defended by John Stuart Mill (1806–1873) in his well-known work On Liberty *(1859) (k), and in his* Considerations on Representative Government *(1861) (l). Like Bentham, Mill was inclined to the view of the less government the better. He argued that a man should be free to do whatever he wished so long as he did not infringe on the liberty of others.*

The subject of this Essay is . . . Civil, or Social Liberty: the nature and limits of the power which can be legitimately exercised by society over the individual. A question seldom stated, and hardly ever discussed, in general terms, but which profoundly influences the practical controversies of the age by its latent presence, and is likely soon to make itself recognised as the vital question of the future. It is so far from being new, that, in a certain sense, it has divided mankind, almost from the remotest ages; but in the stage of progress into which the more civilised portions of the species have now entered, it presents itself under new conditions, and requires a different and more fundamental treatment.

The struggle between Liberty and Authority is the most conspicuous feature in the portions of history with which we are earliest familiar, particularly in that of Greece, Rome, and England. But in old times this contest was between subjects, or some classes of subjects, and the Government. By liberty, was meant protection against the tyranny of the political rulers. The rulers were conceived (except in some of the popular governments of Greece) as in a necessarily antagonistic position to the people whom they ruled. They consisted of a governing One, or a governing tribe or caste, who derived their authority from inheritance or conquest, who, at all events, did not hold it at the pleasure of the governed, and whose supremacy men did not venture, perhaps did not desire, to contest, whatever precautions might be taken against its oppressive exercise. Their power was regarded as necessary, but also as highly dangerous; as a weapon which they would attempt to use against their subjects, no less than against external enemies. To prevent the weaker members of the community from being preyed upon by innumerable vultures, it was needful that there should be an animal of prey stronger than the rest, commissioned to keep them down. But as the king of the vultures would be no less bent upon preying on the flock than any of the minor harpies, it was indispensable to be in a perpetual attitude of defence against his beak and claws. The aim, therefore, of patriots was to set limits to the power which the ruler should be suffered to exercise over the community; and this limitation was what they meant by liberty. It was attempted in two ways. First, by obtaining a recognition of certain immunities, called political liberties or rights, which it was to be regarded as a breach of duty in the ruler to infringe, and which if he did infringe, specific resistance, or general rebellion, was held to be justifiable. A second, and generally a later expedient, was the establishment of constitutional checks, by which the consent of the community, or of a body of some sort, supposed to represent its interests, was made a necessary condition to some of the more important acts of the governing power. To the first of these modes of limitation, the ruling power, in most European countries, was compelled, more or less, to submit. It was not so with the second; and, to attain this, or when already in some degree possessed, to attain it more completely, became everywhere the principal object of the lovers of liberty. And so long as mankind were content to combat one enemy by another, and to be ruled by a master, on condition of being guaranteed more or less efficaciously against his tyranny, they did not carry their aspirations beyond this point.

A time, however, came, in the progress of human affairs, when men ceased to think it a necessity of nature that their governors should be an independent power, opposed in interest to themselves. It appeared to them much better that the various magistrates of the State should be their tenants or delegates, revocable at their pleasure. In that way alone, it seemed, could they have complete security that the powers of government would never be abused to their disadvantage. By degrees this new demand for elective and temporary rulers became the prominent object of the exertions of the popular party, wherever any such party existed; and superseded, to a considerable extent, the previous efforts to limit the power of rulers. As the struggle proceeded for making the ruling power emanate from the periodical choice of the ruled, some persons began to think that too much importance had been attached to the limitation of the power itself. *That* (it might seem) was a resource against rulers whose interests were habitually opposed to those of the people. What was now wanted was, that the rulers should be identified with the people; that their interest and will should be the interest and will of the nation. The nation did not need to be protected against its own will. There was no fear of its tyrannising over itself. Let the rulers be effectually responsible to it, promptly removable by it, and it could afford to trust them with power of which it could itself dictate the use to be made. Their power was but the nation's own power, concentrated, and in a form convenient for exercise. This mode of thought, or rather perhaps of feeling, was common among the last generation of European liberalism, in the Continental section of which it still apparently predominates. Those who admit any limit to what a government may do, except in the case of such governments as they think ought not to exist, stand out as brilliant exceptions among the political thinkers of the Continent. A similar tone of sentiment might by this time have been prevalent in our own country, if the circumstances which for a time encouraged it, had continued unaltered.

But, in political and philosophical theories, as well as in persons, success discloses faults and infirmities which failure might have concealed from observation. The notion, that the people have no need to limit their power over themselves, might seen axiomatic, when popular government was a thing only dreamed about, or read of as having existed at some distant period of the past. Neither was that notion necessarily disturbed by such temporary aberrations as those of the French Revolution, the worst of which were the work of a usurping few, and which, in any case, belonged, not to the permanent working of popular institutions, but to a sudden and convulsive outbreak against monarchical and aristocratic despotism. In time, however, a democratic republic came to occupy a large portion of the earth's surface, and made itself felt as one of the most powerful members of the community of nations; and elective and responsible government became subject to the observations and criticisms which wait upon a great existing fact. It was now perceived that such phrases as "self-government," and "the power of the people over themselves," do not express the true state of the case. The "people" who exercise the power are not always the same people with those over whom it is exercised; and the "self-government" spoken of is not the government of each by himself, but of each by all the rest. The will of the people, moreover, practically means the will of the most numerous or the most active *part* of the people; the majority, or those who succeed in making themselves accepted as the majority; the people, consequently *may* desire to oppress a part of their number; and precautions are as much needed against this as against any other abuse of power. The limitation, therefore, of the power of government over individuals loses none of its importance when the holders of power are regularly accountable to the community, that is, to the strongest party therein. This view of things, recommending itself equally to the intelligence of thinkers and to the inclination of those important classes in European society to whose real or supposed interests democracy is adverse, has had no difficulty in establishing itself; and in political speculations "the tyranny of the majority" is now generally included among the evils against which society requires to be on its guard.

Like other tyrannies, the tyranny of the majority was at first, and is still vulgarly, held in dread, chiefly as operating through the acts of the public authorities. But reflecting persons perceived that when society is itself the tyrant—society collectively over the separate individuals who compose it—its means of tyrannising are not restricted to the acts which it may do by the hands of its political functionaries. Society can and does execute its own mandates: and if it issues wrong mandates instead of right, or any mandates at all in things with which it ought not to meddle, it practises a social tyranny more formidable than many kinds of political oppression, since, though not usually upheld by such extreme penalties, it leaves fewer means of escape, penetrating much more deeply into the details of life, and enslaving the soul itself. Protection, therefore, against the tyranny of the magistrate is not enough: there needs protection also against the tyranny of the prevailing opinion and feeling; against the tendency of society to impose, by other means than civil penalties, its own ideas and practices as rules of conduct on those who dissent from them; to fetter the development, and, if possible, prevent the formation, of any individuality not in harmony with its ways, and compels all characters to fashion themselves upon the model of its own. There is a limit to the legitimate interference of collective opinion with individual independence: and to find that limit, and maintain it against encroachment, is as indispensable to a good condition of human affairs, as protection against political despotism.

But though this proposition is not likely to be contested in general terms, the practical question, where to place the limit—how to make the fitting adjustment between individual independence and social control—is a subject on which nearly everything remains to be done. All that makes existence valuable to any one, depends on the enforcement of restraints upon the actions of other people. Some rules of conduct, therefore, must be imposed, by law in the first place, and by opinion on many things which are not fit subjects for the operation of law. What these rules should be is the principal question in human affairs; but if we except a few of the most obvious cases, it is one of those which least progress has been made in resolving. No two ages, and scarcely any two countries, have decided it alike; and the decision of one age or country is a wonder to another. Yet the people of any given age and country no more suspect any difficulty in it, than if it were a subject on which mankind had always been agreed. The rules which obtain among themselves appear to them self-evident and self-justifying. This all but universal illusion is one of the examples of the magical influence of custom, which is not only, as the proverb says, a second nature, but is continually mistaken for the first. The effect of custom, in preventing any misgiving respecting the rules of conduct which mankind impose on one another, is all the more complete because the subject is one on which it is not generally considered necessary that reasons should be given, either by one person to others or by each to himself. People are accustomed to believe, and have been encouraged in the belief by some who aspire to the character of philosophers, that their feelings, on subjects of this nature, are better than reasons, and render reasons unnecessary. The practical principle which guides them to their opinions on the regulation of human conduct, is the feeling in each person's mind that everybody should be required to act as he, and those with whom he sympathises, would like them to act. No one, indeed, acknowledges to himself that his standard of judgment is his own liking; but an opinion on a point of conduct, not supported by reasons, can only count as one person's preference; and if the reasons, when given, are a mere appeal to a similar preference felt by other people, it is still only many people's liking instead of one. To an ordinary man, however, his own preference, thus supported, is not only a perfectly satisfactory reason, but the only one he generally has for any of his notions of morality, taste, or propriety, which are not expressly written in his religious creed; and his chief guide in the interpretation even of that. Men's opinions, accordingly, on what is laudable or blamable, are affected by all the multifarious causes which influence their wishes in regard to the conduct of others, and which are as numerous as those which determine their wishes on any other subject. Sometimes their reason—at other times their prejudices or superstitions: often their social affections, not seldom their antisocial ones, their envy or jealousy, their arrogance or contemptuousness: but most commonly their desires or fears for themselves—their legitimate or illegitimate self-interest. Wherever there is an ascendant class, a large portion of the morality of the country emanates from its class interests, and its feelings of class superiority. The morality between Spartans and Helots, between planters and negroes, between princes and subjects, between nobles and roturiers, between men and women, has been for the most part the creation of these class interests and feelings: and the sentiments thus generated react in turn upon the moral feelings of the members of the ascendant class, in their relations among themselves. Where, on the other hand, a class, formerly ascendant, has lost its ascendancy, or where its ascendancy is unpopular, the prevailing moral sentiments frequently bear the impress of an impatient dislike of superiority. Another grand determining principle of the rules of conduct, both in act and forbearance, which have been enforced by law or opinion, has been the servility of mankind towards the supposed preferences or aversions of their temporal masters or of their gods. This servility, though essentially selfish, is not hypocrisy; it gives rise to perfectly genuine sentiments of abhorrence; it made men burn magicians and heretics. Among so many baser influences, the general and obvious interests of society have of course had a share, and a large one, in the direction of the moral sentiments: less, however, as a matter of reason, and on their own account, than as a consequence of the sympathies and antipathies which grew out of them: and sympathies and antipathies which had little or nothing to do with the interests of society, have made themselves felt in the establishment of moralities with quite as great force.

The likings and dislikings of society, or of some powerful portion of it, are thus the main thing which has practically determined the rules laid down for general observance, under the penalities of law or opinion. And in general, those who have been in advance of society in thought and feeling, have left this condition of things unassailed in principle, however they may have come into conflict with it in some of its details. They have occupied themselves rather in inquiring what things society ought to like or dislike, than in questioning whether its likings or dislikings should be a law to individuals. They preferred endeavouring to alter the feelings of mankind on the particular points on which they were themselves heretical, rather than make common cause in defence of freedom, with heretics generally. The only case in which the higher ground has been taken on principle and maintained with consistency, by any but an individual here and there, is that of religious belief: a case instructive in many ways, and not least so as forming a most striking instance of the fallibility of what is called the moral sense: for the *odium theologicum*, in a sincere bigot, is one of the most unequivocal cases of moral feeling. Those who first broke the yoke of what called itself the Universal Church, were in general as little willing to permit difference of religious opinion as that church itself. But when the heat of the conflict was over, without giving a complete victory to any party, and each church or sect was reduced to limit its hopes to retaining possession of the ground it already occupied; minorities, seeing that they had no chance of becoming majorities, were under the necessity of pleading to those whom they could not convert, for permission to differ. It is accordingly on this battle field, almost solely, that the rights of the individual against society have been asserted on broad grounds of principle, and the claim of society to exercise authority over dissentients openly controverted. The great writers to whom the world owes what religious liberty it possesses, have mostly asserted freedom of conscience as an indefeasible right, and denied absolutely that a human being is accountable to others for his religious belief. Yet so natural to mankind is intolerance in whatever they really care about, that religious freedom has hardly anywhere been practically realised, except where religious indifference, which dislikes to have its peace disturbed by theological quarrels, has added its weight to the scale. In the minds of almost all religious persons, even in the most tolerant countries, the duty of toleration is admitted with tacit reserves. One person will bear with dissent in matters of church government, but not of dogma; another can tolerate everybody, short of a Papist or a Unitarian; another every one who believes in revealed religion; a few extend their charity a little further, but stop at the belief in a God and in a future state. Wherever the sentiment of the majority is still genuine and intense, it is found to have abated little of its claim to be obeyed.

In England, from the peculiar circumstances of our political history, though the yoke of opinion is perhaps heavier, that of law is lighter, than in most other countries of Europe; and there is considerable jealousy of direct interference, by the legislative or the executive power, with private conduct; not so much from any just regard for the independence of the individual, as from the still subsisting habit of looking on the government as representing an opposite interest to the public. The majority have not yet learnt to feel the power of the government their power, or its opinions their opinions. When they do so, individual liberty will probably be as much exposed to invasion from the government, as it already is from public opinion. But, as yet, there is a considerable amount of feeling ready to be called forth against any attempt of the law to control individuals in things in which they have not hitherto been accustomed to be controlled by it; and this with every little discrimination as to whether the matter is, or is not, within the legitimate sphere of legal control; insomuch that the feeling, highly salutary on the whole, is perhaps quite as often misplaced as well grounded in the particular instances of its application. There is, in fact, no recognised principle by which the propriety or impropriety of government interference is customarily tested. People decide according to their personal preferences. Some, whenever they see any good to be done, or evil to be remedied, would willingly instigate the government to undertake the business; while others prefer to bear almost any amount of social evil, rather than add one to the departments of human interests amenable to governmental control. And men range themselves on one or the other side in any particular case, according to this general direction of their sentiments; or according to the degree of interest which they feel in the particular thing which it is proposed that the government should do, or according to the belief they entertain that the government would, or would not, do it in the manner they prefer; but very rarely on account of any opinion to which they consistently adhere, as to what things are fit to be done by a government. And it seems to me that in consequence of this absence of rule or principle, one side is at present as often wrong as the other; the interference of government is, with about equal frequency, improperly invoked and improperly condemned.

The object of this Essay is to assert one very simple principle, as entitled to govern absolutely the dealings of society with the individual in the way of compulsion and control, whether the means used be physical force in the form of legal penalties, or the moral coercion of public opinion. That principle is, that the sole end for which mankind are warranted, individually or collectively, in interfering with the liberty of action of any of their number, is self-protection. That the only purpose for which power can be rightfully exercised over any member of a civilised community, against his will, is to prevent harm to others. His own good, either physical or moral, is not a sufficient warrant. He cannot rightfully be compelled to do or forbear because it will be better for him to do so, because it will make him happier, because, in the opinions of others, to do so would be wise, or even right. These are good reasons for remonstrating with him, or reasoning with him, or persuading him, or entreating him, but not for compelling him, or visiting him with any evil in case he do otherwise. To justify that, the conduct from which it is desired to deter him must be calculated to produce evil to someone else. The only part of the conduct of any one, for which he is amenable to society, is that which concerns others. In the part which merely concerns himself, his independence is, of right, absolute. Over himself, over his own body and mind, the individual is sovereign.

It is, perhaps, hardly necessary to say that this doctrine is meant to apply only to human beings in the maturity of their faculties. We are not speaking of children, or of young persons below the age which the law may fix as that of manhood or womanhood. Those who are still in a state to require being taken care of by others, must be protected against their own actions as well as against external injury. For the same reason, we may leave out of consideration those backward states of society in which the race itself may be considered as in its nonage. The early difficulties in the way of spontaneous progress are so great, that there is seldom any choice of means for overcoming them; and a ruler full of the spirit of improvement is warranted in the use of any expedients that will attain an end, perhaps otherwise unattainable. Despotism is a legitimate mode of government in dealing with barbarians, provided the end be their improvement, and the means justified by actually effecting that end. Liberty, as a principle, has no application to any state of things anterior to the time when mankind have become capable of being improved by free and equal discussion. Until then, there is nothing for them but implicit obedience to an Akbar or a Charlemagne, if they are so fortunate as to find one. But as soon as mankind have attained the capacity of being guided to their own improvement by conviction or persuasion (a period long since reached in all nations with whom we need here concern ourselves), compulsion, either in the direct form or in that of pains and penalties for non-compliance, is no longer admissible as a means to their own good, and justifiable only for the security of others.

It is proper to state that I forego any advantage which could be derived to my argument from the idea of abstract right, as a thing independent of utility. I regard utility as the ultimate appeal on all ethical questions; but it must be utility in the largest sense, grounded on the permanent interests of a man as a progressive being. Those interests, I contend, authorise the subjection of individual spontaneity to external control, only in respect to those actions of each, which concern the interest of other people. If any one does an act hurtful to others, there is a *prima facie* case for punishing him, by law, or, where legal penalties are not safely applicable, by general disapprobation. There are also many positive acts for the benefit of others, which he may rightfully be compelled to perform; such as to give evidence in a court of justice; to bear his fair share in the common defence, or in any other joint work necessary to the interest of the society of which he enjoys the protection; and to perform certain acts of individual beneficence, such as saving a fellow-creature's life, or interposing to protect the defenceless against ill-usage, things which whenever it is obviously a man's duty to do, he may rightfully be made responsible to society for not doing. A person may cause evil to others not only by his actions but by his inaction, and in either case he is justly accountable to them for the injury. The latter case, it is true, requires a much more cautious exercise of compulsion than the former. To make any one answerable for doing evil to others is the rule; to make him answerable for not preventing evil is, comparatively speaking, the exception. Yet there are many cases clear enough and grave enough to justify that exception. In all things which regard the external relations of the individual, he is *de jure* amenable to those whose interests are concerned, and, if need be, to society as their protector. There are often good reasons for not holding him to the responsibility; but these reasons must arise from the special expediencies of the case: either because it is a kind of case in which he is on the whole likely to act better, when left to his own discretion, than when controlled in any way in which society have it in their power to control him; or because the attempt to exercise control would produce other evils, greater than those which it would prevent. When such reasons as these preclude the enforcement of responsibility, the conscience of the agent himself should step into the vacant judgment seat, and protect those interests of others which have no external protection; judging himself all the more ridigly, because the case does not admit of his being made accountable to the judgment of his fellow-creatures.

But there is a sphere of action in which society, as distinguished from the individual, has, if any, only an indirect interest; comprehending all that portion of a person's life and conduct which affects only himself, or if it also affects others, only with their free, voluntary, and undeceived consent and participation. When I say only himself, I mean directly, and in the first instance; for whatever affects himself, may affect others through himself; and the objection which may be grounded on this contingency, will receive consideration in the sequel. This, then, is the appropriate region of human liberty. It comprises, first, the inward domain of consciousness; demanding liberty of conscience in the most comprehensive sense; liberty of thought and feeling; absolute freedom of opinion and sentiment on all subjects, practical or speculative, scientific, moral, or theological. The liberty of expressing and publishing opinions may seem to fall under a different principle, since it belongs to that part of the conduct of an individual which concerns other people; but, being almost of as much importance as the liberty of thought itself, and resting in great part on the same reasons, is practically inseparable from it. Secondly, the principle requires liberty of tastes and pursuits; of framing the plan of our life to suit our own character; of doing as we like, subject to such consequences as may follow: without impediment from our fellow-creatures, so long as what we do does not harm them, even though they should think our conduct foolish, perverse, or wrong. Thirdly, from this liberty of each individual, follows the liberty, within the same limits, of combination among individuals; freedom to unite, for any purpose not involving harm to others: the persons combining being supposed to be of full age, and not forced or deceived.

No society in which these liberties are not, on the whole, respected, is free, whatever may be its form of government; and none is completely free in which they do not exist absolute and unqualified. The only freedom which deserves the name, is that of pursuing our own good in our own way, so long as we do not attempt to deprive others of theirs, or impede their efforts to obtain it. Each is the proper guardian of his own health, whether bodily, or mental and spiritual. Mankind are greater gainers by suffering each other to live as seems good to themselves, than by compelling each to live as seems good to the rest.

Though this doctrine is anything but new, and, to some persons, may have the air of a truism, there is no doctrine which stands more directly opposed to the general tendency of existing opinion and practice. Society has expended fully as much effort in the attempt (according to its lights) to compel people to conform to its notions of personal as of social excellence. The ancient commonwealths thought themselves entitled to practise, and the ancient philosophers countenanced, the regulation of every part of private conduct by public authority, on the ground that the State had a deep interest in the whole bodily and mental discipline of every one of its citizens; a mode of thinking which may have been admissible in small republics surrounded by powerful enemies, in constant peril of being subverted by foreign attack or internal commotion, and to which even a short interval of relaxed energy and self-command might so easily be fatal that they could not afford to wait for the salutary permanent effects of freedom. In the modern world, the greater size of political communities, and, above all, the separation between spiritual and temporal authority (which placed the direction of men's consciences in other hands than those which controlled their worldly affairs), prevented so great an interference by law in the details of private life; but the engines of moral repression have been wielded more strenuously against divergence from the reigning opinion in self-regarding, than even in social matters; religion, the most powerful of the elements which have entered into the formation of moral feeling, having almost always been governed either by the ambition of a hierarchy, seeking control over every department of human conduct, or by the spirit of Puritanism. And some of those modern reformers who have placed themselves in strongest opposition to the religions of the past, have been noway behind either churches or sects in their assertion of the right of spiritual domination: M. Comte, in particular, whose social system, as unfolded in his *Systeme de Politique Positive,* aims at establishing (though by moral more than by legal appliances) a despotism of society over the individual, surpassing anything contemplated in the political ideal of the most rigid disciplinarian among the ancient philosophers.

Apart from the peculiar tenets of individual thinkers, there is also in the world at large an increasing inclination to stretch unduly the powers of society over the individual, both by the force of opinion and even by that of legislation; and as the tendency of all the changes taking place in the world is to strengthen society, and diminish the power of the individual, this encroachment is not one of the evils which tend spontaneously to disappear, but, on the contrary, to grow more and more formidable. The disposition of mankind, whether as rulers or as fellow-citizens, to impose their own opinions and inclinations as a rule of conduct on others, is so energetically supported by some of the best and by some of the worst feelings incident to human nature, that it is hardly ever kept under restraint by anything but want of power; and as the power is not declining, but growing, unless a strong barrier of moral conviction can be raised against the mischief, we must expect, in the present circumstances of the world, to see it increase.

It will be convenient for the argument, if, instead of at once entering upon the general thesis, we confine ourselves in the first instance to a single branch of it, on which the principle here stated is, if not fully, yet to a certain point, recognised by the current opinions. This one branch is the Liberty of Thought: from which it is impossible to separate the cognate liberty of speaking and of writing. Although these liberties, to some considerable amount, form part of the political morality of all countries which profess religious toleration and free institutions, the grounds, both philosophical and practical, on which they rest, are perhaps not so familiar to the general mind, nor so thoroughly appreciated by many even of the leaders of opinion, as might have been expected. Those grounds, when rightly understood, are of much wider application than to only one division of the subject, and a thorough consideration of this part of the question will be found the best introduction to the remainder. Those to whom nothing which I am about to say will be new, may therefore, I hope, excuse me, if on a subject which for now three centuries has been so often discussed, I venture on one discussion more.

SOURCE. John Stuart Mill, *Utilitarianism, Liberty, and Representative Government*, A. D. Lindsay, ed., London: J. M. Dent & Sons, 1910, pp. 65–67. Everyman's Library Edition. Reprinted by permission of J. M. Dent & Sons, Ltd. and E. P. Dutton & Co., Inc.

1. JOHN STUART MILL, FROM *CONSIDERATIONS ON REPRESENTATIVE GOVERNMENT*, 1861

. . . The ideally best form of government, it is scarcely necessary to say, does not mean one which is practicable or eligible in all states of civilisation, but the one which, in the circumstances in which it is practicable and eligible, is attended with the greatest amount of beneficial consequences, immediate and prospective. A completely popular government is the only polity which can make out any claim to this character. It is pre-eminent in both the departments between which the excellence of a political constitution is divided. It is both more favourable to present good government, and promotes a better and higher form of national character, than any other polity whatsoever.

Its superiority in reference to present well-being rests upon two principles, of as universal truth and applicability as any general propositions which can be laid down respecting human affairs. The first is, that the rights and interests of every or any person are only secure from being disregarded when the person interested is himself able, and habitually disposed, to stand up for them. The second is, that the general prosperity attains a greater height, and is more widely diffused, in proportion to the amount and variety of the personal energies enlisted in promoting it.

Putting these two propositions into a shape more special to their present application; human beings are only secure from evil at the hands of others in proportion as they have the power of being, and are, self-*protecting;* and they only achieve a high degree of success in their struggle with Nature in proportion as they are self-*dependent,* relying on what they themselves can do, either separately or in concert, rather than on what others do for them.

The former proposition—that each is the only safe guardian of his own rights and interests—is one of those elementary maxims of prudence, which every person, capable of conducting his own affairs, implicity acts upon, wherever he himself is interested. Many, indeed, have a great dislike to it as a political doctrine, and are fond of holding it up to obloquy, as a doctrine of universal selfishness. To which we may answer, that whenever it ceases to be true that mankind, as a rule, prefer themselves to others, and those nearest to them to those more remote, from that moment Communism is not only practicable, but the only defensible form of society; and will, when that time arrives, be assuredly carried into effect. For my own part, not believing in universal selfishness, I have no difficulty in admitting that Communism would even now be practicable among the *élite* of mankind, and may become so among the rest. But as this opinion is anything but popular with those defenders of existing institutions who find fault with the doctrine of the general predominance of self-interest, I am inclined to think they do in reality believe that most men consider themselves before other people. It is not, however, necessary to affirm even thus much in order to support the claim of all to participate in the sovereign power. We need not suppose that when power resides in an exclusive class, that class will knowingly and deliberately sacrifice the other classes to themselves: it suffices that, in the absence of its natural defenders, the interest of the excluded is always in danger of being overlooked; and, when looked at, is seen with very different eyes from those of the persons whom it directly concerns. In this country, for example, what are called the working classes may be considered as excluded from all direct participation in the government. I do not believe that the classes who do participate in it have in general any intention of sacrificing the working classes to themselves. They once had that intention; witness the persevering attempts so long made to keep down wages by law. But in the present day their ordinary disposition is the very opposite: they willingly make considerable sacrifices, especially of their pecuniary interest, for the benefit of the working classes, and err rather by too lavish and indiscriminating beneficence; nor do I believe that any rulers in history have been actuated by a more sincere desire to do their duty towards the poorer portion of their countrymen. Yet does Parliament, or almost any of the members composing it, ever for an instant look at any question with the eyes of a working man? When a subject arises in which the labourers as such have an interest, is it regarded from any point of view but that of the employers of labour? I do not say that the working men's view of these questions is in general nearer to the truth than the other: but it is sometimes quite as near; and in any case it ought to be respectfully listened to, instead of being, as it is, not merely turned away from, but ignored. On the question of strikes, for instance, it is doubtful if there is so much as one among the leading members of either House who is not firmly convinced that the reason of the matter is unqualifiedly on the side of the masters, and that the men's view of it is simply absurd. Those who have studied the question know well how far this is from being the case; and in how different, and how infinitely less superficial a manner the point would have to be argued, if the classes who strike were able to make themselves heard in Parliament.

It is an adherent condition of human affairs that no intention, however sincere, of protecting the interests of others can make it safe or salutary to tie up their own hands. Still more obviously true is it, that by their own hands only can any positive and durable improvement of their circumstances in life be worked out. Through the joint influence of these two principles, all free communities have both been more exempt from social injustice and crime, and have attained more brilliant prosperity, than any others, or than they themselves after they lost their freedom. Contrast the free states of the world, while their freedom lasted, with the contemporary subjects of monarchical or oligarchical despotism: the Greek cities with the Persian satrapies; the Italian republics and the free towns of Flanders and Germany, with the feudal monarchies of Europe; Switzerland, Holland, and England, with Austria or ante-revolutionary France. Their superior prosperity was too obvious ever to have been gainsaid: while their superiority in good government and social relations is proved by the prosperity, and is manifest besides in every page of history. If we compare, not one age with another, but the different governments which co-existed in the same age, no amount of disorder which exaggeration itself can pretend to have existed amidst the publicity of the free states can be compared for a moment with the contemptuous trampling upon the mass of the people which pervaded the whole life of the monarchical countries, or the disgusting individual tyranny which was of more than daily occurrence under the systems of plunder which they called fiscal arrangements, and in the secrecy of their frightful courts of justice.

It must be acknowledged that the benefits of freedom, so far as they have hitherto been enjoyed, were obtained by the extension of its privileges to a part only of the community; and that a government in which they are extended impartially to all is a desideratum still unrealised. But though every approach to this has an independent value, and in many cases more than an approach could not, in the existing state of general improvement, be made, the participation of all in these benefits is the ideally perfect conception of free government. In proportion as any, no matter who, are excluded from it, the interests of the excluded are left without the guarantee accorded to the rest, and they themselves have less scope and encouragement than they might otherwise have to that exertion of their energies for the good of themselves and of the community, to which the general prosperity is always proportioned. . . .

SOURCE. John Stuart Mill, *Representative Government,* 1861, A. D. Lindsay, ed., London: J. M. Dent & Sons, 1910, pp. 208–211. Everyman's Library Edition. Reprinted by permission of J. M. Dent & Sons, Ltd. and E. P. Dutton & Co., Inc.

Chapter 9

UNIFICATION AND EMANCIPATION: ITALY, GERMANY, RUSSIA

a. GIUSEPPE MAZZINI, FROM "TO THE ITALIANS"

THE LIBERAL IDEALISM of the Italian unification movement emerges vividly from the essay "To the Italians" by the Italian patriot Giuseppe Mazzini (1805–1872).

It is high time to leave a policy of expedients, of opportunism, of entanglements and crooked ways, of parliamentary hypocrisy, concealment, and compromise, that characterises the languid life of worn-out nations, and return to the virgin, loyal, simple, logical policy that derives directly from a moral standard, that is the consequence of a ruling *principle* that has always inaugurated the young life of peoples that are called to high destinies.

The first condition of this life, is the solemn declaration, made with the unanimous and free consent of our greatest in wisdom and virtue, that Italy, feeling the times to be ripe, rises with one spontaneous impulse, in the name of the Duty and Right inherent in a people, to constitute itself a Nation of free and equal brothers, and demand that rank which by right belongs to it among the Nations that are already formed. The next condition, is the declaration of the body of religious, moral, and political *principles* in which the Italian people believes at the present day, of the common ideal to which it is striving, of the *special* mission that distinguishes it from other peoples, and to which it intends to consecrate itself for its own benefit and for the benefit of Humanity. And the final condition, is to determine the methods to be employed, and the men to whom the country should delegate the function of developing the national conception of life, and the application of its practical consequences to the manifold branches of social activity.

Without this, a *country* may exist, stumbling along from insurrection to insurrection, from revolution to revolution; but there cannot exist a Nation.

And these three conditions can only be fulfilled by a NATIONAL CONTRACT, dictated in Rome by a constituent assembly elected by direct or indirect suffrage, and by all the citizens that Italy contains.

The National Contract is the inauguration, the baptism of the nation. It is the *initiative* that determines the normal life, the successive and peaceful development of the forces and faculties of the country. Without that initiative, which gives life to the exercise of the vote, and directs it to the common *ideal* under the guidance of a *principle* and a *moral* doctrine, even popular suffrage is at the mercy of arbitrary influence, or the passions of the day, or the false suggestions of ambitious agitators. Plebiscites taken under circumstances like these, the perverted and unenlightened expression of mere brute numbers, have, within the space of a few years, led, and will lead again, to a republic, a limited monarchy, and the despotism of a Bonaparte. Until a people if educated to uniformity and brotherhood, the initiative determines in every place and time the character of the solemn acts to which the masses are called.

Everyone knows what is the form of government that we believe to be the logical deduction from the principles in which we believe, and from the national Italian tradition: we define it as *the development and application of a Nation's ideal, duly entrusted by the chosen of the Country to men of recognised capacity and proven virtue. . . .*

Our party is faithful to the ideal of our country's Traditions, but ready to harmonise them with the Traditions of Humanity and the inspirations of conscience; it is tolerant and moral, and it must therefore now confute, without attacking or misconstruing motives. We need not fear that we are forging weapons for the enemy, if we declare the religions of the world to be successive expressions of a series of ages that have educated the human race; if we recognise the religious faculty as eternal in the human soul, eternal, too, the bond between heaven and earth. We can admire in Gregory VII[1] the gigantic energy of will, the sublime moral effort that could not be realised with the instrument that Christianity could lend, and, at the same time, in the name of the progress we have made, declare the Papacy to be for ever dead. We can recognise the Mission which Aristocracy and Monarchy had for other peoples in the past, and yet proclaim, for all of us, the duty and the right to outstrip those worn-out forms. We may, without denying the reverence due to Authority—for that is the real object of all our efforts—claim the task of attacking every Authority that is not based on two conditions—the free and enlightened consent of the governed, and the power of directing the national life and making it fruitful.

We believe in God.

In a providential Law given by Him to life.

In a Law, not of the *Atonement,* not of the *Fall,* and *Redemption* by the *grace* of past or present mediators between God and *man,* but of PROGRESS, unlimited Progress, founded on, and measured by, our works.

---

[1] Gregory VII (1073–1085), a great reform pope of the Middle Ages.

In the *Unity* of Life, misunderstood, as we believe, by the Philosophy of the last two centuries.

In the *Unity* of the Law through both the manifestations of Life, *collective*, and *individual*.

In the immortality of the *Ego,* which is nothing but the application of the Law of PROGRESS revealed beyond doubt now and for ever by Historical Tradition, by Science, by the aspirations of the soul, to the Life that is manifested in the individual.

In Liberty, by which alone exists responsibility, the consciousness and price of *progress.*

In the successive and increasing *association* of all human faculties and powers, as the sole normal means of *progress,* at once collective and individual.

In the *Unity* of the human race, and in the moral *equality* of all the children of God, without distinction of sex, colour, or condition, to be forfeited by *crime* alone.

And hence we believe in the holy, inexorable, dominating idea of DUTY, the sole standard of Life. *Duty* that embraces in each one, according to the sphere in which he moves and the means that he possesses, Family, Fatherland, Humanity. Family the altar of the Fatherland; Fatherland the sanctuary of Humanity; Humanity a part of the Universe, and a temple built to God, who created the Universe, that it might draw near to Him. *Duty,* that bids us promote the progress of others that our own may be effected, and of ourselves that it may profit that of others. *Duty,* without which no *right* exists, that creates the virtue of self-sacrifice, in truth the only pure virtue, holy and mighty in power, the noblest jewel that crowns and hallows the human soul. . . .

The problem that is agitating the world is not the rejection of authority, for without authority, moral anarchy, and therefore sooner or later material anarchy, are inevitable. It is the rejection of all lifeless authority which is founded on the mere fact of its existence in the past, or on privileges of birth, riches, or aught else, and maintained without the free discussion and assent of the citizens, and closed to all progress in the future. It is not the rejection of liberty, whose absence makes tyranny inevitable. It is the restoration of the idea contained in that word to its true meaning—*the power to choose, according to our tendencies, capacity, and circumstances, the means to be employed to reach the end.* It is the rejection of that liberty which is an *end* to itself, and which abandons society and the mission of humanity to the caprice of the impulses and passions of individuals. *Authority* and *Liberty,* conceived as we state them, are equally sacred to us, and should be reconciled in every question awaiting settlement. *All things in Liberty and for Association;* this is the republican formula. Liberty and Association, Conscience and Tradition,

Individual and Nation, the *"I"* and the *"We"* are inseparable elements of human nature, all of them essential to its orderly development. Only in order to co-ordinate them and direct them to a purpose, some point of union is required which is *superior* to all. Hence practical necessity leads us inevitably back to the high principles that we enunciated in theory in an earlier part of our work.

Sovereignty exists neither in the *"I"* nor the *"We"*; it exists in God, the source of Life; in the PROGRESS that defines life; in the Moral Law that defines Duty.

In other terms, Sovereignty is in the IDEAL.

We are all called to do its work.

The knowledge of the *ideal* is given to us—so far as it is understood by the age in which we live—by our intelligence when it is inspired by the love of Good, and proceeds from the Tradition of Humanity to question its own *conscience,* and reconciles these two sole criteria of Truth.

But the knowledge of the *ideal* needs an *interpreter* who may forth-with indicate the means that may best attain to it, and direct its application to the various branches of activity. And as this *interpreter* must embrace within itself the *"I"* and the *"We,"* Authority and Liberty, State and Individual; and as, moreover, it must be *progressive,* it cannot be a man or any order of men selected by chance, or by the prerogative of a privilege unprogressive by its very nature, or birth, or riches, or aught else. Given the principles contained in the contract of faith and brotherhood, this interpreter can only be the People, the Nation.

God and the People. These are the only two terms that survive the analysis of the elements which the Schools have given as the foundation of the social communion. Rome knows by what paths of self-sacrifice, civil virtue, and glory, the banner that bore these two solemn words inscribed upon it, awakened in 1849 the love of Italy for her.

And here for the present we may stop. The Italian Mission is therefore: —

The Unity of the Nation, in its *material* aspect, by the reconquest of the Trentino, of Istria and of Nice; in its *moral* aspect, by National Education, accompanied by the free and protected Instruction of every heterodox doctrine.

Unity of defence, or the *Nation armed.*

Unity of the Contract and every Institution that represents the civil, political, and economic progress o all Italians.

Steady activity of the legislative power; and the administration of the institutions that concern the national progress, to be entrusted, not to the executive power, but to Commissions by delegation from the legislative.

Communal liberty to be decreed so far as regards the special progress of the various localities.

Suppression of all offices intended at the present day to represent an undue influence of the Government over the different local districts.

Division of powers to be a consequence, not of an illogical distribution of *sovereignty*, but of the different functions of government.

A smaller number of State employees and a more equal payment for their services.

Abolition of political oaths.

Universal Suffrage as the beginning of political education.

Legislation tending to advance the intellectual and economic progress of those classes that need it most; and the nation to encourage industrial, agricultural, and labour associations, founded on certain general conditions, and of proven morality and capacity.

Special attention to be given to the uncultivated lands of Italy, to the vast unhealthy zones, to neglected communal property, and to the creation on them of a new class of small proprietors.

A general system of taxation so as to free life—that is, the necessaries of life—from all burdens, and so as to fall proportionately on superfluities, and avoid excessive expenses of collection.

Abolition of all impediments to the free circulation of produce within and without the country.

An economic system based on the saving of all useless expenditure and on the progressive increase of production.

Recognition of every debt contracted by the Nation in the past.

Simplification of the transfer of land.

Abolition of monopolies.

Responsibility of every public servant.

International policy to be governed by the moral *principle* that rules the Nation.

Alliances to be based on uniformity of tendencies and objects.

Especial favour to be shown to every movement that may fraternise Italy with the elements of future or growing Nationalities, with the Greek, Roumanian, or Slave populations, who are destined to solve the problem of Eastern Europe.

These, with many others, are but the consequences of the great *principles* we have enunciated, and will be developed in our Publication; and, if the Italians will help us with their effective assistance, a more popular explanation will be given in a paper which we will add, dedicated specially to the Working Classes.

SOURCE. Giuseppe Mazzini, *The Duties of Man, and Other Essays,* Bolton King, ed., Thomas Okey, tr., London: J. M. Dent and Co., 1894, pp. 159–161, 165–167, 172–176. Everyman's Library Edition.

b. GIUSEPPE GARIBALDI'S PROCLAMATION ON THE LIBERATION OF SICILY

MAZZINI'S DISCIPLE, Giuseppe Garibaldi (1807–1882), a flamboyant adventurer, organized in 1860 a volunteer force to conquer Sicily and southern Italy. Encouraged by Piedmont, which was then in the process of unifying northern Italy, and expressing his support for the Piedmontese King Victor Emmanuel, Garibaldi issued a ringing appeal to the Italian people on the eve of his arrival in Sicily. The response was enthusiastic, and Garibaldi was able very quickly to conquer Sicily and Naples.

Italians!—The Sicilians are fighting against the enemies of Italy, and for Italy. It is the duty of every Italian to succour them with words, money, and arms, and, above all, in person.

The misfortunes of Italy arise from the indifference of one province to the fate of the others.

The redemption of Italy began from the moment that men of the same land ran to help their distressed brothers.

Left to themselves, the brave Sicilians will have to fight, not only the mercenaries of the Bourbon, but also those of Austria and the Priest of Rome.

Let the inhabitants of the free provinces lift their voices in behalf of their struggling brethren, and impel their brave youth to the conflict.

Let the Marches, Umbria, Sabina, Rome, the Neapolitan, rise to divide the forces of our enemies.

Where the cities suffice not for the insurrection, let them send bands of their bravest into the country.

The brave man finds an arm everywhere. Listen not to the voice of cowards, but arm, and let us fight for our brethren, who will fight for us to-morrow.

A band of those who fought with me the country's battles marches with me to the fight. Good and generous, they will fight for their country to the last drop of their blood, nor ask for other reward than a clear conscience.

"Italy and Victor Emmanuel!" they cried, on passing the Ticino. "Italy and Victor Emmanuel!" shall re-echo in the blazing caves of Mongibello.

At this cry, thundering from the great rock of Italy to the Tarpeian, the rotton Throne of tyranny shall crumble, and, as one man, the brave descendants of Vespro shall rise.

To arms! Let me put an end, once for all, to the miseries of so many centuries. Prove to the world that it is no lie that Roman generations inhabited this land.

(Signed)   G. G. GARIBALDI

SOURCE. "Public Documents," *The Annual Register, 1860,* London: 1861, pp. 281–282.

c. FICHTE, "THE PEOPLE AND THE FATHERLAND" FROM *ADDRESSES TO THE GERMAN NATION,* 1807–1808

JOHANN GOTTLIEB FICHTE (1792–1814) delivered a series of "Addresses to the German Nation" in Berlin in 1807–1808 which served as a significant source for later German nationalism. The eighth of these addresses, "The People and the Fatherland," discloses the intense nationalism, arising from the agonizing frustration of centuries of disunion, which exploded with such momentous force into the international politics of the late-nineteenth and twentieth centuries.

Let me make this clear by a simple example. Where is there a man of high mind and noble sentiments who does not desire that in his children and his children's children his own life may be repeated in a nobler and higher scale, that after his death his life may continue on this earth, only ennobled and perfected; who does not long to leave in the minds of those who remain behind him the spirit, the sense, the morality, which perhaps in his case was shocked by perversity and ruin, to rescue these from mortality and leave them as his best treasure to the future world; to strengthen the religious, animate the slothful, and raise the depressed? Where is there a man of high mind and noble sentiments who does not desire by his thought and actions to plant a seed to aid the endlessly increasing perfection of his race, to cast into the time something new, something that as yet has never been, that it may become an unfailing spring of new creation, that so he may pay for his place on earth and the short span of life granted to him with that which is of eternal permanence, so that although he be solitary and unknown to history—for the thirst for fame is an empty vanity—he may leave in his own conscience and faith a public monument to mark the fact that he has been? Where is there a man of high mind and noble sentiments, I ask, but desire this? Only according to the needs of those who are habitually thus minded should this world be regarded and ordered; only on their account is there any world at all. They are the kernel of the world, while they who are otherwise minded are mere parts of a transitory world, so long as they think that only for their sakes the world exists and that it must accommodate itself to them, until all have become as they are.

What is there of proof to fill this demand, this faith of the nobleminded in the imperishability, the eternity of his works? Surely it can be found only in an order of things which is itself eternal, and which may be regarded as able to take unto itself the eternal. Such an order there is. Though it may not be comprehended under one concept, yet it is certainly present. It is the peculiar spiritual nature, the human environment from which a man himself springs, with all his power of thinking and acting and with his faith in the eternity thereof. It is the people, the nation from which he descends and under which he has been trained and has grown to be that which he now is. . . .

This then is the meaning of the word a people, taken in a higher sense and regarded from the standpoint of a spiritual world, namely: that whole body of men living together in society, reproducing themselves from themselves both physically and spiritually, which whole body stands together under certain special laws of the development of the divine part thereof. The participation in these special laws is that which in the eternal world, and therefore in the transitory world as well, unites this mass into a natural and homogeneous whole. This law itself can, in respect to its contents, be well comprehended as a whole, as we have apprehended it in the case of the Germans as a principal race or people; in many of its future determinations it can still further be comprehended through a consideration of the appearance of such a people; but it can never be understood by any one who remains unconsciously under the law, although its existence may be clearly perceived. . . . This law determines and completes what has been called the national character of a people, namely, that law of the development of the original and divine. It is clear from this last consideration, that men who have hitherto described foreign lands do not at all believe in their originality and their continued development, but merely in an unending circulation of apparent life, and by their faith these peoples become according to their faith, but in the higher sense are no people, and since they are not that in reality, they are quite unable to have a national character.

The belief of the noble-minded in the eternal continuance of his activity, even on this earth, is founded, accordingly, on the hope of the eternal continuance of the people from whom he has himself sprung, and of the distinctive character of that people according to that hidden law, without any mixing with, or deprivation by, anything foreign to it or any not belong to the fulness of that law. This distinctive character is the eternal, to which he trusts the eternity of himself and his continued activity; it is the eternal order in which he places that in himself which is eternal; he must desire its continuance, because it is his only means of deliverance, whereby the short span of his moral life may be prolonged to an enduring life. . . .

In this faith our oldest common ancestors, the original people of the new culture, the Teutons, called Germans by the Romans, set themselves bravely in opposition to the overwhelming worldwide rule of the Romans. Did they not see with their own eyes the finest blossom of the Roman provinces beside them, the finer enjoyment in the same, together with laws, courts of justice, lictors' staves and axes in superabundance? Were not the Romans ready and generous enough to let them share in all these benefits? Did they not see proof of the famous Roman clemency in the case of several of their own princes, who allowed themselves to think that war against such benefactors of the human race was rebellion? For the compliant were decorated with the title of king and rewarded with posts of importance as leaders in the Roman army, with Roman sacrificial wreaths; and when they were expelled by their countrymen, the Romans furnished them with a refuge and support in their colonies. Had they no appreciation of the advantages of Roman culture, for better organization of their armies, for example, in which even Arminius himself did not refuse to learn the art of war? It cannot be charged against them that in any one of these respects they were ignorant. Their descendants have appropriated that culture, as soon as they could do so without the loss of their own freedom, and as far as it was possible without loss of their distinctive character. Wherefore, then, have they fought for so many generations in bloody wars which have been repeatedly renewed with undiminished fury? A Roman writer represents their leaders as asking if anything else remained for them but to maintain their freedom or to die before they became slaves. Freedom was their possession, that they might remain Germans, that they might continue to settle their own affairs independently and originally and in their own way, and at the same time to advance their culture and to plant the same independence in the hearts of their posterity. Slavery was what they called all the benefits which the Romans offered them, because through them they would become other than Germans, they would have to become semi-Romans. It was perfectly clear, they assumed, that every man, rather than become this, would die, and that a true German could wish to live only to be and to remain a German, and to have his sons the same.

They have not all died; they have not seen slavery; they have bequeathed freedom to their children. To their constant resistance the whole new world owes that it is as it is. Had the Romans succeeded in subjugating them also, and, as the Romans everywhere did, destroying them as a nation, the entire development of the human race would have taken a different direction, and it cannot be thought a better one. We who are the nearest heirs of their land, their language, and their sentiments, owe to them that we are still Germans, that the stream of original and independent life still bears us on; to them we owe that we have since then become a nation; to them, if now perhaps it is not at an end with us and the last drops of blood inherited from them are not dried in our veins, we owe all that which we have become. To them, even the other tribes, who have become to us aliens but through them our brethren, owe their existence; when they conquered eternal Rome, there were no others of all those peoples present; at that time was won for them the possibility of their future origin. . . .

From all this it follows that the State, as a mere control of the human life as it advances in customary and peaceful course, is not that which is primary and existent for its own sake, but is merely a means for that higher purpose, the eternally, uniformly progressive development of the purely human in the nation; that it is only the image and the love of this eternal progress, which shall in the quiet flow of time mould the higher ideas in the conduct of the State, and which, when the independence of the people is in danger, is alone able to save it. Among the Germans, amid whom as an original people this love of the fatherland was possible, and, as one who knew firmly believed, thus far has also been actual, this could so far with a high degree of confidence count upon the security of its most important affairs. As in the case of the Greeks in old time, so here in the case of the Germans the State and the nation were separated from each other, and each was presented for itself, the former in the various distinct German kingdoms and principalities, the latter visibly in the imperial union,[2] and invisibly, not according to a written constitution but a fundamental law living in the hearts and minds of all, in a multitude of customs and institutions. As far as the German tongue was spoken, so far could every one upon whom the light dawned within that radius regard himself in a twofold aspect as a citizen: on account of his birthplace, to whose care he was first committed, and on account of the entire common fatherland of the German nation. It was permitted each one to obtain for himself over the entire surface of the fatherland that culture which had the greatest affinity with his spirit, or that field of work which was most appropriate to him, and his talent did not grow in its place as a tree grows, but it was permitted him to seek it. Whoever, by the direction which his education took, was estranged from his immediate surroundings, easily found acceptance elsewhere, found new friends in place of those whom he had lost, found time and leisure to explain himself more particularly, and perhaps to win to himself those who had been estranged and so to unite the whole once more. No German prince has ever been able to

---

[2] The Holy Roman Empire, founded by the medieval German King Otto the Great in 962, abolished by Napoleon seven and one-half centuries later, by which time it had long been politically powerless.

compel his subjects to remain among the mountains and rivers where he rules, or to regard themselves as bound to the surface of the earth. A truth which might not be expressed in one place, might be expressed in another, in which place on the contrary those truths were forbidden which were allowed in the first region; and therefore, in spite of all the one-sidedness and narrow-mindedness of the various States, there was to be found in Germany, taken as a whole, the highest freedom of investigation and instruction ever possessed by a people, and the highest culture was, and everywhere remains, the result of the mutual action of the citizens of the German States, and this higher culture came gradually in this form to the vast multitude of the people also, so that it forthwith continued in the whole to educate itself by itself. This essential pledge of the continuance of a German nation detracts in no respect from any German soul who stands at the helm of the government; and although in respect to some original decisions have occurred, as has been thought, otherwise than as the higher German love of fatherland must wish, nevertheless the affairs of the State have at least not been handled directly contrary to what has been desired; no one has been tempted to undermine that love, to exterminate it and to bring a contrary love in its place.

If now, perhaps, the original guidance, not only of the higher culture but of the national power, which should be used as an end only for that and for its continuance, for it is the employment of German wealth and German blood, should be turned in another direction on account of the willingness of the German heart, what would necessarily follow? Here is the point where it is especially necessary that we should not be willing to be deceived in our own affairs, and be courageous enough to see the truth and to confess it; and it is, as far as I know, still allowed us to speak with one another in the German tongue of the fatherland, or at least to sigh; and, believe me, we would not do well if we, on our part, anticipated such a prohibition and clasped the shackles of timidity upon the courage of some who have, no doubt, already thought of the danger.

Picture to yourselves the new power as kind and benevolent as you will, make it as good as God, will you be able to attribute to it divine reason? Let it wish in all seriousness the highest happiness and prosperity of all; will that prosperity which it will be able to comprehend be the German prosperity? I hope then that the main point which I have today presented to you may be well understood by you; I hope that there are many here who have thought and felt that I merely express clearly and in words that which they have already felt in their hearts; I hope these words may stand in the same way toward them.

But several Germans before me have also said very nearly the same things, and the same sentiments, though obscure, have been at the foundation of that striving, always well maintained, against a merely mechanical arrangement and conception of the State. And now I call upon all who are acquainted with the recent foreign literature, to show me what modern sage, poet, or legislator of the same has ever shown thoughts like these, regarding the human race as eternally progressing, and describing all its activity in time as steps in that progress; whether any one, even in that point of time when men have risen to the boldest political conceptions, has ever demanded of the State more than the absence of inequality or internal peace and external national fame, and, where it is at the very best, domestic happiness. If this is their highest, as must follow from what has been pointed out, they will ascribe to us no higher necessities and no higher demands in life, assuming in them benevolent sentiments towards us and absence of all selfishness and all desire to be more than we are, they will believe that we have been well cared for, if we find all which they regard as alone desirable; but that for which alone the nobler of us live has been obliterated from public life, and the people, which has always shown itself sensitive to the suggestions of the nobler, and which one might for the majority hope to raise to the rank of nobility, so far as it is treated as those nobler men would treat it, has been degraded from its rank, dishonored, obliterated from the list of things, in as far as it is merged in what is lower.

He in whom there remains in life and strength those higher demands of life, together with a feeling for divine justice, feels himself led with deep reluctance back to those first days of Christianity, to those men to whom it was said, "Ye shall not resist evil, but if one shall smite thee on the right cheek, turn to him the other also, and if any one will take away thy coat, let him have thy cloak also"; rightfully quoting the last saying, for so long as he sees a cloak on thee, he will contrive some way in which he can take it from thee; when thou art entirely naked thou wilt escape his notice and be let alone by him. Even his higher sense, which honors him, makes the earth for him a hell and a despair; he wishes that he had never been born, that his eyes may close forever before the glance of day and the sooner the better; unending mourning encompasses his days even to the grave; for him who is dear to him he can wish no better gift than a stupid, satiated sense, that with little pain he may approach an eternal life beyond the grave.

These orations have attempted, by the only means remaining after others have been tried in vain, to prevent this annihilation of every noble action that may in the future arise among us, and this degradation of our entire nation. They have attempted to implant in your minds the deep and immovable foundations of the true and almighty love of the fatherland, in the conception of our nation as eternal and the people as citizens of our own eternity through the education of all hearts and minds.

SOURCE. Guy Carelton Lee, ed., *The World's Orators*, New York: G. P. Putnam's Sons, 1900, V, pp. 177–182, 190–193, 195–201.

d. BISMARCK, FROM *REFLECTIONS AND REMINISCENCES*

IT WAS OTTO VON BISMARCK (1815–1898) who, as Chancellor of Prussia, unified all Germany except Austria under the Prussian Hohenzollern monarch through a policy of war and ruthless diplomacy—"blood and iron." In his Reflections and Reminiscences, *the retired statesman expresses himself on the subject of nationalism versus dynasticism in Germany.*

In order that German patriotism should be active and effective, it needs as a rule to hang on the peg of dependence upon a dynasty; independent of dynasty it rarely comes to the rising point, though in theory it daily does so, in parliament, in the press, in public meeting; in practice the German needs either attachment to a dynasty or the goad of anger, hurrying him into action: the latter phenomenon, however, by its own nature is not permanent. It is as a Prussian, a Hanoverian, a Wurtemberger, a Bavarian or a Hessian, rather than as a German, that he is disposed to give unequivocal proof of patriotism; and in the lower orders and the parliamentary groups it will be long before it is otherwise. We cannot say that the Hanoverian, Hessian, and other dynasties were at any special pains to win the affections of their subjects; but nevertheless the German patriotism of their subjects is essentially conditioned by their attachment to the dynasty after which they call themselves. It is not differences of stock, but dynastic relations upon which in their origin the centrifugal elements repose. It is not attachment to Swabian, Lower Saxon, Thuringian, or other particular stock that counts for most, but the dynastic incorporation with the people of some severed portion of a ruling princely family, as in the instances of Brunswick, Brabant, and Wittelsbach dynasties. The cohesion of the kingdom of Bavaria does not rest merely on the Bajuvarian stock as it is found in South Bavaria and in Austria: the Swabian of Augsburg, the Alleman of the Palatinate, the Frank of the Main, though of widely different blood, call themselves Bavarians with as much satisfaction as does the Old-Bavarian at Munich or Landshut, and for no other reason than that they have been connected with the latter for three generations through the common dynasty. It is to dynastic influences that those stocks which present the most marked characteristics, as the Low-German, the *Platt-Deutsch*, the Saxon, owe their greater depth and distinctness of differentiation. The German's love of Fatherland has need of a prince on whom it can concentrate its attachment. Suppose that all the German dynasties were suddenly deposed; there would then be no likelihood that the German national sentiment would suffice to hold all Germans together from the point of view of international law amid the friction of European politics, even in the form of federated Hanse towns and imperial village communes. The Germans would fall a prey to more closely welded nations if they once lost the tie which resides in the princes' sense of community of rank.

History shows that in Germany the Prussian stock is that of which the individual character is most strongly stamped, and yet no one could decisively answer the question whether, supposing the Hohenzollern dynasty and all its rightful successors to have passed away, the political cohesion of Prussia would survive. Is it quite certain that the eastern and the western divisions, that Pomeranians and Hanoverians, natives of Holstein and Silesia, of Aachen and Konigsberg, would then continue as they now are, bound together in the indisruptible unity of the Prussian state? Or Bavaria—if the Wittelbach dynasty were to vanish and leave not a trace behind, would Bavaria continue to hold together in isolated unity? Some dynasties have many memories which are not exactly of the kind to inspire attachment in the heterogeneous fragments out of which their states have, as a matter of history, been formed. Schleswig-Holstein has absolutely no dynastic memories, least of all any opposed to the House of Gottorp, and yet the prospect of the possible formation there of a small, independent, brand-new little court with ministers, court-marshals, and orders, in which the life of a petty state should be sustained at the cost of what Austria and Prussia would manage in the *Bund,* called forth very strong particularist movements in the Elbe duchies. The Grand Duchy of Baden has hardly a dynastic memory since the time of the Margrave Ludwig before Belgrade; the rapid growth of this little principality under French protection in the confederation of the Rhine, the court life of the last princes of the old line, the matrimonial alliance with the Beauharnais house, the Caspar Hauser story, the revolutionary proceedings of 1832, the banishment of the Grand Duke Leopold, the citizens' patron, the banishment of the reigning house in 1849, have not been able to break the power which subservience to dynasty has in that country, and Baden in 1866 fought against Prussia and the German idea because constrained thereto by the dynastic interests of the reigning house.

The other nations of Europe have need of no such go-between for their patriotism and national sentiment. Poles, Hungarians, Italians, Spaniards, Frenchmen would under any or without any dynasty preserve their homogeneous national unity. The Teutonic stocks of the north, the Swedes and the Danes, have shown themselves pretty free from dynastic sentiment; and in England, though external respect for the Crown is demanded by good society, and the formal maintenance of monarchy is held expedient by all parties that have hitherto had any share in government, I do not anticipate the disruption of the nation, or that such sentiments as were common in the time of the Jacobites would attain to any practical form, if in the course of its historical development the British people should come to deem a change of dynasty or the transition to a republican form of government necessary or expedient. The preponderance of dynastic attachment, and the use of a dynasty as the indispensable cement to hold together a definite portion of the nation calling itself by the name of the dynasty is a specific peculiarity of the German Empire. The particular nationalities, which among us have shaped themselves on the bases of dynastic family and possession, include in most cases heterogeneous elements, whose cohesion rests neither on identity of stock nor on similarity of historical development, but exclusively on the fact of some (in most cases questionable) acquisition by the dynasty whether by the right of the strong, or hereditary succession by affinity or compact of inheritance, or by some reversionary grant obtained from the imperial Court as the price of a vote. . . .

The German people and its national life cannot be portioned out as private possessions of princely houses. It has always been clear to me that this reflection applies to the electoral house of Brandenburg as well as to the Bavarian, the Guelf, or other houses; I should have been weaponless against the Brandenburg princely house, if in dealing with it I had needed to reinforce my German national feeling by rupture and resistance; in the predestination of history, however, it so fell out that my courtier-talents sufficed to gain the King, and with him by consequence his army, for the national cause. I have had perhaps harder battles to fight against Prussian particularism than against the particularism of the other German states and dynasties, and my relation to the Emperor William I as his born subject made these battles all the harder for me. Yet in the end, despite the strongly dynastic policy of the Emperor, but thanks to his national policy which, dynastically justified, became ever stronger in critical moments, I always succeeded in gaining his countenance for the German side of our development, and that too when a more dynastic and particularist policy prevailed on all other hands.

SOURCE. *Bismarck, The Man and The Statesman,* A. J. Butler, tr., New York: Harper Bros., 1899, I, pp. 320–326.

e. CZAR ALEXANDER II'S DECREE EMANCIPATING THE RUSSIAN SERFS, 1861

LIBERALISM AND NATIONALISM accomplished far less in Russia than in central and western Europe. As the nineteenth century closed, the authority of the Czar remained unlimited by any legislature or constitution.

Russia continued to be a largely agrarian state, and a middle class was slow in developing. Nevertheless, western ideas were percolating beneath the surface and were to erupt into revolution in 1905 and 1917. Meanwhile, Czar Alexander II (reigned 1855–1881) had undertaken a series of cautious and long-overdue reforms, the most far-reaching of which was his Imperial Ukase emancipating the Russian serfs (March 3, 1861). By his decree some 23,000,000 peasants were freed from servitude.

By the grace of God, we, Alexander II, Emperor and Autocrat of all the Russias, King of Poland, Grand Duke of Finland, etc., to all our faithful subjects, make known:

Called by Divine Providence and by the sacred right of inheritance to the throne of our ancestors, we took a vow in our innermost heart to respond to the mission which is intrusted to us as to surround with our affection and our Imperial solicitude all our faithful subjects of every rank and of every condition, from the warrior, who nobly bears arms for the defence of the country to the humble artisan devoted to the works of industry; from the official in the career of the high offices of the State to the laborer whose plough furrows the soil.

In considering the various classes and conditions of which the State is composed we came to the conviction that the legislation of the empire having wisely provided for the organization of the upper and middle classes and having defined with precision their obligations, their rights, and their privileges, has not attained the same degree of efficiency as regards the peasants attached to the soil, thus designated because either from ancient laws or from custom they have been hereditarily subjected to the authority of the proprietors, on whom it was incumbent at the same time to provide for their welfare. The rights of the proprietors have been hitherto very extended and very imperfectly defined by the law, which has been supplied by tradition, custom, and the good pleasure of the proprietors. . . .

These facts had already attracted the notice of our predecessors of glorious memory, and they had taken measures for improving the conditions of the peasants; but among those measures some were not stringent enough, insomuch that they remained subordinate to the spontaneous initiative of such proprietors who showed themselves animated with liberal intentions; and others, called forth by peculiar circumstances, have been restricted to certain localities or simply adopted as an experiment. It was thus that Alexander I published the regulation for the free cultivators, and that the late Emperor Nicholas, our beloved father, promulgated that one which concerns the peasants bound by contract. In the Western Governments regulations called "inventaires" had fixed the territorial allotments due to the peasants, as well as the amount of their rent dues; but all these reforms have only been applied in a very restricted manner.

We thus came to the conviction that the work of a serious improvement of the condition of the peasants was a sacred inheritance bequeathed to us by our ancestors, a mission which, in the course of events, Divine Providence called upon us to fulfil.

We have commenced this work by an expression of our Imperial confidence towards the nobility of Russia, which has given us so many proofs of its devotion to the Throne, and of its constant readiness to make sacrifices for the welfare of the country.

It is to the nobles themselves, conformable to their own wishes, that we have reserved the task of drawing up the propositions for the new organization of the peasants—propositions which make it incumbent upon them to limit their rights over the peasants, and to accept the onus of a reform which could not be accomplished without some material losses. Our confidence has not been deceived. We have seen the nobles assembled in committees in the districts, through the medium of their confidential agents, making the voluntary sacrifice of their rights as regards the personal servitude of the peasants. These committees, after having collected the necessary data, have formulated their propositions concerning the new organization of the peasants attached to the soil in their relations with the proprietors. . . .

In virtue of the new dispositions above mentioned, the peasants attached to the soil will be invested within a term fixed by the law with all the rights of free cultivators.

The proprietors retaining their rights of property on all the land belonging to them, grant to the peasants for a fixed regulated rental the full enjoyment of their close; and, moreover, to assure their livelihood and to guarantee the fulfilment of their obligations towards the Government, the quantity of arable land is fixed by the said dispositions, as well as other rural appurtenances.

But, in the enjoyment of these territorial allotments, the peasants are obliged, in return, to acquit the rentals fixed by the same dispositions to the profit of the proprietors. In this state, which must be a transitory one, the peasants shall be designated as "temporary bound."

At the same time, they are granted the right of purchasing their close, and, with the consent of the proprietors, they may acquire in full property the arable lands and other appurtenances which are allotted to them as a permanent holding. By the acquisition in full property of the quantity of land fixed, the peasants are free from their obligations towards the proprietors for land thus purchased, and they enter definitely into the condition of free peasants—landholders. . . .

And now, pious and faithful people, make upon the forehead the sacred sign of the cross, and join thy prayers to ours to call down the blessing of the Most High upon thy first free labors, the sure pledge of thy personal well-being and of the public prosperity.

Given at St. Petersburg, the 19th day of February,[3] of the year of Grace 1861, and the seventh of our reign.

ALEXANDER

SOURCE. *Annual Register, 1861*, pp. 207–212, *passim.*

---

[3] March 3 according to the Gregorian Calendar, which was by now universally followed in the West.

PART FIVE

The Mind of the Later Nineteenth Century

EVOLUTION was a basic concept in nineteenth-century thought. Romantics and economists, political theorists and scientists, tended to think of the world as an organism rather than as a machine. Karl Marx conceived of history in evolutionary terms, as a process of change brought on by class conflict. Romantic novelists and poets felt a deep kinship with the medieval past out of which their culture and institutions had developed. And a similar consciousness of the evolutionary connection between past and present is to be found among conservatives of the Burkean tradition. It was in science, however, that the idea of evolution found its most direct and fruitful expression.

Charles Darwin was by no means the first scientist to formulate a theory of evolution. His real contribution was to buttress the theory with firm observational evidence and to provide it with a simple naturalistic explanation—the doctrine of natural selection. Darwinism quickly became a center of explosive controversy. Many Christians regarded it as subversive to their Faith and opposed it vigorously. Some Darwinians attempted to use Darwin's notion of the survival of the fittest to justify the inequalities of the capitalist economic system and the exploitation of backward peoples. Others opposed this ruthless doctrine of social Darwinism with the argument that "survival of the fittest" implied struggle *between species,* not among members of the *same* species.

The German philosopher Friedrich Nietzsche was an evolutionist, too, but he rejected the passivity of Darwin's natural selection in favor of an evolutionary doctrine in which man ennobled himself through his own strivings. Bourgeois mediocrity, mass vulgarity, Christian humility—these were the barriers which man had overcome in order to advance toward his heroic destiny.

The art of the later nineteenth century moved beyond Romanticism into newer forms of expression: the uncompromising realism of Courbet, the poetic subjectivity of the Impressionists, and the increasingly bold distortions of Cézanne and Van Gogh, who sacrificed photographic representationalism for the sake of structural unity and fidelity to the personal vision. The evolution of later nineteenth-century art is marked by a restless dissatisfaction with traditional forms and a search for new and better means by which the artist might communicate his perceptions of the natural world. And more and more, the objective portrayal of a subject gave way to the artist's subjective reaction to it.

Chapter 10

SCIENCE AND PHILOSOPHY

a. CHARLES DARWIN, FROM *THE ORIGIN OF SPECIES*, 1859

THE PUBLICATION OF DARWIN'S The Origin of Species *in 1859 was an event of notable importance in European intellectual history. The excerpts included here are taken from Darwin's own summary of his theory.*

Nothing at first can appear more difficult to believe than that the more complex organs and instincts have been perfected, not by means superior to, though analogous with, human reason, but by the accumulation of innumerable slight variations, each good for the individual possessor. Nevertheless, this difficulty, though appearing to our imagination insuperably great cannot be considered real if we admit the following propositions, namely, that all parts of the organisation and instincts offer, at least, individual differences—that there is a struggle for existence leading to the preservation of profitable deviations of structure or instinct—and, lastly, that gradations in the state of perfection of each organ may have existed, each good of its kind. The truth of these propositions cannot, I think, be disputed.

It is, no doubt, extremely difficult even to conjecture by what gradations many structures have been perfected, more especially amongst broken and failing groups of organic beings, which have suffered much extinction; but we see so many strange gradations in nature, that we ought to be extremely cautious in saying that any organ or instinct, or any whole structure, could not have arrived at its present state by many graduated steps. There are, it must be admitted, cases of special difficulty opposed to the theory of natural selection; . . . but I have attempted to show how these difficulties can be mastered. . . .

Under domestication we see much variability, caused, or at least excited, by changed conditions of life; but often in so obscure a manner, that we are tempted to consider the variations as spontaneous. Variability is governed by many complex laws,—by correlated growth, compensation, the increased use and disuse of parts, and the definite action of the surrounding conditions. There is much difficulty in ascertaining how largely our domestic productions have been modified; but we may safely infer that the amount has been large, and that modifications can be inherited for long periods. As long as the conditions of life remain the same, we have reason to believe that a modification, which has already been inherited for many generations, may continue to be inherited for an almost infinite number of generations. On the other hand, we have evidence that variability when it has once come into play, does not cease under domestication for a very long period; nor do we know that it ever ceases, for new varieties are still occasionally produced by our oldest domesticated productions.

Variability is not actually caused by man; he only unintentionally exposes organic beings to new conditions of life, and then nature acts on the organisation and causes it to vary. But man can and does select the variations given to him by nature, and thus accumulates them in any desired manner. He thus adapts animals and plants for his own benefit or pleasure. He may do this methodically, or he may do it unconsciously by preserving the individuals most useful or pleasing to him without any intention of altering the breed. It is certain that he can largely influence the character of a breed by selecting, in each successive generation, individual differences so slight as to be inappreciable except by an educated eye. This unconscious process of selection has been the great agency in the formation of the most distinct and useful domestic breeds. That many breeds produced by man have to a large extent the character of natural species, is shown by the inextricable doubts whether many of them are varieties or aboriginally distinct species.

There is no reason why the principles which have acted so efficiently under domestication should not have acted under nature. In the survival of favoured individuals and races, during the constantly-recurrent struggle for Existence, we see a powerful and ever-acting form of Selection. The struggle for existence inevitably follows from the high geometrical ratio of increase which is common to all organic beings. This high rate of increase is proved by calculation,—by the rapid increase of many animals and plants during a succession of peculiar seasons, and when naturalised in new countries. More individuals are born than can possibly survive. A grain in the balance may determine which individuals shall live and which shall die,—which variety or species shall increase in number, and which shall decrease, or finally become extinct. As the individuals of the same species come in all respects into the closest competition with each other, the struggle will generally be most severe between them; it will be almost equally severe between the varieties of the same species, and next in severity between the species of the same genus. On the other hand the struggle will often be severe between beings remote in the scale of nature. The slightest advantage in certain individuals, at any age or during any season, over those with which they come into competition, or better adaptation in however slight a degree to the surrounding physical conditions, will, in the long run, turn the balance.

With animals having separated sexes, there will be in most cases a struggle between the males for the possession of the females. The most vigorous males, or those which have most successfully struggled with their conditions of life, will generally leave most progeny. But success will often depend on the males having special weapons, or means of defence, or charms; and a slight advantage will lead to victory.

As geology plainly proclaims that each land has undergone great physical changes, we might have expected to find that organic beings have varied under nature, in the same way as they have varied under domestication. And if there has been any variability under nature, it would be an unaccountable fact if natural selection had not come into play. It has often been asserted, but the assertion is incapable of proof, that the amount of variation under nature is a strictly limited quantity. Man, though acting on external characters alone and often capriciously, can produce within a short period a great result by adding up mere individual differences in his domestic productions; and every one admits that species present individual differences. But, besides such differences, all naturalists admit that natural varieties exist, which are considered sufficiently distinct to be worthy of record in systematic works. No one has drawn any clear distinction between individual differences and slight varieties; or between more plainly marked varieties and sub-species, and species. On separate continents, and on different parts of the same continent when divided by barriers of any kind, and on outlying islands, what a multitude of forms exist, which some experienced naturalists rank as varieties, others as geographical races or sub-species, and others as distinct, though closely allied species!

If then, animals and plants do vary, let it be ever so slightly or slowly, why should not variations or individual differences, which are in any way beneficial, be preserved and accumulated through natural selection, or the survival of the fittest? If man can by patience select variations useful to him, why, under changing and complex conditions of life, should not variations useful to nature's living products often arise, and be preserved or selected? What limit can be put to this power, acting during long ages and rigidly scrutinising the whole constitution, structure, and habits of each creature,—favouring the good and rejecting the bad? I can see no limit to this power, in slowly and beautifully adapting each form to the most complex relations of life. The theory of natural selection, even if we look no farther than this, seems to be in the highest degree probable. . . .

On the view that species are only strongly marked and permanent varieties, and that each species first existed as a variety, we can see why it is that no line of demarcation can be drawn between species, commonly supposed to have been produced by special acts of creation, and varieties which are acknowledged to have been produced by secondary laws. On this same view we can understand how it is that in a region where many species of a genus have been produced, and where they now flourish, these same species should present many varieties; for where the manufactory of species has been active, we might expect, as a general rule, to find it still in action; and this is the case if varieties be incipient species. Moreover, the species of the larger genera, which afford the greater number of varieties or incipient species, retain to a certain degree the character of varieties; for they differ from each other by a less amount of difference than do the species of smaller genera. The closely allied species also of the larger genera apparently have restricted ranges, and in their affinities they are clustered in little groups round other species—in both respects resembling varieties. These are strange relations on the view that each species was independently created, but are intelligible if each existed first as a variety.

As each species tends by its geometrical rate of reproduction to increase inordinately in number; and as the modified descendants of each species will be enabled to increase by as much as they become more diversified in habits and structure, so as to be able to seize on many and widely different places in the economy of nature, there will be a constant tendency in natural selection to preserve the most divergent offspring of any one species. Hence, during a long-continued course of modification, the slight differences characteristic of varieties of the same species, tend to be augmented into the greater differences characteristic of the species of the same genus. New and improved varieties will inevitably supplant and exterminate the older, less improved, and intermediate varieties; and thus species are rendered to a large extent defined and distinct objects. Dominant species belonging to the larger groups within each class tend to give birth to new and dominant forms; so that each large group tends to become still larger, and at the same time more divergent in character. But as all groups cannot thus go on increasing in size, for the world would not hold them, the more dominant groups beat the less dominant. This tendency in the large groups to go on increasing in size and diverging in character, together with the inevitable contingency of much extinction, explains the arrangement of all the forms of life in groups subordinate to groups, all within a few great classes, which has prevailed throughout all time. This grand fact of the grouping of all organic beings under what is called the Natural System is utterly inexplicable on the theory of creation.

As natural selection acts solely by accumulating slight, successive, favourable variations, it can produce no great or sudden modifications; it can act only by short and slow steps. . . . We can see why throughout nature the same general end is gained by an almost infinite diversity of means, for every peculiarity when once acquired is long inherited, and structures already modified in many different ways have to be adapted for the same general purpose. We can, in short, see why nature is prodigal in variety, though niggard in innovation. But why this should be a law of nature if each species has been independently created no man can explain. . . .

If we admit that the geological record is imperfect to an extreme degree, then the facts, which the record does give, strongly support the theory of descent with modification. New species have come on the stage slowly and at successive intervals; and the amount of change, after equal intervals of time, is widely different in different groups. The extinction of species and of whole groups of species, which has played so conspicuous a part in the history of the organic world, almost inevitably follows from the principle of natural selection; for old forms are supplanted by new and improved forms. Neither single species nor groups of species reappear when the chain of ordinary generation is once broken. The gradual diffusion of dominant forms, with the slow modification of their descendants, causes the forms of life, after long intervals of time, to appear as if they had changed simultaneously throughout the world. The fact of the fossil remains of each formation being in some degree intermediate in character between the fossils in the formations above and below, is simply explained by their intermediate position in the chain of descent. . . .

Looking to geographical distribution, if we admit that there has been during the long course of ages much migration from one part of the world to another, owing to former climatal and geographical changes and to the many occasional and unknown means of dispersal, then we can understand, on the theory of descent with modification, most of the great leading facts in Distribution. We can see why there should be so striking a parallelism in the distribution of organic beings throughout space, and in their geological succession throughout time; for in both cases the beings have been connected by the bond of ordinary generation, and the means of modification have been the same. We see the full meaning of the wonderful fact, which has struck every traveller, namely, that on the same continent, under the most diverse conditions, under heat and cold, on mountain and lowland, on deserts and marshes, most of the inhabitants within each great class are plainly related; for they are the descendants of the same progenitors and early colonists. . . .

The similar framework of bones in the hand of a man, wing of a bat, fin of the porpoise, and leg of the horse,—the same number of vertebrae forming the neck of the giraffe and of the elephant,—and innumerable other such facts, at once explain themselves on the theory of descent with slow and slight successive modifications. The similarity of pattern in the wing and in the leg of a bat, though used for such different purpose,—in the jaws and legs of a crab,—in the petals, stamens, and pistils of a flower, is likewise, to a large extent, intelligible on the view of the gradual modification of parts or organs, which were aboriginally alike in an early progenitor in each of these classes. On the principle of successive variations not always supervening at an early age, and being inherited at a corresponding not early period of life, we clearly see why the embryos of mammals, birds, reptiles, and fishes should be so closely similar, and so unlike the adult forms. We may cease marvelling at the embryo of an air-breathing mammal or bird having branchial slits and arteries running in loops, like those of a fish which has to breathe the air dissolved in water by the aid of well-developed branchiae.

Disuse, aided sometimes by natural selection, will often have reduced organs when rendered useless under changed habits or conditions of life; and we can understand on this view the meaning of rudimentary organs. But disuse and selection will generally act on each creature, when it has come to maturity and has to play its full part in the struggle for existence, and will thus have little power on an organ during early life; hence the organ will not be reduced or rendered rudimentary at this early age. The calf, for instance, has inherited teeth, which never cut through the gums of the upper jaw, from an early progenitor having well-developed teeth; and we may believe, that the teeth in the mature animal were formerly reduced by disuse, owing to the tongue and palate, or lips, having become excellently fitted through natural selection to browse without their aid; whereas in the calf, the teeth have been left unaffected, and on the principle of inheritance at corresponding ages have been inherited from a remote period to the present day. On the view of each organism with all its separate parts having been specially created, how utterly inexplicable is it that organs bearing the plain stamp of inutility, such as the teeth in the embryonic calf or the shrivelled wings under the soldered wing-covers of many beetles, should so frequently occur. Nature may be said to have taken pains to reveal her scheme of modification, by means of rudimentary organs, of embryological and homologous structures, but we are too blind to understand her meaning.

I have now recapitulated the facts and considerations which have thoroughly convinced me that species have been modified, during a long course of descent. This has been effected chiefly through the natural selection of numerous successive, slight, favourable variations; aided in an important manner by the inherited effects of the use and disuse of parts; and in an unimportant manner, that is in relation to adaptive structures, whether past or present, by the direct action of external conditions, and by variations which seem to us in our ignorance to arise spontaneously. It appears that I formerly underrated the frequency and value of these latter forms of variation, as leading to permanent modifications of structure independently of natural selection. But as my conclusions have lately been much misrepresented, and it has been stated that I attribute the modification of species exclusively to natural selection, I may be permitted to remark that in the first edition of this work, and subsequently, I placed in a most conspicuous position—namely, at the close of the Introduction—the following words: "I am convinced that natural selection has been the main but not the exclusive means of modification." This has been of no avail. Great is the power of steady misrepresentation; but the history of science shows that fortunately this power does not long endure. . . .

I see no good reason why the views given in this volume should shock the religious feelings of any one. It is satisfactory, as showing how transient such impressions are, to remember that the greatest discovery ever made by man, namely, the law of the attraction of gravity, was also attacked by Leibnitz, "as subversive of natural, and inferentially of revealed, religion." A celebrated author and divine has written to me that "he has gradually learnt to see that it is just as noble a conception of the Deity to believe that He created a few orginal forms capable of self-development into other and needful forms, as to believe that He required a fresh act of creation to supply the voids caused by the action of His laws."

Why, it may be asked, until recently did nearly all the most eminent living naturalists and geologists disbelieve in the mutability of species. It cannot be asserted that organic beings in a state of nature are subject to no variation; it cannot be proved that the amount of variation in the course of long ages is a limited quantity; no clear distinction has been, or can be, drawn between species and well-marked varieties. It cannot be maintained that species when intercrossed are invariably sterile, and varieties invariably fertile; or that sterility is a special endowment and sign of creation. The belief that species were immutable productions was almost unavoidable as long as the history of the world was thought to be of short duration; and now that we have acquired some idea of the lapse of time, we are too apt to assume, without proof, that the geological record is so perfect that it would have afforded us plain evidence of the mutation of species, if they had undergone mutation.

But the chief cause of our natural unwillingness to admit that one species has given birth to other and distinct species, is that we are always slow in admitting great changes of which we do not see the steps. The difficulty is the same as that felt by so many geologists, when Lyell first insisted that long lines of inland cliffs had been formed, and great valleys excavated, by the agencies which we see still at work. The mind cannot possibly grasp the full meaning of the term of even a million years; it cannot add up and perceive the full effects of many slight variations, accumulated during an almost infinite number of generations.

Although I am fully convinced of the truth of the views given in this volume under the form of an abstract, I by no means expect to convince experienced naturalists whose minds are stocked with a multitude of facts all viewed, during a long course of years, from a point of view directly opposite to mine. It is so easy to hide our ignorance under such expressions as the "plan of creation," "unity of design," &c., and to think that we give an explanation when we only re-state a fact. Any one whose disposition leads him to attach more weight to unexplained difficulties than to the explanation of a certain number of facts will certainly reject the theory. A few naturalists, endowed with much flexibility of mind, and who have already begun to doubt the immutability of species, may be influenced by this volume; but I look with confidence to the future,—to young and rising naturalists, who will be able to view both sides of the question with impartiality. Whoever is led to believe that species are mutable will do good service by conscientiously expressing his conviction; for thus only can the load of prejudice by which this subject is over whelmed be removed. . . .

Authors of the highest eminence seem to be fully satisfied with the view that each species has been independently created. To my mind it accords better with what we know of the laws impressed on matter by the Creator, that the production and extinction of the past and present inhabitants of the world should have been due to secondary causes, like those determining the birth and death of the individual. When I view all beings not as special creations, but as the lineal descendants of some few beings which lived long before the first bed of the Cambrian system was deposited, they seem to me to become ennobled. Judging from the past, we may safely infer that not one living species will transmit its unaltered likeness to a distant futurity. And of the species now living very few will transmit progeny of any kind to a far distant futurity; for the manner in which all organic beings are grouped, shows that the greater number of species in each genus, and all the species in many genera, have left no descendants, but have become utterly extinct. We can so far take a prophetic glance into futurity as to foretell that it will be the common and widely-spread species, belonging to the larger and dominant groups within each class, which will ultimately prevail and procreate new and dominant species. As all the living forms of life are the lineal descendants of those which lived long before the Cambrian epoch, we may feel certain that the ordinary succession by generation has never once been broken, and that no cataclysm has desolated the whole world. Hence we may look with some confidence to a secure future of great length. And as natural selection works solely by and for the good of each being, all corporeal and mental endowments will tend to progress towards perfection.

It is interesting to contemplate a tangled bank, clothed with many plants of many kinds, with birds singing on the bushes, with various insections flitting about, and with worms crawling through the damp earth, and to reflect that these elaborately constructed forms, so different from each other, and dependent upon each other in so complex a manner, have all been produced by laws acting around us. These laws, taken in the largest sense, being Growth with Reproduction; Inheritance which is almost implied by reproduction; Variability from the indirect and direct action of the conditions of life, and from use and disuse: a Ratio of Increase so high as to lead to a Struggle for Life, and as a consequence to Natural Selection, entailing Divergence of Character and the Extinction of less-improved forms. Thus, from the war of nature, from famine and death, the most exalted object which we are capable of conceiving, namely, the production of the higher animals, directly follows. There is grandeur in this view of life, with its several powers, having been originally breathed by the Creator into a few forms or into one; and that, whilst this planet has gone cycling on according to the fixed law of gravity, from so simple a beginning endless forms most beautiful and most wonderful have been, and are being evolved.

SOURCE. Charles Darwin, *The Origin of Species,* 6th ed., New York: D. Appleton & Company, 1892, II, 267–268, 270–282, 287–306.

b. SOCIAL DARWINISM:
   HERBERT SPENCER, "POOR LAWS," 1884

IN HERBERT SPENCER'S Social Statics (1884) Darwinian evolution is given a political-economic dimension and is used to support a policy of strict laissez-faire. Spencer argued that the struggle between the fit and unfit, which dominates the world of nature, must not be thwarted in human society by social welfare measures. In the long run, the protection of the unfit will ruin the human race.

Pervading all Nature we may see at work a stern discipline which is a little cruel that it may be very kind. That state of universal warfare mainained throughtout the lower creation, to the great perplexity of many worthy people, is at bottom the most merciful provision which the circumstances admit of. It is much better that the ruminant animal, when deprived by age of the vigour which made its existence a pleasure, should be killed by some beast of prey, than that it should linger out a life made painful by infirmities, and eventually die of starvation. By the destruction of all such, not only is existence ended before it becomes burdensome, but room is made for a younger generation capable of the fullest enjoyment; and, moreover, out of the very act of substitution happiness is derived for a tribe of predatory creatures. Note, further, that their carnivorous enemies not only remove from herbivorous herds individuals past their prime, but also weed out the sickly, the malformed, and the least fleet or powerful. By the aid of which purifying process, as well as by the fighting so universal in the pairing season, all vitiation of the race through the multiplication of its inferior samples is prevented; and the maintenance of a constitution completely adapted to surrounding conditions, and therefore most productive of happiness, is ensured.

The development of the higher creation is a progress towards a form of being, capable of a happiness undiminished by these drawbacks. It is in the human race that the consummation is to be accomplished. Civilization is the last stage of its accomplishment. And the ideal man is the man in whom all the conditions to that accomplishment are fulfilled. Meanwhile, the well-being of existing humanity and the unfolding of it into this ultimate perfection, are both secured by that same beneficial though severe discipline, to which the animate creation at large is subject. It seems hard that an unskilfulness which with all his efforts he cannot overcome, should entail hunger upon the artizan. It seems hard that a labourer incapacitated by sickness from competing with his stronger fellows, should have to bear the resulting privations. It seems hard that widows and orphans should be left to struggle for life or death. Nevertheless, when regarded not separately but in connexion with the interests of universal humanity, these harsh fatalities are seen to be full of beneficence—the same beneficence which brings to early graves the children of diseased parents, and singles out the intemperate and the debilitated as the victims of an epidemic.

There are many very amiable people who have not the nerve to look this matter fairly in the face. Disabled as they are by their sympathies with present suffering, from duly regarding ultimate consequences, they pursue a course which is injudicious, and in the end even cruel. We do not consider it true kindness in a mother to gratify her child with sweetmeats that are likely to make it ill. We should think it a very foolish sort of benevolence which led a surgeon to let his patient's disease progress to a fatal issue, rather than inflict pain by an operation. Similarly, we must call those spurious philanthropists who, to prevent present misery, would entail greater misery on future generations. That rigorous necessity which, when allowed to operate, becomes so sharp a spur to the lazy and so strong a bridle to the random, these paupers' friends would repeal, because of the wailings it here and there produces. Blind to the fact that under the natural order of things society is constantly excreting its unhealthy, imbecile, slow, vacillating, faithless members these unthinking, though well-meaning, men advocate an interference which not only stops the purifying process, but even increases the vitiation—absolutely encourages the multiplication of the reckless and incompetent by offering them an unfailing provision, and *dis*courages the multiplication of the competent and provident by heightening the difficulty of maintaining a family. And thus, in their eagerness to prevent the salutary sufferings that surround us, these sigh-wise and groan-foolish people bequeath to posterity a continually increasing curse.

Returning again to the highest point of view, we find that there is a second and still more injurious mode in which law-enforced charity checks the process of adaptation. To become fit for the social state, man has not only to lose his savageness but he has to acquire the capacities needful for civilized life. Power of application must be developed; such modification of the intellect as shall qualify it for its new tasks must take place; and, above all, there must be gained the ability to sacrifice a small immediate gratification for a future great one. The state of transition will of course be an unhappy state. Misery inevitably results from incongruity between constitution and conditions. Humanity is being pressed against the inexorable necessities of its new position—is being moulded into harmony with them, and has to bear the resulting happiness as best it can. The process *must* be undergone and the sufferings *must* be endured. No power on Earth, no cunningly-devised laws of statesmen, no world-rectifying schemes of the humane, no communist panaceas, no reforms that men ever did broach or ever will broach, can diminish them one jot. Intensified they may be, and are; and in preventing their intensification the philanthropic will find ample scope for exertion. But there is bound up with the change a *normal* amount of suffering, which cannot be lessened without altering the very laws of life. Every attempt at mitigation of this eventuates in exacerbation of it. All that a poor-law or any kindred institution can do, is to partially suspend the transition—to take off for a time, from certain members of society, the painful pressure which is effecting their transformation. At best this is merely to postpone what must ultimately be borne. But it is more than this: it is to undo what has already been done. For the circumstances to which adaptation is taking place cannot be superseded without causing a retrogression; and as the whole process must some time or other be passed through, the lost ground must be gone over again, and the attendant pain borne afresh.

At first sight these considerations seem conclusive against *all* relief to the poor—voluntary as well as compulsory; and it is no doubt true that they imply a condemnation of whatever private charity enables the recipients to elude the necessities of our social existence. With this condemnation, however, no rational man will quarrel. That careless squandering of pence which has fostered into perfection a system of organized begging—which has made skilful mendicancy more profitable than ordinary manual labour—which induces the simulation of diseases and deformities—which has called into existence warehouses for the sale and hire of impostor's dresses—which has given to pity-inspiring babes a market value of 9*d*. per day—the unthinking benevolence which has generated all this, cannot but be disapproved by every one. Now it is only against this injudicious charity that the foregoing arguments tells. To that charity which may be described as helping men to help themselves, it makes no objection—countenances it rather. And in helping men to help themselves, there remains abundant scope for the exercise of a people's sympathies. Accidents will still supply victims on whom generosity may be legitimately expended. Men thrown off the track by unforeseen events, men who have failed for want of knowledge inaccessible to them, men ruined by the dishonesty of others, and men in whom hope long delayed has made the heart sick, may, with advantage to all parties, be assisted. Even the prodigal, after severe hardships has branded his memory with the unbending conditions of social life to which he must submit, may properly have another trial afforded him. And, although by these ameliorations the process of adaptation must be remotely interfered with, yet, in the majority of cases, it will not be so much retarded in one direction as it will be advanced in another.

Objectionable as we find a poor-law to be, even under the supposition that it does what it is intended to do—diminish present suffering—how shall we regard it on finding that in reality it does no such thing—cannot do any such thing? Yet, paradoxical as the assertion looks, this is absolutely the fact. Let but the observer cease to contemplate so fixedly one side of the phenomenon—pauperism and its relief, and begin to examine the other side—rates and the *ultimate* contributors of them, and he will discover that to suppose the sum-total of distress diminishable by act-of-parliament bounty is a delusion.

Here, at any specified period, is a given quantity of food and things exchangeable for food, in the hands or at the command of the middle and upper classes. A certain portion of this food is needed by these classes themselves, and is consumed by them at the same rate, or very near it, be there scarcity or abundance. Whatever variation occurs in the sum-total of food and its equivalents, must therefore affect the remaining portion, not used by these classes for personal sustenance. This remaining portion is paid by them to the people in return for their labour, which is partly expended in the production of a further supply of necessaries, and partly in the production of luxuries. Hence, by how much this portion is deficient, by so much must the people come short. A re-distribution by legislative or other agency cannot make that sufficient for them which was previously insufficient. It can do nothing but change the parties by whom the insufficiency is felt. If it gives enough to some who else would not have enough, it must inevitably reduce certain others to the condition of not having enough.

SOURCE. Herbert Spencer, *Social Statics and Man Versus the State,* New York: D. Appleton & Co., 1892, pp. 149–154, 302–303, 321–333.

c. DARWINISM AND LOVE: PETER KROPOTKIN, FROM *MUTUAL AID, A FACTOR OF EVOLUTION,* 1902

PETER KROPOTKIN, a Russian prince turned scientist and revolutionary, took a very different stand in his work Mutual Aid *(1902). Kropotkin maintained that love, not life-and-death competition, characterized the relationships between members of a single species throughout most of the animal kingdom.*

Two aspects of animal life impressed me most during the journeys which I made in my youth in Eastern Siberia and Northern Manchuria. One of them was the extreme severity of the struggle for existence which most species of animals have to carry on against an inclement Nature; the enormous destruction of life which periodically results from natural agencies; and the consequent paucity of life over the vast territory which fell under my observation. And the other was, that even in those few spots where animal life teemed in abundance, I failed to find—although I was eagerly looking for it—that bitter struggle for the means of existence, *among animals belonging to the same species,* which was considered by most Darwinists (though not always by Darwin himself) as the dominant characteristic of struggle for life, and the main factor of evolution.

The terrible snow-storms which sweep over the northern portion of Eurasia in the later part of the winter, and the glazed frost that often follows them; the frosts and the snow-storms which return every year in the second half of May, when the trees are already in full blossom and insect life swarms everywhere, the early frosts and, occasionally, the heavy snowfalls in July and August, which suddenly destroy myriads of insects, as well as the second broods of the birds in the prairies; the torrential rains, due to the monsoons, which fall in more temperate regions in August and September—resulting in inundations on a scale which is only known in America and in Eastern Asia, and swamping, on the plateaus, areas as wide as European States; and finally, the heavy snowfalls, early in October, which eventually render a territory as large as France and Germany, absolutely impracticable for ruminants, and destroy them by the thousand—these were the conditions under which I saw animal life struggling in Northern Asia. They made me realize at an early date the overwhelming importance in Nature of what Darwin described as "the natural checks to over-multiplication," in comparison to the struggle between individuals of the same species for the means of subsistence, which may go on here and there, to some limited extent, but never attains the importance of the former. Paucity of life, under-population—not over-population—being the distinctive feature of that immense part of the globe which we name Northern Asia, I conceived since then serious doubts—which subsequent study has only confirmed—as to the reality of that fearful competition for food and life within each species, which as an article of faith with most Darwinists, and, consequently, as to the dominant part which this sort of competition was supposed to play in the evolution of new species.

On the other hand, wherever I saw animal life in abundance, as, for instance, on the lakes where scores of species and millions of individuals came together to rear their progeny; in the colonies of rodents; in the migrations of birds which took place at that time on a truly American scale along the Usuri; and especially in a migration of fallow-deer which I witnessed on the Amur, and during which scores of thousands of these intelligent animals came together from an immense territory, flying before the coming deep snow, in order to cross the Amur where it is narrowest—in all these scenes of animal life which passed before my eyes, I saw Mutual Aid and Mutual Support carried on to an extent which made me suspect in it a feature of the greatest importance for the maintenance of life, the preservation of each species, and its further evolution.

And finally, I saw among the semi-wild cattle and horses in Transbaikalia, among the wild ruminants everywhere, the squirrels, and so on, that when animals have to struggle against scarcity of food, in consequence of one of the above-mentioned causes, the whole of that portion of the species which is affected by the calamity, comes out of the ordeal so much impoverished in vigour and health, that *no progressive evolution of the species can be based upon such periods of keen competition.*

Consequently, when my attention was drawn, later on, to the relations between Darwinism and Sociology, I could agree with none of the works and pamphlets that had been written upon this important subject. They all endeavoured to prove that Man, owing to his higher intelligence and knowledge, *may* mitigate the harshness of the struggle for life between men; but they all recognized at the same time that the struggle for the means of existence, of every animal against all its congeners, and of every man against all other men, was "a law of Nature." This view, however, I could not accept, because I was persuaded that to admit a pitiless inner war for life within each species, and to see in that war a condition of progress was to admit something which not only had not yet been proved, but also lacked confirmation from direct observation.

On the contrary, a lecture "On the Law of Mutual Aid," which was delivered at a Russian Congress of Naturalists, in January 1880, by the well-known zoologist, Professor Kessler, the then Dean of the St. Petersburg University, struck me as throwing a new light on the whole subject. Kessler's idea was that besides the *law of Mutual Struggle* there is in Nature *the law of Mutual Aid,* which, for the success of the struggle for life, and especially for the progressive evolution of the species, is far more important than the law of mutual contest. This suggestion—which was, in reality, nothing but a further development of the ideas expressed by Darwin himself in *The Descent of Man*—seemed to me so correct and of so great an importance, that since I became acquainted with it (in 1883) I began to collect materials for further developing the idea, which Kessler had only cursorily sketched in his lecture, but had not lived to develop.

SOURCE. Peter Kropotkin, *Mutual Aid, a Factor of Evolution*, London: William Heinemann, 1902, pp. 1–3.

d. MAN AS HERO: NIETZSCHE, FROM *THE GENEALOGY OF MORALS*, 1887

FRIEDRICH NIETZSCHE (1844–1900) scorned timidity, mediocrity, and abjectness, and put his hope in the man of fearless intelligence and boldness of spirit—the superman who was beyond good and evil. These views are stated with characteristic flair in Nietzsche's The Genealogy of Morals *(1887). They were exaggerated and misused by the later Nazis.*

It is impossible not to recognise at the core of all these aristocratic races the beast of prey; the magnificent *blonde brute,* avidly rampant for spoil and victory; this hidden core needed an outlet from time to time, the beast must get loose again, must return into the wilderness—the Roman, Arabic, German, and Japanese nobility, the Homeric heroes, the Scandinavian Vikings, are all alike in this need. It is the aristocratic races who have left the idea "Barbarian" on all the tracks in which they have marched; nay, a consciousness of this very barbarianism, and even a pride in it, manifests itself even in their highest civilisation (for example, when Pericles says to his Athenians in that celebrated funeral oration, "Our audacity has forced a way over every land and sea, rearing everywhere imperishable memorials of itself for *good* and for *evil*"). This audacity of aristocratic races, mad, absurd, and spasmodic as may be its expression; the incalculable and fantastic nature of their enterprises,—Pericles sets in special relief and glory the *rhathumia* of the Athenians, their nonchalance and contempt for safety, body, life, and comfort, their awful joy and intense delight in all destruction, in all the ecstasies of victory and cruelty,—all these features become crystallised, for those who suffered thereby in the picture of the "barbarian," of the "evil enemy," perhaps of the "Goth" and of the "Vandal." The profound, icy mistrust which the German provokes, as soon as he arrives at power,—even at the present time,—is always still an aftermath of that inextinguishable horror with which for whole centuries Europe has regarded the wrath of the blonde Teuton beast (although between the old Germans and ourselves there exists scarcely a psychological, let alone a physical, relationship). I have once called attention to the embarrassment of Hesiod, when he conceived the series of social ages, and endeavoured to express them in gold, silver, and bronze. He could only dispose of the contradiction, with which he was confronted, by the Homeric world, an age magnificent indeed, but at the same time so awful and so violent by making two ages out of one, which he henceforth placed one behind the other—first, the age of the heroes and demigods, as that world had remained in the memories of the aristocratic families, who found therein their own ancestors; secondly, the bronze age, as that corresponding age appeared to the descendants of the oppressed, spoiled, ill-treated, exiled, enslaved; namely, as an age of bronze, as I have said, hard, cold, terrible, without feelings and without conscience, crushing everything, and bespattering everything with blood. Granted the truth of the theory now believed to be true, that the very *essence of all civilisation* is to *train* out of man, the beast of prey, a tame and civilised animal, a domesticated animal, it follows indubitably that we must regard as the real *tools of civilisation* all those instincts of reaction and resentment, by the help of which the aristocratic races, together with their ideals, were finally degraded and overpowered; though that has not yet come to be synonymous with saying that the bearers of those tools also *represented* the civilisation. It is rather the contrary that is not only probable—nay, it is *palpable* to-day; these bearers of vindictive instincts that have to be bottled up, these descendants of all European and non-European slavery, especially of the pre-Aryan population—these people, I say, represent the *decline* of humanity! These "tools of civilisation" are a disgrace to humanity, and constitute in reality more of an argument against civilisation, more of a reason why civilisation should be suspected. One may be perfectly justified in being always afraid of the blonde beast that lies at the core of all aristocratic races, and in being on one's guard: but who would not a hundred times prefer to be afraid, when one at the same time admires, than to be immune from fear, at the cost of being perpetually obsessed with the loathsome spectacle of the distorted, the dwarfed, the stunted, the envenomed? And is that not our fate? What produces to-day our repulsion towards "man"?—for we *suffer* from "man," there is no doubt about it. It is not fear; it is rather that we have nothing more to fear from men; it is that the worm "man" is in the foreground and pullulates; it is that the "tame man," the wretched mediocre and unedifying creature, has learnt to consider himself a goal and a pinnacle, an inner meaning, an historic principle, a "higher man"; yes, it is that he has a certain right so to consider himself, in so far as he feels that in contrast to that excess of deformity, disease, exhaustion, and effeteness whose odour is beginning to pollute present-day Europe, he at any rate has achieved a relative success, he at any rate still says "yes" to life.

I cannot refrain at this juncture from uttering a sigh and one last hope. What is it precisely which I find intolerable? That which I alone cannot get rid of, which makes me choke and faint? Bad air! Bad air! That something misbegotten comes near me; that I must inhale the odour of the entrails of a misbegotten soul!—That excepted, what can one not endure in the way of need, privation, bad weather, sickness, toil, solitude? In point of fact, one manages to get over everything, born as one is to a burrowing and battling existence; one always returns once again to the light, one always lives again one's golden hour of victory—and then one stands as one was born, unbreakable, tense, ready for something more difficult, for something more distant, like a bow stretched but the tauter by every strain. But from time to time do ye grant me—assuming that "beyond good and evil" there are goddesses who can grant—one glimpse, grant me but one glimpse only, of something perfect, fully realised, happy, mighty, triumphant, or something that still gives cause for fear! A glimpse of a man that justifies the existence of man, a glimpse of an incarnate human happiness that realises and redeems, for the sake of which one may hold fast to *the belief in man!* For the position is this: in the dwarfing and levelling of the European man lurks *our* greatest peril, for it is this outlook which fatigues—we see to-day nothing which wishes to be greater, we surmise that the process is always still backwards, still backwards towards something more attenuated, more inoffensive, more cunning, more comfortable, more mediocre, more indifferent, more Chinese, more Christian—man, there is no doubt about it, grows always "better"—the destiny of Europe lies even in this—that in losing the fear of man, we have also lost the hope in man, yea, the will to be man. The sight of man now fatigues.—What is present-day Nihilism if it is not *that?*—We are tired of *man.*

But let us come back to it; the problem of *another* origin of the good—of the good, as the resentful man has thought it out—demands its solution. It is not surprising that the lambs should bear a grudge against the great birds of prey, but that is no reason for blaming the great birds of prey for taking the little lambs. And when the lambs say among themselves, "Those birds of prey are evil, and he who is as far removed from being a bird of prey, who is rather its opposite, a lamb,—is he not good?" then there is nothing to cavil at in the setting up of this ideal, though it may also be that the birds of prey will regard it a little sneeringly, and perchance say to themselves, "We bear no grudge against them, these good lambs, we even like them: nothing is tastier than a tender lamb." To require of strength that it should *not* express

itself as strength, that it should not be a wish to overpower, a wish to overthrow, a wish to become master, a thirst for enemies and antagonisms and
triumphs, is just as aburd as to require of weakness that it should express
itself as strength. A quantum of force is just such a quantum of movement,
will, action—rather it is nothing else than just those very phenomena of moving, willing, acting, and can only appear otherwise in the misleading errors
of language (and the fundamental fallacies of reason which have become
petrified therein), which understands, and understands wrongly, all working
as conditioned by a worker, by a "subject." And just exactly as the people
separate the lightning from its flash, and interpret the latter as a thing done,
as the working of a subject which is called lightning, so also does the popular
morality separate strength from the expression of strength, as though behind
the strong man there existed some indifferent neutral *substratum,* which
enjoyed a *caprice and option* as to whether or not it should express strength.
But there is no such *substratum,* there is no "being" behind doing, working,
becoming; "the doer" is a mere appanage to the action. The action is everything. In point of fact, the people duplicate the doing, when they make the
lightning lighten, that is a "doing-doing"; they make the same phenomenon
first a cause, and then, secondly, the effect of that cause. The scientists
fail to improve matters when they say, "Force moves, force causes," and so
on. Our whole science is still, in spite of all its coldness, of all its freedom
from passion, a dupe of the tricks of language, and has never succeeded in
getting rid of that superstitious changeling "the subject" (the atom, to give
another instance, is such a changeling, just as the Kantian "Thing-in-itself").
What wonder, if the suppressed and stealthily simmering passions of revenge and hatred exploit for their own advantage their belief, and indeed
hold no belief with a more steadfast enthusiasm than this—"that the strong
has the *option* of being weak, and the bird of prey of being a lamb."
Thereby do they win for themselves the right of attributing to the birds of
prey the *responsibility* for being birds of prey: when the oppressed, down-
trodden, and overpowered say to themselves with the vindictive guile of
weakness, "Let us be otherwise than the evil, namely, good! and good is every
one who does not oppress, who hurts no one, who does not attack, who does
not pay back, who hands over revenge to God, who holds himself, as we do,
in hiding; who goes out of the way of evil, and demands, in short, little
from life; like ourselves the patient, the meek, the just,"—yet all this, in its
cold and unprejudiced interpretation, means nothing more than "once for all,
the weak are weak; it is good to do *nothing for which we are not strong
enough*"; but this dismal state of affairs, this prudence of the lowest order,
which even insects possess (which in a great danger are fain to sham death so
as to avoid doing "too much"), has, thanks to the counterfeiting and self-
deception of weakness, come to masquerade in the pomp of an ascetic, mute,

and expectant virtue, just as though the *very* weakness of the weak—that is, forsooth, its *being*, its working, its whole unique inevitable inseparable reality—were a voluntary result, something wished, chosen, a deed, an act of *merit*. This kind of man finds the belief in a neutral, free-choosing "subject" *necessary* from an instinct of self-preservation, of self-assertion, in which every lie is fain to sanctify itself. The subject (or, to use popular language, the *soul*) has perhaps proved itself the best dogma in the world simply because it rendered possible to the horde of mortal, weak, and oppressed individuals of every kind, that most sublime specimen of self-deception, the interpretation of weakness as freedom, of being this, or being that, as *merit*.

Will any one look a little into—right into—the mystery of how *ideals* are *manufactured* in this world? Who has the courage to do it? Come!

Here we have a vista opened into these grimy workshops. Wait just a moment, dear Mr. Inquisitive and Foolhardy; your eye must first grow accustomed to this false changing light—Yes! Enough! Now speak! What is happening below down yonder? Speak out! Tell what you see, man of the most dangerous curiosity—for now *I* am the listener.

"I see nothing, I hear the more. It is a cautious, spiteful, gentle whispering and muttering together in all the corners and crannies. It seems to me that they are lying; a sugary softness adheres to every sound. Weakness is turned to *merit*, there is no doubt about it—it is just as you say."

Further!

"And the impotence which requites not, is turned to 'goodness,' craven baseness to meekness, submission to those whom one hates, to obedience (namely, obedience to one of whom they say that he ordered this submission—they call him God). The inoffensive character of the weak, the very cowardice in which he is rich, his standing at the door, his forced necessity of waiting, gain here fine names, such as 'patience,' which is also called 'virtue'; not being able to avenge one's self, is called not wishing to avenge one's self, perhaps even forgiveness (for *they* know not what they do—we alone know what they do). They also talk of the 'love of their enemies' and sweat thereby."

Further!

"They are miserable, there is no doubt about it, all these whisperers and counterfeiters in the corners, although they try to get warm by crouching close to each other, but they tell me that their misery is a favour and distinction given to them by God, just as one beats the dogs one likes best; that perhaps this misery is also a preparation, a probation, a training; that perhaps it is still more something which will one day be compensated and paid back with a tremendous interest in gold, nay in happiness. This they call "Blessedness.' "

Further!

"They are now giving me to understand, that not only are they better men than the mighty, the lords of the earth, whose spittle they have got to lick (*not* out of wear, not at all out of fear! But because God ordains that one should honour all authority)—not only are they better men, but that they also have a 'better time,' at any rate, will one day have a 'better time.' But enough! Enough! I can endure it no longer. Bad air! Bad air! These workshops *where ideals are manufactured*—verily they reek with the crassest lies."

Nay. Just one minute! You are saying nothing about the masterpieces of these virtuosos of black magic, who can produce whiteness, milk, and innocence out of any black you like: have you not noticed what a pitch of refinement is attained by their *chief d'oeuvure,* their most audacious, subtle, ingenious, and lying artist-trick? Take care! These cellar-beasts, full of revenge and hate—what do they make, forsooth, out of their revenge and hate? Do you hear these words? Would you suspect, if you trusted only their words, that you are among men of resentment and nothing else?

"I understand, I prick my ears up again (ah! ah! ah! and I hold my nose). Now do I hear for the first time that which they have said so often: 'We good, *we are the righteous*'—what they demand they call not revenge but 'the truimph of *righteousness*'; what they hate is not their enemy, no, they hate 'unrighteousness,' godlessness'; what they believe in and hope is not the hope of revenge, the intoxication of sweet revenge (—"sweeter than honey," did Homer call it?), but the victory of God, of the *righteous God* over the 'godless'; what is left for them to love in this world is not their brothers in hate, but their 'brothers in love,' as they say, all the good and righteous on the earth."

And how do they name that which serves them as a solace against all the troubles of life—their phantasmagoria of their anticipated future blessedness?

"How? Do I hear right? They call it 'the last judgment,' the advent of *their* kingdom, 'the kingdom of God'—but *in the meanwhile* they live in faith,' 'in love,' 'in hope.,"

Enough! Enough!

SOURCE. Friedrich Nietzsche, *The Genealogy of Morals,* William A. Haussmann and John Gray, trs., London: T. Fisher Unwin, 1889.

Chapter 11

Art

a. REALISM

TOWARD THE MIDDLE of the nineteenth century a reaction began to set in against the artistic values of Romanticism. Gustave Courbet (1819–1877), a socialist and a renegade Romantic, became convinced that the emotional and imaginative emphasis of Romanticism was in fact a flight from reality. Courbet turned to a sober, matter-of-fact exposition of ordinary subjects, seeking through artistic understatement to portray the heroism of real life. His Stone Breakers (1849) is a moving expression of the realist point of view, and of the socialist emphasis on the dignity of the worker.

GUSTAVE COURBET, *THE STONE BREAKERS*, 1849

b. IMPRESSIONISM

THE COMING OF IMPRESSIONISM in the 1860's and 1870's marks an important new departure in the history of art—a shift in emphasis from the outside world to the artist's own particular vision of it. Perhaps it was in part the advent of photography that drove painters to strive for a radically unphotographic style in order to assert the integrity and uniqueness of their art. However this may be, the painter's canvas was no longer a "window" to the outside world but a surface on which the artist worked with brush strokes and color to depict his own personal vision. Later Impressionists turned increasingly to the portrayal of subjects under particular conditions of light and atmosphere—a city shrouded by fog, or the reflection of sunlight on a rippling pool. The style is typified in Fishermen on the Seine *by Claude Monet (1840–1926) and* The Road in the Woods *by Alfred Sisley (1839–1899).*

CLAUDE MONET, *FISHERMEN ON THE SEINE*

ALFRED SISLEY, *THE ROAD IN THE WOODS*

c. POST-IMPRESSIONISM

POST-IMPRESSIONISM, which became important in the 1880's, was hardly a style at all. Rather it is a label that is applied to the work of a group of highly individual artists such as Cézanne, Van Gogh, Seurat, and Gauguin, who learned from the Impressionists and went beyond them, each in his own way. In Paul Cézanne (1839–1906) in particular, the emphasis on treating the canvas as a colored surface rather than a window is carried well beyond the limits of the Impressionists. Cézanne was deeply interested in the structure of his compositions, and was willing to sacrifice photographic accuracy in order to achieve formal unity. This quality is evident in his Large Bathers, *in which the figures and the trees are so placed as to create a triangular form for the painting as a whole. His* Mont Sainte-Victoire *(1904–1906) illustrates the solidity of his artistic conception, which contrasts sharply with the Impressionist emphasis on fluidity and change.*

PAUL CÉZANNE, *THE LARGE BATHERS*

PAUL CÉZANNE, *MONT SAINTE-VICTOIRE*

THE DUTCH ARTIST Vincent Van Gogh (1853–1890) transcended Impressionist values in quite a different way. He developed a bold free style and filled his canvases with movement and luminous color. His Wheat Field and Cypress Trees *(1889), and* The Starry Night *(1889, both illustrate his exciting and intensely personal vision.*

VINCENT VAN GOGH, *WHEAT FIELD AND CYPRESS TREES,* 1889

VINCENT VAN GOGH, *THE STARRY NIGHT,* 1889

Chapter 12

INTELLECTUAL ATTITUDES TOWARD IMPERIALISM

a. DIVINE MISSION: JOSIAH STRONG, FROM *OUR COUNTRY*, 1885

THE UPSURGE OF IMPERIALISM in the later nineteenth and early twentieth centuries won the support of a number of writers who justified colonial expansion on the basis of nationalism, social Darwinism, and notions of ethnic superiority. Darwin's concept of the survival of the fittest underwent its own curious evolution; it was adapted to justify such concepts as white supremacy, Nordic superiority, and the manifest destiny of the Anglo-Saxon race. Typical of this trend are the crude racist ideas to be found in Our Country *(1885) by the American clergyman Josiah Strong (1847–1916).*

Every race which has deeply impressed itself on the human family has been the representative of some great idea—one or more—which has given direction to the nation's life and form to its civilization. Among the Egyptians this seminal idea was life, among the Persians it was light, among the Hebrews it was purity, among the Greeks it was beauty, among the Romans it was law. The Anglo-Saxon is the representative of two great ideas, which are closely related. One of them is that of civil liberty. Nearly all of the civil liberty in the world is enjoyed by Anglo-Saxons: the English, the British colonists, and the people of the United States. To some, like the Swiss, it is permitted by the sufferance of their neighbors; others, like the French, have experimented with it; but, in modern times, the peoples whose love of liberty has won it, and whose genius for self-government has preserved it, have been Anglo-Saxons. The noblest races have always been lovers of liberty. That love ran strong in early German blood, and has profoundly influenced the institutions of all the branches of the great German family; but it was left for the Anglo-Saxon branch fully to recognize the right of the individual to himself, and formally to declare it the foundation stone of government.

The other great idea of which the Anglo-Saxon is the exponent is that of a pure *spiritual* Christianity. It was no accident that the great reformation of the sixteenth century originated among a Teutonic, rather than a Latin people. It was the fire of liberty burning in the Saxon heart that flamed up against the absolutism of the Pope. Speaking roughly, the peoples of Europe which are Celtic are Catholic, and those which are Teutonic are Protestant; and where the Teutonic race was purest, there Protestantism spread with the greatest rapidity. . . .

. . . North America is to be the great home of the Anglo-Saxon, the principal seat of his power, the center of his life and influence. Not only does it constitute seven-elevenths of his possessions, but his empire is unsevered, while the remaining four-elevenths are fragmentary and scattered over the earth. Australia will have a great population; but its disadvantages, as compared with North America, are too manifest to need mention. Our continent has room and resources and climate, it lies in the pathway of the nations, it belongs to the zone of power, and already, among Anglo-Saxons, do we lead in population and wealth. . . . America is to have the great preponderance of numbers and of wealth, and by the logic of events will follow the scepter of controlling influence. This will be but the consummation of a movement as old as civilization—a result to which men have looked forward for centuries. John Adams records that nothing was "more ancient in his memory than the observation that arts, sciences and empire had traveled westward. . . .

But we are to have not only the larger portion of the Anglo-Saxon race for generations to come, we may reasonably expect to develop the highest type of Anglo-Saxon civilization. If human progress follows a law of development, if

> Time's noblest offspring is the last,

our civilization should be the noblest; for we are

> The heirs of all the ages in the foremost files of time,

and not only do we occupy the latitude of power, but *our land is the last to be occupied in that latitude*. There is no other virgin soil in the North Temperate Zone. If the consummation of human progress is not to be looked for here, if there is yet to flower a higher civilization, where is the soil that is to produce it? . . .

. . . God, with infinite wisdom and skill, is training the Anglo-Saxon race for an hour sure to come in the world's future. Heretofore there has always been in the history of the world a comparatively unoccupied land westward, into which the crowded countries of the East have poured their surplus populations. But the widening waves of migration, which millenniums ago rolled east and west from the valley of the Euphrates meet to-day on our Pacific coast. There are no more new worlds. . . . The time is coming when the pressure of population on the means of subsistence will be felt here as it is now felt in Europe and Asia. Then will the world enter upon a new stage of its history—*the final competition of races, for which the Anglo-Saxon is being schooled.* Long before the thousand millions are here, the mighty *centrifugal* tendency, inherent in this stock and strengthened in the United States, will assert itself. Then this race of unequaled energy, with all the majesty of numbers and the might of wealth behind it—the representative, let us hope, of the largest liberty, the purest Christianity, the highest civilization—having developed peculiarly aggressive traits calculated to impress its institutions upon mankind, will spread itself over the earth. If I read not amiss, this powerful race will move down upon Mexico, down upon Central and South America, out upon the islands of the sea, over upon Africa and beyond. And can any one doubt that the result of this competition of races will be the "survival of the fittest"? "Any people," says Dr. Bushnell, "that is physiologically advanced in culture, though it be only in a degree beyond another which is mingled with it on strictly equal terms, is sure to live down and finally live out its inferior. Nothing can save the inferior race but a ready and pliant assimilation. Whether the feebler and more abject races are going to be regenerated and raised up, is already very much of a question. What if it should be God's plan to people the world with better and finer material? Certain it is, whatever expectations we may indulge, that there is a tremendous overbearing surge of power in the Christian nations, which, if the others are not speedily raised to some vastly higher capacity, will inevitably submerge and bury them forever. These great populations of Christendom—what are they doing, but throwing out their colonies on every side, and populating themselves, if I may so speak, into the possession of all countries and climes?" To this result no war of extermination is needful; the contest is not one of arms, but of vitality and of civilization. "At the present day," says Mr. Darwin, "civilized nations are everywhere supplanting barbarous nations. . . . "

Some of the stronger races, doubtless, may be able to preserve their integrity; but, in order to compete with the Anglo-Saxon, they will probably be forced to adopt his methods and instruments, his civilization and his religion. . . . The contact of Christian with heathen nations is awaking the latter to new life. Old superstitions are loosening their grasp. The dead crust of fossil faiths is being shattered by the movements of life underneath. In Catholic countries, Catholicism is losing its influence over educated minds, and in some cases the masses have already lost all faith in it. Thus, while on this continent God is training the Anglo-Saxon race for its mission, a complemental work has been in progress in the great world beyond. God has two hands. Not only is he preparing in our civilization the die with which to stamp the nations, but . . . he is preparing mankind to receive our impress.

Is there room for reasonable doubt that this race, unless devitalized by alcohol and tobacco, is destined to dispossess many weaker races, assimilate others, and mold the remainder, until, in a very true and important sense, it has Anglo-Saxonized mankind?

SOURCE. Josiah Strong, *Our Country,* New York: The Baker and Taylor Publishing Company for The American Home Missionary Society, 1885, pp. 159–160, 165–168, 174–178.

b. THE RESPONSIBILITIES OF IMPERIALISM: RUDYARD KIPLING

RUDYARD KIPLING, English author and poet and a firm admirer of the British Empire, viewed imperialism not only as a source of national grandeur but also as a challenge to the Christian responsibility of Englishmen to uplift less civilized peoples. He warned his compatriots that all empires pass and urged them to make good use of what time they had to advance the conditions of their subject peoples.

Recessional (1897)

God of our fathers, known of old,
  Lord of our far-flung battle-line,
Beneath whose awful Hand we hold
  Dominion over palm and pine—
Lord God of Hosts, be with us yet,
Lest we forget—lest we forget!

The tumult and the shouting dies;
  The captains and the kings depart:
Still stands Thine ancient sacrifice,
  An humble and a contrite heart.
Lord God of Hosts, be with us yet,
Lest we forget—lest we forget!

Far-called, our navies melt away;
  On dune and headland sinks the fire:
Lo, all our pomp of yesterday
  Is one with Nineveh and Tyre!
Judge of the Nations, spare us yet,
Lest we forget—lest we forget!

If, drunk with sight of power, we loose
  Wild tongues that have not Thee in awe,
Such boastings as the Gentiles use,
  Or lesser breeds without the Law—
Lord God of Hosts, be with us yet,
Lest we forget—lest we forget!

For heathen heart that puts her trust
  In reeking tube and iron shard,
All valiant dust that builds on dust,
  And guarding, calls not Thee to guard,
For frantic boast and foolish word—
Thy Mercy on Thy People, Lord!

The White Man's Burden (1899)

Take up the White Man's burden—
  Send forth the best ye breed—
Go bind your sons to exile
  To serve your captives' need;
To wait in heavy harness
  On fluttered folk and wild—
Your new-caught, sullen peoples,
  Half devil and half child.

Take up the White Man's burden—
  In patience to abide,
To veil the threat of terror
  And check the show of pride;
By open speech and simple,
  An hundred times made plain,
To seek another's profit,
  And work another's gain.

Take up the White Man's burden—
  The savage wars of peace—
Fill full the mouth of Famine
  And bid the sickness cease;
And when your goal is nearest
  The end for others sought,
Watch Sloth and heathen Folly
  Bring all your hope to nought.

Take up the White Man's burden—
  No tawdry rule of kings,
But toil of serf and sweeper—
  The tale of common things.

The ports ye shall not enter,
  The roads ye shall not tread,
Go make them with your living,
  And mark them with your dead!

Take up the White Man's burden—
  And reap his old reward:
The blame of those ye better,
  The hate of those ye guard—
The cry of hosts ye humour
  (Ah, slowly!) toward the light:—
'Why brought ye us from bondage,
  'Our loved Egyptian night?'

Take up the White Man's burden—
  Ye dare not stoop to less—
Nor call too loud on Freedom
  To cloak your weariness;
By all ye cry or whisper,
  By all ye leave or do,
The silent, sullen peoples
  Shall weigh your Gods and you.

Take up the White Man's burden—
  Have done with childish days—
The lightly proffered laurel,
  The easy, ungrudged praise.
Comes now, to search your manhood
  Through all the thankless years,
Cold-edged with dear-bought wisdom,
  The judgment of your peers!

c. LENIN, FROM *IMPERIALISM: THE HIGHEST STAGE OF CAPITALISM*

MANY OF STRONG'S AND KIPLING'S contemporaries opposed colonialism, and none more vigorously than Lenin. In his Imperialism: the Highest Stage of Capitalism *(1916), he pictured it as the evil product of monopolistic greed and the last phase in the decline of the capitalist system. For a modern criticism of this viewpoint see Chapter 19, e.*

The enormous dimensions of finance capital concentrated in a few hands and creating an extremely extensive and close network of ties and relationships which subordinate not only the small and medium, but also even the very small capitalists and small masters, on the one hand, and the intense struggle waged against other national state groups of financiers for the division of the world and domination over other countries, on the other hand, cause the wholesale transition of the possessing classes to the side of imperialism. The signs of the times are a "general" enthusiasm regarding its prospects, a passionate defence of imperialism, and every possible embellishment of its real nature. The imperialist ideology also penetrates the working class. There is no Chinese Wall between it and the other classes. The leaders of the so-called "Social-Democratic" Party of Germany are today justly called "social-imperialists," that is, socialists in words and imperialists in deeds; but as early as 1902, Hobson noted the existence of "Fabian imperialists" who belonged to the opportunist Fabian Society in England.

Bourgeois scholars and publicists usually come out in defence of imperialism in a somewhat veiled form, and obscure its complete domination and its profound roots; they strive to concentrate attention on partial and secondary details and do their very best to distract attention from the main issue by means of ridiculous schemes for "reform," such as police supervision of the trusts and banks, etc. Less frequently, cynical and frank imperialists speak out and are bold enough to admit the absurdity of the idea of reforming the fundamental features of imperialism. . . .

The question as to whether it is possible to reform the basis of imperialism, whether to go forward to the accentuation and deepening of the antagonisms which it engenders, or backwards, towards allaying these antagonisms, is a fundamental question in the critique of imperialism. As a consequence of the fact that the political features of imperialism are reaction all along the line, and increased national oppression, resulting from the oppression of the financial oligarchy and the elimination of free competition, a petty-bourgeois—democratic opposition has been rising against imperialism in almost all imperialist countries since the beginning of the twentieth century. . . .

In the United States, the imperialist war waged against Spain in 1898 stirred up the opposition of the "anti-imperialists," the last of the Mohicans of bourgeois democracy. They declared this war to be "criminal"; they denounced the annexation of foreign territories as being a violation of the Constitution, and denounced the "Jingo treachery" by means of which Aguinaldo, leader of the native Filipinos, was deceived (the Americans promised him the independence of his country, but later they landed troops and annexed it). They quoted the words of Lincoln:

"When the white man governs himself, that is self-government; but when he governs himself and also governs another man, that is more than self-government—that is despotism."

But while all this criticism shrank from recognising the indissoluble bond between imperialism and the trusts, and, therefore, between imperialism and the very foundations of capitalism; while it shrank from joining up with the forces engendered by large-scale capitalism and its development—it remained a "pious wish." . . .

We have seen that the economic quintessence of imperialism is monopoly capitalism. This very fact determines its place in history, for monopoly that grew up on the basis of free competition, and precisely out of free competition, is the transition from the capitalist system to a higher social-economic order. We must take special note of the four principal forms of monopoly, or the four principal manifestations of monopoly capitalism, which are characteristic of the epoch under review.

Firstly, monopoly arose out of the concentration of production at a very advanced stage of development. This refers to the monopolist capitalist combines, cartels, syndicates and trusts. We have seen the important part that these play in modern economic life. At the beginning of the twentieth century, monopolies acquired complete supremacy in the advanced countries. And although the first steps towards the formation of the cartels were first taken by countries enjoying the protection of high tariffs (Germany, America), Great Britain, with her system of free trade, was not far behind in revealing the same basic phenomenon, namely, the birth of monopoly out of the concentration of production.

Secondly, monopolies have accelerated the capture of the most important sources of raw materials, especially for the coal and iron industries, which are the basic and most highly cartelised industries in capitalist society. The monopoly of the most important sources of raw materials has enormously increased the power of big capital, and has sharpened the antagonism between cartelised and non-cartelised industry.

Thirdly, monopoly has sprung from the banks. The banks have developed from modest intermediary enterprises into the monopolists of finance capital. Some three to five of the biggest banks in each of the foremost capitalist countries have achieved the "personal union" of industrial and bank capital, and have concentrated in their hands the disposal of thousands upon thousands of millions which form the greater part of the capital and income of entire countries. A financial oligarchy, which throws a close net of relations of dependence over all the economic and political institutions of contemporary bourgeois society without exception—such is the most striking manifestation of this monopoly.

Fourthly, monopoly has grown out of colonial policy. To the numerous "old" motives of colonial policy, finance capital has added the struggle for the sources of raw materials, for the export of capital, for "spheres of influence," *i.e.*, for spheres for profitable deals, concessions, monopolist profits and so on; in fine, for economic territory in general. When the colonies of the European powers in Africa, for instance, comprised only one-tenth of that territory (as was the case in 1876), colonial policy was able to develop by methods other than those of monopoly—by the "free grabbing" of territories, so to speak. But when nine-tenths of Africa had been seized (approximately by 1900), when the whole world had been divided up, there was inevitably ushered in a period of colonial monopoly and, consequently, a period of particularly intense struggle for the division and the redivision of the world.

The extent to which monopolist capital has intensified all the contradictions of capitalism is generally known. It is sufficient to mention the high cost of living and the oppression of the cartels. This intensification of contradictions constitutes the most powerful driving force of the transitional period of history, which began from the time of the definite victory of world finance capital.

Monopolies, oligarchy, the striving for domination instead of the striving for liberty, the exploitation of an increasing number of small or weak nations by an extremely small group of the richest or most powerful nations—all these have given birth to those distinctive characteristics of imperialism which compel us to define it as parasitic or decaying capitalism. . . .

The receipt of high monopoly profits by the capitalists in one of the numerous branches of industry, in one of numerous countries, etc., makes it economically possible for them to corrupt certain sections of the working class, and for a time a fairly considerable minority, and win them to the side of the bourgeoisie of a given industry or nation against all the others. The intensification of antagonisms between imperialist nations for the division of the world increases this striving. And so there is created that bond between imperialism and opportunism, which revealed itself first and most clearly in England, owing to the fact that certain features of imperialist development were observable there much earlier than in other countries. . . .

From all that has been said . . . on the economic nature of imperialism, it follows that we must define it as capitalism in transition, or, more precisely, as moribund capitalism. It is very instructive in this respect to note that the bourgeois economists, in describing modern capitalism, frequently employ terms like "interlocking," "absence of isolation," etc.; "in conformity with their functions and course of development," banks are "not purely private business enterprises; they are more and more outgrowing the sphere of purely private business regulation." And this very Riesser, who uttered the words just quoted, declares with all seriousness that the "prophecy" of the Marxists concerning "socialisation" has "not come true"!

What then does this word "interlocking" express? It merely expresses the most striking feature of the process going on before our eyes. It shows that the observer counts the separate trees, but cannot see the wood. It slavishly copies the superficial, the fortuitous, the chaotic. It reveals the observer as one who is overwhelmed by the mass of raw material and is utterly incapable of appreciating its meaning and importance. Ownership of shares and relations between owners of private property "interlock in a haphazard way." But the underlying factor of this interlocking, its very base, is the changing social relations of production. When a big enterprise assumes gigantic proportions, and, on the basis of exact computation of mass data, organises according to plan the supply of primary raw materials to the extent of two-thirds, or three-fourths of all that is necessary for tens of millions of people; when the raw materials are transported to the most suitable place of production, sometimes hundreds or thousands of miles away, in a systematic and organised manner; when a single centre directs all the successive stages of work right up to the manufacture of numerous varieties of finished articles; when these products are distributed according to a single plan among tens and hundreds of millions of consumers (as in the case of the distribution of oil in America and Germany by the American "oil trust")—then it becomes evident that we have socialisation of production, and not mere "interlocking"; that private economic relations and private property relations constitute a shell which is no longer suitable for its contents, a shell which must inevitably begin to decay if its destruction be delayed by artificial means; a shell which may continue in a state of decay for a fairly long period (particularly if the cure of the opportunist abscess is protracted), but which will inevitably be removed.

SOURCE. V. I. Lenin, *Imperialism: The Highest Stage of Capitalism*, New York: International Publishers, 1939, pp. 109–111, 123–124, 126–127. Reprinted by permission of International Publishers Co., Inc.

PART SIX

World Wars and New Authoritarian States, 1914–1945

THE outbreak of World War I was a product of several causes: the intensification of national rivalries resulting in arms races and in the polarization of Europe into two mutually hostile alliance systems; a continuing struggle over colonies and spheres of influence in Asia and Africa; and most immediately, the contest between Austria-Hungary and Russia for hegemony in the Balkans. Here, in the course of the previous century, a number of newly independent states had broken loose from the crumbling Ottoman Empire. Austria-Hungary was particularly sensitive on the matter of Balkan nationalism, for the movement was generating unrest among the Slavic peoples within her own territories. Russia, conscious of her Slavic heritage and anxious to use it to her own political advantage, encouraged Balkan nationalism while Austria-Hungary opposed it.

The Slavic state of Serbia, fiercely independent and hopeful of becoming the nucleus of a unified Balkan nation, was a constant threat to the internal security of Austria-Hungary. When a Serbian terrorist assassinated Archduke Francis Ferdinand, heir to the Austro-Hungarian throne, at Sarajevo on June 28, 1914 a crisis was provoked that led directly to World War I. Austria retaliated by issuing an ultimatum to Serbia containing demands that no independent nation could honorably accept. In the days immediately following, as a consequence of antagonistic alliance systems, the great powers entered the conflict one after another. Russia came to Serbia's defense, Germany joined Austria, France and England joined Russia, most of the smaller European states took one side or the other, and by mid-August Europe was in a state of general war.

World War I was a momentous historical catastrophe—a fundamental turning point in modern history. The fighting dragged on for months and years, taking a fearful toll of European manhood and resources. American intervention in 1917 tipped the scales against the Central Powers, and in September 1918 the German government asked for an armistice on the basis of the moderate peace proposals—the Fourteen Points—of President Woodrow Wilson. The armistice was concluded in November, and the ultimate settlement—the Treaty of Versailles—imposed a series of unexpectedly harsh penalties on Germany and Austria. The Austro-Hungarian kingdom was broken up into its component parts, and Germany was stripped of extensive territories, "permanently" demilitarized, and saddled with a heavy indemnity.

The war had wrought a profound transformation in European politics. Crowns fell in Russia, Austria, and Germany. Russia became Europe's first Communist state; Austria and Germany became republics. The European economy was badly shaken, and European intellectuals became deeply disillusioned. The economic and political turbulence of the postwar years provoked the rise of new authoritarian states, first in Italy, later in Germany in the midst of a great worldwide economic depression. Totalitarianism under Mussolini in Fascist Italy and Hitler in Nazi Germany, and the new Communist regime in Russia, came increasingly into conflict with Europe's parliamentary democracies. Hitler in particular, playing on the themes of anti-Semitism and the "betrayal" at Versailles, re-armed Germany and pursued a policy of systematic aggression against neighboring states. Throughout Europe and the world, so it seemed, the nineteenth-century wave of democratic liberalism was receding.

The causes of World War II are tied to the events of World War I, and its product: the three-way ideological split between liberal democracy, Communism, and right-wing totalitarianism. Ultimately, World War II was brought about by the militant expansionism of the Axis powers—Italy, Japan, and in particular, Germany—and by the rather delayed response of the democracies and Russia to these aggressions.

Step by step, Hitler undid the provisions of the Versailles Treaty. Repeatedly affirming his peaceful intentions, he rearmed Germany, incorporated Austria into his Reich, and, in the Munich agreement of 1938, bluffed England and France into conceding him a portion of Czechoslovakia (the "Sudetenland") which was heavily German in population. Shortly thereafter he occupied the remainder of Czechoslovakia. In August, 1939, he startled the world by concluding a Non-Aggression Pact with the Soviet Union, and a few days afterward, assured of Russian neutrality, he sent his armies into Poland. This last act prompted England and France to declare war.

In 1940 Germany conquered France, occupied much of western and central Europe, and staggered England with devastating air raids. But Hitler's invasion of Russia and the Japanese bombing of Pearl Harbor brought the two supreme powers of the mid-twentieth century into the struggle, and the combined efforts of the United States, the Soviet Union, and Great Britain resulted ultimately in the total defeat of the Axis powers.

Italy capitulated first, then Germany, and finally, in August, 1945, Japan was brought to her knees by the American atomic bomb. The month of August witnessed the end of World War II and the beginning of the atomic age. The Allied powers, in an effort to secure permanent peace through international cooperation, affixed their signatures to the United Nations Charter in June, 1945, and with the crushing of right-wing totalitarianism many people hoped for a new era of peace and civilized behavior among nations. Such hopes were not to be fulfilled.

Chapter 13

WORLD WAR I

a. THE AUSTRO-HUNGARIAN ULTIMATUM TO SERBIA, 1914

THE AUSTRO-HUNGARIAN ULTIMATUM to Serbia, July 23, 1914, following upon the assassination at Sarajevo, is perhaps the key document in the outbreak of World War I. The assassin was a member of a Serbian secret society rather than a direct agent of the Serbian government, but Serbian officials had been aware of the plot, and the government cannot be regarded as innocent. To Austria, the assassination provided a priceless opportunity to humble and humiliate her small but troublesome neighbor, and that was precisely the purpose of the ultimatum. Austria did not expect Serbia to accept it, and Serbian rejection would provide Austria with an excuse for war. Austria banked on the hope that such a war would not spread—that Russia would not come to Serbia's defense. Serbia's response to the ultimatum was conciliatory, but she rejected the demand that Austrian agents be allowed to enter Serbia to join with Serbian officials in the investigation of the assassination. This demand was clearly an affront to Serbia's sovereignty. On July 28, Austria-Hungary declared war against Serbia, and within two weeks the major powers of Europe were at war.

Vienna, July 22, 1914

Your Excellency will present the following note to the Royal Government [of Serbia] on the afternoon of Thursday, July 23:

On the 31 March, 1909, the Royal Serbian Minister at the Court of Vienna made, in the name of his Government, the following statement to the Imperial and Royal Government [of Austria-Hungary]:

Serbia recognizes that her rights were not affected by the situation created in Bosnia and states that she will accordingly accept the decisions that will be reached by the Powers in connection with Article 25 of the Treaty of Berlin. Serbia, in accepting the advice of the Great Powers, binds herself to desist from the protest and opposition which she has engaged in with regard to the annexation since last October, and she furthermore binds herself to change the tenor of her present policy toward Austria-Hungary, and to live with Austria-Hungary on the basis of friendly and neighborly relations in the future.

The history of the past few years, and especially the distressing events of 28th June, have proved the existence of a subversive movement in Serbia, whose object is to separate certain territories from the Austro-Hungarian Monarchy. This movement, which arose under the very eyes of the Serbian Government, later found expression outside of the territory of the Kingdom in acts of terrorism, in a number of assassination attempts, and in murders.

Far from fulfilling the formal obligations contained in its declaration of 31 March, 1909, the Royal Serbian Government has done nothing to put down this movement. It has tolerated the criminal activities of the various unions and associations directed against the Monarchy, the unchecked statements of the press, the glorification of the assassins, the participation of officers and officials in subversive intrigues; it has tolerated an unhealthy propaganda in its public schools; and, finally, it has tolerated every manifestation which could mislead the people of Serbia into hatred of the Monarchy and contempt for its institutions.

This toleration of which the Royal Serbian Government was guilty was still in evidence when the events of 28 June[1] exhibited to the whole world the dreadful consequences of such tolerance.

It is clear from the statements and confessions of the criminal authors of the assassination of 28 June that the murder at Sarajevo was conceived at Belgrade, that the murderers acquired their weapons and bombs from Serbian officers and officials who belonged to the *Narodna Odbrana*,[2] and, finally, that the dispatch of the criminals and their weapons to Bosnia was managed and effected with the connivance of Serbian frontier authorities.

The results brought out by the inquiry no longer allow the Imperial and Royal Government to maintain the attitude of patient tolerance which it has observed for years toward those agitations which center at Belgrade and spread into the territories of the Monarchy. Instead, these results oblige the Imperial and Royal Government to end those intrigues which constitute a continuing menace to the peace of the Monarchy.

To attain this end, the Imperial and Royal Government is compelled to demand that the Serbian Government give official assurance that it will condemn the propaganda directed against Austria-Hungary, that is, the whole of the efforts whose ultimate object is to alienate from the Monarchy territories that belong to it; and that it will undertake to suppress with all the means at its command this criminal and terroristic propaganda.

To give these assurances a character of solemnity, the Royal Serbian Government will publish on the first page of its official organ of July 26/13, the following declaration:

[1] The assassination of the Austrian Arch duke, Francis Ferdinand.

[2] The "Black Hand," a Serbian terrorist society.

"The Royal Serbian Government condemns the propaganda directed against Austria-Hungary, that is, the whole of the efforts whose ultimate object is to alienate from the Austro-Hungarian Monarchy territories that belong to it, and it sincerely regrets the dreadful consequences of these criminal transactions.

"The Royal Serbian Government regrets that Serbian officers and officials have taken part in the abovementioned propaganda and thereby have endangered the friendly and neighborly relations, to the cultivation of which the Royal Government had solemnly pledged itself by its declarations of 31 March, 1909.

"The Royal Government, which disapproves and condemns every plan and every attempt to interfere in the destinies of the population of any portion of Austria-Hungary, regards it as its duty expressly to call to the attention of the officers, officials and the whole population of the kingdom the fact that for the future it will proceed with the utmost rigor against any persons who shall become guilty of any such activities, and will make every effort to suppress such activities."

This declaration shall be brought simultaneously to the attention of the Royal army by an order of the day from His Majesty the King, and by publication in the official organ of the army.

The Royal Serbian Government will furthermore pledge itself:

(1) to suppress every publication which shall incite to hatred and contempt of the Monarchy, and the general tendency of which shall be directed against the territorial integrity of the Monarchy;

(2) to proceed immediately to the dissolution of the *Narodna Odbrana*, to seize all of its means of propaganda, and to proceed likewise against the other unions and associations in Serbia which busy themselves with propaganda against Austria-Hungary; the Royal Government will take all necessary measures to make sure that the dissolved associations will not continue their activities under other names or in other forms;

(3) to eliminate immediately from public instruction in Serbia everything, whether connected with teaching personnel or teaching content that serves or may serve to feed the propaganda against Austria-Hungary;

(4) to remove from military and administrative service all officers and officials who have been guilty of carrying on propaganda against Austria-Hungary, whose names the Imperial and Royal Government reserves the right to make known to the Royal Government when communicating the evidence now in its possession;

(5) to agree to the cooperation in Serbia of the organs of the Imperial and Royal Government in the suppression of the subversive movement directed against the integrity of the Monarchy;

(6) to institute a judicial inquiry against every participant in the conspiracy of 28 June who may be found in Serbian territory; the organs of the Imperial and Royal Government delegated for this purpose will take part in the proceedings;

(7) to undertake immediately the arrest of Major Voislav Tankositch and of Milan Ciganovitch, a Serbian official, who have been compromised by the results of the inquiry;

(8) to prevent by expeditious means the participation of Serbian authorities in the smuggling of weapons and explosives across the frontier; to dismiss from service and to punish severely those members of the Frontier Service at Schabats and Losnitza who assisted the authors of the criminal act at Sarajevo to cross the frontier;

(9) to make explanations to the Imperial and Royal Government concerning the inexcusable statements of high Serbian officials in Serbia and abroad, who, without regard for their official position, have not hesitated to express themselves in a manner hostile toward Austria-Hungary since the assassination of 28 June;

(10) to inform the Imperial and Royal Government immediately of the implementation of the measures comprised in the foregoing points.

The Imperial and Royal Government awaits the reply of the Royal Government by Saturday the twenty-fifth, at 6 p.m. at the latest.

SOURCE. Max Montgelas and Walter Schuckling, eds., *Outbreak of the World War: Documents Collected by Karl Kautsky,* New York: Carnegie Endowment for International Peace, 1924, Supplement I, pp. 603–606. Reprinted by permission of the Carnegie Endowment for International Peace.

b. PRESIDENT WOODROW WILSON'S FOURTEEN POINTS, 1918

THIS SELECTION, omitted from the first edition of Landmarks *because of its widespread availability elsewhere, is included here in response to a number of requests from users of the first edition. It illustrates Wilson's application of liberal idealism to the arena of international affairs. Germany sued for peace on the basis of Wilson's proposals, but the more hardheaded notions of America's European allies resulted in the subjection of Germany to far harsher peace terms (see selection d, below). The Fourteen Points were first presented in Wilson's address of January 8, 1918, to a Joint Session of the United States Congress, and it is from this speech that our excerpt is taken.*

. . . We entered this war because violations of right had occurred which touched us to the quick and made the life of our own people impossible unless they were corrected and the world secured once for all against their recurrence. What we demand in this war, therefore, is nothing peculiar to ourselves. It is that the world be made fit and safe to live in; and particularly that it be made safe for every peace-loving nation which, like our own, wishes to live its own life, determine its own institutions, be assured of justice and fair dealing by the other peoples of the world as against force and selfish aggression. All the peoples of the world are in effect partners in this interest, and for our own part we see very clearly that unless justice be done to others it will not be done to us. The program of the world's peace, therefore, is our program; and that program, the only possible program, as we see it, is this:

I. Open covenants of peace, openly arrived at, after which there shall be no private international understandings of any kind but diplomacy shall proceed always frankly and in the public view.

II. Absolute freedom of navigation upon the seas, outside territorial waters, alike in peace and in war, except as the seas may be closed in whole or in part by international action for the enforcement of international covenants.

III. The removal, so far as possible, of all economic barriers and the establishment of an equality of trade conditions among all the nations consenting to the peace and associating themselves for its maintenance.

IV. Adequate guarantees given and taken that national armaments will be reduced to the lowest point consistent with domestic safety.

V. A free, open-minded, and absolutely impartial adjustment of all colonial claims, based upon a strict observance of the principle that in determining all such questions of sovereignty the interests of the populations concerned must have equal weight with the equitable claims of the government whose title is to be determined.

VI. The evacuation of all Russian territory and such a settlement of all questions affecting Russia as will secure the best and freest cooperation of the other nations of the world in obtaining for her an unhampered and unembarrassed opportunity for the independent determination of her own political development and national policy and assure her of a sincere welcome into the society of free nations under institutions of her own choosing; and, more than a welcome, assistance also of every kind that she may need and may herself desire. The treatment accorded Russia by her sister nations in the months to come will be the acid test of their good will, of their comprehension of her needs as distinguished from their own interests, and of their intelligent and unselfish sympathy.

VII. Belgium, the whole world will agree, must be evacuated and restored, without any attempt to limit the sovereignty which she enjoys in common with all other free nations. No other single act will serve as this will serve to restore confidence among the nations in the laws which they have themselves set and determined for the government of their relations with one another. Without this healing act the whole structure and validity of international law is forever impaired.

VIII. All French territory should be freed and the invaded portions restored, and the wrong done to France by Prussia in 1871 in the matter of Alsace-Lorraine, which has unsettled the peace of the world for nearly fifty years, should be righted, in order that peace may once more be made secure in the interest of all.

IX. A readjustment of the frontiers of Italy should be effected along clearly recognizable lines of nationality.

X. The peoples of Austria-Hungary, whose place among the nations we wish to see safeguarded and assured, should be accorded the freest opportunity of autonomous development.

XI. Rumania, Serbia, and Montenegro should be evacuated; occupied territories restored; Serbia accorded free and secure access to the sea; and the relations of the several Balkan states to one another determined by friendly counsel along historically established lines of allegiance and nationality; and international guarantees of the political and economic independence and territorial integrity of the several Balkan states should be entered into.

XII. The Turkish portions of the present Ottoman Empire should be assured a secure sovereignty, but the other nationalities which are now under Turkish rule should be assured an undoubted security of life and an absolutely unmolested opportunity of autonomous development, and the Dardanelles should be permanently opened as a free passage to the ships and commerce of all nations under international guarantees.

XIII. An independent Polish state should be erected which should include the territories inhabited by indisputably Polish populations, which should be assured a free and secure access to the sea, and whose political and economic independence and territorial integrity should be guaranteed by international covenant.

XIV. A general association of nations must be formed under specific covenants for the purpose of affording mutual guarantees of political independence and territorial integrity to great and small states alike.

In regard to these essential rectifications of wrong and assertions of right we feel ourselves to be intimate partners of all the governments and peoples associated together against the Imperialists. We cannot be separated in interest or divided in purpose. We stand together until the end.

c. GEORGE GROSZ, *FIT FOR ACTIVE SERVICE*

THE BRILLIANT GERMAN PAINTER George Grosz, in his Fit for
Active Service *and similar works, bitterly satirized Prussian militarism.*

d. EXTRACTS FROM THE TREATY OF VERSAILLES, 1919

IN 1918 GERMANY, exhausted by war, was obliged to accept a harsh series of Armistice Demands (November 10, 1918). The final peace settlement—the Treaty of Versailles (June 28, 1919)—was harsher still. The signing of the Treaty was deliberately scheduled to coincide with the fifth anniversary of Sarajevo, and the place of the signing—the Hall of Mirrors in the Versailles Palace—was chosen because it was the setting where the now-defunct German Empire had been proclaimed after the Franco-Prussian War. The clauses of the Treaty, no less than the circumstances of its signing, were calculated to humble Germany.

ARTICLE 31. Germany, recognizing that the Treaties of April 19, 1839, which established the status of Belgium before the war, no longer conform to the requirements of the situation, consents to the abrogation of the said treaties and undertakes immediately to recognize and to observe whatever conventions may be entered into by the Principal Allied and Associated Powers, or by any of them, in concert with the Governments of Belgium and of the Netherlands, to replace the said Treaties of 1839. If her formal adhesion should be required to such conventions or to any of their stipulations, Germany undertakes immediately to give it. . . .

ARTICLE 42. Germany is forbidden to maintain or construct any fortifications either on the left bank of the Rhine or on the right bank to the west of a line drawn 50 kilometres to the East of the Rhine.

ARTICLE 43. In the area defined above the maintenance and the assembly of armed forces, either permanently or temporarily, and military manoeuvres of any kind, as well as the upkeep of all permanent works for mobilization, are in the same way forbidden.

ARGICLE 44. In case Germany violates in any manner whatever the provisions of Articles 42 and 43, she shall be regarded as committing a hostile act against the Powers signatory of the present Treaty and as calculated to disturb the peace of the world.

ARTICLE 45. As compensation for the destruction of the coal-mines in the north of France and as part payment towards the total reparation due from Germany for the damage resulting from the war, Germany cedes to France in full and absolute possession, with exclusive rights of exploitation, unencumbered and free from all debts and charges of any kind, the coal-mines situated in the Saar Basin as defined in Article 48. . . .

ARTICLE 49. Germany renounces in favour of the League of Nations, in the capacity of trustee, the government of the territory defined above.

ARTICLE 50. The stipulations under which the cession of the mines in the Saar Basin shall be carried out, together with the measures intended to guarantee the rights and the well-being of the inhabitants and the government of the territory, as well as the conditions in accordance with which the plebiscite hereinbefore provided for is to be made, are laid down in the Annex hereto. This Annex shall be considered as an integral part of the present Treaty, and Germany declares her adherence to it.

ARTICLE 51. The territories which were ceded to Germany in accordance with the Preliminaries of Peace signed at Versailles on February 26, 1871, and the Treaty of Frankfurt of May 10, 1871, are restored to French sovereignty as from the date of the Armistice of November 11, 1918.

The provisions of the Treaties establishing the delimitation of the frontiers before 1871 shall be restored. . . .

ARTICLE 80. Germany acknowledges and will respect strictly the independence of Austria, within the frontiers which may be fixed in a Treaty between that State and the Principal Allied and Associated Powers; she agrees that this independence shall be inalienable, except with the consent of the Council of the League of Nations.

ARTICLE 81. Germany, in conformity with the action already taken by the Allied and Associated Powers, recognizes the complete independence of the Czecho-Slovak State which will include the autonomous territory of the Ruthenians to the south of the Carpathians. Germany hereby recognizes the frontiers of this State as determined by the Principal Allied and Associated Powers and the other interested States. . . .

ARTICLE 87. Germany, in conformity with the action already taken by the Allied and Associated Powers, recognizes the complete independence of Poland, and renounces in her favour all rights and title over the territory [of Poland].

The boundaries of Poland not laid down in the present Treaty will be subsequently determined by the Principal Allied and Associated Powers.

A Commission consisting of seven members, five of whom shall be nominated by the Principal Allied and Associated Powers, one by Germany and one by Poland, shall be constituted fifteen days after the coming into force of the present Treaty to delimit on the spot the frontier line between Poland and Germany.

The decisions of the Commission will be taken by a majority of votes and shall be binding upon the parties concerned.

ARTICLE 88. In the portion of Upper Silesia included within the boundaries described below, the inhabitants will be called upon to indicate by a vote whether they wish to be attached to Germany or to Poland. . . .

ARTICLE 99. Germany renounces in favour of the Principal Allied and Associated Powers all rights and title over the territories included between the Baltic, the north-eastern fronier of East Prussia as defined in Article 28 of Part II (Boundaries of Germany) of the present Treaty and the former frontier between Germany and Russia.

Germany undertakes to accept the settlement made by the Principal Allied and Associated Powers in regard to these territories, particularly in so far as concerns the nationality of the inhabitants. . . .

ARTICLE 102. The Principal Allied and Associated Powers undertake to establish the town of Danzig, together with the rest of the territory described in Article 100, as a Free City. It will be placed under the protection of the League of Nations. . . .

ARTICLE 119. Germany renounces in favour of the Principal Allied and Associated Powers all her rights and titles over her oversea possessions. . . .

ARTICLE 141. Germany renounces all rights, titles and privileges conferred on her by the General Act of Algeciras of April 7, 1906, and by the Franco-German Agreements of February 9, 1909, and November 4, 1911. All treaties, agreements, arrangements and contracts concluded by her with the Sherifian Empire are regarded as abrogated as from August 3, 1914.

In no case can Germany take advantage of these instruments and she undertakes not to intervene in any way in negotiations relating to Morocco which may take place between France and the other Powers. . . .

ARTICLE 156. Germany renounces, in favour of Japan, all her rights, title and privileges—particularly those concerning the territory of Kiaochow, railways, mines and submarine cables—which she acquired in virtue of the Treaty concluded by her with China on March 6, 1898, and of all other arrangements relative to the Province of Shantung.

All German rights in the Tsingtao-Tsinanfu Railway, including its branch lines, together with its subsidiary property of all kinds, stations, shops, fixed and rolling stock, mines, plant and material for the exploitation of the mines, are and remain acquired by Japan, together with all rights and privileges attaching thereto.

The German State submarine cables from Tsingtao to Shanghai and from Tsingtao to Chefoo, with all the rights, privileges and properties attaching thereto, are similarly acquired by Japan, free and clear of all charges and encumbrances. . . .

ARTICLE 159. The German military forces shall be demobilized and reduced as prescribed hereinafter.

ARTICLE 160. By a date which must not be later than March 31, 1920, the German Army must not comprise more than seven divisions of infantry and three divisions of cavalry.

After that date the total number of effectives in the Army of the States constituting Germany must not exceed one hundred thousand men, including officers and establishments of depots. The Army shall be devoted exclusively to the maintenance of order within the territory and to the control of the frontiers.

The total effective strength of officers, including the personnel of staffs, whatever their composition, must not exceed four thousand.

. . . The Great German General Staff and all similar organizations shall be dissolved and may not be reconstituted in any form. . . .

ARTICLE 179. All fortified works, fortresses and field works situated in German territory to the west of a line drawn fifty kilometres to the east of the Rhine shall be disarmed and dismantled. . . .

ARTICLE 181. After the expiration of a period of two months from the coming into force of the present Treaty the German naval forces in commission must not exceed:

6 battleships of the *Deutschland* or *Lothringen* type,
6 light cruisers,
12 destroyers,
12 torpedo boats,

or an equal number of ships constructed to replace them as provided in Article 190.

No submarines are to be included.

All other warships, except where there is provision to the contrary in the present Treaty, must be placed in reserve or devoted to commercial purposes.

ARTICLE 198. The armed forces of Germany must not include any military or naval air forces. . . .

ARTICLE 231. The Allied and Associated Governments affirm and Germany accepts the responsibility of Germany and her allies for causing all the loss and damage to which the Allied and Associated Governments and their nationals have been subjected as a consequence of the war imposed upon them by the aggression of Germany and her allies.

ARTICLE 232. The Allied and Associated Governments recognize that the resources of Germany are not adequate, after taking into account permanent diminutions of such resources which will result from other provisions of the present Treaty, to make complete reparation for all such loss and damage.

The Allied and Associated Governments, however, require, and Germany undertakes, that she will make compensation for all damage done to the civilian population of the Allied and Associated Powers and to their property during the period of the belligerency of each as an Allied or Associated Power against Germany by such aggression by land, by sea and from the air, and in general all damage as defined in Annex I hereto.

ARTICLE 233. The amount of the above damage for which compensation is to be made by Germany shall be determined by an Inter-Allied Commission, to be called the *Reparation Commission* and constituted in the form and with the powers set forth hereunder and in Annexes II to VII inclusive hereto.

This Commission shall consider the claims and give to the German Government a just opportunity to be heard.

The findings of the Commission as to the amount of damage defined as above shall be concluded and notified to the German Government on or before May 1, 1921, as representing the extent of that Government's obligations.

ARTICLE 234. The Reparation Commissions shall after May 1, 1921, from time to time, consider the resources and capacity of Germany, and, after giving her representatives a just opportunity to be heard, shall have discretion to extend the date, and to modify the form of payments, such as are to be provided for in accordance with Article 233; but not to cancel any part, except with the specific authority of the several Governments represented upon the Commission. . . .

ARTICLE 428. As a guarantee for the execution of the present Treaty by Germany, the German territory situated to the west of the Rhine, together with the bridgeheads, will be occupied by Allied and Associated troops for a period of fifteen years from the coming into force of the present Treaty. . . .

ARTICLE 431. If before the expiration of the period of fifteen years Germany complies with all the undertakings resulting from the present Treaty, the occupying forces will be withdrawn immediately.

SOURCE. United States, 66th Congress, 1st Session, Senate Document No. 49, *Treaty of Peace with Germany*, Washington, 1919.

e. JOHN MAYNARD KEYNES, FROM *THE ECONOMIC CONSEQUENCES OF THE PEACE*, 1920

WORLD WAR I was an agonizing, immensely destructive experience for Europe, and to many thoughtful people the Peace of Versailles did little but to aggravate the calamity. The economic consequences of the war and the peace were forecast in dark colors by the great economist, John Maynard Keynes, immediately after the Versailles settlement. His analysis, only slightly more pessimistic than the reality, does much to explain Europe's political and economic turmoil and the rise of totalitarian regimes during the interwar years.

This chapter must be one of pessimism. The Treaty includes no provisions for the economic rehabilitation of Europe,—nothing to make the defeated Central Empires into good neighbors, nothing to stabilize the new States of Europe, nothing to reclaim Russia; nor does it promote in any way a compact of economic solidarity amongst the Allies themselves; no arrangement was reached at Paris for restoring the disordered finances of France and Italy, or to adjust the systems of the Old World and the New.

The Council of Four[3] paid no attention to these issues, being preoccupied with others,—Clemenceau to crush the economic life of his enemy, Lloyd George to do a deal and bring home something which would pass muster for a week, the President to do nothing that was not just and right. It is an extraordinary fact that the fundamental economic problems of a Europe starving and disintegrating before their eyes, was the one question in which it was impossible to arouse the interest of the Four. Reparation was their main excursion into the economic field, and they settled it as a problem of theology, of politics, of electoral chicane, from every point of view except that of the economic future of the States whose destiny they were handling.

I leave, from this point onwards, Paris, the Conference, and the Treaty, briefly to consider the present situation of Europe, as the War and the Peace have made it; and it will no longer be part of my purpose to distinguish between the inevitable fruits of the War and the avoidable misfortunes of the Peace.

The essential facts of the situation, as I see them, are expressed simply. Europe consists of the densest aggregation of population in the history of the world. This population is accustomed to a relatively high standard of life, in which, even now, some sections of it anticipate improvement rather than deterioration. In relation to other continents Europe is not self-sufficient; in particular it cannot feed itself. Internally the population is not evenly distributed, but much of it is crowded into a relatively small number of dense industrial centers. This population secured for itself a livelihood before the war, without much margin of surplus, by means of a delicate and immensely complicated organization, of which the foundations were supported by coal, iron, transport, and an unbroken supply of imported food and raw materials from other continents. By the destruction of this organization and the interruption of the stream of supplies, a part of this population is deprived of its means of livelihood. Emigration is not open to the redundant surplus. For it would take years to transport them overseas, even, which is not the case, if countries could be found which were ready to receive them. The danger confronting us, therefore, is the rapid depression of the standard of life of the European populations to a point which will mean actual starvation for some (a point already reached in Russia and approximately reached in Austria). Men will not always die quietly. For starvation, which brings to some lethargy and a helpless despair, drives other tem-

---

[3] The chief victorious powers: France (Georges Clemenceau), England (David Lloyd George), the United States (Woodrow Wilson), and Italy (Vittorio Orlando).

peraments to the nervous instability of hysteria and to a mad despair. And these in their distress may overturn the remnants of organization, and submerge civilization itself in their attēmpts to satisfy desperately the overwhelming needs of the individual. This is the danger against which all our resources and courage and idealism must now co-operate.

On the 13th May, 1919, Count Brockdorff-Rantzau addressed to the Peace Conference of the Allied and Associated Powers the Report of the German Economic Commission charged with the study of the effect of the conditions of Peace on the situation of the German population. "In the course of the last two generations," they reported, "Germany has become transformed from an agricultural State to an industrial State. So long as she was an agricultural State, Germany could feed forty million inhabitants. As an industrial State she could insure the means of subsistence for a population of sixty-seven millions; and in 1913 the importation of foodstuffs amounted, in round figures, to twelve million tons. Before the war a total of fifteen million persons in Germany provided for their existence by foreign trade, navigation, and the use, directly or indirectly, of foreign raw material." After rehearsing the main relevant provisions of the Peace Treaty the report continues: "After this diminution of her products, after the economic depression resulting from the loss of her colonies, her merchant fleet and her foreign investments, Germany will not be in a position to import from abroad an adequate quantity of raw material. An enormous part of German industry will, therefore, be condemned inevitably to destruction. The need of importing foodstuffs will increase considerably at the same time that the possibility of satisfying this demand is as greatly diminished. In a very short time, therefore, Germany will not be in a position to give bread and work to her numerous millions of inhabitants, who are prevented from earning their livelihood by navigation and trade. These persons should emigrate, but this is a material impossibility, all the more because many countries and the most important ones will oppose any German immigration. To put the Peace conditions into execution would logically involve, therefore, the loss of several millions of persons in Germany. This catastrophe would not be long in coming about, seeing that the health of the population has been broken down during the War by the Blockade, and during the Armistice by the aggravation of the Blockade of famine. No help, however great, or over however long a period it were continued, could prevent these deaths *en masse.*" "We do not know, and indeed we doubt," the report concludes, "whether the Delegates of the Allied and Associated Powers realize the inevitable consequences which will take place if Germany, an industrial State, very thickly populated, closely bound up with the economic system of the world, and under the necessity of importing enormous quantities of raw material and foodstuffs, suddenly finds herself pushed back to the phase of her development, which corresponds to her economic condition and the numbers of her population as they were half a century ago. Those who sign this Treaty will sign the death sentence of many millions of German men, women and children."

I know of no adequate answer to these words.

SOURCE. John Maynard Keynes, *The Economic Consequences of the Peace*, pp. 226–230. Copyright 1920 by Harcourt Brace Jovanovich, Inc.; renewed, 1948, by Lydia Lopokova Keynes. Reprinted by permission of Harcourt Brace Jovanovich, Inc. and Macmillan London and Basingstoke.

f. T. S. ELIOT, "THE HOLLOW MEN"

T. S. ELIOT'S POEM, "THE HOLLOW MEN," expresses the bitter disillusionment of European man in the postwar world.

The Hollow Men

A penny for the Old Guy

I

We are the hollow men
We are the stuffed men
Leaning together
Headpiece filled with straw. Alas!
Our dried voices, when
We whisper together
Are quiet and meaningless
As wind in dry grass
Or rats' feet over broken glass
In our dry cellar

Shape without form, shade without colour,
Paralysed force, gesture without motion;

Those who have crossed
With direct eyes, to death's other Kingdom
Remember us—if at all—not as lost
Violent souls, but only
As the hollow men
The stuffed men.

II

Eyes I dare not meet in dreams
In death's dream kingdom

These do not appear:
There, the eyes are
Sunlight on a broken column
There, is a tree swinging
And voices are
In the wind's singing
More distant and more solemn
Than a fading star.
Let me be no nearer
In death's dream kingdom
Let me also wear
Such deliberate disguises
Rat's coat, crowskin, crossed staves
In a field
Behaving as the wind behaves
No nearer—

Not that final meeting
In the twilight kingdom

III

This is the dead land
This is cactus land
Here the stone images
Are raised, here they receive
The supplication of a dead man's hand
Under the twinkle of a fading star.

Is it like this
In death's other kingdom
Waking alone
At the hour when we are
Trembling with tenderness
Lips that would kiss
Form prayers to broken stone.

IV

The eyes are not here
There are no eyes here
In this valley of dying stars
In this hollow valley
This broken jaw of our lost kingdoms

In this last of meeting places
We grope together
And avoid speech
Gathered on this beach of the tumid river

Sightless, unless
The eyes reappear
As the perpetual star
Multifoliate rose
Of death's twilight kingdom
The hope only
Of empty men.

      V

Here we go round the prickly pear
Prickly pear prickly pear
Here we go round the prickly pear
At five o'clock in the morning.

Between the idea
And the reality
Between the motion
And the act
Falls the Shadow

                                        For Thine is the Kingdom

Between the conception
And the creation
Between the emotion
And the response
Falls the Shadow

                                                Life is very long

Between the desire
And the spasm
Between the potency
And the existence
Between the essence
And the descent
Falls the Shadow

                                        For Thine is the Kingdom

For Thine is
Life is
For Thine is the

This is the way the world ends
This is the way the world ends
This is the way the world ends
Not with a bang but a whimper.

SOURCE. T. S. Eliot, *Collected Poems, 1909–1962,* New York, Copyright, 1936. Harcourt Brace Jovanovich, Inc.; copyright 1963, 1964 by T. S. Eliot. Reprinted by permission of Harcourt Brace Jovanovich, Inc., and Faber & Faber Ltd.

Chapter 14

RUSSIAN COMMUNISM IN THE INTERWAR YEARS

a. LENIN ON THE COMMUNIST PROGRAMME, 2ND CONGRESS OF THE THIRD COMMUNIST INTERNATIONAL, MOSCOW, 1920

THE RISE OF THE BOLSHEVIKS to power in Russia in the October Revolution of 1917 marked the establishment of the first Communist state. We have already encountered the Communist philosophy in an earlier section (Chapter 7) and have seen how Lenin developed his interpretation of Communist ideology on strict Marxist lines. At the Second Congress of the Third Communist International, Moscow, 1920, Lenin set forth the revolutionary programme of international Communism in uncompromising terms.

1. A characteristic feature of the present moment in the development of the international Communist movement is the fact that in all the capitalist countries the best representatives of the revolutionary proletariat have completely understood the fundamental principles of the Communist International, namely, the dictatorship of the proletariat and the power of the Soviets; and with a loyal enthusiasm have placed themselves on the side of the Communist International. A still more important and great step forward is the unlimited sympathy with these principles manifested by the wider masses not only of the proletariat of the towns, but also by the advanced portion of the agrarian workers.

On the other hand two mistakes or weaknesses in the extraordinarily rapidly increasing international Communist movement have shown themselves. One very serious weakness directly dangerous to the success of the cause of the liberation of the proletariat consists in the fact that some of the old leaders and old parties of the Second International—partly half-unconsciously yielding to the wishes and pressures of the masses, partly consciously deceiving them in order to preserve their former role of agents and supporters of the bourgeoisie inside the Labor movement—are declaring their conditional or even unconditional affiliation to the Third International, while remaining, in reality, in the whole practice of their party and political work, on the level of the Second International. Such a state of things is absolutely inadmissible, because it demoralizes the masses, hinders the development of a strong Communist Party, and lowers their respect for the Third International by threatening repetition of such betrayals as that of the Hungarian Social-Democrats, who had rapidly assumed the disguise of Communists. The second much less important mistake, which is, for the most part, a malady inherent in the party growth of the movement, is the tendency to be extremely "left," which leads to an erroneous valuation of the role and duties of the party in respect to the class and to the mass, and of the obligation of the revolutionary Communists to work in the bourgeois parliaments and reactionary labor unions.

The duty of the Communists is not to gloss over any of the weaknesses of their movement, but to criticize them openly, in order to get rid of them promptly and radically. To this end it is necessary, 1) to establish concretely, especially on the basis of the already acquired practical experience, the meaning of the term: "Dictatorship of the Proletariat" and "Soviet Power," and, 2) to point out what could and should be in all countries the immediate and systematic preparatory work to realizing these formulas; and, 3) to indicate the ways and means of curing our movement of its defects.

2. The victory of Socialism over Capitalism—as the first step to Communism—demands the accomplishment of the three following tasks by the proletariat, as the only really revolutionary class:

The first step is to lay low the exploiters, and above all the bourgeoisie as their chief economic and political representative; to defeat them completely; to crush their resistance; to render impossible any attempts on their part to reimpose the yoke of capitalism and wage-slavery.

The second is to inspire and lead in the footsteps of the revolutionary advance guard of the proletariat, its Communist party—not only the whole proletariat or the great majority, but the entire mass of workers and those exploited by capital; to enlighten, organize, instruct, and discipline them during the course of the bold and mercilessly firm struggle against the exploiters; to wrench this enormous majority of the population in all the capitalist countries out of their state of dependence on the bourgeoisies; to instill in them, through practical experience, confidence in the leading role of the proletariat and its revolutionary advance guard. The third is to neutralize or render harmless the inevitable fluctuations between the bourgeoisie and the proletariat, between bourgeois democracy and Soviet Power, on the part of that rather numerous class in all advanced countries—although constituting a minority of the population—the small owners and proprietors in agriculture, industry, commerce, and the corresponding layers of intellectuals, employees, and so on.

The first and second tasks are independent ones, demanding each of them their special methods of action in respect to the exploiters and to the exploited. The third task results from the two first, demanding only a skilful, timely, supple combination of the methods of the first and second kind, depending on the concrete circumstances of each separate case of fluctuation.

3. Under the circumstances which have been created in the whole world, and especially in the most advanced, most powerful, most enlightened and freest capitalist countries by militarist imperialism—oppression of colonies and weaker nations, the universal imperialist slaughter, the "peace" of Versailles—to admit the idea of a voluntary submission of the capitalists to the will of the majority of the exploited, of a peaceful, reformist passage to Socialism, is not only to give proof of an extreme petty bourgeois stupidity, but it is a direct deception of the workmen, a disguisal of capitalist wage-slavery, a concealment of the truth. This truth is that the bourgeoisie, the most enlightened and democratic portion of the bourgeoisie, is even now not stopping at deceit and crime, at the slaughter of millions of workmen and peasants, in order to retain the right of private ownership over the means of production. Only a violent defeat of the bourgeoisie, the confiscation of its property, the annihilation of the entire bourgeois governmental apparatus, parliamentary, judicial, military, bureaucratic, administrative, municipal, etc., even the individual exile or internment of the most stubborn and dangerous exploiters, the establishment of a strict control over them for the repression of all inevitable attempts at resistance and restoration of capitalist slavery—only such measures will be able to guarantee the complete submission of the whole class of exploiters.

On the other hand, it is the same disguising of capitalism and bourgeois democracy, the same deceiving of the workmen, when the old parties and old leaders of the Second International admit the idea that the majority of the workers and exploited will be able to acquire a clear Socialist consciousness, firm Socialist convictions and character under the conditions of capitalist enslavement, under the yoke of the bourgeoisie, which assumes an endless variety of forms—the more refined and at the same time the more cruel and pitiless, the more cultured the given capitalist nation. In reality it is only when the advance guard of the proletariat, supported by the whole class as the only revolutionary one, or a majority of the same, will have overthrown the exploiters, crushed them, freed all the exploited from their position of slaves, improved their conditions of life immediately at the expense of the expropriated capitalists—only after that, and during the very course of the acute class struggle, it will be possible to bring about the enlightenment, education and organization of the wildest masses of workers and exploited around the proletariat, under its influence and direction; to cure them of their egotism, their non-solidarity, their vices and weaknesses engendered by private ownership, and to transform them into free workers.

4. For victory over capitalism a correct correlation between the leading Communist Party—the revolutionary class, the proletariat—and the masses, i.e., the whole mass of workers and exploited, is essential. If the Communist Party is really the advance guard of the revolutionary class, if it includes the best representatives of the class, if it consists of perfectly conscious and loyal Communists, enlightened by experience gained in the stubborn revolutionary struggle—if it can be bound indissolubly with the entire life of its class, and through the latter with the whole mass of the exploited, and if it can inspire full confidence in this class and this mass, only then is it capable of leading the proletariat in the pitiless, decisive, and final struggle against all the forces of capitalism. On the other hand, only under the leadership of such a Party will the proletariat be able to employ all the forces of its revolutionary onslaught, nullifying the inevitable apathy and partial resistance of the insignificant minority of the demoralized labor aristocracy, the old trade-union and guild leaders, etc. Only then will the proletariat be able to display its power which is immeasurably greater than its share in the population, by reason of the economic organization of capitalist society itself. Lastly, only when practically freed from the yoke of the bourgeoisie and the bourgeois governing apparatus, only after acquiring the possibility of freely (from all capitalist exploitation) organizing into its own Soviets, will the mass—i.e., the total of all the workers and exploited—employ for the first time in history all the initiative and energy of tens of millions of people, formerly crushed by capitalism. Only when the Soviets will become the only State apparatus, will effectual participation in the administration be realized for the entire mass of the exploited, who, even under the most cultured and free bourgeois democracy, remain practically excluded from participation in the administration. Only in the Soviets does the mass really begin to study, not out of books, but out of its own practical experience, the work of Socialist construction, the creation of a new social discipline, a free union of free workers.

6. The conquest of political power by the proletariat does not put a stop to its class struggle against the bourgeoisie; on the contrary, it makes the struggle especially broad, acute, and pitiless. All the groups, parties, leaders of the Labor movement, fully or partially on the side of reformism, the "center," and so on, turn inevitably, during the most acute periods of the struggle, either to the side of the bourgeoisie or to that of the wavering ones, and the most dangerous are added to the number of the unreliable friends of the vanquished proletariat. Therefore the preparation of the dictatorship of the proletariat demands not only an increased struggle against all reformists and "centrist" tendencies, but a modification of the nature of this struggle.

The struggle should not be limited to an explanation of the fallacy of such tendencies, but it should stubbornly and mercilessly denounce any leader in the Labor movement who may be manifesting such tendencies, otherwise the proletariat will not know whom it must trust in the most decisive struggle against the bourgeoisie. The struggle is such, that the slightest hesitation or weakness in the denunciation of those who show themselves to be reformists or "centrists," means a direct increase of the danger that the power of the proletariat may be overthrown by the bourgeoisie, which will on the morrow utilize in favor of the counter-revolution all that which to short-sighted people appears only as a "theoretical difference of opinion" to-day.

7. In particular one cannot stop at the usual doctrinaire refutation of all "collaboration" between the proletariat and the bourgeoisie:

The simple defense of "liberty and equality," under the condition of preserving the right of private ownership of the means of production, becomes transformed under the conditions of the dictatorship of the proletariat—which will never be able to suppress completely all private ownership—into a "collaboration" with the bourgeoisie, which undermines directly the power of the working class. The dictatorship of the proletariat means the strengthening and defense, by means of the ruling power of the State, of the "non-liberty" of the exploiter to continue his work of oppression and exploitation, the "inequality" of the proprietor (i.e., of the person who has taken for himself personally the means of production created by public labor and the proletariat). That which before the victory of the proletariat seems but a theoretical difference of opinion on the question of "democracy," becomes inevitably on the morrow of the victory, a question which can only be decided by force of arms. Consequently, without a radical modification of the whole nature of the struggle against the "centrists" and "defenders of democracy," even a preliminary preparation of the mass for the realization of a dictatorship of the proletariat is impossible.

8. The dictatorship of the proletariat is the most decisive and revolutionary form of class struggle between the proletariat and the bourgeoisie. Such a struggle can be successful only when the revolutionary advance guard of the proletariat leads the majority. The preparation of the dictatorship of the proletariat demands, therefore, not only the elucidation of the bourgeois nature of all reformism, all defense of "democracy," with the preservation of the right to the ownership of the means of production; not only the denunciation of such tendencies, which in practice mean the defense of the bourgeoisie inside the Labor movement—but it demands also the replacing of the old leaders by Communists in all kinds of proletarian organizations, not only political, but industrial, cooperative, educational, etc. The more lasting, complete, and solid the rule of the bourgeois democracy has been in any country, the more has it been possible for the bourgeoisie to appoint as labor leaders men who have been educated by it, imbued with its views and prejudices and very frequently directly or indirectly bribed by it. It is necessary to remove all these representatives of the Labor aristocracy, all such "bour-

geois" workmen, from their posts and replace them by even inexperienced workers, so long as these are in unity with the exploited masses, and enjoy the latter's confidence in the struggle against the exploiters. The dictatorship of the proletariat will demand the appointment of such inexperienced workmen to the most responsible State functions, otherwise the rule of the Labor government will be powerless and it will not have the support of the masses.

9. The dictatorship of the proletariat is the most complete realization of a leadership over all workers and exploited, who have been oppressed, beaten down, crushed, intimidated, dispersed, deceived by the class of capitalists on the part of the only class prepared for such a leading role by the whole history of capitalism. Therefore the preparation of the dictatorship of the proletariat must begin immediately and in all places by means of the following methods among others:

In every organization, union association—beginning with the proletarian ones at first, and afterwards in all those of the non-proletarian workers and exploited masses (political, professional, military, co-operative, educational, sporting, etc., etc.) must be formed groups or nuclei of Communists—mostly open ones, but also secret ones which become necessary in each case when the arrest or exile of their members or the dispersal of their organization is threatened; and these nuclei, in close contact with one another and with the central Party, exchanging experiences, carrying on the work of propaganda, campaign, organization, adapting themselves to all the branches of social life, to all the various forms and subdivisions of the working masses, must systematically train themselves, the Party, the class, and the masses by such multiform work.

At the same time it is most important to work out practically the necessary methods on the one hand in respect to the "leaders" or responsible representatives, who are very frequently hopelessly infected with petty bourgeois and imperialist prejudices; on the other hand, in respect to the masses, who, especially after the imperialist slaughter, are mostly inclined to listen to and accept the doctrine of the necessity of leadership of the proletariat as the only way out of capitalistic enslavement. The masses must be approached with patience and caution, and with an understanding of the peculiarities, the special psychology of each layer, each profession of these masses.

10. In particular one of the groups or nuclei of the Communists deserves the exclusive attention and care of the party, namely, the parliamentary faction, i.e., the group of members of the Party who are members of bourgeois representative institutions. . . . from this very tribune, the Communists must carry on their work of propaganda, agitation, organization, explaining to the masses why the dissolution of the bourgeois parliament (Constituent Assembly) by the national Congress of Soviets was a legitimate proceeding at the time in Russia (as it will be in all countries in due time). . . .

11. One of the chief causes of difficulty in the revolutionary Labor movement in the advanced capitalist countries lies in the fact that owing to colonial dominions and super-dividends of a financial capital, etc., capital has been able to attract a comparatively more solid and broader group of a small minority of the labor aristocracy. The latter enjoy better conditions of pay and are most of all impregnated with the spirit of professional narrow-mindedness, bourgeois and imperialist prejudices. This is the true social "support" of the Second International reformists and centrists, and at the present moment almost the chief social support of the bourgeoisie.

Not even preliminary preparation of the proletariat for the overthrow of the bourgeoisie is possible without an immediate, systematic, widely organized and open struggle against the group which undoubtedly—as experience has already proved—will furnish plenty of men for the White Guards of the bourgeoisie after the victory of the proletariat. All the parties adhering to the Third International must at all costs put into practice the mottoes: "deeper into the masses," "in closer contact with the masses," understanding by the word "masses" the entire mass of workers and those exploited by capitalism, especially the less organized and enlightened. . . .

12. For all countries, even for most free "legal" and "peaceful" ones in the sense of a lesser acuteness in the class struggle, the period has arrived, when it has become absolutely necessary for every Communist party to join systematically lawful and unlawful work, lawful and unlawful organization. . . . It is especially necessary to carry on unlawful work in the army, navy, and police, as, after the imperialist slaughter, all the governments in the world are becoming afraid of the national armies, open to all peasants and workingmen, and they are setting up in secret all kinds of select military organizations recruited from the bourgeoisie and especially provided with improved technical equipment.

On the other hand, it is also necessary, in all cases without exception, not to limit oneself to unlawful work, but to carry on also lawful work overcoming all difficulties, founding a lawful press and lawful organizations under the most diverse, and in case of need, frequently changing names.

SOURCE. V. I. Lenin, *Collected Works*, English ed., Moscow, Vol. IX.

b. "DEMOCRACY" IN THE 1936 CONSTITUTION OF THE USSR

ONE OF THE CHARACTERISTICS of twentieth-century politics is the tendency for governments to describe themselves as "democratic." This approach is evident in a Soviet document of November 28, 1936, asserting the democracy of Stalin's 1936 Constitution of the USSR. Russia nevertheless remained a single-party state whose elections and legislative bodies were firmly controlled by the Communist hierarchy and whose people were kept under the surveillance of the secret police.

Finally, there is one group of critics [who] charge that the draft makes no change in the existing position in the U.S.S.R., that it leaves the dictatorship of the working class intact, does not provide for the freedom of political parties and preserves the present leading position of the Communist Party in the U.S.S.R. At the same time, this group of critics believes that the absence of freedom for parties in the U.S.S.R. is an indication of the violation of fundamental principles of democracy.

I must admit that the Draft New Constitution really does leave in force the regime of the dictatorship of the working class and also leaves unchanged the present leading position of the Communist Party in the U.S.S.R.

If our venerable critics regard this as a shortcoming of the Draft Constitution, this can only be regretted. We Bolsheviks, however, consider this as a merit of the Draft Constitution. As for the freedom of various political parties, we here adhere to somewhat different views. A party is part of a class, its vanguard section. Several parties, and consequently freedom of parties, can only exist in a society, where there are antagonistic classes whose interests are hostile and irreconcilable, where there are, say, capitalists and workers, landlords and peasants, kulaks and poor peasants, and so on. But in the U.S.S.R. there are no longer such classes as capitalists, landlords, kulaks and so on. There are only two classes in the U.S.S.R., workers and peasants, whose interests are not only not antagonistic, but on the contrary, are amicable. Consequently, in the U.S.S.R. there is no ground for the existence of several parties, not therefore, for the existence of freedom for such parties.

In the U.S.S.R. there are grounds for only one party, the Communist Party. In the U.S.S.R. only one party can exist, the Communist Party, a party which boldly defends the interests of workers and peasants to the very end. And there can hardly be any doubts about the fact that it defends the interests of these classes not so badly.

They talk about democracy, but what is democracy? Democracy in capitalist countries where there are antagonistic classes is, in the last analysis, democracy for the strong, democracy for a propertied minority. Democracy in the U.S.S.R., on the other hand, is democracy for the toilers, is democracy for all. But from this it follows that the principles of democracy are violated, not by the draft of a new Constitution of the U.S.S.R., but by bourgeois constitutions. This is why I think that the Constitution of the U.S.S.R. is the only thoroughly democratic Constitution in the world.

SOURCE. *International Press Correspondence,* English edition, November 28, 1936, p. 139.

Chapter 15

DEPRESSION, FASCISM, AND NAZISM

a. THE GREAT DEPRESSION: ROOSEVELT'S INAUGURAL ADDRESS, 1933

IN 1929 THE COLLAPSE of the American stock market, aggravating economic problems already existing in Europe, brought on a great worldwide depression that lasted through the greater part of the 1930's. Domestic economic crises caused national leaders such as President Roosevelt to turn away from the liberal idea of international commercial cooperation and freedom of trade. The result was a destructive global trade war that worsened the economic picture in Europe and America. Traditional doctrines of political and economic liberalism, undermined by the horrors of World War I, were further discredited by the chaos of depression and social unrest, in the midst of which Hitler led his Nazi party to power in Germany.

In his Inaugural Address of March 4, 1933, President Franklin D. Roosevelt analyzed the depression in America and suggested several lines of action against it, all of which represent modifications or rejections of the old liberal doctrines of Adam Smith and his followers: for example, "the less government the better," an uncontrolled free-enterprise economy, and unrestricted international trade.

I am certain that my fellow Americans expect that on my induction into the Presidency I will address them with a candor and a decision which the present situation of our Nation impels. This is preeminently the time to speak the truth, the whole truth, frankly and boldly. Nor need we shrink from honestly facing conditions in our country today. This great Nation will endure as it has endured, will revive and will prosper. So, first of all, let me assert my firm belief that the only thing we have to fear is fear itself—nameless, unreasoning, unjustified terror which paralyzes needed efforts to convert retreat into advance. In every dark hour of our national life a leadership of frankness and vigor has met with that understanding and support of the people themselves which is essential to victory. I am convinced that you will again give that support to leadership in these critical days.

In such a spirit on my part and on yours we face our common difficulties. They concern, thank God, only material things. Values have shrunken to fantastic levels; taxes have risen; our ability to pay has fallen; government of all kinds is faced by serious curtailment of income; the means of exchange are frozen in the currents of trade; the withered leaves of industrial enterprise lie on every side; farmers find no markets for their produce; the savings of many years in thousands of families are gone.

More important, a host of unemployed citizens face the grim problem of existence, and an equally great number toil with little return. Only a foolish optimist can deny the dark realities of the moment.

Yet our distress comes from no failure of substance. We are stricken by no plague of locusts. Compared with the perils which our forefathers conquered because they believed and were not afraid, we have still much to be thankful for. Nature still offers her bounty and human efforts have multiplied it. Plenty is at our doorstep, but a generous use of it languishes in the very sight of the supply. Primarily this is because rulers of the exchange of mankind's goods have failed through their own stubbornness and their own incompetence, have admitted their failure, and have abdicated. Practices of the unscrupulous money changers stand indicted in the court of public opinion, rejected by the hearts and minds of men.

True they have tried, but their efforts have been cast in the pattern of an outworn tradition. Faced by failure of credit they have proposed only the lending of more money. Stripped of the lure of profit by which to induce our people to follow their false leadership, they have resorted to exhortations, pleading tearfully for restored confidence. They know only the rules of a generation of self-seekers. They have no vision, and when there is no vision the people perish.

The money changers have fled from their high seats in the temple of our civilization. We may now restore that temple to the ancient truths. The measure of the restoration lies in the extent to which we apply social values more noble than mere monetary profit.

Happiness lies not in the mere possession of money; it lies in the joy of achievement, in the thrill of creative effort. The joy and moral stimulation of work no longer must be forgotten in the mad chase of evanescent profits. These dark days will be worth all they cost us if they teach us that our true destiny is not to be ministered unto but to minister to ourselves and to our fellow men.

Recognition of the falsity of material wealth as the standard of success goes hand in hand with the abandonment of the false belief that public office and high political position are to be valued only by the standards of pride of place and personal profit; and there must be an end to a conduct in banking and in business which too often has given to a sacred trust the likeness of callous and selfish wrongdoing. Small wonder that confidence languishes, for it thrives only on honesty, on honor, on the sacredness of obligations, on faithful protection, on unselfish performance; without them it cannot live.

Restoration calls, however, not for changes in ethics alone. This Nation asks for action, and action now.

Our greatest primary task is to put people to work. This is no unsolvable problem if we face it wisely and courageously. It can be acomplished in part by direct recruiting by the Government itself, treating the task as we would treat the emergency of a war, but at the same time, through this employment, accomplishing greatly needed projects to stimulate and reorganize the use of our natural resources.

Hand in hand with this we must frankly recognize the overbalance of population in our industrial centers and, by engaging on a national scale in a redistribution, endeavor to provide a better use of the land for those best fitted for the land. The task can be helped by definite efforts to raise the values of agricultural products and with this the power to purchase the output of our cities. It can be helped by preventing realistically the tragedy of the growing loss through foreclosure of our small homes and our farms. It can be helped by insistence that the Federal, State, and local governments act forthwith on the demand that their cost be drastically reduced. It can be helped by the unifying of relief activities which today are often scattered, uneconomical, and unequal. It can be helped by national planning for and supervision of all forms of transportation and of communications and other utilities which have a definitely public character. There are many ways in which it can be helped, but it can never be helped merely by talking about it. We must act 'and act quickly.

Finally, in our progress toward a resumption of work we require two safeguards against a return of the evils of the old order: there must be a strict supervision of all banking and credits and investments, so that there will be an end to speculation with other people's money; and there must be provision for an adequate but sound currency.

These are the lines of attack. I shall presently urge upon a new Congress, in special session, detailed measures for their fulfillment, and I shall seek the immediate assistance of the several States.

Through this program of action we address ourselves to putting our own national house in order and making income balance outgo. Our international trade relations, though vastly important, are in point of time and necessity secondary to the establishment of a sound national economy. I favor as a practical policy the putting of first things first. I shall spare no effort to restore world trade by international economic readjustment, but the emergency at home cannot wait on that accomplishment.

b. MUSSOLINI, "THE POLITICAL AND SOCIAL DOCTRINE OF FASCISM," 1932

BENITO MUSSOLINI (1883–1945) rose to power in Italy in 1922, well before the coming of the Great Depression. His rightwing ideology was vague and incoherent, based on the cloudy concept of "national rebirth" and on a fervent hostility to leftist radicalism. In an article in the Enciclopaedia Italiana *(1932), Mussolini clarified Fascist doctrine and presented in a somewhat more systematic form his notions of activism, militarism, ultra-nationalism, and human nature (which Mussolini sees in vaguely Nietzschean terms).*

When, in the now distant March of 1919, I summoned a meeting at Milan through the columns of the *Popolo d'Italia* of the surviving members of the Interventionist Party who had themselves been in action, and who had followed me since the creation of the Fascist Revolutionary Party (which took place in the January of 1915), I had no specific doctrinal attitude in mind. I had a living experience of one doctrine only—that of Socialism, from 1903–4 to the winter of 1914—that is to say, about a decade: and from Socialism itself, even though I had taken part in the movement first as a member of the rank and file and then later as a leader, yet I had no experience of its doctrine in practice. My own doctrine, even in this period, had always been a doctrine of action. . . .

The years which preceded the March to Rome were years of great difficulty, during which the necessity for action did not permit of research or any complete elaboration of doctrine. The battle had to be fought in the towns and villages. There was much discussion, but—what was more important and more sacred—men died. They knew how to die. Doctrine, beautifully defined and carefully elucidated, with headlines and paragraphs, might be lacking; but there was to take its place something more decisive—Faith. Even so, anyone who can recall the events of the time through the aid of books, articles, votes of congresses, and speeches of great and minor importance—anyone who knows how to research and weigh evidence—will find that the fundamentals of doctrine were cast during the years of conflict. It was precisely in those years that Fascist thought armed itself, was refined, and began the great task of organization. The problem of the relation between the individual citizen and the State; the allied problems of authority and liberty; political and social problems as well as those specifically national—a solution was being sought for all these while at the same time the struggle against Liberalism, Democracy, Socialism, and the Masonic bodies was being carried on. . . .

Fascism, the more it considers and observes the future and the development of humanity quite apart from political considerations of the moment, believes neither in the possibility nor the utility of perpetual peace. It thus repudiates the doctrine of Pacifism—born of a renunciation of the struggle and an act of cowardice in the face of sacrifice. War alone brings up to its highest tension all human energy and puts the stamp of nobility upon the peoples who have the courage to meet it. All other trials are substitutes, which never really put men into the position where they have to make the great decision—the alternative of life or death. Thus a doctrine which is founded upon this harmful postulate of peace is hostile to Fascism. And thus hostile to the spirit of Fascism, though accepted for what use they can be in dealing with particular political situations, are all the international leagues and societies which, as history will show, can be scattered to the winds when once strong national feeling is aroused by any motive— sentimental, ideal, or practical. This anti-pacifist spirit is carried by Fascism even into the life of the individual; the proud motto of the Squadrista, *"Me ne frego"* (I do not fear), written on the bandage of the wound, is an act of philosophy not only stoic, the summary of a doctrine not only political—it is the education to combat, the acceptance of the risks which combat implies, and a new way of life for Italy. Thus the Fascist accepts life and loves it, knowing nothing of and despising suicide: he rather conceives of life as duty and struggle and conquest, life which should be high and full, lived for oneself, but above all for others—those who are at hand and those who are far distant, contemporaries, and those who will come after. . . . .

Such a conception of life makes Fascism the complete opposite of that doctrine, the base of the so-called scientific and Marxian Socialism, the materialist conception of history; according to which the history of human civilization can be explained simply through the conflict of interests among the various social groups and by the change and development in the means and instruments of production. That the changes in the economic field—new discoveries of raw materials, new methods of working them, and the inventions of science—have their importance no one can deny; but that these factors are sufficient to explain the history of humanity excluding all others is an absurd delusion. Fascism, now and always, believes in holiness and in heroism; that is to say, in actions influenced by no economic motive, direct or indirect. And if the economic conception of history be denied, according to which theory men are no more than puppets, carried to and fro by the waves of chance, while the real directing forces are quite out of their control, it follows that the existence of an unchangeable and unchanging class war is also denied—the natural progeny of the economic conception of history. And above all Fascism denies that class war can be the preponderant force in the transformation of society. These two fundamental concepts of Socialism being thus refuted, nothing is left of it but the sentimental aspiration—as old as humanity itself—towards a social convention in which the sorrows and sufferings of the humblest shall be alleviated. But here again Fascism repudiates the conception of "economic" happiness, to be realized by Socialism and, as it were, at a given moment in economic evolution to assure to everyone the maximum of well-being. Fascism denies the materialist conception of happiness as a possibility, and abandons it to its inventors, the economists of the first half of the nineteenth century: that is to say, Fascism denies the validity of the equation, well-being = happiness, which would reduce men to the level of animals, caring for one thing only—to be fat and well-fed—and would thus degrade humanity to a purely physical existence.

After Socialism, Fascism combats the whole complex system of democratic ideology, and repudiates it, whether in its theoretical premises or in its practical application. Fascism denies that the majority, by the simple fact that it is a majority, can direct human society; it denies that numbers alone can govern by means of a periodical consultation, and it affirms the immutable, beneficial, and fruitful inequality of mankind, which can never be permanently leveled through the mere operation of a mechanical process such as universal suffrage. The democratic regime may be defined as from time to time giving the people the illusion of sovereignty, while the real effective sovereignty lies in the hands of other concealed and irresponsible forces. Democracy is a regime nominally without a king, but it is ruled by many kings—more absolute, tyrannical, and ruinous than one sole king, even though a tyrant. This explains why Fascism, having first in 1922 (for reasons of expediency) assumed an attitude tending towards republicanism, renounced this point of view before the March to Rome; being convinced that the question of political form is not today of prime importance, and after having studied the examples of monarchies and republics past and present reached the conclusion that monarchy or republicanism are not to be judged, as it were, by an absolute standard; but that they represent forms in which the evolution—political, historical, traditional, or psychological—of a particular country has expressed itself.

Fascism has taken up an attitude of complete opposition to the doctrines of Liberalism, both in the political field and the field of economics. There should be no undue exaggeration (simply with the object of immediate success in controversy) of the importance of Liberalism in the last century, nor should what was but one among many theories which appeared in that period be put forward as a religion for humanity for all time, present and to come. . . . Germany attained her national unity quite outside the doctrines of Liberalism—a doctrine which seems entirely foreign to the German mind, a mind essentially monarchic—while Liberalism is the logical and, indeed, historical forerunner of anarchy. The stages in the achievement of German unity are the three wars of '64, '66, and '70, which were guided by such "Liberals" as Von Moltke and Bismarck. As for Italian unity, its debt to Liberalism is completely inferior in contrast to that which it owes to the work of Mazzini and Garibaldi, who were not Liberals. Had it not been for the intervention of the anti-Liberal Bismarck at Sadowa and Sedan it is very probable that we should never have gained the province of Venice in '66, or been able to enter Rome in '70. From 1870 to 1914 a period began during which even the very high priests of the religion themselves had to recognize the gathering twilight of their faith—defeated as it was by the decadence of literature and atavism in practice—that is to say, Nationalism, Futurism, Fascism. The era of Liberalism, after having accumulated an infinity of Gordian knots, tried to untie them in the slaughter of the World War—and never has any religion demanded of its votaries such a monstrous sacrifice. Perhaps the Liberal Gods were athirst for Blood? But now, today, the Liberal faith must shut the doors of its deserted temples, deserted because the peoples of the world realize that its worship—agnostic in the field of economics and indifferent in the field of politics and morals—well lead, as it has already led, to certain ruin. In addition to this, let it be pointed out that all the political hopes of the present day are anti-Liberal, and it is therefore supremely ridiculous to try to classify this sole creed as outside the judgment of history, as though history were a hunting ground reserved for the professors of Liberalism alone—as though Liberalism were the final unalterable verdict of civilization.

But the Fascist negation of Socialism, Democracy, and Liberalism must not be taken to mean that Fascism desires to lead the world back to the state of affairs before 1789, the date which seems to be indicated as the opening year of the succeeding semi-Liberal century: we do not desire to turn back.

. . . Absolute monarchy has been and can never return, any more than blind acceptance of ecclesiastical authority.

So, too, the privileges of the feudal system "have been," and the division of society into castes impenetrable from outside, and with no intercommunication among themselves: the Fascist conception of authority has nothing to do with such a polity. A party which entirely governs a nation is a fact entirely new to history, there are no possible references or parallels. Fascism uses in its construction whatever elements in the Liberal, Social, or Democratic doctrines still have a living value; it maintains what may be called the certainties which we owe to history, but it rejects all the rest—that is to say, the conception that there can be any doctrine of unquestioned efficacy for all times and all peoples. Given that the nineteenth century was the century of Socialism, Liberalism, and Democracy: political doctrines pass, but humanity remains; and it may rather be expected that this will be a century of Fascism. For if the nineteenth century was the century of individualism (Liberalism always signifying individualism) it may be expected that this will be the century of collectivism, and hence the century of the State. It is a perfectly logical deduction that a new doctrine can utilize all the still vital elements of previous doctrines.

No doctrine has ever been born completely new, completely defined and owing nothing to the past; no doctrine can boast a character of complete originality; it must always derive, if only historically, from the doctrines which have preceded it and develop into further doctrines which will follow. Thus the scientific Socialism of Marx is the heir of the Utopian Socialism of Fourier, of the Owens and of Saint-Simon; thus again the Liberalism of the eighteenth century is linked with all the advanced thought of the seventeenth century, and thus the doctrines of Democracy are the heirs of the Encyclopedists. Every doctrine tends to direct human activity towards a determined objective; but the action of men also reacts upon the doctrine, transform it, adapts it to new needs, or supersedes it with something else. A doctrine then must be no mere exercise in words, but a living act; and thus the value of Fascism lies in the fact that it is veined with pragmatism, but at the same time has a will to exist and a will to power, a firm front in face of the reality of "violence."

The foundation of Fascism is the conception of the State, its character, its duty, and its aim. Fascism conceives of the State as an absolute, in comparison with which all individuals or groups are relative, only to be conceived of in their relation to the State. The conception of the Liberal State is not that of a directing force, guiding the play and development, both material and spiritual, of a collective body, but merely a force limited to the function of recording results: on the other hand, the Fascist State is itself conscious, and has itself a will and a personality—thus it may be called the "ethic" State. In i929, at the first five-yearly assembly of the Fascist regime, I said:

"For us Fascists, the State is not merely a guardian, preoccupied solely with the duty of assuring the personal safety of the citizens; nor is it an organization with purely material aims, such as to guarantee a certain level of well-being and peaceful conditions of life; for a mere council of administration would be sufficient to realize such objects. Nor is it a purely political creation, divorced from all contact with the complex material reality which makes up the life of the individual and the life of the people as a whole. The State, as conceived of and as created by Fascism, is a spiritual and moral fact in itself, since its political, juridical, and economic organization of the nation is a concrete thing: and such an organization must be in its origins and development a manifestation of the spirit. The State is the guarantor of security both internal and external, but it is also the custodian and transmitter of the spirit of the people, as it has grown up through the centuries in language, in customs, and in faith. And the State is not only a living reality of the present, it is also linked with the past and above all with the future, and thus transcending the brief limits of individual life, it represents the immanent spirit of the nation. The forms in which States express themselves may change, but the necessity for such forms is eternal. It is the State which educates its citizens in civic virtue, gives them a consciousness of their mission and welds them into unity; harmonizing their various interests through justice, and transmitting to future generations the mental conquests of science, of art, of law and the solidarity of humanity. It leads men from primitive tribal life to the highest expression of human power which is Empire; it links up through the centuries the names of those of its members who have died for its existence and in obedience to its laws, it holds up the memory of the leaders who have increased its territory and the geniuses who have illuminated it with glory as an example to be followed by future generations. When the conception of the State declines, and disunifying and centrifugal tendencies prevail, whether of individuals or of particular groups, the nations where such phenomena appear are in their decline."

From 1929 until today, evolution, both political and economic, has everywhere gone to prove the validity of these doctrinal premises. Of such gigantic importance is the State. It is the force which alone can provide a solution to the dramatic contradictions of capitalism. . . . Fascism desires the State to be a strong and organic body, at the same time reposing upon broad and popular support. The Fascist State has drawn into itself even the economic activities of the nation, and, through the corporative social and educational institutions created by it, its influence reaches every aspect of the national life and includes, framed in their respective organizations, all the political, economic and spiritual forces of the nation. A State which reposes upon the support of millions of individuals who recognize its authority, are continually conscious of its power and are ready at once to serve it, is not the old tyrannical State of the medieval lord nor has it anything in common with the absolute governments either before or after 1789. The individual in the Fascist State is not annulled but rather multiplied, just in the same way that a soldier in a regiment is not diminished but rather increased by the number of his comrades. The Fascist State organizes the nation, but leaves a sufficient margin of liberty to the individual; the latter is deprived of all useless and possibly harmful freedom, but retains what is essential; the deciding power in this question cannot be the individual, but the State alone.

The Fascist State is not indifferent to the fact of religion in general, or to that particular and positive faith which is Italian Catholicism. The State professes no theology, but a morality, and in the Fascist State religion is considered as one of the deepest manifestations of the spirit of man; thus it is not only respected but defended and protected. The Fascist State has never tried to create its own God, as at one moment Robespierre and the wildest extremists of the Convention tried to do; nor does it vainly seek to obliterate religion from the hearts of men as does Bolshevism; Fascism respects the

God of the ascetics, the saints and hereos, and equally, God, as He is perceived and worshipped by simple people.

The Fascist State is an embodied will to power and government; the Roman tradition is here an ideal of force in action. According to Fascism, government is not so much a thing to be expressed in territorial or military terms as in terms of morality and the spirit. It must be thought of as an empire—that is to say, a nation which directly or indirectly rules other nations, without the need for conquering a single square yard of territory. For Fascism, the growth of empire, that is to say the expansion of the nation, is an essential manifestation of vitality, and its opposite a sign of decadence. Peoples which are rising, or rising again after a period of decadence, are always imperialist: any renunciation is a sign of decay and of death.

Fascism is the doctrine best adapted to represent the tendencies and the aspirations of a people, like the people of Italy, who are rising again after many centuries of abasement and foreign servitude. But empire demands discipline, the co-ordination of all forces and a deeply felt sense of duty and sacrifice: this fact explains many aspects of the practical working of the regime, the character of many forces in the State, and the necessarily severe measures which must be taken against those who would oppose this spontaneous and inevitable movement of Italy in the twentieth century, and would oppose it by recalling the outworn ideology of the nineteenth century—repudiated wheresoever there has been the courage to undertake great experiments of social and political transformation: for never before has the nation stood more in need of authority, of direction, and of order. If every age has its own characteristic doctrine, there are a thousand signs which point to Fascism as the characteristic doctrine of our time. For if a doctrine must be a living thing, this is proved by the fact that Fascism has created a living faith; and that this faith is very powerful in the minds of men, is demonstrated by those who have suffered and died for it.

Fascism has henceforth in the world the universality of all those doctrines which, in realizing themselves, have represented a stage in the history of the human spirit.

SOURCE. Benito Mussolini in *International Conciliation*, No. 306, January 1935, pp. 5–17. Reprinted by permission of the Carnegie Endowment for International Peace.

c. NAZISM: ADOLF HITLER, SPEECH OF SEPTEMBER 1, 1933

NAZISM, AN IDEOLOGICAL BLOOD-BROTHER TO FASCISM, was the political philosophy of Hitler's National Socialist Party. Nazi thought is developed in a speech by Adolf Hitler, who assumed political control in depression-ridden Germany in 1933 and established the "Third Reich." At Nuremberg on September 1, 1933, Hitler stressed the dangers of Bolshevism, the ineptitude of liberal democracy, and the virility and popular basis of National Socialism.

When in the year 1919 the National Socialist Movement came into being in order to create a new Reich in place of the Marxist-democratic Republic, such an enterprise seemed hopeless and foolish. Above all, the caviling intellectuals with their superficial historical education had no more than a pitying smile for such an undertaking. Most of them very well knew that Germany would fall on evil times. The greater part of the so-called intelligentsia understood very well that the rules of the November Republic were either too evil or too incompetent to lead our people. But they did not recognize that this new regime could not be overcome by those forces which for fifty years have steadily retreated before the attacks of Marxism, finally, in the hour of greatest emergency, to capitulate miserably. Perhaps part of the reason for this was that the political leaders of the nation were aging, outdated. They could not or would not recognize the time necessary for the restoration of the strength of a nation.

Strength cannot be found in an organization which has none. It was therefore an error when in 1919 and 1920 the men who recognized the distress of the Fatherland thought that a change in the leadership of the bourgeois parties would suddenly give them the strength to annihilate the inner enemy. . . .

When one has glorified a false democracy for seventy years, one cannot attempt a dictatorship in the seventy-first year. It leads to ridiculous experiments.

With few exceptions, age destroys the mental as well as the physical powers of generation. Because each man wishes to see for himself the growth and the fruits of his struggle, he seeks for easier, that is, quicker ways to transform his ideas into realities. The rootless intellectual, lacking all understanding of organic development, tries to evade the law of growth by hasty experiments. Nationalism, on the other hand, was ready from the very first to undertake the long and painful task of building up anew the structure which would later destroy Marxism. But because this way was not understood by the superficial intelligence of our politicalized bourgeoisie, the new Movement could at first develop only among those groups who were not miseducated, who were uncomplicated and therefore closer to nature.

What the intellect of the intellectual could not see was grasped immediately by the soul, the heart, the instinct of this simple, primitive, but healthy man. It is another one of the tasks of the future to re-establish the unity between feeling and intellect; that is, to educate an unspoiled generation which will perceive with clear understanding the eternal law of development and at the same time will consciously return to the primitive instinct.

National Socialism directed its appeal for the formation of a new Movement to the broad masses of the people. Its first task was to inspire by suggestion those few whom it had first won over with the belief that they would one day be the saviors of their Fatherland. This problem of educating men to believe and have faith in themselves was as necessary as it was difficult. Men who socially and economically belonged to subordinate, and frequently oppressed groups, had to be given the political conviction that some day they would represent the leadership of the nation.

While the former leaders of the bourgeois world talked about "quite progress" and declaimed profound treatises at tea parties, National Socialism began its march into the heart of the people. We held hundreds of thousands of demonstrations. A hundred and a hundred thousand times our speakers spoke in meeting halls, in small, smoky taverns, and in great sports arenas. And each demonstration not only won us new adherents, but above all made the others firm in their belief and filled them by suggestion with the kind of self-confidence without which success is not possible. The others talked about democracy and kept away from the people. National Socialism talked about authority, but it fought and wrestled with the people as no movement in Germany had ever done.

For all time to come this city shall be the place where our Movement will hold its Party Congress, for it was here that for the first time we proclaimed the new will of Germany. . . .

The National Socialist Revolution has overthrown the republic of treason and perjury, and in its place has created once more a Reich of honor, loyalty, and decency. It is our great good fortune that we did not have to bring about this Revolution as leaders of the "historic minority" against the majority of the German nation. We rejoice that at the end of our struggle but before the final turn in our destiny, the overwhelming majority of the German people had already declared itself for our principles. Thus it was possible to accomplish one of the greatest revolutions in history with hardly any bloodshed. As a result of the splendid organization of the movement which brought about this Revolution, at no moment did we lose control of it.

Aside from the Fascist Revolution in Italy, no similar historic action is comparable in discipline and order with the National Socialist uprising. It is particularly pleasing that today the great majority of the German people stand loyal and united behind the new regime. . . .

Our perilous political situation was accompanied by a no less dangerous economic situation. The rapid decline of the past winter seemed to be leading to a complete collapse. The great historian, Mommsen, once characterized the Jews in the life of nations as a "ferment of decomposition." In Germany this decomposition had already made great progress. National Socialism opposed with fierce resoluteness this creeping "decline of the West," because we were convinced that those inner values which are natural to the civilized nations of Europe, and to our own German nation in particular, had not yet been completely destroyed. . . .

As sole possessor of State power, the Party must recognize that it bears the entire responsibility for the course of German history. The work of education which the Movement must carry on is tremendous. For it is not enough to organize the State in accordance with pacific principles; it is necessary to educate the people inwardly. Only if the people has an intimate sympathy with the principles and methods which inspire and move the organization of its State, will there grow up a living organism instead of a dead, because purely formal and mechanistic, organization.

Among the tasks we face, the most important is the question of eliminating unemployment. The danger in unemployment is not only a material one. It is neither logical, nor moral, nor just, to continue taking away from those who are able to work a part of the fruits of their industry in order to maintain those unable to work—no matter for what reasons they are unable. It is more logical to distribute the work itself instead of distributing wages. No one has a moral right to demand that others should work for him so that he will not have to work himself. Each has a right to demand that the political organization of his nation, the State, find ways and means to give work to all.

We are following paths for which there is hardly any model in history. It is thus at any time possible that one or another measure that we take today may prove unworkable. It is thus all the more necessary to put a stop to that carping criticism which tends only towards disintegration. It is no matter whether a thousand critics live or die, what does matter is whether a people shall be conquered and ruined and in consequence as a community lose its life. All those who since November, 1918, through their mad or criminal action hurled our people into their present misfortunes, those who proclaimed such phrases as "Freedom," "Brotherliness," and "Equality," as the *leitmotiv* of their action—they do not share today the fate and the sufferings of the victims of their policy! Millions of our German fellow-countrymen through them have been given over to the hardest stress imaginable. Need, misery, hunger, do violence to their existence. Those who misled them indeed enjoy abroad the freedom to slander their own people for foreign gold, the liberty to deliver them up to the hatred of their neighbors: they would, if they could, see them attacked and shot down, defenseless, on the battlefield. . . .

The rise and the astonishing final victory of the National Socialist Movement would never have happened if the Party had ever formulated the principle that in our ranks everyone can do as he likes. This watchword of democratic freedom led only to insecurity, indiscipline, and at length to the downfall and destruction of all authority. Our opponents' objection that we, too, once made use of these rights, will not hold water; for we made use of an unreasonable right, which was part and parcel of an unreasonable system, in order to overthrow the unreason of this system. No fruit falls which is not ripe for falling. When old Germany fell, it betrayed its inner weakness, just as the November Republic[1] has revealed its weakness to everyone by now.

By its political education, therefore, the Party will have to fortify the mind of the German people against any tendency to regression. While we deny the parliamentary-democratic principle, we champion most definitely the right of the people itself to determine its own life. In the parliamentary system we do not recognize any true expression of the will of the people, but we see in it a perversion, if not a violation, of that will. The will of a people to maintain its existence appears first and in its most useful form in its best brains.

The greater the tasks with which we are faced, the greater must be the authority of those who must accomplish these tasks. It is important that the self-assurance of the leaders of the whole organizaton in their decisions should arouse in the members and followers of the Party an untroubled confidence. For the people will justifiably never understand it if they are suddenly asked to discuss problems which their leaders cannot cope with. It is conceivable that even wise men should not in questions of special difficulty be able to reach complete clarity. But it means a capitulation of all leadership if it hands over precisely those questions to public discussion and allows the public to state its views. For the leaders thereby imply that the masses have more judgment than they themselves have. This cannot be the attitude of the National Socialist party. The Party must be convinced that it will be able to cope with all problems, that because it has chosen its human material in living struggle, its leaders are politically the most competent men in Germany.

Our Party must follow the same law that it wishes to see the masses of the nation follow. It must, therefore, constantly educate itself to recognize authority, to submit voluntarily to the highest discipline, so that it will be able to educate the followers of the Party to do the same. And in doing this the Party must be hard and logical. . . .

[1] The Weimar Republic, which governed Germany from the end of World War I until the rise of Hitler.

Power and the brutal application of power can accomplish much. But in the long run no state of affairs is secure unless it is firmly rooted in logic. Above all: The National Socialist Movement must profess its faith in that heroism which is content to face all opposition and every trial rather than for a moment to be false to the principles which it has recognized to be right. The Movement must be filled with one fear alone—the fear lest the time should ever come when it could be charged with dishonesty or thoughtlessness.

To save a nation one must think heroically. But the heroic thinker must always be willing to renounce the approval of his contemporaries where truth is at stake.

May the very manner of this demonstration renew our understanding that the Government of the nation must never harden into a purely bureaucratic machine; it must ever remain a living leadership, a leadership which does not view the people as an object of its activity, but which lives within the people, feels with the people and fights for the people. Forms and organizations can pass, but what does and must remain is the living substance of flesh and blood. All of us desire that the German people shall remain forever upon this earth, and we believe that by our struggle we are but carrying out the will of the Creator, who imbued all creatures with the instinct for self-preservation. Long live our nation. Long live the National Socialist party!

d. THE NATIONAL SOCIALIST COMMANDMENTS, 1940

THE THOROUGHGOING AUTHORITARIANISM of the National Socialist Party is illustrated by excerpts from the Nazi Party Organization Book *(1940) dealing with the duties of party members.*

The National Socialist commandments:

The Führer[2] is always right!

Never go against discipline!

Don't waste your time in idle chatter or in self-satisfying criticism, but take hold and do your work!

Be proud but not arrogant!

Let the program be your dogma. It demands of you the greatest devotion to the movement.

You are a representative of the party; control your bearing and your manner accordingly!

Let loyalty and unselfishness be your highest precepts!

[2] Führer is the German word for "leader" and, in the Nazi era, referred specifically to Adolf Hitler.

Practice true comradeship and you will be a true socialist!
Treat your racial comrades as you wish to be treated by them!
In battle be hard and silent!
Spirit is not unruliness!
That which promotes the movement, Germany, and your people, is right!
If you act according to these commandments, you are a true soldier of your
Führer.

SOURCE. *National Socialism,* Washington: U. S. Government Printing Office, 1943, p. 195.

e. NAZI MEDICAL EXPERIMENTS:
TESTIMONY OF DR. FRANZ BLAHA,
A CZECHOSLOVAKIAN PRISONER

*THE UNPARALLELED BARBARISM of the Nazis was not fully compre-
hended until the close of World War II, when Allied armies uncovered the
full horror of the German concentration camps and testimony at the Nuremberg War Crimes Trials disclosed in detail the Nazi medical experiments and
the mass murders of Jews. The next two documents require no further comment.*

From the middle of 1941 to the end of 1942 some 500 operations on healthy
prisoners were performed [at Dachau]. These were for the instructions of the
SS medical students and doctors and included operations on the stomach, gall
bladder and throat. These were performed by students and doctors of only 2
years' training, although they were very dangerous and difficult. Ordinarily
they would not have been done except by surgeons with at least 4 years' surg-
ical practice. Many prisoners died on the operating table and many others
from later complications. I performed autopsies on all of these bodies. The
doctors who supervised these operations were Lang, Muermelstadt, Wolter,
Ramsauer, and Kahr. Standartenführer Dr. Lolling frequently witnessed
these operations.

During my time at Dachau I was familiar with many kinds of medical
experiments carried on there on human victims. These persons were never
volunteers but were forced to submit to such acts. Malaria experiments on
about 1,200 people were conducted by Dr. Klaus Schilling between 1941 and
1945. Schilling was personally ordered by Himmler to conduct these experiments. The victims were either bitten by mosquitoes or given injections of
malaria sporozoites taken from mosquitoes. Different kinds of treatment were
applied including quinine, pyrifer, neosalvarsan, antipyrin, pyramidon, and a
drug called 2516 Behring. I performed autopsies on the bodies of people who

died from these malaria experiments. Thirty to 40 died from the malaria itself. Three hundred to four hundred died later from diseases which were fatal
because of the physical condition resulting from the malaria attacks. In addition there were deaths resulting from poisoning due to overdoses of neosalvarsan and pyramidon. Dr. Schilling was present at my autopsies on the
bodies of his patients.

In 1942 and 1943 experiments on human beings were conducted by Dr.
Sigmund Rascher to determine the effects of changing air pressure. As many
as 25 persons were put at one time into a specially constructed van in which
pressure could be increased or decreased as required. The purpose was to find
out the effects on human beings of high altitude and of rapid descents by par-
achute. Through a window in the van I have seen the people lying on the
floor of the van. Most of the prisoners used died from these experiments, from
internal hemorrhage of the lungs or brain. The survivors coughed blood when
taken out. It was my job to take the bodies out and as soon as they were
found to be dead to send the internal organs to Munich for study. About 400
to 500 prisoners were experimented on. The survivors were sent to invalid
blocks and liquidated shortly afterwards. Only a few escaped.

Rascher also conducted experiments on the effect of cold water on human
beings. This was done to find a way for reviving airmen who had fallen into
the ocean. The subject was placed in ice cold water and kept there until he
was unconscious. Blood was taken from his neck and tested each time his
body temperature dropped one degree. This drop was determined by a rectal
thermometer. Urine was also periodically tested. Some men stood it as long
as 24 to 36 hours. The lowest body temperature reached was 19 degrees cen-
tigrade, but most men died at 25 or 26 degrees. When the men were removed
from the ice water attempts were made to revive them by artificial sunshine,
with hot water, by electrotherapy, or by animal warmth. For this last experiment prostitutes were used and the body of the unconscious man was placed
between the bodies of two women. Himmler was present at one such experiment. I could see him from one of the windows in the street between the
blocks. I have personally been present at some of these cold water experiments when Rascher was absent, and I have seen notes and diagrams on
them in Rascher's laboratory. About 300 persons were used in these experiments. The majority died. Of those who survived, many became mentally
deranged. Those who did not die were sent to invalid blocks and were killed
just as were the victims of the air pressure experiments. I know only two who
survived a Yugoslav and a Pole, both of whom are mental cases.

Liver puncture experiments were performed by Dr. Brachtl on healthy
people and on people who had diseases of the stomach and gall bladder. For
this purpose a needle was jabbed into the liver of a person and a small piece
of the liver was extracted. No anaesthetic was used. The experiment is very
painful and often had serious results, as the stomach or large blood vessels

were often punctured, resulting in hemorrhage. Many persons died of these tests for which Polish, Russian, Czech, and German prisoners were employed. Altogether about 175 people were subjected to these experiments.

Phlegmone experiments were conducted by Dr. Shütz, Dr. Babor, Dr. Kieselwetter and Professor Lauer. Forty healthy men were used at a time, of which twenty were given intramuscular and twenty intravenous injections of pus from diseased persons. All treatment was forbidden for 3 days, by which time serious inflammation and in many cases general blood poisoning had occurred. Then each group was divided again into groups of 10. Half were given chemical treatment with liquid and special pills every 10 minutes for 24 hours. The remainder were treated with sulfanamide and surgery. In some cases all the limbs were amputated. My autopsy also showed that the chemical treatment had been harmful and had even caused perforations of the stomach wall. For these experiments Polish, Czech, and Dutch priests were ordinarily used. Pain was intense in such experiments. Most of the 600 to 800 persons who were used finally died. Most of the others became permanent invalids and were later killed.

In the fall of 1944 there were 60 to 80 persons who were subjected to salt water experiments. They were locked in a room and for 5 days were given nothing for food but salt water. During this time their urine, blood, and excrement were tested. None of these prisoners died, possibly because they received smuggled food from other prisoners. Hungarians and Gypsies were used for these experiments.

It was common practice to remove the skin from dead prisoners. I was commanded to do this on many occasions. Dr. Rascher and Dr. Wolter in particular asked for this human skin from human backs and chests. It was chemically treated and placed in the sun to dry. After that it was cut into various sizes for use as saddles, riding breeches, gloves, house slippers, and ladies' handbags. Tattooed skin was especially valued by SS men. Russians, Poles, and other inmates were used in this way, but it was forbidden to cut out the skin of a German. This skin had to be from healthy prisoners and free from defects. Sometimes we did not have enough bodies with good skin and Rascher would say, "All right, you will get the bodies." The next day we would receive 20 or 30 bodies of young people. They would have been shot in the neck or struck on the head so that the skin would be uninjured. Also we frequently got requests for the skulls or skeletons of prisoners. In those cases we boiled the skull or the body. Then the soft parts were removed and the bones were bleached and dried and reassembled. In the case of skulls it was important to have a good set of teeth. When we got an order for skulls from Oranienburg the SS men would say, "We will try to get you some with good teeth." So it was dangerous to have good skin or good teeth.

SOURCE. Nuremberg Document # 3249-PS.

f. THE MASS MURDERS OF JEWS: TESTIMONY OF RUDOLF HOESS

. . . I have been constantly associated with the administration of concentration camps since 1934, serving at Dachau until 1938; then as Adjutant in Sachsenhausen from 1938 to 1 May 1940, when I was appointed Commandant of Auschwitz. I commanded Auschwitz until 1 December 1943, and estimate that at least 2,500,000 victims were executed and exterminated there by gassing and burning, and at least another half million succumbed to starvation and disease making a total dead of about 3,000,000. This figure represents about 70 or 80 percent of all persons sent to Auschwitz as prisoners, the remainder having been selected and used for slave labor in the concentration camp industries; included among the executed and burned were approximately 20,000 Russian prisoners of war (previously screened out of prisoner-of-war cages by the Gestapo) who were delivered at Auschwitz in Wehrmacht transports operated by regular Wehrmacht officers and men. The remainder of the total number of victims included about 100,000 German Jews, and great numbers of citizens, mostly Jewish, from Holland, France, Belgium, Poland, Hungary, Czechoslovakia, Greece, or other countries. We executed about 400,000 Hungarian Jews alone at Auschwitz in the summer of 1944. . . .

. . .

The "final solution" of the Jewish question meant the complete extermination of all Jews in Europe. I was ordered to establish extermination facilities at Auschwitz in June 1941. At that time, there were already in the General Government three other extermination camps: Belzek, Treblinka, and Wolzek. These camps were under the Einsatzkommando of the Security Police and SD. I visited Treblinka to find out how they carried out their exterminations. The camp commandant at Treblinka told me that he had liquidated 80,000 in the course of one-half year. He was principally concerned with liquidating all the Jews from the Warsaw Ghetto. He used monoxide gas, and I did not think that his methods were very efficient. So when I set up the extermination building at Auschwitz, I used Cyklon B, which was a crystallized prussic acid which we dropped into the death chamber from a small opening. It took from 3 to 15 minutes to kill the people in the death chamber, depending upon climatic conditions. We knew when the people were dead because their screaming stopped. We usually waited about one-half hour before we opened the doors and removed the bodies. After the bodies were removed our special Kommandos took off the rings and extracted the gold from the teeth of the corpses. . . .

Another improvement we made over Treblinka was that we built our gas chamber to accommodate 2,000 people at one time whereas at Treblinka their gas chambers only accommodated 200 people each. The way we selected our victims was as follows: We had two SS doctors on duty at Auschwitz to examine the incoming transports of prisoners. The prisoners would be marched by one of the doctors who would make spot decisions as they walked by. Those who were fit for work were sent into the camp. Others were sent immediately to the extermination plants. Children of tender years were invariably exterminated since by reason of their youth they were unable to work. Still another improvement we made over Treblinka was that at Treblinka the victims almost always knew that they were to be exterminated and at Auschwitz we endeavored to fool the victims into thinking that they were to go through a delousing process. Of course, frequently they realized our true intentions and we sometimes had riots and difficulties due to that fact. Very frequently women would hide their children under the clothes, but of course when we found them we would send the children in to be exterminated. We were required to carry out these exterminations in secrecy but of course the foul and nauseating stench from the continuous burning of bodies permeated the entire area and all of the people living in the surrounding communities knew that exterminations were going on at Auschwitz.

SOURCE. Nuremberg Document # 3868-PS.

Chapter 16

THE ROAD TO WORLD WAR II

a. HITLER ON PEACE AND WAR: SPEECH TO THE REICHSTAG, 1935; THE HOSSBACH NOTES, 1937

IN DIRECT VIOLATION of the Versailles Treaty, Hitler undertook a policy of German rearmament and at the same time took pains to assure the world of his peaceful intentions. In a speech delivered in Berlin on May 21, 1935, Hitler affirmed his dedication to peace. But a far different and doubtless more accurate picture of Hitler's policy emerges from the Hossbach notes. On November 5, 1937, Hitler conferred secretly with his foreign minister, his war minister, and the commanders-in-chief of his army, navy and air force. The minutes of this conference, taken by Hitler's adjutant, Colonel Hossbach, disclose the Fuehrer's intentions to conduct wars of aggression in Europe.

SPEECH OF 1935

. . . Members of the German Reichstag:

I have been at pains to give you a picture of the problems which confront us today. However great the difficulties and worries may be in individual questions, I consider that I owe it to my position as Füehrer and Chancellor of the Reich not to admit a single doubt as to the possibility of maintaining peace. The peoples wish for peace. It must be possible for the Governments to maintain it. I believe that the restoration of the German defense force will contribute to this peace. Not because we intend to increase it beyond all bounds, but because the simple fact of its existence has got rid of a dangerous vacuum in Europe. Germany does not intend to increase her armaments beyond all bounds. We have not got ten thousand bombing planes and we shall not build them. . . .

I cannot better conclude my speech of today to you, my fellow-fighters and trustees of the nation, than by repeating our confession of faith in peace. The nature of our new constitution makes it possible for us in Germany to put a stop to the machinations of war agitators. May the other nations too be able to give bold expression to their real inner longing for peace. Whoever lights the torch of war in Europe can wish for nothing but chaos. We, however, live in the firm conviction that in our time will be fulfilled, not the decline but the

268

renaissance of the West. That Germany may make an imperishable contribution to this great work is our proud hope and our unshakable belief.

The Hossbach Notes, 1937

The Füehrer stated initially that the subject matter of today's conference was of such high importance, that its further detailed discussion would probably take place in Cabinet sessions. However, he, the Füehrer, had decided NOT to discuss this matter in the larger circle of the Reich Cabinet, because of its importance. His subsequent statements were the result of detailed deliberations and of the experiences of his 4 and 1/2 years in Government; he desired to explain to those present his fundamental ideas on the possibilities and necessities of expanding our foreign policy and in the interests of a far-sighted policy he requested his statement be looked upon in the case of his death as his last will and testament.

The Füehrer then stated:

The aim of the Germany policy is the security and preservation of the nation, and its propagation. This is, consequently, a problem of space.

The German nation is composed of 85 million people, which, because of the number of individuals and the compactness of habitation, form a homogeneous European racial body which cannot be found in any other country. On the other hand it justifies the demand for larger living space more than for any other nation. If no political body exists in space, corresponding to the German racial body, [this void] will represent the greatest danger to the preservation of the German nation at its present high level. An arrest of the deterioration of the German element in Austria and Czechoslovakia is just as little possible as the preservation of the present state in Germany itself. . . . The German future is therefore dependent exclusively on the solution of the need for living space. . . .

The question for Germany is where the greatest possible conquest could be made at lowest cost. . . .

The German question can be solved only by way of force, and this is never without risk. The battles of Frederick the Great for Silesia, and Bismarck's wars against Austria and France had been a tremendous risk and the speed of the Russian action in 1870 had prevented Austria from participating in the war. If we place the decision to apply force at the head of the following expositions, then we are left to reply to the question "when" and "how."

b. THE MUNICH AGREEMENT, 1938

BEGUILED BY HITLER'S SPEECHES and anxious to avoid military conflict, England and France responded to German demands with a policy of appeasement. In the Munich Agreement of September 29, 1938, they submitted to German annexation of the Czechoslovakian Sudetenland which Hitler claimed on the ground that its population was heavily German.

Germany, the United Kingdom, France, and Italy, taking into consideration the agreement, which has been already reached in principle for the cession to Germany of the Sudeten German territory, have agreed on the following terms and conditions governing the said cession and the measures consequent thereon, and by this agreement they each hold themselves responsible for the steps necessary to secure its fulfillment:

1. The evacuation will begin on the 1st October.

2. The United Kingdom, France, and Italy agree that the evacuation of the territory shall be completed by the 10th October, without any existing installations having been destroyed and that the Czechoslovak Government will be held responsible for carrying out the evacuation without damage to the said installations.

3. The conditions governing the evacuation will be laid down in detail by an international commission composed of representatives of Germany, the United Kingdom, France, Italy, and Czechoslovakia.

4. The occupation by stages of the predominantly German territory by German troops will begin on the 1st October. The four territories marked on the attached map will be occupied by German troops in the following order: the territory marked No. I on the 1st and 2nd of October, the territory marked No. II on the 2nd and 3rd of October, the territory marked No. III on the 3rd, 4th and 5th of October, the territory marked No. IV on the 6th and 7th of October. The remaining territory of preponderantly German character will be ascertained by the aforesaid international commission forthwith and be occupied by German troops by the 10th of October.

5. The international commission referred to in paragraph 3 will determine the territories in which a plebiscite is to be held. These territories will be occupied by international bodies until the plebiscite has been completed. The same commission will fix the conditions in which the plebiscite is to be held, taking as a basis the conditions of the Saar plebiscite. The commission will also fix a date, not later than the end of November, on which the plebiscite will be held.

6. The final determination of the frontiers will be carried out by the international commission. This commission will also be entitled to recommend to the four Powers, Germany, the United Kingdom, France and Italy, in cer-

tain exceptional cases minor modifications in the strictly ethnographical determination of the zones which are to be transferred without plebiscite.

7. There will be a right of option into and out of the transferred territories, the option to be exercised within six months from the date of this agreement. A German-Czechoslovak commission shall determine the details of the option, consider ways of facilitating the transfer of population and settle questions of principle arising out of the said transfer.

8. The Czechoslovak Government will within a period of four weeks from the date of this agreement release from their military and police forces any Sudeten Germans who may wish to be released, and the Czechoslovak Government will within the same period release Sudeten German prisoners who are serving terms of imprisonment for political offences.

ADOLF HITLER
NEVILLE CHAMBERLAIN
EDOUARD DALADIER
BENITO MUSSOLINI

SOURCE. Great Britain, House of Commons, XXX (1937–38), *Accounts and Papers*, XV. Cmd. 5848, "Further Documents Respecting Czechoslovakia, Including the Agreement Concluded at Munich on September 29, 1938," Miscellaneous No. 8 (1938), pp. 3–4.

c. THE PERSONAL AGREEMENT BETWEEN HITLER AND CHAMBERLAIN, 1938

ON THE NEXT DAY, September 30, Prime Minister Neville Chamberlain announced to the British people in an airport speech that Hitler had reassured him personally of his peaceful intentions.

. . . This morning I had another talk with the German Chancellor, Herr Hitler, and here is a paper which bears his name upon it as well as mine. Some of you perhaps have already heard what it contains, but I would just like to read it to you.

We, the German Führer and Chancellor and the British Prime Minister, of Anglo-German relations is of the first importance for the two countries and for Europe.

We regard the agreement signed last night and the Anglo-German Naval Agreement as symbolic of the desire of our two peoples never to go to war with one another again.

We are resolved that the method of consultation shall be the method adopted to deal with any other questions that may concern our two countries, and we are determined to continue our efforts to remove possible sources of difference and thus to assure the peace of Europe.

d. THE RUSSO-GERMAN NONAGGRESSION PACT, 1939

NEVERTHELESS, IN MARCH, 1939, German troops marched into Prague, and Czechoslovakia became a German protectorate. Hitler now began speaking ominously about Poland's persecution of its German inhabitants. The path to the conquest of Poland was cleared by a totally unexpected treaty of nonaggression between Germany and the Soviet Union (August 23, 1939) which in fact opened the way for aggression by both parties in Poland and the Baltic states.

ARTICLE I

Both High Contracting Parties obligate themselves to desist from any act of violence, any aggressive action, and any attack on each other, either individually or jointly with other powers. . . .

Secret Additional Protocol

On the occasion of the signature of the Nonaggression Pact between the German Reich and the Union of Socialist Soviet Republics the undersigned plenipotentiaries of each of the two parties discussed in strictly confidential conversations the question of the boundary of their respective spheres of influence in Eastern Europe. These conversations led to the following conclusions:

1. In the event of a territorial and political rearrangement in the areas belonging to the Baltic States (Finland, Estonia, Latvia, Lithuania), the northern boundary of Lithuania shall represent the boundary of the spheres of influence of Germany and the U.S.S.R. In this connection the interest of Lithuania in the Vilna area is recognized by each party.

2. In the event of a territorial and political rearrangement of the areas belonging to the Polish state the spheres of influence of Germany and the U.S.S.R. shall be bounded approximately by the line of the rivers Narew, Vistula, and San.

The question of whether the interests of both parties make desirable the maintenance of an independent Polish state and how such a state should be bounded can only be definitely determined in the course of further political developments.

In any event both Governments will resolve this question by means of a friendly agreement.

3. With regard to Southeastern Europe attention is called by the Soviet side to its interest in Bessarabia. The German side declares its complete political disinterestedness in these areas.

4. This protocol shall be treated by both parties as strictly secret.

Moscow, August 23, 1939.

For the Government
of the German Reich:
    V. Ribbentrop

Plenipotentiary of the
Government of the U.S.S.R.
    V. Molotov

SOURCE. R. G. Sontag and J. Beddie, eds., *Nazi-Soviet Relations, 1939–1941*, Washington, D. C.: U. S. Department of State, 1948, pp. 76 and 78.

e. TRANSCRIPT OF A CONVERSATION BETWEEN RIBBENTROP AND STALIN, 1939

THE CYNICISM of the Russo-German pact drove many European and American Communists out of the Party. The fundamental dishonesty of Hitler's fervent anti-Bolshevik assertions is attested by the secret transcript of a conversation between the German Foreign Minister Ribbentrop and Joseph Stalin on the night following the signing of the Nonaggression Pact. With Hitler's invasion of Poland on September 1, and the declaration of war by Britain and France against Germany two days later, World War II began.

Memorandum of a Conversation Held on the Night of August 23rd to 24th, between the Reich Foreign Minister, on the One Hand, and Herr Stalin and the Chairman of the Council of People's Commissars Molotov, on the Other Hand.

VERY SECRET!

STATE SECRET

The following problems were discussed: . . .

Italy:

HERR STALIN inquired of the Reich Foreign Minister as to Italian aims. Did not Italy have aspirations beyond the annexation of Albania—perhaps for Greek territory? Small, mountainous, and thinly populated Albania was, in his estimation, of no particular use to Italy.

The REICH FOREIGN MINISTER replied that Albania was important to Italy for strategic reasons. Moreover, Mussolini was a strong man who could not be intimidated.

This he had demonstrated in the Abyssinian conflict, in which Italy had asserted its aims by its own strength against a hostile coalition. Even Germany was not yet in a position at that time to give Italy appreciable support.

Mussolini welcomed warmly the restoration of friendly relations between Germany and the Soviet Union. He had expressed himself as gratified with the conclusion of the Nonaggression Pact. . . .

England:

HERREN STALIN and MOLOTOV commented adversely on the British Military Mission in Moscow, which had never told the Soviet Government what it really wanted.

The REICH FOREIGN MINISTER stated in this connection that England had always been trying and was still trying to disrupt the development of good relations between Germany and the Soviet Union. England was weak and wanted to let others fight for its presumptuous claim to world domination.

HERR STALIN eagerly concurred and observed as follows: the British Army was weak; the British Navy no longer deserved its previous reputation. England's air arm was being increased, to be sure, but there was a lack of pilots. If England dominates the world in spite of this, this was due to the stupidity of the other countries that always let themselves be bluffed. It was ridiculous, for example, that a few hundred British should dominate India.

The REICH FORIEGN MINISTER concurred and informed Herr Stalin confidentially that England had recently put out a new feeler which was connected with certain allusions to 1914. It was a matter of a typically English, stupid maneuver. The Reich Foreign Minister had proposed to the Führer to inform the British that every hostile British act, in case of a German-Polish conflict, would be answered by a bombing attack on London.

HERR STALIN remarked that the feeler was evidently Chamberlain's letter to the Führer, which Ambassador Henderson delivered on August 23 at the Obersalzberg. Stalin further expressed the opinion that England, despite its weakness, would wage war craftily and stubbornly.

France:

HERR STALIN expressed the opinion that France, nevertheless, had an army worthy of consideration.

The REICH FOREIGN MINISTER, on his part, pointed out to Herren Stalin and Molotov the numerical inferiority of France. While Germany had available an annual class of more than 300,000 soldiers, France could muster only 150,000 recruits annually. The West Wall was five times as strong as the Maginot Line. If France attempted to wage war with Germany, she would certainly be conquered.

Anti-Comintern Pact:

The REICH FOREIGN MINISTER observed that the Anti-Comintern Pact was basically directed not against the Soviet Union but against the Western democracies. He knew, and was able to infer from the tone of the Russian press, that the Soviet Government fully recognized this fact.

HERR STALIN interposed that the Anti-Comintern Pact had in fact frightened principally the City of London and the small British merchants.

The REICH FORIEGN MINISTER concurred and remarked jokingly that Herr Stalin was surely less frightened by the Anti-Comintern Pact than the City of London and the small British merchants. What the German people thought of this matter is evident from a joke which had originated with the Berliners, well known for their wit and humor, and which had been going the rounds for several months, namely, "Stalin will yet join the Anti-Comintern Pact." . . .

When they took their leave, HERR STALIN addressed to the Reich Foreign Ministers words to this effect:

The Soviet Government takes the new Pact very seriously. He could guarantee on his word of honor that the Soviet Union would not betray its partner.

Moscow, August 24, 1939.

HENCKE

Accordingly, the Governments of Germany, Italy and Japan have agreed as follows:

ARTICLE 1. Japan recognizes and respects the leadership of Germany and Italy in the establishment of a new order in Europe.

ARTICLE 2. Germany and Italy recognize and respect the leadership of Japan in the establishment of a new order in Greater East Asia.

ARTICLE 3. Germany, Italy and Japan agree to co-operate in their efforts on the aforesaid lines. They further undertake to assist one another with all political, economic and military means if one of the three Contracting Powers is attacked by a Power at present not involved in the European War or in the Chinese-Japanese conflict.

ARTICLE 4. With a view to implementing the present pact, joint technical commissions, the members of which are to be appointed by the governments of Germany, Italy, and Japan, will meet without delay.

ARTICLE 6. The present pact shall become valid immediately upon signature and shall remain in force ten years. . . .

Done in triplicate at Berlin, the 27th day of September, 1940, in the eighteenth year of the Fascist era. . . .

SOURCE. German Library of Information, *Facts in Review*, New York, 1941, II, p. 486.

Chapter 17

WORLD WAR II

a. WINSTON CHURCHILL'S FIRST ADDRESS TO COMMONS, 1940

THE RESOLUTION OF THE BRITISH was strengthened by the determined policies and eloquent speeches of its wartime Prime Minister, Winston Churchill, who, on May 13, 1940, delivered his first and most memorable address to the House of Commons.

. . . In this crisis I hope I may be pardoned if I do not address the House at any length today. I hope that any of my friends and colleagues, or former colleagues, who are affected by the political reconstruction, will make allowance, all allowance, for any lack of ceremony with which it has been necessary to act. I would say to the House, as I said to those who have joined this Government; "I have nothing to offer but blood, toil, tears and sweat."

We have before us an ordeal of the most grievous kind. We have before us many, many long months of struggle and of suffering. You ask, what is our policy? I will say: It is to wage war, by sea, land, and air, with all our might and with all the strength that God can give us: to wage war against a monstrous tyranny, never surpassed in the dark, lamentable catalogue of human crime. That is our policy. You ask, what is our aim? I can answer in one word: It is victory, victory at all costs, victory in spite of all terror, victory, however long and hard the road may be; for without victory there is no survival. Let that be realized; no survival for the British Empire; no survival for all that the British Empire has stood for, no survival for the urge and impulse of the ages, that mankind will move forward towards its goal. But I take up my task with buoyancy and hope. I feel sure that our cause will not be suffered to fail among men. At this time I feel entitled to claim the aid of all, and I say, "Come, then, let us go forward together with our united strength."

SOURCE. Great Britain, House of Commons, *Parliamentary Debates*, 5th Series, CCCLX, p. 1502.

b. THE AXIS PACT, 1940

ON SEPTEMBER 27, 1940, with war raging in Europe, Germany, Italy, and Japan concluded a pact of alliance known as the Rome–Berlin–Tokyo Axis.

The Governments of Germany, Italy, and Japan consider it the prerequisite of lasting peace that every nation in the world shall receive the space to which it is entitled. They have, therefore, decided to stand by and co-operate with one another in their efforts in Greater East Asia and the regions of Europe respectively. In doing this it is their prime purpose to establish and maintain a new order of things, calculated to promote the mutual prosperity and welfare of the peoples concerned.

It is, furthermore, the desire of the three Governments to extend cooperation to other nations . . . who are inclined to direct their efforts along lines similar to their own for the purpose of realizing their ultimate object, world peace.

c. THE ATLANTIC CHARTER, 1941

MEANWHILE THE UNITED STATES, although not yet formally a belligerent, was providing massive aid to Britain. On August 14, 1941, President Franklin D. Roosevelt and Prime Minister Churchill, meeting aboard a battleship in mid-ocean, issued an important declaration of common aims known as the Atlantic Charter which became a basis of Allied war goals.

The President of the United States of America and the Prime Minister, Mr. Churchill, representing His Majesty's Government in the United Kingdom, being met together, deem it right to make known certain common principles in the national policies of their respective countries on which they base their hopes for a better future for the world.

First, their countries seek no aggrandizement, territorial or other;

Second, they desire to see no territorial changes that do not accord with the freely expressed wishes of the peoples concerned;

Third, they respect the right of all peoples to choose the form of government under which they will live; and they wish to see sovereign rights and self-government restored to those who have been forcibly deprived of them;

Fourth, they will endeavor, with due respect for their existing obligations, to further the enjoyment by all States, great or small, victor or vanquished, of access, on equal terms, to the trade and to the raw materials of the world which are needed for their economic prosperity;

Fifth, they desire to bring about the fullest collaboration between all nations in the economic field with the object of securing, for all, improved labor standards, economic adjustment and social security;

Sixth, after the final destruction of the Nazi tyranny, they hope to see established a peace which will afford all nations the means of dwelling in safety within their own boundaries, and which will afford assurance that all the men in all the lands may live out their lives in freedom from fear and want;

Seventh, such a peace should enable all men to traverse the high seas and oceans without hindrance;

Eighth, they believe that all of the nations of the world, for realistic as well as spiritual reasons, must come to the abandonment of the use of force. Since no future peace can be maintained if land, sea or air armaments continue to be employed by nations which threaten, or may threaten, aggression outside of their frontiers, they believe, pending the establishment of a wider and permanent system of general security, that the disarmament of such nations is essential. They will likewise aid and encourage all other practicable measures which will lighten for peaceloving peoples the crushing burden of armaments.

FRANKLIN D. ROOSEVELT
WINSTON S. CHURCHILL

SOURCE. *Congressional Record,* LXXXVII, 77th Congress, 1st Session, p. 7217.

d. PRESIDENT ROOSEVELT'S WAR MESSAGE
TO CONGRESS, 1941

WITH THE JAPANESE ATTACK on Pearl Harbor on December 7, 1941, America entered fully into the war. On December 8, President Roosevelt delivered a war message to Congress, and the two Houses responded with a formal declaration of war against Japan, Germany and Italy.

Yesterday, December 7, 1941—A date which will live in infamy—the United States of America was suddenly and deliberately attacked by naval and air forces of the Empire of Japan.

The United States was at peace with that nation and, at the solicitation of Japan, was still in conversation with its Government and its Emperor looking toward the maintenance of peace in the Pacific.

Indeed, one hour after Japanese air squadrons had commenced bombing Oahu, the Japanese Ambassador to the United States and his colleague delivered to the Secretary of State a formal reply to a recent American message. While this reply stated that it seemed useless to continue the existing diplomatic negotiations, it contained no threat or hint of war or armed attack.

It will be recorded that the distance of Hawaii from Japan makes it obvious that the attack was deliberately planned many days or even weeks ago. During the intervening time, the Japanese Government has deliberately sought to deceive the United States by false statements and expressions of hope for continued peace.

The attack yesterday on the Hawaiian Islands has caused severe damage to American naval and military forces. Very many American lives have been lost. In addition, American ships have been reported torpedoed on the high seas between San Francisco and Honolulu.

Yesterday the Japanese Government also launched an attack against Malaya.

Last night Japanese forces attacked Hong Kong.

Last night Japanese forces attacked Guam.

Last night Japanese forces attacked the Philippine Islands.

Last night the Japanese attacked Wake Island.

This morning the Japanese attacked Midway Island.

Japan has, therefore, undertaken a surprise offensive extending throughout the Pacific area. The facts of yesterday speak for themselves. The people of the United States have already formed their opinions and well understand the implications to the very life and safety of our nation.

As Commander in Chief of the army and navy I have directed that all measures be taken for our defense.

Always will we remember the character of the onslaught against us.

No matter how long it may take us to overcome this premeditated invasion, the American people in their righteous might will win through the absolute victory.

I believe I interpret the will of the Congress and of the people when I assert that we will not only defend ourselves to the uttermost but will make very certain that this form of treachery shall never endanger us again.

Hostilities exist. There is no blinking at the fact that our people, our territory and our interests are in grave danger.

With confidence in our armed forces—with the onbounding determination of our people—we will gain the inevitable triumph—so help us God.

I ask that the Congress declare that since the unprovoked and dastardly attack by Japan on Sunday, December 7, a state of war has existed between the United States and the Japanese Empire.

FRANKLIN D. ROOSEVELT

e. THE JAPANESE AGREEMENT FROM THE YALTA TREATY, 1945

PRIOR TO THE PEARL HARBOR ATTACK, Hitler had launched a surprise invasion of Russia in violation of the 1939 Nonaggression Pact. The hope of Germany against Russia, and of Japan against the United States, lay in quick victories and early surrenders or armistice favorable to the Axis powers. The survival of Russia and the United States, and their policy of no peace without total victory, doomed the Axis powers to a hopeless struggle against overwhelming manpower and industrial might.

Shortly before the end of the war, Roosevelt, Churchill, and Stalin met at Yalta in the Crimea (February 4–11, 1945) in order to reach agreement on aspects of the coming postwar settlement. Stalin made territorial demands in violation of the Atlantic Charter, and Roosevelt and Churchill, anxious to obtain Russian participation in the war against Japan, bowed to Stalin's wishes.

The leaders of the three great powers—the Soviet Union, the United States of America, and Great Britain— have agreed that in two or three months after Germany has surrendered and the war in Europe has terminated, the Soviet Union shall enter into the war against Japan on the side of the Allies on condition that:

1. The *status quo* in Outer Mongolia (the Mongolian People's Republic) shall be preserved;

2. The former rights of Russia violated by the treacherous attack of Japan in 1904 shall be restored, viz.:

a. The southern part of Sakhalin as well as the islands adjacent to it shall be returned to the Soviet Union;

b. The commercial port of Dairen shall be internationalized, the preeminent interests of the Soviet Union in this port being safeguarded, and the lease of Port Arthur as a naval base of U.S.S.R. restored;

c. The Chinese Eastern Railroad and the South Manchurian Railroad, which provides an outlet to Dairen, shall be jointly operated by the establishment of a joint Soviet-Chinese company, it being understood that the preeminent interests of the Soviet Union shall be safeguarded and that China shall retain full sovereignty in Manchuria;

3. The Kurile Islands shall be handed over to the Soviet Union. It is understood that the agreement concerning Outer Mongolia and the ports and railroads referred to above will require concurrence of Generalissimo Chiang Kai-shek. The President [*Roosevelt*] will take measures in order to obtain this concurrence on advice from Marshal Stalin.

The heads of the three great powers have agreed that these claims of the Soviet Union shall be unquestionably fulfilled after Japan has been defeated.

For its part, the Soviet Union expresses its readiness to conclude with the National Government of China a pact of friendship and alliance between the U.S.S.R. and China in order to render assistance to China with its armed forces for the purpose of liberating China from the Japanese yoke.

JOSEPH V. STALIN
FRANKLIN D. ROOSEVELT
WINSTON S. CHURCHILL

SOURCE. Department of State Press Release, No. 239, March 24, 1947.

f. THE POTSDAM DECLARATION, 1945

AT A TIME WHEN the success of the atomic bomb was yet uncertain, it seemed to Roosevelt that Russian entry into the struggle with Japan would shorten the war considerably. Nevertheless, some of postwar observers regarded the Yalta concessions as a blunder on the part of the Unites States. Two months after the defeat of Nazi Germany, the "Big Three" met again at Potsdam, with Stalin representing the Soviet Union and President Harry S. Truman now representing the United States. The new British Labour Prime Minister, Clement Attlee, replaced Winston Churchill midway through the conference. The Potsdam Declaration (August 2, 1945) dealt with the problems of German occupation and political and economic reconstitution.

The Allied Armies are in occupation of the whole of Germany and the German people have begun to atone for the terrible crimes committed under the leadership of those whom in the hour of their success, they openly approved and blindly obeyed.

Agreement has been reached at this conference on the political and economic principles of a co-ordinated Allied policy toward defeated Germany during the period of Allied control.

The purpose of this agreement is to carry out the Crimea [Yalta] Declaration on Germany. German militarism and Nazism will be extirpated and the Allies will take in agreement together, now and in the future, the other measures necessary to assure that Germany never again will threaten her neighbors or the peace of the world.

It is not the intention of the Allies to destroy or enslave the German people. It is the intention of the Allies that the German people be given the opportunity to prepare for the eventual reconstruction of their life on a democratic and peaceful basis. If their own efforts are steadily directed to this end, it will be possible for them in due course to take their place among the free and peaceful peoples of the world.

The text of the agreement is as follows:

1. In accordance with the agreement on control machinery in Germany, supreme authority in Germany is exercised on instructions from their respective governments, by the Commanders-in-Chief of the armed forces of the United States of America, the United Kingdom, the Union of Soviet Socialist Republics, and the French Republic, each in his own zone of occupation, and also jointly, in matters affecting Germany as a whole, in their capacity as members of the Control Council.

2. So far as practicable, there shall be uniformity of treatment of the German population throughout Germany.

3. The purposes of the occupation of Germany by which the Control Council shall be guided are:

(i) The complete disarmament and demilitarization of Germany and the elimination or control of all German industry that could be used for military production. To these ends:

(a) All German land, naval and air forces, the S.S., S.A., S.D., and Gestapo, with all their organizations, staffs and institutions, including the General Staff, the Officers' Corps, Reserve Corps, military schools, war veterans' organizations and all other military and quasi-military organizations, together with all clubs and associations which serve to keep alive the military tradition in Germany, shall be completely and finally abolished in such manner as permanently to prevent the revival or reorganization of German militarism and Nazism.

(b) All arms, ammunition and implements of war and all specialized facilities for their production shall be held at the disposal of the Allies or destroyed. The maintenance and production of all aircraft and all arms, ammunition and implements of war shall be prevented.

(ii) To convince the German people that they have suffered a total military defeat and that they cannot escape responsibility for what they have brought upon themselves, since their own ruthless warfare and the fanatical Nazi resistance have destroyed German economy and made chaos and suffering inevitable.

(iii) To destroy the National Socialist Party and its affiliated and supervised organizations, to dissolve all Nazi institutions, to ensure that they are not revived in any form, and to prevent all Nazi and militarist activity or propaganda.

(iv) To prepare for the eventual reconstruction of German political life on a democratic basis and for eventual peaceful cooperation in international life by Germany.

4. All Nazi laws which provided the basis of the Hitler regime or established discrimination on grounds of race, creed, or political opinion shall be abolished. No such discrimination, whether legal, administrative or otherwise, shall be tolerated.

5. War criminals and those who have participated in planning or carrying out Nazi enterprises involving or resulting in atrocities or war crimes shall be arrested and brought to judgment. Nazi leaders, influential Nazi supporters and high officials of Nazi organizations and institutions and any other persons dangerous to the occupation or its objectives shall be arrested and interned.

6. All members of the Nazi party who have been more than nominal participants in its activities and all other persons hostile to allied purposes shall be removed from public and semi-public office, and from positions of responsibility in important private undertakings. Such persons shall be replaced by persons who, by their political and moral qualities, are deemed capable of assisting in developing genuine democratic institutions in Germany.

7. German education shall be so controlled as completely to eliminate Nazi militarist doctrines and to make possible the successful development of democratic ideas.

8. The judicial system will be reorganized in accordance with the principles of democracy, of justice under law, and of equal rights for all citizens without distinction of race, nationality or religion.

9. The administration of affairs in Germany should be directed towards the decentralization of the political structure and the development of local responsibility. To this end:

(i) Local self-government shall be restored throughout Germany on democratic principles and in particular through elective councils as rapidly as is consistent with military security and the purposes of military occupation;

(ii) All democratic political parties with rights of assembly and of public discussion shall be allowed and encouraged throughout Germany;

(iii) Representative and elective principles shall be introduced into regional, provincial and state (land) administration as rapidly as may be justified by the successful application of these principles in local self-government;

(iv) For the time being no central German government shall be established. Notwithstanding this, however, certain essential central German administrative departments, headed by state secretaries, shall be established, particularly in the fields of finance, transport, communications, foreign trade and industry. Such departments will act under the direction of the Control Council.

10. Subject to the necessity for maintaining military security, freedom of speech, press and religion shall be permitted, and religious institutions shall be respected. Subject likewise to the maintenance of military security, the formation of free trade unions shall be permitted.

SOURCE. U. S. Department of State, *Bulletin,* XIII, No. 319, August 5, 1945, pp. 154–156.

g. PRESIDENT TRUMAN ANNOUNCES THE BOMBING OF HIROSHIMA, 1945

A FEW DAYS after the Potsdam Declaration the war with Japan came to an end with the dropping of atomic bombs on Hiroshima and Nagasaki. In a speech of August 6, President Harry S. Truman announced America's first use of the awesome new weapon that was soon to hold the entire world in a precarious balance of terror.

Sixteen hours ago an American airplane dropped one bomb on Hiroshima, an important Japanese Army base. That bomb had more power than 20,000 tons of TNT. . . .

The Japanese began the war from the air at Pearl Harbor. They have been repaid manyfold. And the end is not yet. With this bomb we have now added a new and revolutionary increase in destruction to supplement the growing power of our armed forces. In their present form these bombs are now in production and even more powerful forms are in development.

It is an atomic bomb. It is a harnessing of the basic power of the universe. The force from which the sun draws its power has been loosed against those who brought war to the Far East.

Before 1939, it was the accepted belief of scientists that it was theoretically possible to release atomic energy. But no one knew any practical method of doing it. By 1942, however, we knew that the Germans were working feverishly to find a way to add atomic energy to the other engines of war with which they hoped to enslave the world. But they failed. We may be grateful to Providence that the Germans got the V-1's and the V-2's late and in limited quantities and even more grateful that they did not get the atomic bomb at all.

The battle of the laboratories held fateful risks for us as well as the battles of the air, land, and sea, and we have now won the battle of the laboratories as we have won the other battles.

Beginning in 1940. . . . American and British scientists working together . . . entered the race of discovery against the Germans. . . .

In the United States the laboratory work and the production plants, on which a substantial start had already been made, would be out of the reach of enemy bombing, while at the time Britain was exposed to constant air attack and was still threatened with the possibility of invasion.

For these reasons Prime Minister Churchill and President Roosevelt agreed that it would be wise to carry on the project here. We now have two great plants and many lesser works devoted to the production of atomic power. Employment during peak construction numbered 125,000. . . . Few know what they have been producing. . . . We have spent two billion dollars on the greatest scientific gamble in history—and won. . . .

We are now prepared to obliterate more rapidly and completely every productive enterprise the Japanese have above ground in any city. . . . Let there be no mistake; we shall completely destroy Japan's power to make war.

It was to spare the Japanese people from destruction that the ultimatum of July 26 was issued at Potsdam. Their leaders promptly rejected that ultimatum. If they do not now accept our terms they may expect a rain of ruin from the air, the like of which has never been seen on this earth. . . .

The fact that we can release atomic energy ushers in a new age in man's understanding of nature's forces. . . . It has never been the habit of the scientists of this country or the policy of the Government to withhold from the world scientific knowledge. . . .

But under present circumstances it is not intended to divulge the terminal processes of production of all the military applications pending further examination of possible methods of protecting us and the rest of the world from the danger of sudden destruction.

I shall recommend that the Congress of the United States consider promptly the establishment of an appropriate commission to control the production and use of atomic power.

h. EXCERPTS FROM THE UNITED NATIONS CHARTER, 1945

WITH THE SIGNING of the United Nations Charter on June 26, 1945, the world took a new step in the direction of international cooperation and world government. The postwar career of the United Nations has been disappointing to many, for the development of the Cold War tended to weaken the peace-enforcing machinery of the Security Council. Nevertheless, the United Nations played a significant role in the Korean War, the Suez crisis, the Congo crisis, and other postwar conflicts. More generally, the United Nations constitutes an international political response—much delayed—to the world-wide interpretration of economic systems and cultures that had been gaining momentum ever since the fifteenth century.

WE THE PEOPLES OF THE UNITED NATIONS DETERMINED

to save succeeding generations from the scourge of war, which twice in our lifetime has brought untold sorrow to mankind, and

to reaffirm faith in fundamental human rights, in the dignity and worth of the human person, in the equal rights of men and women and of nations large and small, and

to establish conditions under which justice and respect for the obligations arising from treaties and other sources of international law can be maintained, and

to promote social progress and better standards of life in larger freedom,

AND FOR THESE ENDS

to practice tolerance and live together in peace with one another as good neighbors, and

to unite our strength to maintain international peace and security, and

to ensure, by the acceptance of principles and the institution of methods, that armed force shall not be used, save in the common interest, and

to employ international machinery for the promotion of the economic and social advancement of all peoples,

HAVE RESOLVED TO COMBINE OUR EFFORTS TO ACCOMPLISH THESE AIMS.

Accordingly, our respective Governments, through representatives assembled in the city of San Francisco, who have exhibited their full powers found to be in good and due form, have agreed to the present Charter of the United Nations and do hereby establish an international organization to be known as the United Nations.

Chapter 1. Purposes and Principles

ARTICLE 1

The Purposes of the United Nations are:

1. To maintain international peace and security, and to that end: to take effective collective measures for the prevention and removal of threats to the peace, and for the suppression of acts of aggression or other breaches of the peace, and to bring about by peaceful means, and in conformity with the principles of justice and international law, adjustment or settlement of international disputes or situations which might lead to a breach of the peace;

2. To develop friendly relations among nations based on respect for the principle of equal rights and self-determination of peoples, and to take other appropriate measures to strengthen universal peace;

3. To achieve international cooperation in solving international problems of an economic, social, cultural, or humanitarian character, and in promoting and encouraging respect for human rights and for fundamental freedoms for all without distinction as to race, sex, language, or religion; and

4. To be a center for harmonizing the actions of nations in the attainment of these common ends.

ARTICLE 2

The Organization and its Members, in pursuit of the Purposes stated in Article 1, shall act in accordance with the following Principles.

1. The Organization is based on the principle of the sovereign equality of all its Members.

2. All Members, in order to ensure to all of them the rights and benefits resulting from membership, shall fulfil in good faith the obligations assumed by them in accordance with the present Charter.

3. All Members shall settle their international disputes by peaceful means in such a manner that international peace and security, and justice, are not endangered.

4. All Members shall refrain in their international relations from the threat or use of force against the territorial integrity or political independence of any state, or in any other manner inconsistent with the Purposes of the United Nations.

5. All Members shall give the United Nations every assistance in any action it takes in accordance with the present Charter, and shall refrain from giving assistance to any state against which the United Nations is taking preventive or enforcement action.

6. The Organization shall ensure that states which are not Members of the United Nations act in accordance with these Principles so far as may be necessary for the maintenance of international peace and security.

7. Nothing contained in the present Charter shall authorize the United Nations to intervene in matters which are essentially within the domestic jurisdiction of any state or shall require the Members to submit such matters to settlement under the present Charter; but this principle shall not prejudice the application of enforcement measures under Chapter VII.

Chapter II. Membership

ARTICLE 3

The original Members of the United Nations shall be the states which, having participated in the United Nations Conference on International Organization at San Francisco, or having previously signed the Declaration by United Nations of January 1, 1942, sign the present Charter and ratify it in accordance with Article 110.

ARTICLE 4

1. Membership in the United Nations is open to all other peace-loving states which accept the obligations contained in the present Charter and, in the judgment of the Organization, are able and willing to carry out these obligations.

2. The admission of any such state to membership in the United Nations will be effected by a decision of the General Assembly upon the recommendation of the Security Council.

ARTICLE 5

A Member of the United Nations against which preventive or enforcement action has been taken by the Security Council may be suspended from the exercise of the rights and privileges of membership by the General Assembly upon the recommendation of the Security Council. The exercise of these rights and privileges may be restored by the Security Council.

ARTICLE 6

A Member of the United Nations which has persistently violated the Principles contained in the present Charter may be expelled from the Organization by the General Assembly upon the recommendation of the Security Council.

Chapter III. Organs

ARTICLE 7

1. There are established as the principal organs of the United Nations: a General Assembly, a Security Council, an Economic and Social Council, a Trusteeship Council, an International Court of Justice, and a Secretariat.
2. Such subsidiary organs as may be found necessary may be established in accordance with the present Charter.

ARTICLE 8

The United Nations shall place no restrictions on the eligibility of men and women to participate in any capacity and under conditions of equality in its principal and subsidiary organs. . . .

Chapter VI. Pacific Settlement of Disputes

ARTICLE 33

1. The parties to any dispute, the continuance of which is likely to endanger the maintenance of international peace and security, shall, first of all, seek a solution by negotiation, enquiry, mediation, conciliation, arbitration, judicial settlement, resort to regional agencies or arrangements, or other peaceful means of their own choice.
2. The Security Council shall, when it deems necessary, call upon the parties to settle their dispute by such means.

ARTICLE 34

The Security Council may investigate any dispute, or any situation which might lead to international friction or give rise to a dispute, in order to determine whether the continuance of the dispute or situation is likely to endanger the maintenance of international peace and security.

ARTICLE 35

1. Any Member of the United Nations may bring any dispute, or any situation of the nature referred to in Article 34, to the attention of the Security Council or of the General Assembly.
2. A state which is not a Member of the United Nations may bring to the attention of the Security Council or of the General Assembly any dispute to which it is a party if it accepts in advance, for the purposes of the dispute, the obligations of pacific settlement provided in the present Charter. . . .

Chapter VII. Action with Respect to Threats to the Peace, Breaches of the Peace, and Acts of Aggression

ARTICLE 39

The Security Council shall determine the existence of any threat to the peace, breach of the peace, or act of aggression and shall make recommendations, or decide what measures shall be taken in accordance with Articles 41 and 42, to maintain or restore international peace and security.

ARTICLE 40

In order to prevent an aggravation of the situation, the Security Council may, before making the recommendations or deciding upon the measures provided for in Article 39, call upon the parties concerned to comply with such provisional measures as it deems necessary or desirable. Such provisional measures shall be without prejudice to the rights, claims, or position of the parties concerned. The Security Council shall duly take account of failure to comply with such provisional measures.

ARTICLE 41

The Security Council may decide what measures not involving the use of armed force are to be employed to give effect to its decisions, and it may call upon the Members of the United Nations to apply such measures. These may include complete or partial interruption of economic relations and of rail, sea, air, postal, telegraphic, radio, and other means of communication, and the severance of diplomatic relations.

ARTICLE 42

Should the Security Council consider that measures provided for in Article 41 would be inadequate or have proved to be inadequate, it may take such action by air, sea, or land forces as may be necessary to maintain or restore international peace and security. Such action may include demonstration, blockade, and other operations by air, sea, or land forces of Members of the United Nations. . . .

ARTICLE 51

Nothing in the present Charter shall impair the inherent right of individual or collective self-defense if an armed attack occurs against a Member of the United Nations, until the Security Council has taken measures necessary to maintain international peace and security. Measures taken by Members in the exercise of this right of self-defense shall be immediately reported to the Security Council and shall not in any way affect the authority and responsibility of the Security Council under the present Charter to take at any time such action as it deems necessary in order to maintain or restore international peace and security. . . .

Chapter IX. International Economic and Social Cooperation

ARTICLE 55

With a view to the creation of conditions of stability and well-being which are necessary for peaceful and friendly relations among nations based on respect for the principle of equal rights and self-determination of peoples, the United Nations shall promote:

a. higher standards of living, full employment, and conditions of economic and social progress and development;

b. solutions of international economic, social, health, and related problems; and international cultural and educational cooperation; and

c. universal respect for, and observance of, human rights and fundamental freedoms for all without distinction as to race, sex, language, or religion. . . .

SOURCE. Reprinted by permission of The United Nations.

PART SEVEN

The Contemporary World

THE hopes for peace expressed in the United Nations Charter, and widely shared among the peoples of the victorious powers, were dampened in the early postwar years as the spirit of Russo-American cooperation gave way to the Cold War. Simply put, America and her allies committed themselves to a policy of opposing the spread of Communism—to a policy of containment—whereas the Soviet Union remained dedicated to the Marxist/Leninist idea that Communism was the wave of the future and must necessarily expand. Russia quickly discovered the secret of nuclear weapons, and presently both countries were spending immense sums on nuclear bomb stockpiles and delivery systems sufficient to annihilate each other several times over. Accordingly, the implications of full-scale war changed fundamentally: no longer a possible (though hazardous) option for advancing national policy, total war had now become an act of national suicide, carrying with it the threat of destroying all humanity. Of necessity, therefore, armed clashes involving the interests of the two superpowers were indirect or limited. America declined to intervene when Russian armies crushed anti-Soviet revolutionary regimes in Hungary and Czechoslovakia. Russia witheld its armies from Korea and Vietnam. America abstained from a full-scale invasion of Cuba. Both countries refrained from using their atomic weapons and agreed to limit nuclear testing. And Russia, with certain exceptions, supported the advance of Communism by encouraging domestic "wars of liberation" rather than by armed invasions.

The struggle of the superpowers was waged in the midst of a worldwide anticolonial revolution. It was not always possible to distinguish between Marxist social revolutions and colonial wars of independence, and the Western nations, in pursuing their policy of containing Communism, sometimes found themselves pitted against national independence movements in the nonwhite world. America's war against Communism in Vietnam, for example, was viewed by many not as a bloody episode in the Cold War but as a cruel, fruitless effort by neocolonial whites to suppress Vietnamese independence. Here, as elsewhere, the Cold War—originally a duel between two predominately white superstates—became entangled in the liberation struggles of nonwhite peoples.

The drive for independence from traditional colonial status was almost everywhere successful. The old colonial system lay in ruins, and with the emergence of politically free Afro-Asian countries, Europe's age-long dominion over the nonwhite world was crumbling. Japan was becoming one of the world's great economic powers. China, with a revolutionary Communist regime deeply hostile toward America and, increasingly, toward Russia, was arming herself with nuclear weapons, struggling toward industrialization, and building herself into a third superpower.

But elsewhere in Asia, and throughout Africa, nonwhite peoples found themselves caught in a trap of poverty and rampant population growth. At the very time that poverty was disappearing in large areas of Europe and North America, it was deepening throughout much of the Third World. With advances in transportation and communication—particularly television—peoples of the world were becoming better known to one another than ever before, and the prodigious contrast between the wealthy and the wretched of the earth intensified the aspirations and anger of the poor while it prodded the consciences of the more sensitive among the rich. Young people in the West began to reject the affluent life as empty of meaning, productive of environmental pollution, wasteful of resources, and an affront to human brotherhood. Yet it seemed doubtful that the solution to poverty and starvation in the Third World was to be found in the rejection of the work-affluence ethic in the West. Indeed, it seemed unlikely that any solution to human poverty could be found unless population growth was radically reduced. The threat of suffocating overpopulation joined the threat of atomic annihilation to darken the spirits of rich and poor alike.

Throughout the twentieth century, the population explosion has been accompanied by an "information explosion" that has driven the intelligentsia into ever-narrowing fields of specialization and has vastly increased the difficulties of the man aspiring to be both broadly and deeply educated. It has been an age of widening schism between the sciences and humanities, of striking contradiction between the wonders of technology and the vulgarities of mass culture.

Freudian psychology—a dominant theme in the twentieth century—has placed heavy emphasis on the dark, subconscious levels of the human mind, thereby tending to discredit the old belief that man is an essentially rational being. Yet in no other century has man's reason produced such spectacular triumphs. In the field of technology, rockets have carried men to the moon and instruments towards the planets, and the older industrial revolution has given way to a new electronic revolution. Cybernetics has become basic to modern thought and modern life: remarkably sophisticated "thinking machines" have been used to plot economic trends, predict electron results, calculate the orbits of rockets and artificial satellites, and automate factories. Automation, indeed, is in the process of transforming the economies of the advanced industrial states, vastly increasing the efficiency of production and also sharply reducing the need for unskilled labor and aggravating the unemployment problem.

Notable progress has occurred in medicine, biology, and the physical sciences. Einstein's relativity theories are beyond the grasp of all but a few, yet they have had the effect of eroding man's confidence in a comprehendible Newtonian universe. The triumphs of medicine and sanitation have reduced suffering and saved lives but have also fed the population explosion. Biological breakthroughs, encouraging though they are, have opened the ominous possibilities of selective human breeding and "manufactured men." The optimistic rationalism of the Enlightenment is dying.

Twentieth-century art has evolved in a bewildering variety of directions. In painting, the emphasis of the later nineteenth century was on the work of art itself rather than on the outside world that it depicted. This trend has become increasingly pronounced in the present century, and the drift from objectivism to subjectivism has been carried to its ultimate degree in the work of abstract expressionists such as Jackson Pollock, who made no attempt whatever to represent the natural world but created paintings that were pure expressions of design and color. Sculptors, too, have made use of ever-increasing distortions of objective reality in order to communicate their own personal vision of things, and have sometimes devoted themselves to creating shapes, masses, and mobiles that represent no outside reality at all. Representational painting and sculpture continued to hold the allegiance of the most artists, but modern representationalism remains intensely subjective, reflecting the emphasis on the individual observer and his interpreting psyche suggested in the scientific theories of Einstein and Freud.

Man in the twentieth century, surrounded by technological marvels and an abstruse science, often living in huge, impersonal cities, has been haunted by a sense of loneliness and loss of identity. Some individuals have turned to the contemporary philosophy of existentialism. Jean Paul Sartre, Albert Camus, and other existentialist writers have been deeply conscious of the alienation of modern man from his society and his world. They have suggested, as answers, an unreserved acceptance of responsibility for the actions of all human beings, a new existential identification with humanity, a reaffirmation of man's freedom to make significant moral decisions, and an ultimate acceptance of the world despite its absurdity.

Yet such answers do not always satisfy. There remain the everpresent threats of catastrophe through soaring population or atomic war. And there remains, too, the sense of disorientation in these latter days of a civilization whose earlier syntheses and solutions—Christian, rationalist-scientific, nationalist, liberal-democratic, Marxist—have lost their hold on some of our most astute and sensitive minds. If this disorientation has plunged some into a well of despair, it has driven others toward an intensified search for values adequate to the human situation today.

Chapter 18

BALANCE OF TERROR: THE COLD WAR

a. THE BARUCH PROPOSALS OF ATOMIC CONTROL

THE TERRIFYING POTENTIAL of atomic weaponry prompted Bernard Baruch, speaking for the United States government, to present to the United Nations Atomic Energy Commission in June, 1946, a series of proposals for international atomic control. Russia, which had not yet developed the bomb, nevertheless rejected the proposals on the grounds of the inspection provisions and the absence of a veto power in the proposed new atomic authority.

My Fellow Members of the United Nations Atomic Energy Commission, and My Fellow Citizens of the World:

We are here to make a choice between the quick and the dead.

That is our business.

Behind the black portent of the new atomic age lies a hope which, seized upon with faith, can work our salvation. If we fail, then we have damned every man to be the slave of Fear. Let us not deceive ourselves: We must elect World Peace or World Destruction.

Science has torn from nature a secret so vast in its potentialities that our minds cower in fear from the terror it creates. Yet terror is not enough to inhibit the use of the atomic bomb. The terror created by weapons has never stopped man from employing them. For each new weapon a defense has been produced, in time. But now we face a condition in which adequate defense does not exist.

Science, which gave us this dread power, shows that it can be made a giant help to humanity, but science does *not* show us how to prevent its baleful use. So we have been appointed to obviate that peril by finding a meeting of the minds and hearts of our people. Only in the will of mankind lies the answer.

It is to express this will and make it effective that we have been assembled. We must provide the mechanisms to assure that atomic energy is used for peaceful purposes and preclude its use in war. To that end, we must provide immediate, swift, and sure punishment of those who violate the agreements that are reached by the nations. Penalization is essential if peace is to be more than a feverish interlude between wars. . . .

I now submit the following measures as representing the fundamental features of a plan which could give effect to certain of the conclusions which I have epitomized.

1. *General*. The Authority should set up a thorough plan for control of the field of atomic energy, through various forms of ownership, dominion, licenses, operation, inspection, research, and management by competent personnel. After this is provided for, there should be as little interference as may be with the economic plans and the present private, corporate, and state relationships in the several countries involved.

2. *Raw Materials*. The Authority should have as one of its earliest purposes to obtain and maintain complete and accurate information on world supplies of uranium and thorium and to bring them under its dominion. The precise pattern of control for various types of deposits of such materials will have to depend upon the geological, mining, refining, and economic facts involved in different situations.

The Authority should conduct continuous surveys so that it will have the most complete knowledge of the world geology of uranium and thorium. Only after all current information on world sources of uranium and thorium is known to us all can equitable plans be made for their production, refining, and distribution.

3. *Primary Production Plants*. The Authority should exercise complete managerial control of the production of fissionable materials. This means that it should control and operate all plants producing fissionable materials in dangerous quantities and must own and control the product of these plants.

4. *Atomic Explosives*. The Authority should be given sole and exclusive right to conduct research in the field of atomic explosives. Research activities in the field of atomic explosives are essential in order that the Authority may keep in the forefront of knowledge in the field of atomic energy and fulfil the objective of preventing illicit manufacture of bombs. Only by maintaining its position as the best-informed agency will the Authority be able to determine the line between intrinsically dangerous and non-dangerous activities.

5. *Strategic Distribution of Activities and Materials*. The activities entrusted to the Authority because they are intrinsically dangerous to security should be distributed throughout the world. Similarly, stockpiles of raw materials and fissionable materials should not be centralized.

6. *Non-dangerous Activities*. A function of the Authority should be promotion of the peacetime benefits of atomic energy.

Atomic research (except in explosives), the use of research reactors, the production of radioactive tracers by means of non-dangerous reactors, the use of such tracers, and to some extent the production of power should be open to nations and their citizens under reasonable licensing arrangements from the Authority. Denatured materials, whose use we know also requires suitable safeguards, should be furnished for such purpcses by the Authority under lease or other arrangement. Denaturing seems to have been overestimated by the public as a safety measure.

7. *Definition of Dangerous and Non-dangerous Activities.* Although a reasonable dividing line can be drawn between dangerous and non-dangerous activities, it is not hard and fast. Provision should, therefore, be made to assure constant reexamination of the questions and to permit revision of the dividing line as changing conditions and new discoveries may require.

8. *Operations of Dangerous Activities.* Any plant dealing with uranium and thorium after it once reaches the potential of dangerous use must be not only subject to the most rigorous and competent inspection by the Authority, but its actual operation shall be under the management, supervision, and control of that authority.

9. *Inspection.* By assigning intrinsically dangerous activities exclusively to the Authority, the difficulties of inspection are reduced. If the Authority is the only agency which may lawfully conduct dangerous activities, then visible operation by others than the Authority will constitute an unambiguous danger signal. Inspection will also occur in connection with the licensing function of the Authority.

10. *Freedom of Access.* Adequate ingress and egress for all qualified representatives of the Authority must be assured. Many of the inspection activities of the Authority should grow out of, and be incidental to, its other functions. Important measures of inspection will be associated with the tight control of raw materials, for this is a keynote of the plan. The continuing activities of prospecting, survey, and research in relation to raw materials will be designed not only to serve the affirmative development functions of the authority but also to assure that no surreptitious operations are conducted in the raw-material field by nation or their citizens.

11. *Personnel.* The personnel of the Authority should be recruited on a basis of proven competence but also as far as possible on an international basis.

12. *Progress by Stages.* A primary step in the creation of the system of control is the setting forth, in comprehensive terms, of the functions, responsibilities, powers, and limitations of the Authority. Once a charter for the Authority has been adopted, the Authority and the system of control for which it will be responsible will require time to become fully organized and effective. The plan of control will, therefore, have to come into effect in successive stages. These should be specifically fixed in the charter or means should otherwise be set forth in the charter for transitions from one stage to another, as contemplated in the resolution of the United Nations Assembly which created this Commission.

13. *Disclosures*. In the deliberations of the United Nations Commission on Atomic Energy, the United States is prepared to make available the information essential to a reasonable understanding of the proposals which it advocates. Further disclosures must be dependent, in the interests of all, upon the effective ratification of the treaty. When the Authority is actually created, the United States will join the other nations in making available the further information essential to that organization for the performance of its functions. As the successive stages of international control are reached, the United States will be prepared to yield, to the extent required by each stage, national control of the activities in this field to the Authority.

14. *International Control*. There will be questions about the extent of control to be allowed to national bodies, when the Authority is established. Purely national authorities for control and development of atomic energy should to the extent necessary for the effective operation of the Authority be subordinate to it. This is neither an endorsement nor a disapproval of the creation of national authorities. The Commission should evolve a clear demarcation of the scope of duties and responsibities of such national authorities.

SOURCE. U. S. Department of State, *The United States and the United Nations*, Report Series No. 7, Washington, D. C.: 1947, pp. 169–178.

b. THE MARSHALL PLAN, 1947

THE WIDENING SPLIT between the United States and the Soviet Union, the slow pace of economic recovery in Western Europe, and the growth of Communist parties in the western European states were all factors underlying the American program of massive economic aid to Europe known as the Marshall Plan. Described by Secretary of State George C. Marshall in an address at Harvard University on June 5, 1947, it resulted in the spending of some four and a half billion dollars during its first year of operation. It was markedly successful in building European prosperity and curbing the spread of European Communism.

I need not tell you, gentlemen, that the world situation is very serious. That must be apparent to all intelligent people. I think one difficulty is that the problem is one of such enormous complexity that the very mass of facts presented to the public by press and radio make it exceedingly difficult for the man in the street to reach a clear appraisement of the situation. Furthermore, the people of this country are distant from the troubled areas of the earth and it is hard for them to comprehend the plight and consequent reactions on their governments in connection with our efforts to promote peace in the world.

In considering the requirements for the rehabilitation of Europe the physical loss of life, the visible destruction of cities, factories, mines and railroads was correctly estimated, but it has become obvious during recent months that this visible destruction was probably less serious than the dislocation of the entire fabric of European economy. For the past ten years conditions have been highly abnormal.

The feverish preparation for war and the more feverish maintenance of the war effort engulfed all aspects of national economies. Machinery has fallen into disrepair or is entirely obsolete. Under the arbitrary and destructive Nazi rule, virtually every possible enterprise was geared into the German war machine. Long-standing commericial ties, private institutions, banks, insurance companies and shipping companies disappeared, through loss of capital, absorption through nationalization or by simple destruction.

In many countries, confidence in the local currency has been severely shaken. The breakdown of the business structure of Europe during the war was complete. Recovery has been seriously retarded by the fact that two years after the close of hostilities a peace agreement with Germany and Austria has not been agreed upon. But even given a more prompt solution of these difficult problems, the rehabilitation of the economic structure of Europe quite evidently will require a much longer time and greater effort than had been foreseen.

There is a phase of this matter which is both interesting and serious. The farmer has always produced the foodstuffs to exchange with the city dweller for the other necessities of life. The division of labor is the basis of modern civilization. At the present time it is threatened with breakdown. The town and city industries are not producing adequate goods to exchange with the food-producing farmer. Raw materials and fuel are in short supply. Machinery is lacking or worn out.

The farmer or the peasant cannot find the goods for sale which he desires to purchase. So the sale of his farm produce for money which he cannot use, seems to him an unprofitable transaction. He, therefore, has withdrawn many fields from crop cultivation and is using them for grazing. He feeds more grain to stock and finds for himself and his family an ample supply of food, however short he may be on clothing and the other ordinary gadgets of civilization. Meanwhile, people in the cities are short of food and fuel. So the governments are forced to use their foreign money and credits to procure these necessities abroad. This process exhausts funds which are urgently needed for reconstruction. Thus a very serious situation is rapidly developing which bodes no good for the world. The modern system of the division of labor upon which the exchange of products is based is in danger of breaking down.

The truth of the matter is that Europe's requirements for the next three or four years of foreign food and other essential products—principally from America—are so much greater than her present ability to pay that she must have substantial additional help, or face economic, social and political deterioration of a very grave character.

The remedy lies in breaking the vicious circle and restoring the confidence of the European people in the economic future of their own countries and of Europe as a whole. The manufacturer and the farmer throughout wide areas must be able and willing to exchange their products for currencies, the continuing value of which is not open to question.

Aside from the demoralizing effect on the world at large and the possibilities of disturbances arising as a result of the desperation of the people concerned, the consequences to the economy of the United States should be apparent to all. It is logical that the United States should do whatever it is able to do to assist in the return of normal economic health to the world, without which there can be no political stability and no assured peace.

Our policy is directed not against any country or doctrine but against hunger, poverty, desperation and chaos. Its purpose should be the revival of a working economy in the world so as to permit the emergence of political and social conditions in which free institutions can exist. Such assistance, I am convinced, must not be on a piecemeal basis as various crises develop. Any assistance that this government may develop in the future should provide a cure rather than a mere palliative.

Any government that is willing to assist in the task of recovery will find full cooperation, I am sure, on the part of the United States Government. Any government which maneuvers to block the recovery of other countries cannot expect help from us. Furthermore, governments, political parties or groups which seek to perpetuate human misery in order to profit therefrom politically or otherwise will encounter the opposition of the United States.

It is already evident that, before the United States Government can proceed much further in its efforts to alleviate the situation and help start the European world on its way to recovery, there must be some agreement among the countries of Europe as to the requirements of the situation and the part those countries themselves will take in order to give proper effect to whatever action might be undertaken by this Government. It would be neither fitting nor efficacious for this Government to undertake to draw up unilaterally a program designed to place Europe on its feet economically. This is the business of the Europeans. The initiative, I think, must come from Europe. The role of this country should consist of friendly aid in the drafting of a European program and of later support of such a program so far as it may be practical for us to do so. The program should be a joint one, agreed to by a number, if not all European nations.

An essential part of any successful action on the part of the United States is an understanding on the part of the people of America of the character of the problem and the remedies to be applied. Political passion and prejudice should have no part. With foresight, and a willingness on the part of our people to face up to the vast responsibility which history has clearly placed upon our country, the difficulties I have outlined can and will be overcome.

c. THE NORTH ATLANTIC TREATY, 1949

AS A FURTHER STEP against Soviet expansion in Europe, a mutual defense alliance—the North Atlantic Treaty—was drawn up in the fall of 1948. On April 4, 1949, the Treaty was signed by Great Britain, France, The Netherlands, Belgium, Luxembourg, Canada, the United States, Norway, Denmark, Iceland, Italy, and Portugal. The North Atlantic Treaty Organization (NATO) became the chief international organ for coordinating the military defense of western Europe.

PREAMPLE. The parties to this treaty reaffirm their faith in the purposes and principles of the Charter of the United Nations and their desire to live in peace with all peoples and all governments.

They are determined to safeguard the freedom, common heritage and civilization of their peoples, founded on the principles of democracy, individual liberty and the rule of law.

They seek to promote stability and well-being in the North Atlantic area.

They are resolved to unite their efforts for collective defense and for the preservation of peace and security.

They therefore agree to this North Atlantic Treaty:

ARTICLE 1. The parties undertake, as set forth in the Charter of the United Nations, to settle any international disputes in which they may be involved by peaceful means in such a manner that international peace and security, and justice, are not endangered, and to refrain in their international relations from the threat or use of force in any manner inconsistent with the purposes of the United Nations.

ARTICLE 2. The parties will contribute toward the further development of peaceful and friendly international relations by strengthening their free institutions, by bringing about a better understanding of the principles upon which these institutions are founded, and by promoting conditions of stability and well-being. They will seek to eliminate conflict in their international economic policies and will encourage economic collaboration between any or all of them.

ARTICLE 3. In order more effectively to achieve the objectives of this treaty, the parties, separately and jointly, by means of continuous and effective self-help and mutual aid, will maintain and develop their individual and collective capacity to resist armed attack.

ARTICLE 4. The parties will consult together whenever, in the opinion of any of them, the territorial integrity, political independence or security of any of the parties is threatened.

ARTICLE 5. The parties agree that an armed attack against one or more of them in Europe or North America shall be considered an attack against them all; and consequently they agree that, if such an armed attack occurs, each of them, in exercise of the right of individual or collective self-defense recognized by Article 51 of the Charter of the United Nations, will assist the party or parties so attacked by taking forthwith, individually and in concert with the other parties, such action as it deems necessary, including the use of armed force, to restore and maintain the security of the North Atlantic area.

Any such armed attack and all measures taken as a result thereof shall immediately be reported to the Security Council. Such measures shall be terminated when the Security Council has taken the measures necessary to restore and maintain international peace and security.

ARTICLE 6. For the purpose of Article 5 an armed attack on one or more of the parties is deemed to include an armed attack on the territory of any of the parties in Europe or North America, on the Algerian Departments of France, on the occupation forces of any party in Europe, on the islands under the jurisdiction of any party in the North Atlantic area north of the Tropic of Cancer or on the vessels or aircraft in this area of any of the parties.

ARTICLE 7. This treaty does not affect, and shall not be interpreted as affecting, in any way the rights and obligations under the Charter of the parties which are members of the United Nations, or the primary responsibility of the Security Council for the maintenance of international peace and security.

ARTICLE 8. Each party declares that none of the international engagements now in force between it and any other of the parties or any third state is in conflict with the provisions of this treaty, and undertakes not to enter into any international engagement in conflict with this treaty.

ARTICLE 9. The parties hereby establish a Council, on which each of them shall be represented, to consider matters concerning the implementation of this treaty. The Council shall be so organized as to be able to meet promptly at any time. The Council shall set up such subsidiary bodies as may be necessary; in particular it shall establish immediately a defense committee which shall recommend measures for the implementation of Articles 3 and 5.

ARTICLE 10. The parties may, by unanimous agreement, invite any other European state in a position to further the principles of this treaty and to contribute to the security of the North Atlantic area to accede to this treaty. Any state so invited may become a party to the treaty by depositing its instrument of accession with the Government of the United States of America. The Government of the United States of America will inform each of the parties of the deposit of each such instrument of accession.

ARTICLE 11. This treaty shall be ratified and its provisions carried out by the parties in accordance with their respective constitutional processes. The instruments of ratification shall be deposited as soon as possible with the Government of the United States of America, which will notify all the other signatories of each deposit. The treaty shall enter into force between the states which have ratified it as soon as the ratifications of the majority of the signatories, including the ratifications of Belgium, Canada, France, Luxembourg, the Netherlands, the United Kingdom and the United States, have been deposited and shall come into effect with respect to other states on the date of the deposit of their ratifications.

ARTICLE 12. After the treaty has been in force for ten years, or at any time thereafter, the parties shall, if any of them so requests, consult together for the purpose of reviewing the treaty, having regard for the factors then affecting peace and security in the North Atlantic area, including the development of universal as well as regional arrangements under the Charter of the United Nations for the maintenance of international peace and security.

ARTICLE 13. After the treaty has been in force for twenty years, any party may cease to be a party one year after its notice of denunciation has been given to the Government of the United States of America, which will inform the Governments of the other parties of the deposit of each notice of denunciation.

ARTICLE 14. This treaty, of which the English and French texts are equally authentic, shall be deposited in the archives of the Government of the United States of America. Duly certified copies thereof will be transmitted by that Government to the Governments of the other signatories.

IN WITNESS WHEREOF, the undersigned plenipotentiaries have signed this treaty.

d. THE HUNGARIAN REBELLION, NOVEMBER 1956

IN THE AUTUMN OF 1956, as the American presidential campaign between Dwight D. Eisenhower and Adlai E. Stevenson was drawing to its conclusion, two major world crises broke out almost simultaneously: the invasion of Egypt by English, French, and Israeli forces in response to Egypt's earlier nationalization of the Suez Canal, and the rebellion against the Communist regime in Hungary. An anti-Communist Hungarian government, headed by Premier Imre Nagy, held power briefly, but the rebellion was quickly crushed by the tanks and troops of Soviet Russia. The final moments of the rebellion are dramatically captured in Premier Nagy's last message to the Hungarian people and the free world.

Premier Imre Nagy's Final Message

This fight is the fight for freedom by the Hungarian people against the Russian intervention, and it is possible that I shall only be able to stay at my post for one or two hours. The whole world will see how the Russian armed forces, contrary to all treaties and conventions, are crushing the resistance of the Hungarian people. They will also see how they are kidnapping the Prime Minister of a country which is a Member of the United Nations, taking him from the capital, and therefore it cannot be doubted at all that this is the most brutal form of intervention. I should like in these last moments to ask the leaders of the revolution, if they can, to leave the country. I ask that all that I have said in my broadcast, and what we have agreed on with the revolutionary leaders during meetings in Parliament, should be put in a memorandum, and the leaders should turn to all the peoples of the world for help and explain that today it is Hungary and tomorrow, or the day after tomorrow, it will be the turn of other countries because the imperialism of Moscow does not know borders, and is only trying to play for time.

SOURCE. "United Nations Report of the Special Committee on the Problem of Hungary," *General Assembly Official Records*, 11th Session Supplement #18 A/3592.

ENGLAND, FRANCE, AND ISRAEL withdrew from Egypt on the strength of United Nations and world opposition, but appeals by the United Nations General Assembly for Russian withdrawal from Hungary were ignored. The rebellion was extinguished, but the policy of the Soviet Union dealt a serious blow to the prestige of world Communism and provoked numerous resignations from the Party.

United Nations Resolution On Hungary, November 4, 1956

The General Assembly,

Considering that the United Nations is based on the principle of the sovereign equality of all its Members,

Recalling that the enjoyment of human rights and of fundamental freedom in Hungary was specifically guaranteed by the Peace Treaty between Hungary and the Allied and Associated Powers signed at Paris on 10 February 1947 and that the general principle of these rights and this freedom is affirmed for all peoples in the Charter of the United Nations,

Convinced that recent events in Hungary manifest clearly the desire of the Hungarian people to exercise and to enjoy fully their fundamental rights, freedom and independence,

Condemning the use of Soviet military forces to suppress the efforts of the Hungarian people to reassert their rights,

Noting moreover the declaration of 30 October 1956 by the Government of the Union of Soviet Socialist Republics of its avowed policy of non-intervention in the internal affairs of other States,

Noting the communication of 1 November 1956 (A/3251) of the Government of Hungary to the Secretary-General regarding demands made by that Government to the Government of the Union of Soviet Socialist Republics for the instant and immediate withdrawal of Soviet forces,

Noting further the communication of 2 November 1956 (S/3726) from the Government of Hungary to the Secretary-General asking the Security Council to instruct the Government of the Union of Soviet Socialist Republics and the Government of Hungary to start the negotiations immediately on withdrawal of Soviet forces,

Noting that the intervention of Soviet military forces in Hungary has resulted in grave loss of life and widespread bloodshed among the Hungarian people,

Taking note of the radio appeal of Prime Minister Imre Nagy of 4 November 1956,

1. *Calls upon* the Government of the Union of Soviet Socialist Republics to desist forthwith from all attack on the people of Hungary and from any form of intervention, in particular armed intervention, in the internal affairs of Hungary;

2. *Calls upon* the Union of Soviet Socialist Republics to cease the introduction of additional armed forces into Hungary and to withdraw all of its forces without delay from Hungarian territory;

3. *Affirms* the rights of the Hungarian people to a government responsive to its national aspirations and dedicated to its independence and well-being;

4. *Requests* the Secretary-General to investigate the situation caused by foreign intervention in Hungary, to observe the situation directly through representatives named by him, and to report thereon to the General Assembly at the earliest moment, and as soon as possible suggest methods to bring an end to the foreign intervention in Hungary in accordance with the principles of the Charter of the United Nations;

5. *Calls upon* the Government of Hungary and the Government of the Union of Soviet Socialist Republics to permit observers designated by the Secretary-General to enter the territory of Hungary, to travel freely therein, and to report their findings to the Secretary-General;

6. *Calls upon* all Members of the United Nations to co-operate with the Secretary-General and his representatives in the execution of his functions:

7. *Requests* the Secretary-General in consultation with the heads of appropriate specialized agencies to inquire, on an urgent basis, into the needs of the Hungarian people for food, medicine and other similar supplies, and to report to the General Assembly as soon as possible;

8. *Requests* all Members of the United Nations, and invites national and international humanitarian organizations to co-operate in making available such supplies as may be required by the Hungarian people.

564th Plenary Meeting
4 November 1956

SOURCE. Resolution 1004 (ES II).

e. KHRUSHCHEV ON THE COLD WAR: 1960, 1961

BY THE LATER 1950's signs of a slight thaw in the Cold War were beginning to appear. Communist China held to the traditional position that war between the Communist states and their opponents was inevitable, but Premier Nikita Khrushchev advanced the notion of peaceful coexistence, maintaining that atomic war would be a catastrophe for all concerned and that the Communist victory could be achieved through peaceful economic competition with the capitalist states. He expressed these views succinctly in an address to the Roumanian Communist Party in Bucharest on June 21, 1960.

Comrades, questions of international relations, questions of war and peace, have always deeply concerned the mass of the people. That is natural. More than once in history the anti-national policy of the imperialists, their desire for a redivision of the world, for the seizure of new colonies, have subjected mankind to the horrors of devastating wars. But no matter how terrible wars have been in the past, if the imperialist circles should succeed in unleashing another world war, its calamities would be incomparably more terrible. For millions of people might burn in the conflagration of hydrogen explosions, and for some states a nuclear war would be literally a catastrophe. That is why the Marxist-Leninist parties, in all their activity, have always been consistent champions of a reasonable peaceloving policy, of the prevention of another world war. . . .

This is a policy of coexistence, a policy of consolidating peace, easing international tension and doing away with the cold war.

The thesis that in our time war is not inevitable has a direct bearing on the policy of peaceful coexistence proclaimed at the 20th and 21st Congresses of our party. Lenin's propositions about imperialism remain in force and are still a lodestar for us in our theory and practice. But it should not be forgotten that Lenin's propositions on imperialism were advanced and developed tens of years ago, when the world did not know many things that are now decisive for historical development, for the entire international situation.

Some of Lenin's propositions on imperialism date back to the period when there was no Soviet Union, when the other socialist countries did not exist.

The powerful Soviet Union, with its enormous economic and military potential, is now growing and gaining in strength; the great socialist camp, which now numbers over 1,000 million people, is growing and gaining in strength; the organisation and political consciousness of the working class have grown, and even in the capitalist countries it is actively fighting for peace. Such factors are in operation now as, for instance, the broad movement of peace champions; the number of countries coming out for peace among nations is increasing. It should also be pointed out that imperialism no longer has such a rear to fall back upon as the colonial system which it had formerly.

Besides, comrades, one cannot mechanically repeat now on this question what Vladimir Ilyich Lenin said many decades ago on imperialism, and go on asserting that imperialist wars are inevitable until socialism triumphs throughout the world. We are now living in such a period when the forces of socialism are increasingly growing and becoming stronger, where ever-broader masses of the working people are rallying behind the banner of Marxism-Leninism.

History will possibly witness such a time when capitalism is preserved only in a small number of states, maybe states for instance, as small as a button on a coat. Well? And even in such conditions would one have to look up in a book what Vladimir Ilyich Lenin quite correctly said for his time, would one just have to repeat that wars are inevitable since capitalist countries exist?

Of course, the essence of capitalism, of imperialism, does not change even if it is represented by small countries. It is common knowledge that a wolf is just as bloodthirsty a beast of prey as a lion or a tiger, although he is much weaker. That is why man fears less to meet a wolf than a tiger or a lion. Of course, small beasts of prey can also bite, essentially they are the same but they have different possibilities, they are not so strong and it is easier to render them harmless.

Therefore one cannot ignore the specific situation, the changes in the correlation of forces in the world and repeat what the great Lenin said in quite different historical conditions. If Lenin could rise from his grave he would take such people, as one says, to task and would teach them how one must understand the essence of the matter.

We live in a time when we have neither Marx, nor Engels, nor Lenin with us. If we act like children who, studying the alphabet, compile words from letters, we shall not go very far. Marx, Engels and Lenin created their immortal works which will not fade away in centuries. They indicated to mankind the road to communism. And we confidently follow this road. On the basis of the teaching of Marxism-Leninism we must think ourselves, profoundly study life, analyse the present situation and draw the conclusions which benefit the common cause of communism.

One must not only be able to read but also correctly understand what one has read and apply it in the specific conditions of the time in which we live, taking into consideration the existing situation, and the real balance of forces. A political leader acting in this manner shows that he not only can read but can also creatively apply the revolutionary teaching. If he does not do this, he resembles a man about whom people say: "He looks into a book, but sees nothing!"

All this gives grounds for saying with confidence that under present conditions war is not inevitable.

He who fails to understand this does not believe in the strength and creative abilities of the working class, underestimates the power of the socialist camp, does not believe in the great force of attraction of socialism, which has demonstrated its superiority over capitalism with the utmost clarity.

Is the possibility of the imperialists unleashing war under present conditions ruled out? We have said several times and we repeat once again: No, it is not. But. . . . the imperialists do not want to trigger off war in order to perish in it. . . . Therefore today even the stupid, frenzied representatives of the imperialist circles will think twice about our power before they start a military gamble. . . .

The U.S.S.R. pursued a policy of peace even when it stood alone, facing the powerful camp of imperialist states. We are also pursuing this policy now when the forces of peace are undoubtedly superior to the forces of war and aggression.

This position of ours stems from our firm belief in the stability of the socialist system, in our system. . . .

No world war is needed for the triumph of socialist ideas throughout the world. These ideas will get the upper hand in the peaceful competition between the countries of socialism and capitalism.

In a speech of October 17, 1961, to the 22nd Congress of the Communist Party of the Soviet Union (C.S.P.U.), Khrushchev elaborated on the theory of peaceful coexistence and summarized the Russian position in world politics.

Comrades, the chief content of the period following the Twentieth Congress of the C.P.S.U. is the competition between the two world social systems—the socialist and capitalist systems. It has become the pivot, the main feature of world development in the present historical period. Two lines, two historical tendencies in social development, are becoming more and more evident. One of them is the line of social progress, of peace and creative activity. The other is the line of reaction, oppression and war.

If we imagine the whole globe as the scene of this competition, we see that socialism has been winning one position after another from the old world. In the first place capitalism has been seriously cramped by socialism in a decisive sphere of human activity, that of material production. The socialist system's share in world production has increased and its rates of development greatly exceed those of the most advanced capitalist countries. It is obvious to everyone that the socialist countries are able to develop colossal productive forces and create a real abundance of material and spiritual values.

While conducting an unswerving policy we have not forgotten the threat of war on the part of the imperialists. Everything necessary has been done to ensure the superiority of our country in defense. The achievements of socialist production and Soviet science and technology have enabled us to effect a real revolution in matters military. Our country and the entire socialist camp now possess vast power, ample to provide a reliable defense for the great gains of socialism against the inroads of imperialist aggressors. The growing defense power of the Soviet Union and the other socialist countries, and the world peace forces have not allowed the imperialists to divert the competition between the two systems from the path of peace on to that of armed conflict, of war. The Soviet Union, while pursuing the Leninist policy of peaceful coexistence, has resolutely exposed and checked imperialist provocations.

The fact that it has been possible to prevent war, and that Soviet people and the peoples of other countries have been able to enjoy the benefits of peaceful life must be regarded as the chief result of the activities of our Party and its Central Committee in increasing the might of the Soviet state and in implementing a Leninist foreign policy, as a result of the work of the fraternal parties of the socialist states and the greater activity of the peace forces in all countries.

During recent years, as we know, the imperialists have made a number of attempts to ignite the fires of a new war and test the strength of the socialist system. During the past five years the U.S.A. and its closest allies have frequently resorted to brutal force, have resorted to arms. But on each occasion the Soviet Union and all the socialist countries have checked the aggressor in good time. Of particular, fundamental importance were the actions of the socialist countries in defense of the peoples struggling for their liberty and independence. The masses are getting to realize more and more that the Soviet Union and all the socialist countries are a reliable support in the struggle the peoples are waging for their liberty and independence, for progress and peace.

In the course of the peaceful competition between the two systems capitalism has suffered a profound moral defeat in the eyes of all peoples. Ordinary people are being daily convinced that capitalism cannot solve any of the urgent problems facing mankind. It is becoming ever more obvious that these problems can be solved only through socialism. Faith in the capitalist system and the capitalist path of development is dwindling. Monopoly capital is losing influence and resorting more frequently to the intimidation and suppression of the people, to methods of open dictatorship to implement its domestic policy, and to aggressive acts against other countries. The masses, however, are offering increasing resistance to reaction.

It is no secret that intimidation and threats are not a sign of strength but are evidence of the weakening of capitalism and the deepening of its general crisis. As the saying goes, "If you couldn't hang on by the mane, you won't hold on by the tail!" The reactionaries in some countries are still able, in defiance of constitutions, to dissolve parliaments, cast the best representatives of the people into prison and dispatch cruisers and marines to subdue the "unruly." All this may put off for a time the fatal hour of capitalist rule. Such measures of repression, however, expose, to a still greater extent, the predatory nature of imperialism. The imperialists are cutting off the branch on which they are sitting. There are no barriers in the world that can stem mankind's advance along the road of progress.

Events show that our Party's policy, elaborated by the Twentieth Congress, was a correct and true one: the Congress noted that the main feature of our epoch was the emergence of socialism beyond the bounds of one country and its conversion into a world system. In the period since that Congress there has been further important progress—the world socialist system is becoming a decisive factor in the development of society.

The Party drew the conclusion that the collapse of colonialism is inevitable. Under the powerful blows of the national liberation movement the colonial system has, to all intents and purposes, fallen to pieces.

The Party propounded the important thesis that wars between states are not inevitable in the present epoch, that they can be prevented. The events of the past years serve to confirm this, too. They show that the mighty forces that stand watch over the peace have today effective means of preventing the imperialists from launching a world war. The superiority of the forces of peace and socialism over those of imperialism and war has become more evident.

To put it briefly, comrades, for us those six years have been good years on a world scale.

SOURCE. Soviet Embassy, *Soviet News*, #4229, June 22, 1960.

f. VIETNAM: FROM PRESIDENT JOHNSON'S NEWS CONFERENCE, July 28, 1965

THE AMERICAN POLICY OF CONTAINMENT and the Communist doctrine of expansion through wars of "national liberation" collided in Vietnam. The Vietnam War, although "limited," was immensely destructive and seemingly endless. Formerly a part of French Incochina, Vietnam was divided after the French withdrawal into Communist North Vietnam and non-Communist South Vietnam. The government of South Vietnam, backed by the United States, had increasing difficulty in subduing a rebellion of South Vietnamese Communists, the Viet Cong, aided by the North Vietnamese. In 1965 the United States began bombing North Vietnam and significantly increasing the number of American troops in South Vietnam. Some argued that this policy was strategically unwise and a dangerous threat to world peace. President Lyndon B. Johnson attempted to refute these argu-

ments in a news conference of July 28, 1965, in which he announced his intention to nearly double the American military force in Vietnam. Further increases over the next three years were to raise American troop strength in Vietnam to over half a million.

MY FELLOW AMERICANS:

Not long ago I received a letter from a woman in the Midwest. She wrote:

Dear Mr. President:
In my humble way I am writing to you about the crisis in Viet-Nam. I have a son who is now in Viet-Nam. My husband served in World War II. Our country was at war, but now, this time, it is just something that I don't understand. Why?

Well, I have tried to answer that question dozens of times and more in practically every State in this Union. I have discussed it fully in Baltimore in April, in Washington in May, in San Francisco in June. Let me again, now, discuss it here in the East Room of the White House.

Why must young Americans, born into a land exultant with hope and with golden promise, toil and suffer and sometimes die in such a remote and distant place?

The answer, like the war itself, is not an easy one, but it echoes clearly from the painful lessons of half a century. Three times in my lifetime in two world wars and in Korea Americans have gone to far lands to fight for freedom. We have learned at a terrible and a brutal cost that retreat does not bring safety and weakness does not bring peace.

It is this lesson that has brought us to Viet-Nam. This is a different kind of war. There are no marching armies or solemn declarations. Some citizens of South Viet-Nam at times with understandable grievances have joined in the attack on their own government.

But we must not let this mask the central fact that this is really war. It is guided by North Viet-Nam and it is spurred by Communist China. Its goal is to conquer the South, to defeat American power, and to extend the Asiatic dominion of communism.

There are great stakes in the balance.

Most of the non-Communist nations of Asia cannot, by themselves and alone, resist the growing might and the grasping ambition of Asian communism.

Our power, therefore, is a very vital shield. If we are driven from the field in Viet-Nam, then no nation can ever again have the same confidence in American promise, or in American protection.

In each land the forces of independence would be considerably weakened and an Asia so threatened by Communist domination would certainly imperil the security of the United States itself.

We did not choose to be the guardians at the gate, but there is no one else.

Nor would surrender in Viet-Nam bring peace, because we learned from Hitler at Munich that success only feeds the appetite of aggression.The battle would be renewed in one country and then another country, bringing with it perhaps even larger and crueler conflict, as we have learned from the lessons of history.

Moreover, we are in Viet-Nam to fulfill one of the most solemn pledges of the American Nation. Three Presidents—President Eisenhower, President Kennedy, and your present President—over 11 years have committed themselves and have promised to help defend this small and valiant nation.

Strengthened by that promise, the people of South Viet-Nam have fought for many long years. Thousands of them have died. Thousands more have been crippled and scarred by war. We just cannot now dishonor our word, or abandom our commitment, or leave those who believed us and who trusted us to the terror and repression and murder that would follow.

This, then, my fellow Americans, is why we are in Viet-Nam.

What are our goals in that war-strained land?

First, we intend to convince the Communists that we cannot be defeated by force of arms or by superior power. They are not easily convinced. In recent months they have greatly increased their fighting forces and their attacks and the number of incidents.

I have asked the Commanding General, General Westmoreland, what more he needs to meet this mounting aggression. He has told me. We will meet his needs.

I have today ordered to Viet-Nam the Air Mobile Division and certain other forces which will raise our fighting strength from 75,000 to 125,000 men almost immediately. Additional forces will be needed later, and they will be sent as requested.

This will make it necessary to increase our active fighting forces by raising the monthly draft call from 17,000 over a peroid of time to 35,000 per month, and for us to step up our campaign for voluntary enlistments. . . .

We do not want an expanding struggle with consequences that no one can perceive, nor will we bluster or bully or flaunt our power, but we will not surrender and we will not retreat.

For behind our American pledge lies the determination and resources I believe, of all of the American Nation.

Second, once the Communists know, as we know, that a violent solution is impossible, then a peacefull solution is inevitable.

We are ready now, as we have always been, to move from the battlefield to the conference table. I have stated publicly and many times, again and again, American's willingness to begin unconditional discussions with any government at any place at any time. . . .

I have directed Ambassador Goldberg to go to New York today and to present immediately to Secretary General U Thant a letter from me requesting that all the resources, energy, and immense prestige of the United Nations be employed to find ways to halt aggression and to bring peace in Viet-Nam.
    . . .

Let me also add now a personal note. I do not find it easy to send the flower of our youth, our finest young men, into battle. I have spoken to you today of the divisions and the forces and the battalions and the units, but I know them all, every one. I have seen them in a thousand streets, of a hundred towns, in every State in this Union—working and laughing and building, and filled with hope and life. I think I know, too, how their mothers weep and how their families sorrow.

This is the most agonizing and the most painful duty of your President.

There is something else, too. When I was young, poverty was so common that we didn't know it had a name. An education was something that you had to fight for, and water was really life itself. I have now been in public life 35 years, more than three decades, and in each of those 35 years I have seen good men, and wise leaders, struggle to bring the blessings of this land to all of our people.

And now I am the President. It is now my opportunity to help every child get an education, to help every Negro and every American citizen have an equal opportunity, to have every family get a decent home, and to help bring healing to the sick and dignity to the old.

As I have said before, that is what I have lived for, that is what I have wanted all my life since I was a little boy, and I do not want to see all those hopes and all those dreams of so many people for so many years now drowned in the wasteful ravages of cruel wars. I am going to do all I can do to see that that never happens.

But I also know, as a realistic public servant, that as long as there are men who hate and destroy, we must have the courage to resist, or we will see it all, all that we have built, all that we hope to build, all of our dreams for freedom—all, *all* will be swept away on the flood of conquest.

So, too, this shall not happen. We will stand in Viet-Nam.

SOURCE. *Weekly Compilation of Presidential Documents,* Vol. I, No. 1, August 2, 1965.

g. THE PENTAGON PAPERS:
CABLEGRAM FROM PRESIDENT JOHNSON
TO AMBASSADOR LODGE, MARCH 20, 1964

*FROM THE TOP-SECRET DOCUMENTS of the United States govern-
ment relating to Vietnam, made public in 1971, the following cable of President Johnson to Henry Cabot Lodge, American ambassador to South
Vietnam in Saigon, outlines American thinking on the escalation of the war
and discloses opposition to the compromise solution of letting South Vietnam
become a neutral state.*

1. We have studied your 1776 and I am asking State to have Bill Bundy
make sure that you get out latest planning documents on ways of applying
pressure and power against the North. I understand that some of this was
discussed with you by McNamara mission in Saigon, but as plans are refined
it would be helpful to have your detailed comments. As we agreed in our
previous messages to each other, judgment is reserved for the present on
overt military action in view of the consensus from Saigon conversations of
McNamara mission with General Khanh and you on judgment that movement against the North at the present would be premature. We have [sic]
share General Khanh's judgment that the immediate and essential task is to
strengthen the southern base. For this reason our planning for action against
the North is on a contingency basis at present, and immediate problem in this
area is to develop the strongest possible military and political base for possible later action. There is additional international reason for avoiding immediate overt action in that we expect a showdown between the Chinese and
Soviet Communist parties soon and action against the North will be more
practicable after than before a showdown. But if at any time you feel that
more immediate action is urgent, I count on you to let me know specifically
the reasons for such action, together with your recommendations for its size
and shape.
2. On dealing with de Gaulle, I continue to think it may be valuable for
you to go to Paris after Bohlen has made his first try. (State is sending you
draft instruction to Bohlen, which I have not yet reviewed, for your comment.) It ought to be possible to explain in Saigon that your mission is precisely for the purpose of knocking down the idea of neutralization where-
ever it rears its ugly head and on this point I think that nothing is more important than to stop neutralist talk wherever we can by whatever means we
can. I have made this point myself to Manfield and Lippmann and I expect
to use every public opportunity to restate our position firmly. You may want
to convey our concern on this point to General Khanh and get his ideas on the

best possible joint program to stop such talk in Saigon, in Washington, and in Paris. I imagine that you have kept General Khanh abreast of our efforts in Paris. After we see the results of the Bohlen approach you might wish to sound him out on Paris visit by you.

h. THE PENTAGON PAPERS: AMERICAN OBJECTIVES IN VIETNAM, JANUARY 19, 1966

NEARLY TWO YEARS AFTER THE PRECEDING DOCUMENT, and about a half year after President Johnson's escalation announcement (above, f), America's prospects for victory in Vietnam were dim. In the following memorandum, Assistant Secretary of Defense McNaughton discusses basic American objectives in Vietnam and possible grounds for settlement. The "neutralization" possibility now seems less distasteful than in 1964.

The present U.S. objective in Vietnam is to avoid humiliation. The reasons why we *went into* Vietnam to the present depth are varied; but they are now largely academic. Why we have not *withdrawn* from Vietnam is, by all odds, *one* reason: (1) to preserve our reputation as a guarantor, and thus to preserve our effectiveness in the rest of the world. We have not hung on (2) to save a friend, or (3) to deny the Communists the added acres and heads (because the dominoes don't fall for that reason in this case), or even (4) to prove that "wars of national liberation" won't work (except as our reputation is involved). At each decision point we have gambled; at each point, to avoid the damage to our effectiveness of defaulting on our commitment, we have upped the ante. We have not defaulted, and the ante (and commitment) is now very high. It is important that we behave so as to protect our reputation. At the same time, since it is our *reputation* that is at stake, it is important that we not construe our obligation to be more than do the countries whose opinions of us *are* our reputation.

We are in an escalating military stalemate. There is an honest difference of judgment as to the success of the present military efforts in the South. There is no question that the U.S. deployments thwarted the VC[1] hope to achieve a quick victory in 1965. But there is a serious question whether we are now defeating the VC/PAVN[2] main forces and whether planned U.S.

[1] Viet Cong.

[2] Viet Cong/People's Army of North Vietnam.

deployments will more than hold our position in the country. Population and area control has not changed significantly in the past year; and the best judgment is that, even with the Phase IIA deployments, we will probably be faced is early 1967 with a continued stalemate at a higher level of forces and casualties.

U.S. commitment to SVN.[3] Some will say that we have defaulted if we end up, at any point in the relevant future, with anything less than a Western-oriented, non-Communist, independent government, exercising effective sovereignty over all of South Vietnam. This is not so. As stated above, the U.S. end is solely to preserve our reputation as a guarantor. It follows that the "softest" credible formulation of the U.S. commitment is the following:

    a. DRV does not take over South Vietnam by force. This does not *necessarily* rule out:

    b. A coalition government including Communists.

    c. A free decision by the South to succumb to the VC or to the North.

    d. A neutral (or even anti-U.S.) government in SVN.

    e. A live-and-let-live "reversion to 1959." Futhermore, we must recognize that even if we fail to in achieving this "soft" formulation, we could over time come out with minimum damage:

    f. If the reason was GVN[4] gross wrongheadedness or apathy.

    g. If victorious North Vietnam "went Titoist."

    h. If the Communist take-over was fuzzy and very slow.

i. PRESIDENT NIXON ON CHINA, 1971

AT THE HEIGHT OF HOSTILITIES IN 1968 to 1969, well over 500,000 American troops were supporting the pro-Western government of South Vietnam. The Viet Cong rebels were supported by substantial numbers of North Vietnamese troops and by supplies (but not troops) from Russia and China. American troops brought the rebellion under control but were unable to crush it. The American government, faced with a war it could not win, and with a war-weary, increasingly disillusioned, bitterly divided populace, was forced to a fundamental reevaluation of its postwar policy of containing Communism through military intervention. America's failure in Vietnam, together with growing hostility between Russia and China, marked the end of the Cold War in its traditional sense and the emergence of less polar-

[3] South Vietnam.

[4] Government of South Vietnam.

ized, more complex configurations in world politics. President Richard M. Nixon's decision to visit China in 1972 attested to his realization that international relations were no longer simply a duel between two power blocs with two antagonistic ideologies.

Good evening:

I have requested this television time tonight to announce a major development in our efforts to build a lasting peace in the world.

As I have pointed out on a number of occasions over the past three years, there can be no stable peace and enduring peace without the participation of the People's Republic of China and its 750 million people. That is why I have undertaken initiatives in several areas to open the door for more normal relations between our two countries.

In pursuance of that goal, I sent Dr. Kissinger, my Assistant for National Security Affairs, to Peking during his recent world tour for the purpose of having talks with Premier Chou En-lai.

The announcement I shall now read is being issued simultaneously in Peking and in the United States:

"Premier Chou En-lai and Dr. Henry Kissinger, President Nixon's Assistant for National Security Affairs, held talks in Peking from July 9 to 11, 1971. Knowing of President Nixon's expressed desire to visit the People's Republic of China, Premier Chou En-lai on behalf of the Government of the People's Republic of China has extended an invitation to President Nixon to visit China at an appropriate date before May, 1972."

"President Nixon has accepted the invitation with pleasure."

"The meeting between the leaders of China and the United States is to seek the normalization of relations between the two countries and also to exchange views on questions of concern to the two sides."

In anticipation of the inevitable speculation which will follow this announcement, I want to put our policy in the clearest possible context. Our action in seeking a new relationship with the People's Republic of China will not be at the expense of our old friends.

It is not directed against any other nation. We seek friendly relations with all nations. Any nation can be our friend without being any other nation's enemy.

I have taken this action because of my profound conviction that all nations will gain from a reduction of tensions and a better relationship between the United States and the People's Republic of China.

It is in this spirit that I will undertake what I deeply hope will become a journey for peace, peace not just for our generation but for future generations on this earth we share together.

Thank you and good night.

Chapter 19

THE THIRD WORLD

a. GANDHI: NONVIOLENCE

IN THE SHADOW OF THE POSTWAR STRUGGLE between the Russian and American blocs there gradually emerged a third group of nations — "Neutralist," uncommitted, pursuing goals of their own. The new group came to be called the "Third World." And although European countries such as Sweden and Yugoslavia often identified with the uncommitted nations, the Third World countries were predominately nonwhite, Afro-Asian, poor, and newly free. Aware that Russian and American leaders, although different in ideology, were similar in pigmentation, they represented the beginnings of a counterthrust against the long domination of the world by white peoples of European ancestry.

If the Third World is equated with the nonwhite world, then China and Japan belong to it, even though the former is enthusiastically Marxist and the latter is democratic, industrialized, and affluent. But the archetypal Third World nation is poor, uncommitted in the superpower duel, and newly independent. Most Third World countries share the searing experience of colonial subservience and the triumphant memory of recent liberation. They also share the realization that their colonial experience has precluded any return to a precolonial social order and that their new society must incorporate, on its own terms, many of the technological, constitutional, and ideological tools that had given power to their former masters.

Our first selection explores the process of liberation itself and the methodology of nonviolence, which in Gandhi's hands becomes more than a mere strategy for decolonization. Gandhi sees nonviolence as a potent ethical principle appropriate to all people dedicated to far-reaching political and social change. Thus, Gandhi, the great architect of Indian independence from British rule, contributed creatively and substantially to a tradition that has included such figures as the Buddha, Jesus, St. Francis, and—most recently— Martin Luther King. Like them, he found in nonviolence an extraordinarily positive and effective means of changing society and human lives.

I am but a poor struggling soul yearning to be wholly good —wholly truthful and wholly non-violent in thought, word and deed; but ever failing to reach the ideal which I know to be true. It is a painful climb, but the pain of it is a positive pleasure to me. Each step upward makes me feel stronger and fit for the next.

I am endeavouring to see God through service of humanity, for I know that God is neither in heaven, nor down below, but in every one.

Indeed religion should pervade every one of our actions. Here religion does not mean sectarianism. It means a belief in ordered moral government of the universe. It is not less real because it is unseen. This religion transcends Hinduism, Islam, Christianity, etc. It does not supersede them. It harmonizes them and gives them reality. . . .

To see the universal and all-pervading Spirit of truth face to face one must be able to love the meanest of creation as oneself. And a man who aspires after that cannot afford to keep out of any field of life. That is why my devotion to truth has drawn me into the field of politics; and I can say without the slightest hesitation, and yet in all humility, that those who say that religion has nothing to do with politics do not know what religion means. . . .

If I found myself entirely absorbed in the service of the community, the reason behind it was my desire for self-realization. I had made the service. And service for me was the service of India, because it came to me without my seeking, because I had an aptitude for it. . . .

We want freedom for our country, but not at the expense or exploitation of others, not so as to degrade other countries. I do not want the freedom of India if it means the extinction of England or the disappearance of Englishmen. I want the freedom of my country so that other countries may learn something from my free country, so that the resources of my country might be utilized for the benefit of mankind. Just as the cult of patriotism teaches us today that the individual has to die for the family, the family has to die for the village, the village for the district, the district for the province, and the province for the country, even so, a country has to be free in order that it may die, if necessary, for the benefit of the world. My love therefore of nationalism or my idea of nationalism, is that my country may become free, that if need be, the whole country may die, so that the human race may live. There is no room for race-hatred there. Let that be our nationalism.

There is no limit to extending our services to our neighbours across State-made frontiers. God never made those frontiers.

My goal is friendship with the whole world and I can combine the greatest love with the greatest opposition to wrong.

For me patriotism is the same as humanity. I am patriotic because I am human and humane. It is not exclusive, I will not hurt England or Germany to serve India. Imperialism has no place in my scheme of life. The law of a patriot is not different from that of the patriarch. And a patriot is so much the less a patriot if he is a lukewarm humanitarian. There is no conflict between private and political law.

Our non-co-operation is neither with the English nor with the West. Our non-co-operation is with the system the English have established, with the material civilization and its attendant greed and exploitation of the weak.

Our non-co-operation is a retirement within ourselves. Our non-co-operation is a refusal to co-operate with the English administrators on their own terms. We say to them: 'Come and co-operate with us on our terms and it will be well for us, for you and the world.' We must refuse to be lifted off our feet. A drowning man cannot save others. In order to be fit to save others, we must try to save ourselves. Indian nationalism is not exclusive, nor aggressive, nor destructive. It is health giving, religious and therefore humanitarian. India must learn to live before she can aspire to die for humanity. . . .

As to the habit of looking to the West for light, I can give little guidance if the whole of my life has not provided any. Light used to go out from the East. If the Eastern reservoir has become empty, naturally the East will have to borrow from the West. I wonder if light, if it is light and not a miasma, can ever be exhausted. As a boy I learnt that it grew with the giving. Anyway I have acted in that belief and have, therefore, traded on the ancestral capital. It has never failed me. This, however, does not mean that I must act like a frog in the well. There is nothing to prevent me from profiting by the light that may come from the West. Only I must take care that I am not overpowered by the glamor of the West. I must not mistake the glamor for true light.

I do not subscribe to the superstition that everything is good because it is ancient. I do not believe either that anything is good because it is Indian.

I have always held that social justice, even unto the least and lowliest, is impossible of attainment by force. I have believed that it is possible by proper training of the lowliest by non-violent means to secure the redress of the wrongs suffered by them. That means is non-violent non-co-operation. At times, non-co-operation becomes as much a duty as co-operation. No one is bound to co-operate in one's own undoing or slavery. Freedom received through the effort of others, however benevolent, cannot be retained when such effort is withdrawn. In other words, such freedom is not real freedom. But the lowliest can feel its glow, as soon as they learn the art of attaining it through non-violent non-co-operation.

Civil disobedience is the inherent right of a citizen. He dare not give it up without ceasing to be a man. Civil disobedience is never followed by anarchy. Criminal disobedience can lead to it. Every State puts down criminal disobedience by force. It perishes if it does not. But to put down civil disobedience is to attempt to imprison conscience. . . .

Non-violence is 'not a resignation from all real fighting against wickedness'. On the contrary, the non-violence of my conception is a more active and real fight against wickedness than retaliation whose very nature is to increase wickedness. I contemplate a mental and therefore a moral opposition to immoralities. I seek entirely to blunt the edge of the tyrant's sword, not by putting up against it a sharper-edged weapon, but by disappointing his expectation that I would be offering physical resistance. The resistance of the soul that I should offer would elude him. It would at first dazzle him and at last compel recognition from him, which recognition would not humiliate but would uplift him. It may be urged that this is an ideal state. And so it is. . . .

Non-violence cannot be taught to a person who fears to die and has no power of resistance. A helpless mouse is not non-violent because he is always eaten by pussy. He would gladly eat the murderess if he could, but he ever tries to flee from her. We do not call him a coward, because he is made by nature to behave no better than he does. But a man who, when faced by danger, behaves like a mouse, is rightly called a coward. He harbours violence and hatred in his heart and would kill his enemy if he could without hurting himself. He is a stranger to non-violence. All sermonizing on it will be lost on him. Bravery is foreign to his nature. Before he can understand non-violence he had to be taught to stand his ground and even suffer death, in the attempt to defend himself against the aggressor who bids fair to overwhelm him. To do otherwise would be to confirm his cowardice and take him farther away from non-violence. Whilst I may not actually help anyone to retaliate, I must not let a coward seek shelter behind non-violence so-called. Not knowing the stuff of which non-violence is made, many have honestly believed that running away from danger every time was a virtue compared to offering resistance, especially when it was fraught with danger to one's life. As a teacher of non-violence I must, so far as it is possible for me, guard against such an unmanly belief. . . .

Passive resistance is a method of securing rights by personal suffering; it is the reverse of resistance by arms. When I refuse to do a thing that is repugnant to my conscience, I use soul-force. For instance, the government of the day has passed a law which is applicable to me. I do not like it. If by using violence I force the government to repeal the law, I am employing what may be termed body-force. If I do not obey the law and accept the penalty for its breach, I use soul-force. It involves sacrifice of self.

Everybody admits that sacrifice of self is infinitely superior to sacrifice of others. Moreover, if this kind of force is used in a cause that is unjust, only the person using it suffers. He does not make others suffer for his mistakes. Men have before now done many things which were subsequently found to have been wrong. No man can claim that he is absolutely in the right or that a particular thing is wrong because he thinks so, but it is wrong for him so long as that is his deliberate judgement. It is therefore meet that he should not do that which he knows to be wrong, and suffer the consequence whatever it may be. This is the key to the use of soul-force. . . .

Complete civil disobedience is rebellion without the element of violence in it. An out-and-out civil resister simply ignores the authority of the State. He becomes an outlaw claiming to disregard every unmoral State law. Thus, for instance, he may refuse to pay taxes, he may refuse to recognize the authority in his daily intercourse. He may refuse to obey the law of trespass and claim to enter military barracks in order to speak to the soldiers, he may refuse to submit to limitations upon the manner of picketing and may picket within the proscribed area. In doing all this he never uses force and never resists force when it is used against him. In fact, he invites imprisonment and other uses of force against himself. This he does because and when he finds the bodily freedom he seemingly enjoys to be an intolerable burden. He argues to himself that a State allows personal freedom only in so far as the citizen submits to its regulations. Submission to the State law is the price a citizen pays for his personal liberty. Submission, therefore, to a State law wholly or largely unjust is an immoral barter for liberty. A citizen who thus realizes the evil nature of a State is not satisifed to live on its sufferance, and therefore appears to the others who do not share his belief to be a nuisance to society whilst he is endeavouring to compel the State, without committing a moral breach, to arrest him. Thus considered, civil resistance is a most powerful expression of a soul's anguish and an eloquent protest against the continuance of an evil State. Is not this the history of all reform? Have not reformers, much to the disgust of their fellows, discarded even innocent symbols associated with an evil practice?

When a body of men disown the State under which they have hitherto lived, they nearly establish their own government. I say nearly, for they do not go to the point of using force when they are resisted by the State. Their 'business', as of the individual, is to be locked up or shot by the State, unless it recognizes their separate existence, in other words bows to their will. Thus three thousand Indians in South Africa after due notice to the Government of the Transvaal crossed the Transvaal border in 1914 in defiance of the Transvaal Immigration Law and compelled the government to arrest them. When it failed to provoke them to violence or to coerce them into submission, it yielded to their demands. A body of civil resisters is, therefore, like an army subject to all the discipline of a soldier, only harder because of want of excitement of an ordinary soldier's life. And as a civil resistance army is or ought to be free from passion because free from the spirit of retaliation, it requires the fewest number of soldiers. Indeed one *perfect* civil resister is enough to win the battle of Right against Wrong.

SOURCE. Mahatma Gandhi, *All Men are Brothers,* UNESCO, Switzerland, 1958, pp. 11, 20, 27, 89, 96, 138, 148, 149, 173.

b. THOUGHTS OF CHAIRMAN MAO TSE-TUNG

CHINA WAS NEVER A COLONY, yet in the nineteenth and early twentieth centuries she was repeatedly defeated, humbled, and deprived of rights and territories by European powers (and by Japan). After World War II this immense, populous nation, with proud imperial traditions reaching far into the past, again became a significant world power. A drawn-out Communist revolution led by Mao Tse-Tung triumphed in 1949, and under the centralized discipline of the new regime, China advanced toward industrialization and developed nuclear armaments. China in time split with Russia over territorial and doctrinal differences. Both states professed Marxism-Leninism, but the revisions of Khrushchev seemed unacceptably compromising to the Chinese leadership, still close to the militancy of revolution. In China, Marxism-Leninism was expanded and given new direction by Chairman Mao, who adapted a philosophy of industrial class struggle to the needs of a preindustrial peasantry. His contribution takes on singular importance in view of Communism's failure in advanced industrial nations and its success in nonindustrial Cuba and Vietnam.

The excerpts below are drawn from a variety of Mao's writings over the years. The date of each is given at the end of the quotation, and the statements should be understood not simply as pieces of abstract wisdom but as observations of a deeply involved political leader, first of the revolution and later of the Chinese regime.

ON REVOLUTION

It is up to us to organize the people. As for the reactionaries in China, it is up to us to organize the people to overthrow them. Everything reactionary is the same; if you don't hit it, it won't fall. This is like sweeping the floor; as a rule, where the broom does not reach, the dust will not vanish of itself. (1945)

The enemy will not perish of himself. Neither the Chinese reactionaries nor the aggressive forces of U.S. imperialism in China will step down from the stage of history of their own accord. (1948)

A revolution is not a dinner party, or writing an essay, or painting a picture, or doing embroidery; it cannot be so refined, so leisurely and gentle, so temperate, kind, courteous, restrained and magnanimous.[1] A revolution is an insurrection, an act of violence by which one class overthrows another. (1927)

ON THE POWER OF THE MASSES

The people, and the people alone, are the motive force in the making of world history. (1945)

[1] European Economic Community.

The masses are the real heroes, while we ourselves are often childish and ignorant, and without this understanding it is impossible to acquire even the most rudimentary knowledge. (1941)

The masses have boundless creative power. They can organize themselves and concentrate on places and branches of work where they can give full play to their energy; they can concentrate on production in breadth and depth and create more and more welfare undertakings for themselves. (1955)

The present upsurge of the peasant movement is a colossal event. In a very short time, in China's central, southern and nothern provinces, several hundred million peasants will rise like a mighty storm, like a hurricane, a force so swift and violent that no power, however great, will be able to hold it back. They will smash all the trammels that bind them and rush forward along the road to liberation. They will sweep all the imperialists, warlords, corrupt officials, local tyrants and evil gentry into their graves. Every revolutionary party and every revolutionary comrade will be put to the test, to be accepted or rejected as they decide. There are three alternatives. To march at their head and lead them? To trail behind them, gesticulating and criticising? Or to stand in their way and oppose them? Every Chinese is free to choose, but events will force you to make the choice quickly. (1927.)

Twenty-four years of experience tell us that the right task, policy and style of work invariably conform with the demands of the masses at a given time and place and invariably strengthen our ties with the masses, and the wrong task, policy and style of work invariably disagree with the demands of the masses at a given time and place and invariably alienate us from the masses. The reason why such evils as dogmatism, empiracism, commandism, tailism, sectarianism, bureaucracy and an arrogant attitude in work are definitely harmful and intolerable, and why anyone suffering from these maladies must overcome them, is that they alienate us from the masses. (1945)

To link oneself with the masses, one must act in accordance with the needs and wishes of the masses. All work done for the masses must start from their needs and not from the desire of any individual, however well-intentioned. It often happens that objectively the masses need a certain change, but subjectively they are not yet conscious of the need, not yet willing or determined to make the change. In such cases, we should wait patiently. We should not make the change until, through our work, most of the masses have become conscious of the need and are willing and determined to carry it out. Otherwise we shall isolate ourselves from the masses. Unless they are conscious and willing, any kind of work that requires their participation will turn out to be a mere formality and will fail. . . . There are two principles here: one is the actual needs of the masses rather than what we fancy they need, and the other is the wishes of the masses, who must make up their own minds instead of our making up their minds for them. (1944)

ON MILITARY AND PARTY DISCIPLINE

Within the ranks of the people, democracy is correlative with centralism and freedom with discipline. They are the two opposites of a single entity, contradictory as well as united, and we should not onesidedly emphasize one to the denial of the other. Within the ranks of the people, we cannot do without freedom, nor can we do without discipline; we cannot do without democracy, nor can we do without centralism. This unity of democracy and centralism, of freedom and discipline, constitutes our democratic centralism. Under this system, the people enjoy extensive democracy and freedom, but at the same time they have to keep within the bounds of socialist discipline. (1957)

We must affirm anew the discipline of the Party, namely:

(1) the individual is subordinate to the organization;

(2) the minority is subordinate to the majority;

(3) the lower level is subordinate to the higher level; and

(4) the entire membership is subordinate to the Central Committee.

Whoever violates these articles of discipline disrupts Party unity. (1938)

The Three Main Rules of Discipline are as follows:

(1) Obey orders in all your actions.

(2) Do not take a single needle or piece of thread from the masses.

(3) Turn in everything captured.

The Eight Points for Attention are as follows:

(1) Speak politely.

(2) Pay fairly for what you buy.

(3) Return everything you borrow.

(4) Pay for anything you damage.

(5) Do not hit or swear at people.

(6) Do not damage crops.

(7) Do not take liberties with women.

(8) Do not ill-treat captives. (1947)

c. THE ASIAN-AFRICAN CONFERENCE AT BANDUNG, 1955

ON APRIL 18, 1955, a highly publicized and symbolically significant conference of Afro-Asian countries opened at Bandung in the newly independent Republic of Indonesia, formerly the Dutch East Indies. The conference was important in solidifying the Afro-Asian world as a self-conscious force in international politics. President Soekarno of Indonesia, in his opening address, touched on some of the common experiences, concerns, and hopes of the uncommitted decolonized nations. Soekarno subsequently fell from power in a sanguinary revolt that brought a more conservative regime to power in Indonesia.

Your Excellencies, Ladies and Gentlemen.

Sisters and Brothers!

It is my great honour and privilege on this historic day to bid you welcome to Indonesia. On behalf of the people and Government of Indonesia—your hosts—I beg your understanding and forebearance if some circumstances in our country do not meet your expectation. We have, I assure you, done our best to make your stay amongst us memorable for both our guests and your hosts. We hope that the warmth of our welcome will compensate for whatever material shortcomings there may be.

As I survey this hall and the distinguished guests gathered here, my heart is filled with emotion. This is the first intercontinental conference of coloured peoples in the history of mankind! I am proud that my country is your host. I am happy that you were able to accept the invitations extended by the five Sponsoring Countries. But also I cannot restrain feelings of sadness when I recall the tribulations through which many of our peoples have so recently passed, tribulations which have exacted a heavy toll in life, in material things, and in the things of the spirit. . . .

Sisters and Brothers, how terrifically dynamic is our time! I recall that, several years ago, I had occasion to make a public analysis of colonialism, and that I then drew attention to what I called the "Life-line of imperialism." This line runs from the Straits of Gibraltar, through the Mediterranean, the Suez Canal, the Red Sea, the Indian Ocean, the South China Sea and the Sea of Japan. For most of that enormous distance, the territories on both sides of this lifeline were colonies, the peoples were unfree, their futures mortgaged to an alien system. Along that life-line, that main artery of imperialism, there was pumped the life-blood of colonialism.

And today in this hall are gathered together the leaders of those same peoples. They are no longer the victims of colonialism. They are no longer the tools of others and the playthings of forces they cannot influence. Today, you are representatives of free peoples, peoples of a different stature and standing in the world. . . .

The last few years have seen enormous changes. Nations, States, have awoken from a sleep of centuries. The passive peoples have gone, the outward tranquillity has made place for struggle and activity. Irresistible forces have swept the two continents. The mental, spiritual and political face of the whole world has been changed, and the process is still not complete.

There are new conditions, new concepts, new problems, new ideals abroad in the world. Hurricanes of national awakening and reawakening have swept over the land, shaking it, changing it, changing it for the better. . . .

We are of many different nations, we are of many different social backgrounds and cultural patterns. Our ways of life are different. Our national characters, or colours or motifs—call it what you will—are different. Our racial stock is different, and even the colour of our skin is different. But what does that matter? Mankind is united or divided by considerations other than these. Conflict comes not from variety of skins, nor from variety of religion, but from variety of desires.

All of us, I am certain, are united by more important things than those which superficially divide us. We are united, for instance, by a common detestation of colonialism in whatever form it appears. We are united by a common detestation of racialism. And we are united by a common determination to preserve and stabilise peace in the world. Are not these aims mentioned in the letter of invitation to which you responded?

I freely confess it—in these aims I am not disinterested or driven by purely impersonal motives.

How is it possible to be disinterested about colonialism? For us, colonialism is not something far and distant. We have known it in all its ruthlessness. We have seen the immense human wastage it causes, the poverty it causes, and the heritage it leaves behind when, eventually and reluctantly, it is driven out by the inevitable march of history. My people, and the peoples of many nations of Asia and Africa know these things, for we have experienced them.

Indeed, we cannot yet say that all parts of our countries are free already. Some parts still labour under the lash. And some parts of Asia and Africa which are not represented here still suffer from the same condition.

Yes, some parts of our nations are not yet free. That is why all of us cannot yet feel that journey's end has been reached. No people can feel themselves free, so long as part of their motherland is unfree. Like peace, freedom is indivisible. There is no such thing as being half free, as there is no such thing as being half alive.

We are often told "Colonialism is dead." Let us not be deceived or even soothed by that. I say to you, colonialism is not yet dead. How can we say it is dead, so long as vast areas of Asia and Africa are unfree.

And, I beg of you, do not think of colonialism only in the classic form which we of Indonesia, and our brothers in different parts of Asia and Africa, knew. Colonialism has also its modern dress, in the form of economic control, intellectual control, actual physical control by a small but alien community within a nation. It is a skillful and determined enemy, and it appears in many guises. It does not give up its loot easily. Wherever, whenever, and however it appears, colonialism is an evil thing, and one which must be eradicated from the earth.

The battle against colonialism has been a long one, and do you know that today is a famous anniversary in that battle? On the eighteenth day of April, one thousand seven hundred and seventy five, just one hundred and eighty years ago, Paul Revere rode at midnight through the New England countryside, warning of the approach of British troops and of the opening of the American War of Independence, the first successful anti-colonial war in history. About this midnight ride the poet Longfellow wrote:

A cry of defiance and not of fear,
A voice in the darkness, a knock at the door,
And a word that shall echo for evermore. . . .

Yes, it shall echo for evermore, just as the other anti-colonial words which gave us comfort and reassurance during the darkest days of our struggle shall echo for evermore. But remember, that battle which began 180 years ago is not yet completely won, and it will not have been completely won until we can survey this our own world, and can say that colonialism is dead.

So, I am not disinterested when I speak of the fight against colonialism.

Nor am I disinterested when I speak of the battle for peace. How can any of us be disinterested about peace?

Not so very long ago we argued that peace was necessary for us because an outbreak of fighting in our part of the world would imperil our precious independence, so recently won at such great cost.

Today, the picture is more black. War would not only mean a threat to our independence, it may mean the end of civilisation and even of human life. There is a force loose in the world whose potentiality for evil no man truly knows. Even in practice and rehearsal for war the effects may well be building up into something of unknown horror.

Not so long ago it was possible to take some little comfort from the idea that the clash, if it came, could perhaps be settled by what were called "conventional weapons"—bombs, tanks, cannon and men. Today that little grain of comfort is denied us, for it has been made clear that the weapons of ultimate horror will certainly be used, and the military planning of nations is on that basis. The unconventional has become the conventional, and who knows what other examples of misguided and diabolical scientific skill have been discovered as a plague on humanity. . . .

What can we do? The peoples of Asia and Africa wield little physical power. Even their economic strength is dispersed and slight. We cannot indulge in power politics. Diplomacy for us is not a matter of the big stick. Our statesmen, by and large, are not backed up with serried ranks of jet bombers.

What can we do? We can do much! We can inject the voice of reason into world affairs. We can mobilise all the spiritual, all the moral, all the political strength of Asia and Africa on the side of peace. Yes, we! We, the peoples of Asia and Africa, 1,400,000,000 strong, far more than half the human population of the world, we can mobilise what I have called the *Moral Violence of Nations* in favour of peace. We can demonstrate to the minority of the world which lives on the other continents that we, the majority, are for peace, not for war, and that whatever strength we have will always be thrown on to the side of peace. . . .

Let us not be bitter about the past, but let us keep our eyes firmly on the future. Let us remember that no blessing of God is so sweet as life and liberty. Let us remember that the stature of all mankind is diminished so long as nations or parts of nations are still unfree. Let us remember that the highest purpose of man is the liberation of man from his bonds of fear, his bonds of human degradation, his bonds of poverty—the liberation of man from the physical, spiritual and intellectual bonds which have for too long stunted the development of humanity's majority.

And let us remember, Sisters and Brothers, that for the sake of all that, we Asians and Africans must be united.

SOURCE. *Let a New Asia and a New Africa be Born!*, Ministry of Foreign Affairs, Republic of I donesia [1955].

d. GEORGE LICHTHEIM, "BEYOND IMPERIALISM"

THE WIDESPREAD INCIDENCE OF DECOLONIZATION inevitably raises the question: Is independence largely an illusion? Have political bonds between colony and mother country simply given way to economic bonds? In the economic sense, does colonialism continue? In answering these questions, George Lichtheim reevaluates Lenin's theory of imperialism (see above, Chapter 12, c).

It seems appropriate to conclude . . . with some brief reflections on the well-worn theme of imperialism. Has the colonial chapter really been closed, or is there some truth in the assertion that Western relations with the backward, tropical, and subtropical countries have been no more than superficially revamped and are currently about to enter what is described as a "neocolonialist" stage of economic exploitation veiled by the formal trappings of independence? The charge, when directed against Britain and France, is the more plausible since it can be argued that something of the kind has indeed marked the relations between the United States and most Latin American countries over the past century. It can also be held that, quite irrespective of power relationships, the "normal" exchange of goods and services between developed and undeveloped areas inevitably works out to the detriment of the latter, unless a conscious effort is made to correct the imbalance.

The point at issue, however, is not whether Western capital investment in the past—with or without overt political control, i.e., "imperialism" in the strict sense of the term—has damaged and distorted the economies of backward areas, but whether this phase has now given way to a different kind of relationship. Socialists have traditionally denounced the capitalist-imperialist nexus, without denying that it was responsible for *some* degree of progress. The current controversy turns upon the question whether "planned" development—as instanced among others by the relations between the EEC[1] and the African states—represents something radically new or a continuation of the old "unequal relationship" at a higher level. European socialists—who have taken a prominent part in helping to liquidate the old colonial system— could in principle subscribe to all, or most, of the charges hurled against it by Leninists and/or radical nationalists and still maintain that it is absurd to talk of neocolonialism when considering the relationship of Asia or Africa to Europe under present conditions. They might also argue that it is perverse to saddle them with the sins of U.S. "private enterprise" in Latin America. The analogy would hold only if Afro-European relations were typified by what has been going on in the formerly Belgian Congo since 1960. But, in fact, the extraordinary doings of the Union Minière in Katanga represent a type of "monopoly-capitalist" activity that is rapidly going out of fashion. The notion that this kind of primitive skulduggery typifies the present order of things is really not worth controverting. Nor is it apparent that these antics form part of a global pattern that could with any plausibility be interpreted in Leninist terms, i.e., as an attempt on the part of "the monopolists and their governments" to secure physical possession of strategic raw materials.

This point leads to what is really the decisive consideration, namely the growing irrelevance of theoretical arguments derived from the pre-1914, or even the pre-1939, era. Every year that passes makes it plainer that shortage of colonial raw materials, and the need by hook or crook to seize control of them, simply does not describe the reality of present-day industrial capitalism, whether planned or unplanned. The exact opposite is the case: Many of these raw materials are being superseded by industrial techniques making use of products available in the industrially developed countries themselves. The real danger facing the backward countries is that their exports will be squeezed out by the development of synthetics. Statistics relating to the consumption of raw materials in industrial countries since the early 1950's indicate that the use of crude materials (cotton, wool, rubber, jute, copper, etc.) has lagged far behind the consumption of synthetics and other processed materials (synthetic rubber, aluminum, plastic materials and fibers, etc.). In consequence of these developments, the flow of capital tends to be diverted from extractive industries (mining, plantations) towards manufacturing. On balance, this is clearly an advantage to the developing countries, though of course it does nothing to solve their surplus-labor problem. The new forms of foreign investment are directly linked to new techniques, and they also demand workers with modern skills, though fewer in number than did the old mining and plantation economy, which reached its peak on the eve of the 1914–18 war. Even if it be argued that this inflow of foreign capital results in a political partnership with the local bourgeoisie, the latter is at any rate becoming a genuine entrepreneurial class (i.e., in Communist parlance a "national" bourgeoisie) rather than a reactionary "comprador" class living off the crumbs of foreign exploitation. In fact, this is precisely what is happening; that it should be happening because Western industrial society has itself been revolutionized by new techniques is quite in accordance with Marxist principles—though Soviet propagandists, for obvious reasons, have no interest in proclaiming the fact.

The Leninist model of a stagnant Western capitalism clutching at the lifeline of colonial superprofits extrapolated certain features of an era that came to an end with the 1914–18 war, though even then the bulk of foreign investment did not go to the colonies but to developed countries in Europe or the Americas. Since then, the economic importance of the colonial hinterland has dwindled to such an extent that it has become a major political preoccupation of the rival blocs (East and West) to raise public funds for development purposes, largely in the hope (which may be frustrated) of securing political sympathies and averting a desperate outbreak on the part of chronically underfed and overpopulated countries. Such private investment as can be prevailed upon—not without difficulty—to venture forth into the hinterland typically yields a lower rate of profit than capital invested in Europe or North America. The few notable exceptions to this rule—principally oil—do not seriously alter the general picture. Oil investments indeed belong to the earlier phase, which is why they are always quoted by writers anxious to prove that the Leninist model is still operative. In terms of the real problems encountered by countries such as India or Brazil, they are of course quite marginal, and where—as in the Middle East and North Africa—they have genuine importance, the post-independence pattern makes it certain that they are going to be used for the purpose of financing industrialization—as is right and proper. By contrast, the fantastic games still played in Arabia and along the Persian Gulf by newly oil-rich sheikhs and princelings make good copy for journalists and propagandists, but their political significance is minute.

In our age, when the emergent countries are clamoring for capital investments which the developed industrial centers are reluctant to make available, it may seem odd that nationalists should go on quoting Lenin's theses on colonial exploitation as a feature of the "highest" stage of a supposedly over-ripe and moribund capitalism; but such intellectual lags are not unusual. Moreover, it can be held that the emergent countries are entitled to demand planned public investment in basic services and/or modern manufacturing industries rather than a continuation of the old wasteful system, which developed a few sectors of the economy while distorting or neglecting the remainder. This is a legitimate argument between the Western countries and the ruling elites of their former dependencies. It has nothing to do with the weird notion that Africa is a stamping-ground for "monopolists" in search of profits denied to them at home. The real problem arises from the enormous claims levied upon the European countries by their less-developed partners, now understandably in a hurry to industrialize, and simultaneously faced with a population explosion.

In the case of Algeria, to take one notable example, it has been calculated that merely to hold living standards at their present level—in the face of a population growth curve that has doubled its numbers from 5 to 10 million since 1920 and promises to raise it to 15 million by 1980—the former metropolis would have to invest between $5 billion and $6 billion in Algerian industry—exclusive of oil production and pipeline construction—over the next twenty years. A plan to raise living standards by 2 per cent annually would require the investment of $10 billion; raising standards by 4 per cent a year would call for some $20 billion by 1980. Clearly such efforts are more likely to be made (if at all) by a semi-authoritarian regime in France than by a parliamentary democracy dependent on the voters. This may be among the reasons why all factions of Algerian nationalism greatly prefer the Gaullist regime to its predecessor.

If the Leninist formula of equating capital exports with colonialism is outmoded, the nationalist argument that without massive injection of public capital the vicious circle of poverty, overpopulation, and inadequate investment cannot be broken is well-founded. So is the insistence that such investments must in the main be guided to the key sectors of the economy, not left to short-range considerations of profitability. It is within these terms—familiar to European socialists, and increasingly to intelligent conservatives and liberals as well—that the argument now tends to work itself out. It gains nothing from being presented in terms of stale controversies between Leninists and *laissez-fairists*. Now that the leading European countries have been shorn of their colonial possessions (without suffering the threatened disaster), while their former dependencies are experimenting with "mixed" public and private economies, it becomes possible to transcend the dispute over "imperialism as the highest stage of capitalism." Clearly, the colonial chapter is closed, while the maturation of Europe's industrial economy involves both an exceedingly fast rate of growth and a conscious departure from the state of affairs summed up in the phrase "anarchy of production." Whatever else imperialism may have been, it was plainly not the last stage in the development of the society that is now about to give itself a supranational political organization.

SOURCE. George Lichtheim, *The New Europe,* New York, Frederick A. Praeger, 1963, pp. 169–174.

Chapter 20

TWENTIETH CENTURY SCIENCE AND SOCIAL SCIENCE

a. EINSTEIN, "THE STRUCTURE OF SPACE ACCORDING TO THE GENERAL THEORY OF RELATIVITY"

THE TWENTIETH CENTURY, like the sixteenth and seventeenth, has been an age in which former certainties have crumbled. The optimistic convictions of Enlightenment rationalism have turned sour in an epoch of world wars, overpopulation, and nuclear weaponry. Concurrently, the Newtonian universe, on which so much Enlightenment thinking was based, has given way to the far less comprehendible universe of Albert Einstein. The new universe was set forth in Einstein's Special Theory of Relativity (1905) and his General Theory of Relativity (1915). It is understandable only through mathematics, not through mechanical models or visualization. Some of its significant concepts are (1) that no description of the universe can exclude the observer, and that each observer is at the "center" of his own universe; (2) that the universe is not infinite but that space "curves"; (3) that time is a dimension no less than length, width and depth, and that time slows down as the observer approaches the speed of light (relative to a stationary observer). In short, time and space are not absolutes but are affected by mass and velocity and are relative to the person perceiving them.

According to the general theory of relativity, the geometrical properties of space are not independent, but they are determined by matter. Thus we can draw conclusions about the geometrical structure of the universe only if we base our considerations on the state of the matter as being something that is known. We know from experience that, for a suitably chosen co-ordinate system, the velocities of the stars are small as compared with the velocity of transmission of light. We can thus as a rough approximation arrive at a conclusion as to the nature of the universe as a whole, if we treat the matter as being at rest.

We already know from our previous discussion that the behaviour of measuring-rods and clocks is influenced by gravitational fields, *i.e.* by the distribution of matter. This in itself is sufficient to exclude the possibility of the exact validity of Euclidean geometry in our universe. But it is conceivable that our universe differs only slightly from a Euclidean one, and

337

this notion seems all the more probable, since calculations show that the metrics of surrounding space is influenced only to an exceedingly small extent by masses even of the magnitude of our sun. We might imagine that, as regards geometry, our universe behaves analogously to a surface which is irregularly curved in its individual parts, but which nowhere departs appreciably from a plane: something like the rippled surface of a lake. Such a universe might fittingly be called a quasi-Euclidean universe. As regards its space it would be infinite. But calculation shows that in a quasi-Euclidean universe the average density of matter would necessarily be *nil*. Thus such a universe could not be inhabited by matter everywhere. . . .

If we are to have in the universe an average density of matter which differs from zero, however small may be that difference, then the universe cannot be quasi-Euclidean. On the contrary, the results of calculation indicate that if matter be distributed uniformly, the universe would necessarily be spherical (or elliptical). Since in reality the detailed distribution of matter is not uniform, the real universe will deviate in individual parts from the spherical, *i.e.* the universe will be quasi-spherical. But it will be necessarily finite. In fact, the theory supplies us with a simple connection between the space-expanse of the universe and the average density of matter in it.

SOURCE. Albert Einstein, *Relativity, The Special and General Theory,* Robert W. Lawson, tr., New York, Henry Holt & Co., 1921, pp. 135–137. Reprinted by permission of Peter Smith, Publisher.

b. JOSÉ ORTEGA Y GASSET, FROM "THE HISTORICAL SIGNIFICANCE OF THE THEORY OF EINSTEIN"

A PERCEPTIVE, NONSCIENTIFIC ANALYSIS of some of the likely effects of Relativity theory on man and society is provided by the Spanish philosopher, José Ortega y Gasset.

The provincial spirit has always, and with good reason, been accused of stupidity. Its nature involves an optical illusion. The provincial does not realise that he is looking at the world from a decentralised position. He supposes, on the contrary, that he is at the centre of the whole earth, and accordingly passes judgment on all things as if his vision were directed from that centre. This is the cause of the deplorable complacency which produces such comic effects. All his opinions are falsified as soon as they are formulated because they originate from a pseudo-centre. On the other hand, the dweller in the capital knows that his city, however large it may be, is only one point of the cosmos, a decentralised corner of it. He knows, further, that the world has no centre, and that it is therefore necessary, in all our judgements, to discount the peculiar perspective that reality offers when it is looked at from our own point of view. This is the reason why the provincial always thinks his neighbour of the great city a sceptic, though the fact is that the latter is only better informed.

The theory of Einstein has shown modern science, with its exemplary discipline—the *nuova scienza* of Galileo, the proud physical philosophy of the West—to have been labouring under an acute form of provincialism. Euclidian geometry, which is only applicable to what is close at hand, had been extended to the whole universe. In Germany today the system of Euclid is beginning to be called "proximate geometry" in contradistinction to other collections of axioms which, like those of Riemann, are long-range geometries.

The refutation of this provincial geometry, like that of all provincialism, has been accomplished by means of an apparent limitation, an exercise of modesty in the claims of its conqueror. Einstein is convinced that to talk of Space is a kind of megalomania which inevitably introduces error. We are not aware of any more extensions than those we measure, and we cannot measure more than our instruments can deal with. These are our organ of scientific vision; they determine the spatial structure of the world we know. But as every other being desirous of constructing a system of physics from some other place in the earth is in the same case the result is that there is no real limitation involved at all.

There is no question, then, of our relapsing into a subjectivist interpretation of knowledge, according to which the truth is only true for a pre-determined subjective personality. According to the theory of relativity, the event *A*, which from the mundane point of view precedes the event *B* in time, will, from another place in the universe—Sirius, for example—seem to succeed *B*. There cannot be a more complete inversion of reality. Does it mean that either our own imagination or else that of the mind resident in Sirius is at fault? Not at all. Neither the human mind nor that in Sirius alters the conformation of reality. The fact of the matter is that one of the qualities proper to reality is that of possessing perspective, that is, of organising itself in different ways so as to be visible from different points. Space and time are the objective ingredients of physical perspective, and it is natural that they should vary according to the point of view. . . .

If there had been among the infinite number of points of view an exceptional one to which it might have been possible to assign a superior correspondence with nature, we could have considered the rest as deforming agents or as "purely subjective." Galileo and Newton believed that this was the case when they spoke of absolute space, that is to say, of a space contemplated from a point of view which is in no way concrete. Newton calls absolute space *sensorium Die,* the visual organ of God; or, we might say, divine perspective. But we have scarcely thought out in all its implications this idea of a perspective which is not seen from any determined and exclusive place when we discover its contradictory and absurd nature. There is no absolute space because there is no absolute perspective. To be absolute, space has to cease being real—a space full of phenomena—and become an abstraction.

The theory of Einstein is a marvellous proof of the harmonious multiplicity of all possible points of view. If the idea is extended to morals and aesthetics, we shall come to experience history and life in a new way.

The individual who desires to master the maximum amount possible of truth will not now be compelled, as he was for centuries enjoined, to replace his spontaneous point of view with another of an exemplary and standardised character, which used to be called the "vision of things *sub specie aeternitatis.*" The point of view of eternity is blind: it sees nothing and does not exist. Man will henceforth endeavour, instead, to be loyal to . . . his individuality.

It is the same with nations. Instead of regarding non-European cultures as barbarous, we shall now begin to respect them, as methods of confronting the cosmos which are equivalent to our own. There is a Chinese perspective which is fully as justified as the Western.

SOURCE José Ortega y Gasset, *The Modern Theme,* James Cleugh, tr., New York, Harper Torchbooks, 1961, pp. 139–144. Copyright © 1933, 1961 by José Ortega y Gasset, Reprinted by permission of Curtis Brown, Ltd., and The C. W. Daniel Company Limited., London.

c. MAX PLANCK, FROM "THE MEANING AND LIMITS OF EXACT SCIENCE"

TWENTIETH-CENTURY SCIENTISTS have been concerned not only with the inadequacies of scientific theories of the past but also with the validity or "reality" of scientific knowledge itself. This question is explored by the important physicist Max Planck who sees behind the universe of scientific theory an irrational reality that science, by its very nature, cannot penetrate. His remarks are taken from a lecture delivered in November 1941.

What is the direction of [scientific] progress, and what is its ultimate goal? The direction, evidently, is the constant improvement of the world picture by reducing the real elements contained in it to a higher reality of a less naïve character. The goal, on the other hand, is the creation of a world picture, with real elements which no longer require an improvement, and therefore represent the ultimate reality. A demonstrable attainment of this goal will—or can—never be ours. But in order to have at least a name for it, for the time being, we call the ultimate reality "the real world," in the absolute, metaphysical sense of the word, *real*. This is to be construed as expressing the fact that the *real* world—in other words, objective nature—stands behind everything explorable. In contrast to it, the scientific world picture gained by experience—the *phenomenological world*—remains always a mere approximation, a more or less well divined model. As there is a material object behind every sensation, so there is a metaphysical reality behind everything that human experience shows to be real. Many philosophers object to the word, *"behind."* They say: "Since in exact science all concepts and all measures are reducible to sensations, in the last analysis the meaning of every scientific finding also refers only to the sense world, and it is inadmissible, or at least superfluous, to postulate the existence behind this world of a metaphysical world, totally inaccessible to direct scientific inquiry and examination." The only proper reply to this argument is, simply, that in the above sentence the word, *behind*, must not be interpreted in an external or spatial sense. Instead of "behind," we could just as well say, *"in"* or *"within."* Metaphysical reality does not stand spatially *behind* what is given in experience, but lies fully *within* it. "Nature is neither core nor shell—she is everything at once." The essential point is that the world of sensation is not the only world which may conceivably exist, but that there is still another world. To be sure, this other world is not directly accessible to us, but its existence is indicated, time and again, with compelling clarity, not only by practical life, but also by the labors of science. For the great marvel of the scientific world picture, becoming progressively more complete and perfect, necessarily impels the investigator to seek its ultimate form. And since one must assume the existence of that which one seeks, the scientist's assumption of the actual existence of a "real world," in the absolute sense of the word, eventually grows into a firm conviction which nothing can shake any more. This firm belief in the absolute *Real* in nature is what constitutes for him the given, self-evident premise of his work; it fortifies repeatedly his hope of eventually groping his way still a little nearer to the essence of objective Nature, and of thereby gaining further clues to her secrets.

Since the real world, in the absolute sense of the word, is independent of individual personalities, and in fact of all human intelligence, every discovery made by any individual acquires a completely universal significance. This gives the inquirer, wrestling with his problem in quiet seclusion, the assurance that every discovery will win the unhesitating recognition of all experts throughout the entire world, and in this feeling of the importance of his work lies his happiness. It compensates him fully for many a sacrifice which he must make in his daily life.

The sublime nature of such a goal must, necessarily, dwarf into insignificance any doubt engendered by the difficulties encountered while shaping the scientific world picture. It is particularly important to emphasize this in our own day, for nowadays such difficulties are sometimes regarded as serious impediments to the salutary progress of scientific work. It is an odd fact that experimental difficulties are so regarded to a lesser degree than theoretical ones. The circumstance that with the increasing demands on the accuracy of measurements the instruments, too, become more intricate, is understood and accepted as a matter of course. But the fact that in the endeavor to improve continually the expansion of systematic interrelations, it is necessary to use definitions and concepts which diverge more and more from traditional forms and intuitive notions, is sometimes cited as a reproach against theoretical research, and is even viewed as indicating that theoretical research is entirely on the wrong track.

Nothing could be more shortsighted than such a view. For if we stop to think that the improvement of the world picture goes hand in hand with an approach to the metaphysically "real world," the expectation that the definitions and concepts of the objectively real world picture will not diverge too much from the framework created by the classical world picture, amounts basically to a demand that the metaphysically real world be completely intelligible in terms of ideas derived from the former naive world picture. This is a demand that can be never fulfilled. We simply cannot expect to recognize and discern the finer structure of something, so long as we flatly refuse to view it otherwise than with the naked eye. Yet, in this respect there is no reason for fear. The development of the scientific world picture is a matter of absolute necessity. The experiences gained with the refined instruments of measurement demand inexorably that certain firmly-rooted intuitive notions be abandoned and replaced by new, more abstract conceptual structures, for which the appropriate intuitions are still to be found and developed. Thus, they are the landmarks to guide theoretical research on its road from the naive concept of reality to the metaphysical "Real."

But significant as the achievements may be, and near as the desired goal may seem, there always remains a gaping chasm, unbridgeable from the point of view of exact science, between the real world of phenomenology and the real world of metaphysics. This chasm is the source of a constant tension, which can never be balanced, and which is the inexhaustible source of the insatiable thirst for knowledge within the true research scientist. But at the same time, we catch here a glimpse of the boundaries which exact science is unable to cross. May its results be ever so deep and far-reaching, it can never succeed in taking the last step which would take it into the realm of metaphysics. The fact that although we feel inevitably compelled to postulate the existence of a *real world,* in the absolute sense, we can never fully comprehend its nature, constitutes the irrational element which exact science can never shake off. . . .

SOURCE. Max Planck, *Scientific Autobiography and Other Papers,* Frank Gaynor, tr., New York: Philosophical Library, 1949. pp. 100–106. Reprinted by permission of Philosophical Library, Inc., Publishers.

d. SIGMUND FREUD, FROM *THE EGO AND THE ID*

SIGMUND FREUD (1865–1939) was the real founder of modern psychology. With his emphasis on the subconscious parts of the human mind—the id *in particular—he demonstrated the irrational basis of many human actions. The Freudian vision of human irrationality has made a deep impact on the thoughts and attitudes of the twentieth century. Freud summarized some of the basic elements of his psychology in his book* The Ego and the Id *(1927) from which representative passages are extracted here.*

The division of the psychical into what is conscious and what is unconscious is the fundamental premise of psycho-analysis; and it alone makes it possible for psycho-analysis to understand the pathological processes in mental life, which are as common as they are important, and to find a place for them in the framework of science. To put it once more, in a different way: psycho-analysis cannot situate the essence of the psychical in consciousness, out is obliged to regard consciousness as a quality of the psychical, which may be present in addition to other qualities or may be absent.

If I could suppose that everyone interested in psychology would read this book, I should also be prepared to find that at this point some of my readers would already stop short and would go no further; for here we have the first shibboleth of psycho-analysis. To most people who have been educated in philosophy the idea of anything psychical which is not also conscious is so inconceivable that it seems to them absurd and refutable simply by logic. I believe this is only because they have never studied the relevant phenomena of hypnosis and dreams, which—quite apart from pathological manifestations—necessitate this view. Their psychology of consciousness is incapable of solving the problems of dreams and hypnosis.

'Being conscious' is in the first place a purely descriptive term, resting on perception of the most immediate and certain character. Experience goes on to show that a psychical element (for instance, an idea) is not as a rule conscious for a protracted length of time. On the contrary, a state of consciousness is characteristically very transitory; an idea that is conscious now is no longer so a moment later, although it can become so again under certain conditions that are easily brought about. In the interval the idea was—we do not know what. We can say that it was *latent,* and by this we mean that it was *capable of becoming conscious* at any time. Or, if we say that it was *unconscious,* we shall also be giving a correct description of it. Here 'unconscious' coincides with 'latent and capable of becoming conscious.' The philosophers would no doubt object: 'No, the term "unconscious" is not applicable here; so long as the idea was in a state of latency it was not anything psychical at all.' To contradict them at this point would lead to nothing more profitable than a verbal dispute.

But we have arrived at the term or concept of the unconscious along another path, by considering certain experiences in which mental *dynamics* play a part. We have found—that is, we have been obliged to assume—that very powerful mental processes or ideas exist (and here a quantitative or *economic* factor comes into question for the first time) which can produce all the effects in mental life that ordinary ideas do (including effects that can in their turn become conscious as ideas), though they themselves do not become conscious. It is unnecessary to repeat in detail here what has been explained so often before. It is enough to say that at this point psycho-analytic theory steps in and asserts that the reason why such ideas cannot become conscious is that a certain force opposes them, that otherwise they could become conscious, and that it would then be apparent how little they differ from other elements which are admittedly psychical. The fact that in the technique of psychoanalysis a means has been found by which the opposing force can be removed and the ideas in question made conscious renders this theory irrefutable. The state in which the ideas existed before being made conscious is called by us *repression,* and we assert that the force which instituted the repression and maintains it is perceived as *resistance* during the work of analysis.

Thus we obtain our concept of the unconscious from the theory of repression. The repressed is the prototype of the unconscious for us. We see, however, that we have two kinds of unconscious—the one which is latent but capable of becoming conscious, and the one which is repressed and which is not, in itself and without more ado, capable of becoming conscious. This piece of insight into psychical dynamics cannot fail to affect terminology and description. The latent, which is unconscious only descriptively, not in the dynamic sense, we call *preconscious;* we restrict the term *unconscious* to the dynamically unconscious repressed; so that now we have three terms, conscious *(Cs.)*, preconscious *(Pcs.)*, and unconscious *(Ucs.)*, whose sense is no longer purely descriptive. The *Pcs.* is presumably a great deal closer to the *Cs.* than is the *Ucs.*, and since we have called the *Ucs.* psychical we shall with even less hesitation call the latent *Pcs.* psychical. But why do we not rather, instead of this, remain in agreement with the philosophers and, in a consistent way, distinguish the *Pcs.* as well as the *Ucs.* from the conscious psychical? The philosophers would then propose that the *Pcs.* and the *Ucs.* should be described as two species or stages of the 'psychoid,' and harmony would be established. But endless difficulties in exposition would follow; and the one important fact, that these two kinds of 'psychoid' coincide in almost every other respect with what is admittedly psychical, would be forced into the background in the interests of a prejudice dating from a period in which these psychoids, or the most important part of them, were still unknown.

We can now play about comfortably with our three terms, *Cs.*, *Pcs.*, and *Ucs.*, so long as we do not forget that in the descriptive sense there are two kinds of unconscious, but in the dynamic sense only one. For purposes of exposition this distinction can in some cases be ignored, but in others it is of course indispensable. At the same time, we have become more or less accustomed to this ambiguity of the unconscious and have managed pretty well with it. As far as I can see, it is impossible to avoid this ambiguity; the distinction between conscious and unconscious is in the last resort a question of perception, which must be answered 'yes' or 'no,' and the act of perception itself tells us nothing of the reason why a thing is or is not perceived. No one has a right to complain because the actual phenomenon expresses the dynamic factor ambiguously.

In the further course of psycho-analytic work, however, even these distinctions have proved to be inadequate and, for practical purposes, insufficient. This has become clear in more ways than one; but the decisive instance is as follows. We have formed the idea that in each individual there is a coherent organization of mental processes; and we call this his *ego*. It is to this ego that consciousness is attached; the ego controls the approaches to motility—that is, to the discharge of excitations into the external world; it is the mental agency which supervises all its own constituent processes, and which goes to sleep at night, though even then it exercises the censorship on dreams. From this ego proceed the repressions, too, by means of which it is sought to exclude certain trends in the mind not merely from consciousness but also from other forms of effectiveness and activity. In analysis these trends which have been shut out stand in opposition to the ego, and the analysis is faced with the task of removing the resistances which the ego displays against concerning itself with the repressed. Now we find during analysis that, when we put certain tasks before the patient, he gets into difficulties; his associations fail when they should be coming near the repressed. We then tell him that he is dominated by a resistance; but he is quite unaware of the fact, and, even if he guesses from his unpleasurable feelings that a resistance is now at work in him, he does not know what it is or how to describe it. Since, however, there can be no question but that this resistance emanates from his ego and belongs to it, we find ourselves in an unforeseen situation. We have come upon something in the ego itself which is also unconscious, which behaves exactly like the repressed—that is, which produces powerful effects without itself being conscious and which requires special work before it can be made conscious. From the point of view of analytic practice, the consequence of this discovery is that we land in endless obscurities and difficulties if we keep to our habitual forms of expression and try, for instance, to derive neuroses from a conflict between the conscious and the unconscious. We shall have to substitute for this antithesis another, taken from our insight into the structural conditions of the mind—the antithesis between the coherent ego and the repressed which is split off from it.

For our conception of the unconscious, however, the consequences of our discovery are even more important. Dynamic considerations caused us to make our first correction; our insight into the structure of the mind leads to the second. We recognize that the *Ucs.* does not coincide with the repressed; it is still true that all that is repressed is *Ucs.*, but not all that is *Ucs.* is repressed. A part of the ego, too—and Heaven knows how important a part—may be *Ucs.*, undoubtedly is *Ucs.* And this *Ucs.* belonging to the ego is not latent like the *Pcs.;* for if it were, it could not be activated without becoming *Cs.*, and the process of making it conscious would not encounter such great difficulties. When we find ourselves thus confronted by the necessity of postulating a third *Ucs.*, which is not repressed, we must admit that the characteristic of being unconscious begins to lose significance for us. It becomes a quality which can have many meanings, a quality which we are unable to make, as we should have hoped to do, the basis of far-reaching and inevitable conclusions. Nevertheless we must beware of ignoring this characteristic, for the property of being conscious or not is in the last resort our one beacon-light in the darkness of depth-psychology. . . .

. . . the ego seeks to bring the influence of the external world to bear upon the id and its tendencies, and endeavours to substitute the reality principle for the pleasure principle which reigns unrestrictedly in the id. For the ego, perception plays the part which in the id falls to instinct. The ego represents what may be called reason and common sense, in contrast to the id, which contains the passions. All this falls into line with popular distinctions which we are all familiar with; at the same time, however, it is only to be regarded as holding good on the average or 'ideally.'

The functional importance of the ego is manifested in the fact that normally control over the approaches to motility devolves upon it. Thus in its relation to the id it is like a man on horseback, who has to hold in check the superior strength of the horse; with this difference, that the rider tries to do so with his own strength while the ego uses borrowed forces. The analogy may be carried a little further. Often a rider, if he is not to be parted from his horse, is obliged to guide it where it wants to go; so in the same way the ego is in the habit of transforming the id's will into action as if it were its own. . . .

The relation of the ego to consciousness has been entered into repeatedly; yet there are some important facts in this connection which remain to be described here. Accustomed as we are to taking our social or ethical scale of values along with us wherever we go, we feel no surprise at hearing that the scene of the activities of the lower passions is in the unconscious; we expect, moreover, that the higher any mental function ranks in our scale of values the more easily it will find access to consciousness assured to it. Here, however, psycho-analytic experience disappoints us. On the one hand, we have evidence that even subtle and difficult intellectual operations which ordinarily require strenuous reflection can equally be carried out preconsciously and without coming into consciousness. Instances of this are quite incontestable; they may occur, for example, during the state of sleep, as is shown when someone finds, immediately after waking, that he knows the solution to a difficult mathematical or other problem with which he had been wrestling in vain the day before.

There is another phenomenon, however, which is far stranger. In our analyses we discover that there are people in whom the faculties of self-criticism and conscience—mental activities, that is, that rank as extremely high ones—are unconscious and unconsciously produce effects of the greatest importance; the example of resistance remaining unconscious during analysis is therefore by no means unique. But this new discovery, which compels us, in spite of our better critical judgement, to speak of an 'unconscious sense of guilt,' bewilders us far more than the other and sets us fresh problems, especially when we gradually come to see that in a great number of neuroses an unconscious sense of guilt of this kind plays a decisive economic part and puts the most powerful obstacles in the way of recovery. If we come back once more to our scale of values, we shall have to say that not only what is lowest but also what is highest in the ego can be unconscious. . . .

If the ego were merely the part of the id modified by the influence of the perceptual system, the representative in the mind of the real external world, we should have a simple state of things to deal with. But there is a further complication.

The considerations that led us to assume the existence of a grade in the ego, a differentiation within the ego, which may be called the 'ego ideal' or 'super-ego,' have been stated elsewhere. They still hold good. The fact that this part of the ego is less firmly connected with consciousness is the novelty which calls for explanation. . . .

An interpretation of the normal, conscious sense of guilt (conscience) presents no difficulties; it is based on the tension between the ego and the ego ideal and is the expression of a condemnation of the ego by its critical agency. The feelings of inferiority so well known in neurotics are presumably not far removed from it. In two very familiar maladies the sense of guilt is over-strongly conscious; in them the ego ideal displays particular severity and often rages against the ego in a cruel fashion. The attitude of the ego ideal in these two conditions, obsessional neurosis and melancholia, presents, alongside of this similarity, differences that are no less significant.

In certain forms of obsessional neurosis the sense of guilt is over-noisy but cannot justify itself to the ego. Consequently the patient's ego rebels against the imputation of guilt and seeks the physician's support in repudiating it. It would be folly to acquiesce in this, for to do so would have no effect. Analysis eventually shows that the super-ego is being influenced by processes that have remained unknown to the ego. It is possible to discover the repressed impulses which are really at the bottom of the sense of guilt. Thus in this case the super-ego knew more than the ego about the unconscious id.

In melancholia the impression that the super-ego has obtained a hold upon consciousness is even stronger. But here the ego ventures no objection; it admits its guilt and submits to the punishment. We understand the difference. In obsessional neurosis what were in question were objectionable impulses which remained outside the ego, while in melancholia the object to which the super-ego's wrath applies has been taken into the ego through identification.

It is certainly not clear why the sense of guilt reaches such an extraordinary strength in these two neurotic disorders; but the main problem presented in this state of affairs lies in another direction. We shall postpone discussion of it until we have dealt with the other cases in which the sense of guilt remains unconscious.

It is essentially in hysteria and in states of a hysterical type that this is found. Here the mechanism by which the sense of guilt remains unconscious is easy to discover. The hysterical ego fends off a distressing perception with which the criticisms of its super-ego threaten it . . . by an act of repression. It is the ego, therefore, that is responsible for the sense of guilt remaining unconscious. We know that as a rule the ego carries out repressions in the service and at the behest of its super-ego; but this is a case in which it has turned the same weapon against its harsh taskmaster. In obsessional neurosis, as we know, the phenomena of reaction-formation predominate; but here [in hysteria] the ego succeeds only in keeping at a distance the material to which the sense of guilt refers.

One may go further and venture the hypothesis that a great part of the sense of guilt must normally remain unconscious, because the origin of conscience is intimately connected with the Oedipus complex, which belongs to the unconscious. If anyone were inclined to put forward the paradoxical proposition that the normal man is not only far more immoral than he believes but also far more moral than he knows, psychoanalysis, on whose findings the first half of the assertion rests, would have no objection to raise against the second half.[1]

It was a surprise to find that an increase in this *Ucs.* sense of guilt can turn people into criminals. But it is undoubtedly a fact. In many criminals, especially youthful ones, it is possible to detect a very powerful sense of guilt which existed before the crime, and is therefore not its result but its motive. It is as if it was a relief to be able to fasten this unconscious sense of guilt on to something real and immediate. . . .

From the point of view of instinctual control, of morality, it may be said of the id that it is totally non-moral, of the ego that it strives to be moral, and of the super-ego that it can be super-moral and then become as cruel as only the id can be. It is remarkable that the more a man checks his aggressiveness towards the exterior the more severe—that is aggressive—he becomes in his ego ideal. The ordinary view sees the situation the other way round: the standard set up by the ego ideal seems to be the motive for the suppression of aggressiveness. The fact remains, however, as we have stated it: the more a man controls his aggressiveness, the more intense becomes his ideal's inclination to aggressiveness against his ego. It is like a displacement, a turning round upon his own ego. But even ordinary normal morality has a harshly restraining, cruelly prohibiting quality. It is from this, indeed, that the conception arises of a higher being who deals out punishment inexorably. . . .

Our ideas about the ego are beginning to clear, and its various relationships are gaining distinctness. We now see the ego in its strength and in its weaknesses. It is entrusted with important functions. By virtue of its relation to the perceptual system it gives mental processes an order in time and submits them to 'reality-testing.' By interposing the processes of thinking, it secures a postponement of motor discharges and controls the access to motility. This last power is, to be sure, a question more of form than of fact; in the matter of action the ego's position is like that of a constitutional monarch, without whose sanction no law can be passsed but who hesitates long before imposing his veto on any measure put forward by Parliament. All the experiences of life that originate from without enrich the ego; the id, however, is its second external world, which it strives to bring into subjection to itself. . . . With the aid of the super-ego, in a manner that is still obscure to us, it draws upon the experiences of past ages stored in the id.

---

[1] This proposition is only apparently a paradox; it simply states that human nature has a far greater extent, both for good and for evil, than it thinks it has—i.e. than its ego is aware of through conscious perception.

There are two paths by which the contents of the id can penetrate into the ego. The one is direct, the other leads by way of the ego ideal; which of these two paths they take may, for some mental activities, be of decisive importance. The ego develops from perceiving instincts to controlling them, from obeying instincts to inhibiting them. In this achievement a large share is taken by the ego ideal, which indeed is partly a reaction-formation against the instinctual process of the id. Psycho-analysis is an instrument to enable the ego to achieve a progressive conquest of the id.

From the other point of view, however, we see this same ego as a poor creature owing service to three masters and consequently menaced by three dangers: from the external world, from the libido of the id, and from the severity of the super-ego. Three kinds of anxiety correspond to these three dangers, since anxiety is the expression of a retreat from danger. As a frontier-creature, the ego tries to mediate between the world and the id, to make the id pliable to the world and, by means of its muscular activity, to make the world fall in with the wishes of the id. . . . it disguises the id's conflicts with reality and, if possible, its conflicts with the super-ego too. In its position midway between the id and reality, it only too often yields to the temptation to become sycophantic, opportunist and lying, like a politician who sees the truth but wants to keep his place in popular favour. . . .

We know that the fear of death makes its appearance under two conditions (which, moreover, are entirely analogous to situations in which other kinds of anxiety develop), namely, as a reaction to an external danger and as an internal process, as for instance in melancholia. Once again a neurotic manifestation may help us to understand a normal one.

The fear of death in melancholia only admits of one explanation: that the ego gives itself up because it feels itself hated and persecuted by the super-ego, instead of loved. To the ego, therefore, living means the same as being loved—being loved by the super-ego, which here again appears as the representative of the id. The super-ego fulfils the same function of protecting and saving that was fulfilled in earlier days by the father and later by Providence or Destiny. But, when the ego finds itself in an excessive real danger which it believes itself unable to overcome by its own strength, it is bound to draw the same conclusion. It sees itself deserted by all protecting forces and lets itself die. Here, moreover, is once again the same situation as that which underlay the first great anxiety-state of birth and the infantile anxiety of longing—the anxiety due to separation from the protecting mother.

These considerations make it possible to regard the fear of death, like the fear of conscience, as a development of the fear of castration. The great of anxiety between the ego and the super-ego (fear of castration, of conscience, of death).

The id, to which we finally come back, has no means of showing the ego either love or hate. It cannot say what it wants; it has achieved no unified will. Eros and the death instinct struggle within it; we have seen with what weapons the one group of instincts defends itself against the other. It would be possible to picture the id as under the domination of the mute but powerful death instincts, which desire to be at peace and (prompted by the pleasure principle) to put Eros, the mischief-maker, to rest; but perhaps that might be to undervalue the part played by Eros.

SOURCE. Sigmund Freud. "The Ego and the Id." from *The Standard Edition of the Complete Psychological Works of Sigmund Freud,* Volume XIX, translated from the German and edited by James Strachey, London: The Hogarth Press, 1961, pp. 13–18, 25–28, 50–52, 54–56, and 58–59. Copyright 1960 by James Strachey. Reprinted by permission of Sigmund Freud Copyrights Ltd., The Institute of Psycho-Analysis, The Hogarth Press Ltd. and W. W. Norton & Company, Inc.

e. ERICH FROMM, FROM *THE SANE SOCIETY,* 1955

ERICH FROMM learned from Freud and went beyond him into an area that Fromm called "humanistic psychoanalysis." The experience of love, Fromm believed, was the key to being sane and being human.

MAN'S NEED—AS THEY STEM FROM THE CONDITIONS OF HIS EXISTENCE

Man's life is determined by the inescapable alternative between regression and progression, between return to animal existence and arrival at human existence. Any attempt to return is painful, it inevitably leads to suffering and mental sickness, to death either physiologically or mentally (insanity). Every step forward is frightening and painful too, until a certain point has been reached where fear and doubt have only minor proportions. Aside from the physiologically nourished cravings (hunger, thirst, sex), all essential human cravings are determined by this polarity. Man has to solve a problem, he can never rest in the given situation of a passive adaptation to nature. Even the most complete satisfaction of all his instinctive needs does not solve his *human* problem; his most intensive passions and needs are not those rooted in his body, but those rooted in the very peculiarity of his existence.

There lies also the key to humanistic psychoanalysis. Freud, searching for the basic force which motivates human passions and desires, believed he had found it in the libido. But powerful as the sexual drive and all its derivations are, they are by no means the most powerful forces within man and their frustration is not the cause of mental disturbance. The most powerful forces motivating man's behavior stem from the condition of his existence, the "human situation."

Man cannot live statically because his inner contradictions drive him to seek for an equilibrium, for a new harmony instead of the lost animal harmony with nature. After he has satisfied his animal needs, he is driven by his human needs. While his body tells him what to eat and what to avoid—his conscience ought to tell him which needs to cultivate and satisfy, and which needs to let wither and starve out. But hunger and appetite are functions of the body with which man is born—conscience, while potentially present, requires the guidance of men and principles which develop only during the growth of culture.

All passions and strivings of man are attempts to find an answer to his existence or, as we may also say, they are an attempt to avoid insanity. (It may be said in passing that the real problem of mental life is not why some people become insane, but rather why most avoid insanity.) Both the mentally healthy and the neurotic are driven by the need to find an answer, the only difference being that one answer corresponds more to the total needs of man, and hence is more conducive to the unfolding of his powers and to his happiness than the other. All cultures provide for a patterned system in which certain solutions are predominant, hence certain strivings and satisfactions. Whether we deal with primitive religions, with theistic or non-theistic religions, they are all attempts to give an answer to man's existential problem. The finest, as well as the most barbaric cultures have the same function—the difference is only whether the answer given is better or worse. The deviate from the cultural pattern is just as much in search of an answer as his more well-adjusted brother. His answer may be better or worse than the one given by his culture—it is always another answer to the same fundamental question raised by human existence. In this sense all cultures are religious and every neurosis is a private form of religion, provided we mean by religion an attempt to answer the problem of human existence. Indeed, the tremendous energy in the forces producing mental illness, as well as those behind art and religion, could never be understood as an outcome of frustrated or sublimated physiological needs; they are attempts to solve the problem of being born human. All men are idealists and cannot help being idealists, provided we mean by idealism the striving for the satisfaction of needs which are specifically human and transcend the physiological needs of the organism. The difference is only that one idealism is a good and adequate solution, the other a bad and destructive one. The decision as to what is good and bad has to be made on the basis of our knowledge of man's nature and the laws which govern its growth.

What are these needs and passions stemming from the existence of man?

A. RELATEDNESS VERSUS NARCISSISM

Man is torn away from the primary union with nature, which characterizes animal existence. Having at the same time reason and imagination, he is aware of his aloneness and separateness; of his powerlessness and ignorance; of the accidentalness of his birth and of his death. He could not face this state of being for a second if he could not find new ties with his fellow man which replace the old ones, regulated by instincts. Even if all his physiological needs were satisfied, he would experience his state of aloneness and individuation as a prison from which he had to break out in order to retain his sanity. In fact, the insane person is the one who has completely failed to establish any kind of union, and is imprisoned, even if he is not behind barred windows. The necessity to unite with other living beings, to be related to them, is an imperative need on the fulfillment of which man's sanity depends. This need is behind all phenomena which constitute the whole gamut of intimate human relations, of all passions which are called love in the broadest sense of the word.

There are several ways in which this union can be sought and achieved. Man can attempt to become one with the world by *submission* to a person, to a group, to an institution, to God. In this way he transcends the separateness of his individual existence by becoming part of somebody or something bigger than himself, and experiences his identity in connection with the power to which he has submitted. Another possibility of overcoming separateness lies in the opposite direction: man can try to unite himself with the world by having *power* over it, by making others a part of himself, and thus transcending his individual existence by domination. The common element in both submission and domination is the symbiotic nature of relatedness. Both persons involved have lost their integrity and freedom; they live on each other and from each other, satisfying their craving for closeness, yet suffering from the lack of inner strength and self-reliance which would require freedom and independence, and furthermore constantly threatened by the conscious or unconscious hostility which is bound to arise from the symbiotic relationship. The realization of the submissive (masochistic) or the domineering (sadistic) passion never leads to satisfaction. They have a self-propelling dynamism, and because no amount of submission, or domination (or possession, or fame) is enough to give a sense of identity and union, more and more of it is sought. The ultimate result of these passions is defeat. It cannot be otherwise; while these passions aim at the establishment of a sense of union, they destroy the sense of integrity. The person driven by any one of these passions actually becomes dependent on others; instead of developing his own individual being, he is dependent on those to whom he submits, or whom he dominates.

There is only one passion which satisfies man's need to unite himself with the world, and to acquire at the same time a sense of integrity and individuality, and this is *love*. *Love is union* with somebody, or something, outside oneself, *under the condition of retaining the separateness and integrity of one's own self.* It is an experience of sharing, of communion, which permits the full unfolding of one's own inner activity. The experience of love does away with the necessity of illusions. There is no need to inflate the image of the other person, or of myself, since the reality of active sharing and loving permits me to transcend my individualized existence, and at the same time to experience myself as the bearer of the active powers which constitute the act of loving. What matters is the particular *quality* of loving, not the object. Love is in the experience of human solidarity with our fellow creatures, it is in the erotic love of man and woman, in the love of the mother for the child, and also in the love for oneself, as a human being; it is in the mystical experience of union. In the act of loving, I am one with All, and yet I am myself, a unique, separate, limited, mortal human being. Indeed out of the very polarity between separateness and union, love is born and reborn.

Love is one aspect of what I have called the productive orientation: the active and creative relatedness of man to his fellow man, to himself and to nature. In the realm of *thought*, this productive orientation is expressed in the proper grasp of the world by reason. In the realm of *action*, the productive orientation is expressed in productive work, the prototype of which is art and craftsmanship. In the realm of *feeling*, the productive orientation is expressed in love, which is the experience of union with a other person, with all men, and with nature, under the condition of retaining one's sense of integrity and independence. In the experience of love the paradox happens that two people become one, and remain two at the same time. Love in this sense is never restricted to one person. If I can love only one person, and nobody else, if my love for one person makes me more alienated and distant from my fellow man, I may be attached to this person in any number of ways, yet I do not love. If I can say, "I love you," I say, "I love in you all of humanity, all that is alive; I love in you also myself." Self-love, in this sense, is the opposite of selfishness. The latter is actually a greedy concern with oneself which springs from and compensates for the lack of genuine love for oneself. Love, paradoxically, makes me more independent because it makes me stronger and happier—yet it makes me one with the loved person to the extent that individuality seems to be extinguished for the moment. In loving I experience "I am you," you—the loved person, you—the stranger, you—everything alive. In the experience of love lies the only answer to being human, lies sanity. . . .

B. TRANSCENDENCE—CREATIVENESS VERSUS DESTRUCTIVENESS

Another aspect of the human situation, closely connected with the need for relatedness, is man's situation as a *creature,* and his need to transcend this very state of the passive creature. Man is thrown into this world without his knowledge, consent or will, and he is removed from it again without his consent or will. In this respect he is not different from the animals, from the plants, or from inorganic matter. But being endowed with reason and imagination, he cannot be content with the passive role of the creature, with the role of dice cast out of a cup. He is driven by the urge to transcend the role of the creature, the accidentalness and passivity of his existence, by becoming a "creator."

Man can create life. This is the miraculous quality which he indeed shares with all living beings, but with the difference that he alone is aware of being created and of being a creator. Man can create life, or rather, woman can create life, by giving birth to a child, and by caring for the child until it is sufficiently grown to take care of his own needs. Man—man and woman—can create by planting seeds, by producing material objects, by creating art, by creating ideas, by loving one another. In the act of creation man transcends himself as a creature, raises himself beyond the passivity and accidentalness of his existence into the realm of purposefulness and freedom. In man's need for transcendence lies one of the roots for love, as well as for art, religion and material production.

To create presupposes activity and care. It presupposes love for that which one creates. How then does man solve the problem of transcending himself, if he is not capable of creating, if he cannot love? *There is another answer to this need for transcendence: if I cannot create life, I can destroy it. To destroy life makes me also transcend it.* Indeed, that man can destroy life is just as miraculous a feat as that he can create it, for life is *the* miracle, the inexplicable. In the act of destruction, man sets himself above life; he transcends himself as a creature. Thus, the ultimate choice for man, inasmuch as he is driven to transcend himself, is to create or to destroy, to love or to hate. The enormous power of the will for destruction which we see in the history of man, and which we have witnessed so frightfully in our own time, is rooted in the nature of man, just as the drive to create is rooted in it. To say that man is capable of developing his primary potentiality for love and reason does not imply the naïve belief in man's goodness. Destructiveness is a secondary potentiality, rooted in the very existence of man, and having the same intensity and power as any passion can have. But—and this is the essential point of my argument—it is only the *alternative* to creativeness. Creation and destruction, love and hate, are not two instincts which exist independently. They are both answers to the same need for transcendence, and the will to destroy must rise when the will to create cannot be satisfied. However, the satisfaction of the need to create leads to happiness; destructiveness to suffering, most of all, for the destroyer himself.

SOURCE. Eric Fromm, *The Sane Society,* Fawcett Publications, Connecticut, copyright (c) 1955 by Erich Fromm, pp. 33–38, 41–42. Reprinted by permission of Holt, Rinehart and Winston, Inc. and Routledge and Kegan Paul Ltd., London.

Chapter 21.

TWENTIETH CENTURY ART

a. PAINTING

IN THE LATER NINETEENTH CENTURY, painters recoiled increasingly from photographic representationalism, rejected the notion of a painting as a window to the natural world, and concentrated increasingly on the aspects of design and color in the painting itself. These trends continued to develop during the twentieth century. For the sake of formal structure and the communication of the artists' personal perceptions and emotions, painters moved farther and farther from objective realism and engaged in increasingly bold distortions of their subjects. In the cubist style of Pablo Picasso and others, illustrated in highly developed form by Picasso's Three Musicians *(1921), the human form becomes merely a point of departure for the artist's fantastic imagination and boundless inventiveness. This characteristic is further developed in works such as Joan Miro's* Dutch Interior. *The impression that these works convey is at once comic, grotesque, and tragic.*

PABLO PICASSO, *THREE MUSICIANS,* 1921

JOAN MIRÓ, *DUTCH INTERIOR*, 1928

THE QUALITY OF TRAGEDY takes priority in the works of the more conservative Catholic artist Georges Rouault (1871–1958), whose early work in stained glass carries over in the heavy, dark outlines which he used in his paintings. His fundamental theme is that of passion—human and divine—and his painings, whether of scriptural subjects or of prostitutes and clowns, are infused with his vision of the tragic corruption of humanity and the possibility of redemption through Christ. *His* Christ Mocked by the Soldiers *(1932), like so much of his own art and that of his contemporaries, is a powerful and deeply personal statement. In surrealist works such as René Magritte's* Castle of the Pyrenees *(1955), the imaginative reorganization of the natural order, evident in Picasso's* Three Musicians *and Miro's* Dutch Interior, *is brought to the point of pure fantasy.*

GEORGES ROUAULT, *CHRIST MOCKED BY THE SOLDIERS*, 1932

RENÉ MAGRITTE, *CASTLE OF THE PYRENES*, 1955

THE ABSTRACT EXPRESSIONIST STYLE carried the trend toward subjectivity beyond the reordering of nature to the point of a total break with the outside world. The style is exemplified by the painting entitled Number One *(1948) by Jackson Pollock (1912–56). To the question, "What is it?" the abstract expressionist would answer, "It is a painting." The answer reflects the basic artistic trend of the past century.*

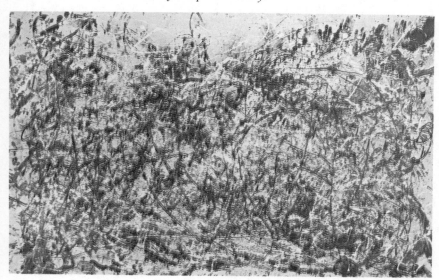

JACKSON POLLOCK, *NUMBER ONE*, 1948

ABSTRACT EXPRESSIONISM acquired great vogue in the middle decades of the twentieth century, but many painters continued to produce representational paintings and retained the artist's traditional relationship with the outside world. In the late 1950's several artists turned to an irreverent and witty new style known as pop art which emphasized imaginative presentations of the inanely ordinary. The face of an old bureau drawer might be mounted on a canvas, an American flag might be set in a frame, the artist might paint his own version of a commercial sign or highway marker.

POP ART, ARISOL, *THE FAMILY,* 1962

b. SCULPTURE

TWO EXAMPLES of twentieth-century sculpture are given here. Both re-flect a tendency toward primitivism and the subordination of objective ac-curacy to inner meaning. Henry Moore's King and Queen *(1952–1953) are huge, faceless figures which give the impression of having been eroded by sea or wind. Jacques Lipchitz'* Figure *(1926–1930) possesses the Picasso-like quality of a wildly inventive reordering of the human form.*

HENRY MOORE, *KING AND QUEEN,* 1952–1953

JACQUES LIPCHITZ, *FIGURE,* 1926–1930

c. ARCHITECTURE

PERHAPS THE LEADING EXPONENT of the severe International Style in modern architecture is Ludwig Mies van der Rohe (b. 1888). His Lake Shore Drive Apartment Houses, Chicago, 1950–1952, are characteristic masterpieces of the style that has dominated mid-twentieth-century architecture. As the Lake Shore Apartments were being constructed, a radically new architectural style was finding expression in Le Corbusier's church of Notre-Dame-du-Haut, erected in Ronchamp, France, between 1950 and 1955. Le Corbusier rejected the geometric purism of the International Style in favor of a flowing, organic quality akin to that of contemporary sculpture. His Notre-Dame-du-Haut is a significant landmark in the development of modern architecture—a structure which is serving as the inspiration for many of the more advanced architects of today. The work of the American architect, Edward Durell Stone is representative of a somewhat different kind of departure from the International Style. Stone has pioneered in a new trend away from the austerity of Mies van der Rohe and his followers toward a reassertion of decorative values and a search for beauty through tasteful ornamentation. His prize-winning United States Embassy at New Delhi (completed in 1959) is a graceful, placid, harmoniously balanced structure faced with a decorative screen, its outlines clearly defined by a cornice, its entrance strongly emphasized, its interior merging into an inner court. Stone was remarkably successful in adapting his own techniques and values to the traditional architectural style of India and thereby creating a work of art that is appropriate to its setting.

LUDWIG MIES VAN DER ROHE, LAKE SHORE DRIVE
APARTMENT HOUSES, CHICAGO, 1950–1952

LE CORBUSIER, NOTRE-DAME-DU-HAUT, RONCHAMP, FRANCE, 1950–1955

EDWARD DURELL STONE, UNITED STATES EMBASSY, NEW DELHI, INDIA

Chapter 22

THE HUMAN PREDICAMENT

a. NORBERT WIENER ON MAN AND MACHINE

THE GREAT CYBERNETICIST NORBERT WIENER (b. 1894) comments here on the impact of cybernetics and automation on human society and the future of man.

I have spoken of the actuality and the imminence of this new possibility of widespread automation of production using machines based on the principle of feedback. What can we expect of its economic and social consequences? In the first place, we can expect an abrupt and final cessation of the demand for the type of factory labor performing purely repetitive tasks. In the long run, the deadly uninteresting nature of the repetitive task may make this a good thing and the source of leisure necessary for man's full cultural development. It may also produce cultural results as trivial and wasteful as the greater part of those so far obtained from the radio and the movies.

Be that as it may, the intermediate period of the introduction of the new means . . . will lead to an immediate transitional period of disastrous confusion. We have a good deal of experience as to how the industrialists regard a new industrial potential. Their whole propaganda is to the effect that it must not be considered as the business of the government but must be left open to whatever entrepreneurs wish to invest money in it. We also know that they have very few inhibitions when it comes to taking all the profit out of an industry that there is to be taken, and then letting the public pick up the pieces. This is the history of the lumber and mining industries, and is part of what we have called in another chapter the traditional American philosophy of progress.

Under these circumstances, industry will be flooded with the new tools to the extent that they appear to yield immediate profits, irrespective of what long-time damage they can do. We shall see a process parallel to the way in which the use of atomic energy for bombs has been allowed to compromise the very necessary potentialities of the long-time use of atomic power to replace our oil and coal supplies, which are within centuries, if not decades, of utter exhaustion. Note well that atomic bombs do not compete with power companies.

370

Let us remember that the automatic machine, whatever we think of any feelings it may have or may not have, is the precise economic equivalent of slave labor. Any labor which competes with slave labor must accept the economic conditions of slave labor. It is perfectly clear that this will produce an unemployment situation, in comparison with which the present recession and even the depression of the thirties will seem a pleasant joke. This depression will ruin many industries—possibly even the industries which have taken advantage of the new potentialities. However, there is nothing in the industrial tradition which forbids an industrialist to make a sure and quick profit, and to get out before the crash touches him personally.

Thus the new industrial revolution is a two-edged sword. It may be used for the benefit of humanity, but only if humanity survives long enough to enter a period in which such a benefit is possible. It may also be used to destroy humanity, and if it is not used intelligently it can go very far in that direction. There are, however, hopeful signs on the horizon. Since the publication of the first edition of this book, I have participated in two big meetings with representatives of business management, and I have been delighted to see that awareness on the part of a great many of those present of the social dangers of our new technology and the social obligations of those responsible for management to see that the new modalities are used for the benefit of man, for increasing his leisure and enriching his spiritual life, rather than merely for profits and the worship of the machine as a new brazen calf. There are many dangers still ahead, but the roots of good will are there, and I do not feel as thoroughly pessimistic as I did at the time of the publication of the first edition of this book.[1]

In the well-known Paris journal, *Le Monde,* for December 28, 1948, a certain Dominican friar, Père Dubarle, has written a very penetrating review of my book *Cybernetics.* I shall quote a suggestion of his which carries out some of the dire implications of the chess-playing machine grown up and encased in a suit of armor.

One of the most fascinating prospects thus opened is that of the rational conduct of human affairs, and in particular of those which interest communities and seem to present a certain statistical regularity, such as the human phenomena of the development of opinion. Can't one imagine a machine to collect this or that type of information, as for example information on production and the market; and then to determine as a function of the average psychology of human beings, and of the quantities which it is possible to measure in a determined instance, what the most probable development of the situation might be? Can't one even conceive a State apparatus covering all systems of political decisions, either under a regime of many states distributed over the earth, or under the apparently much more simple regime of a human government of this planet? At present nothing prevents our thinking of this. We may dream of the time

[1] Wiener is writing in 1954; The first edition was published in 1950.

when the *machine à gouverner* may come to supply—whether for good or evil—the present obvious inadequacy of the brain when the latter is concerned with the customary machinery of politics. . . . The *machines a gouverner* will define the State as the best-informed player at each particular level; and the State is the only supreme coordinator of all partial decisions. These are enormous privileges; if they are acquired scientifically, they will permit the State under all circumstances to beat every player of a human game other than itself by offering this dilemma: either immediate ruin, or planned co-operation. This will be the consequences of the game itself without outside violence. The lovers of the best of worlds have something indeed to dream of!

Despite all this, and perhaps fortunately, the *machine à gouverner* is not ready for a very near tomorrow. For outside of the very serious problems which the volume of information to be collected and to be treated rapidly still pose, the problems of the stability of prediction remain beyond what we can seriously dream of controlling. For human processes are assimilable to games with incompletely defined rules, and above all, with the rules themselves functions of the time. The variation of the rules depends both on the effective detail of the situations engendered by the game itself, and on the system of psychological reactions of the players in the face of the results obtained at each instant.

It may even be more rapid than these. A very good example of this seems to be given by what happened to the Gallop Poll in the 1948 election.[2] All this not only tends to complicate the degree of the factors which influence prediction, but perhaps to make radically sterile the mechanical manipulation of human situations. As far as one can judge, only two conditions here can guarantee stabilization in the mathematical sense of the term. These are, on the one hand, a sufficient ignorance on the part of the mass of the players exploited by a skilled player, who moreover may plan a method of paralyzing the consciousness of the masses; or on the other, sufficient good-will to allow one, for the sake of the stability of the game, to refer his decisions to one or a few players of the game who have arbitrary privileges. This is a hard lesson of cold mathematics, but it throws a certain light on the adventure of our century: hesitation between an indefinite turbulence of human affairs and the rise of a prodigious Leviathan. In comparison with this, Hobbes' *Leviathan* was nothing but a pleasant joke. We are running the risk nowadays of a great World State, where deliberate and conscious primitive injustice may be the only possible condition for the statistical happiness of the masses: a world worse than hell for every clear mind. Perhaps it would not be a bad idea for the teams at present creating cybernetics to add to their *cadre* of technicians, who have come from all horizons of science, some serious anthropologists, and perhaps a philosopher who has some curiosity as to world matters.

Wiener continues: The *machine à gouverner* of Père Dubarle is not frightening because of any danger that it may achieve autonomous control over humanity. It is far too crude and imperfect to exhibit a one-thousandth part of the purposive independent behavior of the human being. Its real danger, however, is the quite different one that such machines, though helpless by themselves, may be used by a human being or a block of human beings to increase their control over the rest of the human race or that political leaders may at-

---

[2] In 1948 the Gallop Poll and most other polls incorrectly predicted the election of Thomas E. Dewey to the presidency of the United States.

tempt to control their populations by means not of machines themselves but through political techniques as narrow and indifferent to human possibility as if they had, in fact, been conceived mechanically. The great weakness of the machine—the weakness that saves us so far from being dominated by it—is that it cannot yet take into account the vast range of probability that characterizes the human situation. The dominance of the machine presupposes a society in the last stages of increasing entropy, where probability is negligible and where the statistical differences among individuals are nil. Fortunately we have not yet reached such a state.

But even without the state machine of Père Dubarle we are already developing new concepts of war, of economic conflict, and of propaganda on the basis of von Neumann's *Theory of Games,* which is itself a communicational theory, as the developments of the 1950s have already shown. This theory of games, as I have said in an earlier chapter, contributes to the theory of language, but there are in existence government agencies bent on applying it to military and quasi-military aggressive and defensive purposes.

The theory of games is, in its essence, based on an arrangement of players or coalitions of players each of whom is bent on developing a strategy for accomplishing its purposes, assuming that its antagonists, as well as itself, are each engaging in the best policy for victory. This great game is already being carried on mechanistically, and on a colossal scale. While the philosophy behind it is probably not acceptable to our present opponents, the Communists, there are strong signs that its possibilities are already being studied in Russia as well as here, and that the Russians, not content with accepting the theory as we have presented it, have conceivably refined it in certain important respects. In particular, much of the work, although not all, which we have done on the theory of games, is based on the assumption that both we and our opponents have unlimited capabilities and that the only restrictions within which we play depend on what we may call the cards dealt to us or the visible positions on the chess board. There is a considerable amount of evidence, rather in deed than in words, that the Russians have supplemented this attitude to the world game by considering the psychological limits of the players and especially their fatigability as part of the game itself. A sort of *machine a gouverner* is thus now essentially in operation on both sides of the world conflict, although it does not consist in either case of a single machine which makes policy, but rather of a mechanistic technique which is adapted to the exigencies of a machine-like group of men devoted to the formation of policy.

Père Dubarle has called the attention of the scientist to the growing military and political mechanization of the world as a great superhuman apparatus working on cybernetic principles. In order to avoid the manifold dangers of this, both external and internal, he is quite right in his emphasis on the need for the anthropologist and the philosopher. In other words, we must know as scientists what man's nature is and what his built-in purposes are, even when we must wield this knowledge as soldiers and as statesmen; and we must know why we wish to control him.

When I say that the machine's danger to society is not from the machine itself but from what man makes of it, I am really underlining the warning of Samuel Butler. In *Erewhon* he conceives machines otherwise unable to act, as conquering mankind by the use of men as the subordinate organs. Nevertheless, we must not take Butler's foresight too seriously, as in fact at his time neither he nor anyone around him could understand the true nature of the behavior of automata, and his statements are rather incisive figures of speech than scientific remarks.

Our papers have been making a great deal of American "know-how" ever since we had the misfortune to discover the atomic bomb. There is one quality more important than "know-how" and we cannot accuse the United States of any undue amount of it. This is "know-what" by which we determine not only how to accomplish our purposes, but what our purposes are to be. I can distinguish between the two by an example. Some years ago, a prominent American engineer bought an expensive player-piano. It became clear after a week or two that this purchase did not correspond to any particular interest in the music played by the piano but rather to an overwhelming interest in the piano mechanism. For this gentleman, the player-piano was not a means of producing music, but a means of giving some inventor the chance of showing how skillful he was at overcoming certain difficulties in the production of music. This is an estimable attitude in a second-year high-school student. How estimable it is in one of those on whom the whole cultural future of the country depends, I leave to the reader.

In the myths and fairy tales that we read as children we learned a few of the simpler and more obvious truths of life, such as that when a djinnee is found in a bottle, it had better be left there; that the fisherman who craves a boon from heaven too many times on behalf of his wife will end up exactly where he started; that if you are given three wishes, you must be very careful what you wish for. These simple and obvious truths represent the childish equivalent of the tragic view of life which the Greeks and many modern Europeans possess, and which is somehow missing in this land of plenty.

The Greeks regarded the act of discovering fire with very split emotions. On the one hand, fire was for them as for us a great benefit to all humanity. On the other, the carrying down of fire from heaven to earth was a defiance of the Gods of Olympus, and could not but be punished by them as a piece of insolence towards their prerogatives. Thus we see the great figure of Prometheus, the fire-bearer, the prototype of the scientist; a hero but a hero damned, chained on the Caucasus with vultures gnawing at his liver. We read the ringing lines of Aeschylus in which the bound god calls on the whole world under the sun to bear witness to what torments he suffers at the hands of the gods.

The sense of tragedy is that the world is not a pleasant little nest made for our protection, but a vast and largely hostile environment, in which we can achieve great things only by defying the gods; and that this defiance inevitably brings its own punishment. It is a dangerous world, in which there is no security, save the somewhat negative one of humility and restrained ambitions. It is a world in which there is a condign punishment, not only for him who sins in conscious arrogance, but for him whose sole crime is ignorance of the gods and the world around him.

If a man with this tragic sense approaches, not fire, but another manifestation of original power, like the splitting of the atom, he will do so with fear and trembling. He will not leap in where angels fear to tread, unless he is prepared to accept the punishment of the fallen angels. Neither will he calmly transfer to the machine made in his own image the responsibility for his choice of good and evil, without continuing to accept a full responsibility for that choice.

I have said that the modern man, and especially the modern American, however much "know-how" he may have, has very little "know-what." He will accept the superior dexterity of the machine-made decisions with out too much inquiry as to the motives and principles behind these. In doing so, he will put himself sooner or later in the position of the father in W. W. Jacobs' *The Monkey's Paw,* who has wished for a hundred pounds, only to find at his door the agent of the company for which his son works, tendering him one hundred pounds as a consolation for his son's death at the factory. Or again, he may do it in the way of the Arab fisherman in the *One Thousand and One Nights,* when he broke the Seal of Solomon on the lid of the bottle which contained the angry djinnee.

Let us remember that there are game-playing machines both of the Monkey's Paw type and of the type of the Bottled Djinnee. Any machine constructed for the purpose of making decisions, if it does not possess the power of learning, will be completely literal-minded. Woe to us if we let it decide our conduct, unless we have previously examined the laws of its action, and know fully that its conduct will be carried out on principles acceptable to us! On the other hand, the machine like the djinnee, which can learn and can make decisions on the basis of its learning, will in no way be obliged to make such decisions as we should have made, or will be acceptable to us. For the man who is not aware of this, to throw the problem of his responsibility on the machine, whether it can learn or not, is to cast his responsibility to the winds, and to find it coming back seated on the whirlwind.

I have spoken of machines, but not only of machines having brains of brass and thews of iron. When human atoms are knit into an organization in which they are used, not in their full right as responsible human beings, but as cogs and levers and rods, it matters little that their raw material is flesh and blood. *What is used as an element in a machine, is in fact an element in the machine.* Whether we entrust our decisions to machines of metal, or to those machines of flesh and blood which are bureaus and vast laboratories and armies and corporations, we shall never receive the right answers to our questions unless we ask the right questions. The *Monkey's Paw* of skin and bone is quite as deadly as anything cast out of steel and iron. The djinnee which is a unifying figure of speech for a whole corporation is just as fearsome as if it were a glorified conjuring trick.

The hour is very late, and the choice of good and evil knocks at our door.

SOURCE. Norbert Wiener, *The Human Use of Human Beings: Cybernetics and Society,* Boston: Houghton Mifflin Co., 1954, Doubleday Anchor edition, pp. 161–162, 178–186. Copyright 1950, 1954 by Norbert Wiener. Reprinted by permission of Houghton Mifflin Co.

b. ALDOUS HUXLEY ON POPULATION AND ECOLOGY

ALDOUS HUXLEY, author of Brave New World *and a number of other important novels, turns here to nonfiction and looks ahead to a future of potential catastrophe through overpopulation.*

In politics, the central and fundamental problem is the problem of power. Who is to exercise power? And by what means, by what authority, with what purpose in view, and under what controls? Yes, under what controls? For, as history has made it abundantly clear, to possess power is *ipso facto* to be tempted to abuse it. In mere self-preservation we must create and maintain institutions that make it difficult for the powerful to be led into those temptations which, succumbed to, transform them into tyrants at home and imperialists abroad.

For this purpose what kind of institutions are effective? And, having created them, how can we guarantee them against obsolescence? Circumstances change, and, as they change, the old, the once so admirably effective devices for controlling power cease to be adequate. What then? Specifically, when advancing science and acceleratingly progressive technology alter man's long-established relationship with the planet on which he lives, revolutionize his societies, and at the same time equip his rulers with new and immensely more powerful instruments of domination, what ought we to do? What *can* we do?

Very briefly let us review the situation in which we now find ourselves and, in the light of present facts, hazard a few guesses about the future.

On the biological level, advancing science and technology have set going a revolutionary process that seems to be destined for the next century at least, perhaps for much longer, to exercise a decisive influence upon the destinies of all human societies and their individual members. In the course of the last fifty years extremely effective methods for lowering the prevailing rates of infant and adult mortality were developed by Western scientists. These methods were very simple and could be applied with the expenditure of very little money by very small numbers of not very highly trained technicians. For these reasons, and because everyone regards life as intrinsically good and death as intrinsically bad, they were in fact applied on a worldwide scale. The results were spectacular. In the past, high birth rates were balanced by high death rates. Thanks to science, death rates have been halved but, except in the most highly industrialized, contraceptive-using countries, birth rates remain as high as ever. An enormous and accelerating increase in human numbers has been the inevitable consequence.

At the beginning of the Christian era, so demographers assure us, our planet supported a human population of about two hundred and fifty millions. When the Pilgrim Fathers stepped ashore, the figure had risen to about five hundred millions. We see, then, that in the relatively recent past it took sixteen hundred years for the human species to double its numbers. Today world population stands at three thousand millions. By the year 2000, unless something appallingly bad or miraculously good should happen in the interval, six thousand millions of us will be sitting down to breakfast every morning. In a word, twelve times as many people are destined to double their numbers in one-fortieth of the time.

This is not the whole story. In many areas of the world human numbers are increasing at a rate much higher than the average for the whole species. In India, for example, the rate of increase is now 2.3 per cent per annum. By 1990 its four hundred and fifty million inhabitants will have become nine hundred million inhabitants. A comparable rate of increase will raise the population of China to the billion mark by 1980. In Ceylon, in Egypt, in many of the countries of South and Central America, human numbers are increasing at an annual rate of 3 per cent. The result will be a doubling of their present populations in approximately twenty-three years.

On the social, political, and economic levels, what is likely to happen in an underdeveloped country whose people double themselves in a single generation, or even less? An underdeveloped society is a society without adequate capital resources (for capital is what is left over after primary needs have been satisfied, and in underdeveloped countries most people never satisfy their primary needs); a society without a sufficient force of trained teachers, administrators, and technicians; a society with few or no industries and few or no developed sources of industrial power; a society, finally, with enormous arrears to be made good in food production, education, road building, housing, and sanitation. A quarter of a century from now, when there will be twice as many of them as there are today, what is the likelihood that the members of such a society will be better fed, housed, clothed, and schooled than at present? And what are the chances in such a society for the maintenance, if they already exist, or the creation, if they do not exist, of democratic institutions?

Not long ago Mr. Eugene Black, the former president of the World Bank, expressed the opinion that it would be extremely difficult, perhaps even impossible, for an underdeveloped country with a very rapid rate of population increase to achieve full industrialization. All its resources, he pointed out, would be absorbed year by year in the task of supplying, or not quite supplying, the primary needs of its new members. Merely to stand still, to maintain its current subhumanly inadequate standard of living, will require hard work and the expenditure of all the nation's available capital. Available capital may be increased by loans and gifts from abroad; but in a world where the industrialized nations are involved in power politics and an increasingly expensive armament race, there will never be enough foreign aid to make much difference. And even if the loans and gifts to underdeveloped countries were to be substantially increased, any resulting gains would be largely nullified by the uncontrolled population explosion.

The situation of these nations with such rapidly increasing populations reminds one of Lewis Carroll's parable in *Through the Looking Glass,* where Alice and the Red Queen start running at full speed and run for a long time until Alice is completely out of breath. When they stop, Alice is amazed to see that they are still at their starting point. In the looking glass world, if you wish to retain your present position, you must run as fast as you can. If you wish to get ahead, you must run at least twice as fast as you can.

If Mr. Black is correct (and there are plenty of economists and demographers who share his opinion), the outlook for most of the world's newly independent and economically non-viable nations is gloomy indeed. To those that have shall be given. Within the next ten or twenty years, if war can be avoided, poverty will almost have disappeared from the highly industrialized and contraceptive-using societies of the West. Meanwhile, in the underdeveloped and uncontrolledly breeding societies of Asia, Africa, and Latin America the condition of the masses (twice as numerous, a generation from now, as they are today) will have become no better and may even be decidedly worse than it is at present. Such a decline is foreshadowed by current statistics of the Food and Agriculture Organization of the United Nations. In some underdeveloped regions of the world, we are told, people are somewhat less adequately fed, clothed, and housed than were their parents and grandparents thirty and forty years ago. And what of elementary education? UNESCO recently provided an answer. Since the end of World War II heroic efforts have been made to teach the whole world how to read. The population explosion has largely stultified these efforts. The absolute number of illiterates is greater now than at any time.

The contraceptive revolution which, thanks to advancing science and technology, has made it possible for the highly developed societies of the West to offset the consequences of death control by a planned control of births, has had as yet no effect upon the family life of people in underdeveloped countries. This is not surprising. Death control, as I have already remarked, is easy, cheap, and can be carried out by a small force of technicians. Birth control, on the other hand, is rather expensive, involves the whole adult population, and demands of those who practice it a good deal of forethought and directed will-power. To persuade hundreds of millions of men and women to abandon their tradition-hallowed views of sexual morality, then to distribute and teach them to make use of contraceptive devices or fertility-controlling drugs—this is a huge and difficult task, so huge and so difficult that it seems very unlikely that it can be successfully carried out, within a sufficiently short space of time, in any of the countries where control of the birth rate is most urgently needed.

Extreme poverty, when combined with ignorance, breeds that lack of desire for better things which has been called "wantlessness"—the resigned acceptance of a subhuman lot. But extreme poverty, when it is combined with the knowledge that some societies are affluent, breeds envious desires and the expectation that these desires must of necessity, and very soon, be satisfied. By means of the mass media (those easily exportable products of advancing science and technology) some knowledge of what life is like in affluent societies has been widely disseminated throughout the world's underdeveloped regions. But, alas, the science and technology which have given the industrial West its cars, refrigerators, and contraceptives have given the people of Asia, Africa, and Latin America only movies and radio broadcasts, which they are too simple-minded to be able to criticize, together with a population explosion, which they are still too poor and too tradition-bound to be able to control by deliberate family planning.

In the context of a 3, or even of a mere 2 per cent annual increase in numbers, high expectations are foredoomed to disappointment. From disappointment, through resentful frustration, to widespread social unrest the road is short. Shorter still is the road from social unrest, through chaos, to dictatorship, possibly of the Communist party, more probably of generals and colonels. It would seem, then, that for two-thirds of the human race now suffering from the consequences of uncontrolled breeding in a context of industrial backwardness, poverty, and illiteracy, the prospects for democracy, during the next ten or twenty years, are very poor.

From underdeveloped societies and the probable political consequences of their explosive increase in numbers we now pass to the prospect for democracy in the fully industrialized, contraceptive-using societies of Europe and North America.

It used to be assumed that political freedom was a necessary pre-condition of scientific research. Ideological dogmatism and dictatorial institutions were supposed to be incompatible with the open-mindedness and the freedom of experimental action, in the absence of which discovery and invention are impossible. Recent history has proved these comforting assumptions to be completely unfounded. It was under Stalin that Russian scientists developed the A-bomb and, a few years later, the H-bomb. And it is under a more-than-Stalinist dictatorship that Chinese scientists are now in process of performing the same feat.

Another disquieting lesson of recent history is that, in a developing society, science and technology can be used exclusively for the enhancement of military power, not at all for the benefit of the masses. Russia has demonstrated, and China is now doing its best to demonstrate, that poverty and primitive conditions of life for the overwhelming majority of the population are perfectly compatible with the wholesale production of the most advanced and sophisticated military hardware. Indeed, it is by deliberately imposing poverty on the masses that the rulers of developing industrial nations are able to create the capital necessary for building an armament industry and maintaining a well equipped army, with which to play their parts in the suicidal game of international power politics.

We see, then, that democratic institutions and libertarian traditions are not at all necessary to the progress of science and technology, and that such progress does not of itself make for human betterment at home and peace abroad. Only where democratic institutions already exist, only where the masses can vote their rulers out of office and so compel them to pay attention to the popular will, are science and technology used for the benefit of the majority as well as for increasing the power of the State. Most human beings prefer peace to war, and practically all of them would rather be alive than dead. But in every part of the world men and women have been brought up to regard nationalism as axiomatic and war between nations as something cosmically ordained by the Nature of Things. Prisoners of their culture, the masses, even when they are free to vote, are inhibited by the fundamental postulates of the frame of reference within which they do their thinking and their feeling from decreeing an end to the collective paranoia that governs international relations. As for the world's ruling minorities, by the very fact of their power they are chained even more closely to the current system of ideas and the prevailing political customs; for this reason they are even less capable than their subjects of expressing the simple human preference for life and peace.

Some day, let us hope, rulers and ruled will break out of the cultural prison in which they are now confined. Some day . . . And may that day come soon! For, thanks to our rapidly advancing science and technology, we have very little time at our disposal. The river of change flows ever faster, and somewhere downstream, perhaps only a few years ahead, we shall come to the rapids, shall hear, louder and ever louder, the roaring of a cataract.

Modern war is a product of advancing science and technology. Conversely, advancing science and technology are products of modern war. It was in order to wage war more effectively that first the United States, then Britain and the USSR, financed the crash programs that resulted so quickly in the harnessing of atomic forces. Again, it was primarily for military purposes that the techniques of automation, which are now in process of revolutionizing industrial production and the whole system of administrative and bureaucratic control, were first developed. "During World War II," writes Mr. John Diebold, "the theory and use of feedback was studied in great detail by a number of scientists both in this country and in Britain. The introduction of rapidly moving aircraft very quickly made traditional gun-laying techniques of anti-aircraft warfare obsolete. As a result, a large part of scientific manpower in this country was directed towards the development of self-regulating devices and systems to control our military equipment. It is out of this work that the technology of automation as we understand it today has developed."

The headlong rapidity with which scientific and technological changes, with all their disturbing consequences in the fields of politics and social relations, are taking place is due in large measure to the fact that, both in the USA and the USSR, research in pure and applied science is lavishly financed by military planners whose first concern is in the development of bigger and better weapons in the shortest possible time. In the frantic effort, on one side of the Iron Curtain, to keep up with the Joneses—on the other, to keep up with the Ivanovs—these military planners spend gigantic sums on research and development. The military revolution advances under forced draft, and as it goes forward it initiates an uninterrupted succession of industrial, social, and political revolutions. It is against this background of chronic upheaval that the members of a species, biologically and historically adapted to a slowly changing environment, must now live out their bewildered lives.

Old-fashioned war was incompatible, while it was being waged, with democracy. Nuclear war, if it is ever waged, will prove in all likelihood to be incompatible with civilization, perhaps with human survival. Meanwhile, what of the preparations for nuclear war? If certain physicists and military planners had their way, democracy, where it exists, would be replaced by a system of regimentation centered upon the bomb shelter. The entire population would have to be systematically drilled in the ticklish operation of going underground at a moment's notice, systematically exercised in the art of living troglodytically under conditions resembling those in the hold of an eighteenth-century slave ship. The notion fills most of us with horror. But if we fail to break out of the ideological prison of our nationalistic and militaristic culture, we may find ourselves compelled by the military consequences of our science and technology to descend into the steel and concrete dungeons of total and totalitarian civil defense.

In the past, one of the most effective guarantees of liberty was governmental inefficiency. The spirit of tyranny was always willing; but its technical and organizational flesh was weak. Today the flesh is as strong as the spirit. Governmental organization is a fine art, based upon scientific principles and disposing of marvelously efficient equipment. Fifty years ago an armed revolution still had some chance of success. In the context of modern weaponry a popular uprising is foredoomed. Crowds armed with rifles and home-made grenades are no match for tanks. And it is not only to its armament that a modern government owes its overwhelming power. It also possesses the strength of superior knowledge derived from its communication systems, its stores of accumulated data, its batteries of computers, its network of inspection and administration.

Where democratic institutions exist and the masses can vote their rulers out of office, the enormous powers with which science, technology, and the arts of organization have endowed the ruling minority are used with discretion and a decent regard for civil and political liberty. Where the masses can exercise no control over their rulers, these powers are used without compunction to enforce ideological orthodoxy and to strengthen the dictatorial state. The nature of science and technology is such that it is peculiarly easy for a dictatorial government to use them for its own anti-democratic purposes. Well financed, equipped and organized, an astonishingly small number of scientists and technologists can achieve prodigious results. The crash program that produced the A-bomb and ushered in a new historical era was planned and directed by some four thousand theoreticians, experimenters, and engineers. To parody the words of Winston Churchill, never have so many been so completely at the mercy of so few.

Throughout the nineteenth century the State was relatively feeble, and its interest in, and influence upon, scientific research were negligible. In our day the State is everywhere exceedingly powerful and a lavish patron of basic and *ad hoc* research. In Western Europe and North America the relations between the State and its scientists on the one hand and individual citizens, professional organizations, and industrial, commercial, and educational institutions on the other are fairly satisfactory. Advancing science, the population explosion, the armament race, and the steady increase and centralization of political and economic power are still compatible, in countries that have a libertarian tradition, with democratic forms of government. To maintain this compatibility in a rapidly changing world, bearing less and less resemblance to the world in which these democratic institutions were developed—this, quite obviously, is going to be increasingly difficult.

A rapid and accelerating population increase that will nullify the best efforts of underdeveloped societies to better their lot and will keep two-thirds of the human race in a condition of misery in anarchy or of misery under dictatorship, and the intensive preparations for a new kind of war that, if it breaks out, may bring irretrievable ruin to the one-third of the human race now living prosperously in highly industrialized societies—these are the two main threats to democracy now confronting us. Can these threats be eliminated? Or, if not eliminated, at least reduced?

My own view is that only by shifting our collective attention from the merely political to the basic biological aspects of the human situation can we hope to mitigate and shorten the time of troubles into which, it would seem, we are now moving. We cannot do without politics; but we can no longer afford to indulge in bad, unrealistic politics. To work for the survival of the species as a whole and for the actualization in the greatest possible number of individual men and women of their potentialities for good will, intelligence, and creativity—this, in the world of today, is good, realistic politics. To cultivate the religion of idolatrous nationalism, to subordinate the interests of the species and its individual members to the interests of a single national state and its ruling minority—in the context of the population explosion, missiles, and atomic warheads, this is bad and thoroughly unrealistic politics. Unfortunately, it is to bad and unrealistic politics that our rulers are now committed.

Ecology is the science of the mutual relations of organisms with their environment and with one another. Only when we get it into our collective head that the basic problem confronting twentieth-century man is an ecological problem will our politics improve and become realistic. How does the human race propose to survive and, if possible, improve the lot and the intrinsic quality of its individual members? Do we propose to live on this planet in symbiotic harmony with our environment? Or, preferring to be wantonly stupid, shall we choose to live like murderous and suicidal parasites that kill their host and so destroy themselves?

Committing that sin of overweening bumptiousness, which the Greeks called *hubris,* we behave as though we were not members of earth's ecological community, as though we were privileged and, in some sort, supernatural beings and could throw our weight around like gods. But in fact we are, among other things, animals—emergent parts of the natural order. If our politicians were realists, they would think rather less about missiles and the problem of landing a couple of astronauts on the moon, rather more about hunger and moral squalor and the problem of enabling three billion men, women, and children, who will soon be six billions, to lead a tolerably human existence without, in the process, ruining and befouling their planetary environment.

Animals have no souls; therefore, according to the most authoritative Christian theologians, they may be treated as though they were things. The truth, as we are now beginning to realize, is that even things ought not to be treated as *mere* things. They should be treated as though they were parts of a vast living organism. "Do as you would be done by." The Golden Rule applies to our dealings with nature no less than to our dealings with our fellow-men. If we hope to be well treated by nature, we must stop talking about "mere things" and start treating our planet with intelligence and consideration.

Power politics in the context of nationalism raises problems that, except by war, are practically insoluble. The problems of ecology, on the other hand, admit of a rational solution and can be tackled without the arousal of those violent passions always associated with dogmatic ideology and nationalistic idolatry. There may be arguments about the best way of raising wheat in a cold climate or of re-afforesting a denuded mountain. But such arguments never lead to organized slaughter. Organized slaughter is the result of arguments about such questions as the following: Which is the best nation? The best religion? The best political theory? The best form of government? Why are other people so stupid and wicked? Why can't they see how good and intelligent *we* are? Why do they resist our beneficent efforts to bring them under our control and make them like ourselves?

To questions of this kind the final answer has always been war. "War," said Clausewitz, "is not merely a political act, but also a political instrument, a continuation of political relationships, a carrying out of the same by other means." This was true enough in the eighteen thirties, when Clausewitz published his famous treatise; and it continued to be true until 1945. Now, pretty obviously, nuclear weapons, long-range rockets, nerve gases, bacterial aerosols, and the "Laser" (that highly promising, latest addition to the world's military arsenals) have given the lie to Clausewitz. All-out war with modern weapons is no longer a continuation of previous policy; it is a complete and irreversible break with previous policy.

Power politics, nationalism, and dogmatic ideology are luxuries that the human race can no longer afford. Nor, as a species, can we afford the luxury of ignoring man's ecological situation. By shifting our attention from the now completely irrelevant and anachronistic politics of nationalism and military power to the problems of the human species and the still inchoate politics of human ecology we shall be killing two birds with one stone—reducing the threat of sudden destruction by scientific war and at the same time reducing the threat of more gradual biological disaster.

The beginnings of ecological politics are to be found in the special services of the United Nations Organization. UNESCO, the Food and Agriculture Organization, the World Health Organization, the various Technical Aid Services—all these are, partially or completely, concerned with the ecological problems of the human species. In a world where political problems are thought of and worked upon within a frame of reference whose coordinates are nationalism and military power, these ecology-oriented organizations are regarded as peripheral. If the problems of humanity could be thought about and acted upon within a frame of reference that has survival for the species, the well-being of individuals, and the actualization of man's desirable potentialities as its coordinates, these peripheral organizations would become central. The subordinate politics of survival, happiness, and personal fulfillment would take the place now occupied by the politics of power, ideology, nationalistic idolatry, and unrelieved misery.

In the process of reaching this kind of politics we shall find, no doubt, that we have done something, in President Wilson's prematurely optimistic words, "to make the world safe for democracy."

February 1963

SOURCE. Aldous Huxley, *The Politics of Ecology*, Center for the Study of Democratic Institutions, The Fund for the Republic, Inc., Santa Barbara, 1963, pp. 1–7. Reprinted, with permission, from a publication of the Center for the Study of Democratic Institutions in Santa Barbara, Calif.

c. JEAN PAUL SARTRE, "FREEDOM AND RESPONSIBILITY"

JEAN PAUL SARTRE (born 1905) is perhaps the most widely known of the twentieth-century existentialists. In "Freedom and Responsibility," from his book Being and Nothingness, *Sartre presents some of his most important ethical ideas. Man is responsible for the world and for himself, Sartre argues, and man's responsibility is a necessary consequence of his freedom.*

Although the considerations which are about to follow are of interest primarily to the ethicist, it may nevertheless be worthwhile after these descriptions and arguments to return to the freedom of the for-itself and to try to understand what the fact of this freedom represents for human destiny.

The essential consequence of our earlier remarks is that man being condemned to be free carries the weight of the whole world on his shoulders; he is responsible for the world and for himself as a way of being. We are taking the world "responsibility" in its ordinary sense as "consciousness (of) being the incontestable author of an event or of an object." In this sense the responsibility of the for-itself is overwhelming since he is the one by whom it happens that *there is* a world; since he is also the one who makes himself be, then whatever may be the situation in which he finds himself, the for-itself must wholly assume this situation with its peculiar coefficient of adversity, even though it be insupportable. He must assume the situation with the proud consciousness of being the author of it, for the very worst disadvantages or the worst threats which can endanger my person have meaning only in and through my project; and it is on the ground of the engagement which I am that they appear. It is therefore senseless to think of complaining since nothing foreign has decided what we feel, what we live, or what we are.

Furthermore this absolute responsibility is not resignation; it is simply the logical requirement of the consequences of our freedom. What happens to me happens through me, and I can neither affect myself with it nor revolt against it nor resign myself to it. Moreover everything which happens to me is *mine*. By this we must understand first of all that I am always equal to what happens to me *qua* man, for what happens to a man through other men and through himself can be only human. The most terrible situations of war, the worst tortures do not create a non-human state of things; there is no non-human situation. It is only through fear, flight, and recourse to magical types of conduct that I shall decide on the non-human, but this decision is human, and I shall carry the entire responsibility for it. But in addition the situation is *mine* because it is the image of my free choice of myself, and everything which it presents to me is *mine* in that this represents me and symbolizes me. Is it not I who decide the coefficient of adversity in things and even their unpredictability by deciding myself?

Thus there are no *accidents* in a life; a community event which suddenly bursts forth and involves me in it does not come from the outside. If I am mobilized in a war, this war is *my* war; it is in my image and I deserve it. I deserve it first because I could always get out of it by suicide or by desertion; these ultimate possibilities are those which must always be present for us when there is a question of envisaging a situation. For lack of getting out of it, I have *chosen* it. This can be due to inertia, to cowardice in the face of public opinion, or because I prefer certain other values to the value of the refusal to join in the war (the good opinion of my relatives, the honor of my family, *etc.*). Anyway you look at it, it is a matter of a choice. This choice will be repeated later on again and again without a break until the end of the war. Therefore we must agree with the statement by J. Romains, "In war there are no innocent victims." If therefore I have preferred war to death or to dishonor, everything takes place as if I bore the entire responsibility for this war. Of course others have declared it, and one might be tempted perhaps to consider me as a simple accomplice. But this notion of complicity has only a juridical sense, and it does not hold here. For it depended on me that for me and by me this war should not exist, and I have decided that it does exist. There was no compulsion here, for the compulsion could have got no hold on a freedom. I did not have any excuse; for as we have said repeatedly in this book, the peculiar character of human-reality is that it is without excuse. Therefore it remains for me only to lay claim to this war.

But in addition the war is *mine* because by the sole fact that it arises in a situation which I cause to be and that I can discover it there only by engaging myself for or against it, I can no longer distinguish at present the choice which I make of myself from the choice which I make of the war. To live this war is to choose myself through it and to choose it through my choice of myself. There can be no question of considering it as "four years of vacation" or as a "reprieve," as a "recess," the essential part of my responsibilities being elsewhere in my married, family, or professional life. In this war which I have chosen I choose myself from day to day, and I make it mine by making myself. If it is going to be four empty years, then it is I who bear the responsibility for this.

Finally, as we pointed out earlier, each person is an absolute choice of self from the standpoint of a world of knowledges and of techniques which this choice both assumes and illumines; each person is an absolute upsurge at an absolute date and is perfectly unthinkable at another date. It is therefore a waste of time to ask what I should have been if this war had not broken out, for I have chosen myself as one of the possible meanings of the epoch which imperceptibly led to war. I am not distinct from this same epoch; I could not be transported to another epoch without contradition. Thus *I am* this war which restricts and limits and makes comprehensible the period which preceded it. In this sense we may define more precisely the responsibility of the for-itself if to the earlier quoted statement, "There are no innocent victims," we add the words, "We have the war we deserve." Thus, totally free, undistinguishable from the period for which I have chosen to be the meaning, as profoundly responsible for the war as if I had myself declared it, unable to live without integrating it in *my* situation, engaging myself in it wholly and stamping it with my seal, I must be without remorse or regrets as I am without excuse; for from the instant of my upsurge into being, I carry the weight of the world by myself alone without anything or any person being able to lighten it.

Yet this responsibility is of a very particular type. Someone will say, "I did not ask to be born." This is a naive way of throwing greater emphasis on our facticity. I am responsible for everything, in fact, except for my very responsibility, for I am not the foundation of my being. Therefore everything takes place as if I were compelled to be responsible. I am *abandoned* in the world, not in the sense that I might remain abandoned and passive in a hostile universe like a board floating on the water, but rather in the sense that I find myself suddenly alone and without help, engaged in a world for which I bear the whole responsibility without being able, whatever I do, to tear myself away from this responsibility for an instant. For I am responsible for my very desire of fleeing responsibilities. To make myself passive in the world, to refuse to act upon things and upon Others is still to choose myself, and suicide is one mode among others of being-in-the-world. Yet I find an absolute responsibility for the fact that my facticity (here the fact of my birth) is directly inapprehensible and even inconceivable, for this fact of my birth never appears as a brute fact but always across a projective reconstruction of my for-itself. I am ashamed of being born or I am astonished at it or I rejoice over it, or in attempting to get rid of my life I affirm that I live and I assume this life as bad. Thus in a certain sense I *choose* being born. This choice itself is integrally affected with facticity since I am not able not to choose, but this facticity in turn will appear only in so far as I surpass it toward my ends. Thus facticity is everywhere but inapprehensible; I never encounter anything except my responsibility. That is why I can not ask, "*Why* was I born?" or curse the day of my birth or declare that I did not ask to be born, for these various attitudes toward my birth— *i.e.*, toward the *fact* that I realize a presence in the world—are absolutely nothing else but ways of assuming this birth in full responsibility and of making it *mine*. Here again I encounter only myself and my projects so that finally my abandonment—*i.e.*, my facticity—consists simply in the fact that I am condemned to be wholly responsible for myself. I am the being which *is* in such a way that in its being its being is in question. And this "is" of my being *is* as present and inapprehensible.

Under these conditions since every event in the world can be revealed to me only as an *opportunity* (an opportunity made use of, lacked, neglected, *etc.*), of better yet since everything which happens to us can be considered as a *chance* (*i.e.*, can appear to us only as a way of realizing this being which is in question in our being) and since others as transcendences-transcended are themselves only *opportunities* and *chances,* the responsibility of the for-itself extends to the entire world as a peopled-world. It is precisely thus that the for-itself apprehends itself in anguish; that is, as a being which is neither the foundation of its own being nor of the Other's being nor of the in-itselfs which form the world, but a being which is compelled to decide the meaning of being—within it and everywhere outside of it. The one who realizes in anguish his condition as *being* thrown into a responsibility which extends to his very abandonment has no longer either remorse or regret or excuse; he is no longer anything but a freedom which perfectly reveals itself and whose being resides in this very revelation. But as we pointed out at the beginning of this work, most of the time we flee anguish in bad faith.

SOURCE. Jean Paul Sartre, *Being and Nothingness,* Hazel E. Barnes, tr., reprinted in *Existentialism and Human Emotion,* New York: Philosophical Library, 1957, pp. 52–59. Copyright 1957 by Philosophical Library Co., Inc. Reprinted by permission of the Philosophical Library Co., Inc., and Methuen & Co., London.

d. PAUL TILLICH ON ALIENATION AND RECONCILIATION

CHRISTIANITY HAS BEEN A CENTRAL PRINCIPLE in Western Civilization—as a creative organizing force, as a source of bloody sectarian struggle, as an inexhaustable reservoir of popular revivals, as a symbol of political and intellectual conservatism against which advanced non-Christian thinkers, ever since the eighteenth century, have oriented their new ideas and their revolutions. Christianity and its God have been pronounced dead repeatedly, yet today, as attendance drops in the established churches, it is soaring in college departments of religious studies. Something of a New Testament revival appears to be making inroads in the youth culture, and Jesus Christ has become a superstar. At a more traditional level, the neo-orthodox theologian Paul Tillich has used the Christian doctrines of sin and grace to elucidate the contemporary (and timeless) problem of alienation.

There are few words more strange to most of us than "sin" and "grace." They are strange, just because they are so well-known. During the centuries they have received distorting connotations, and have lost so much of their genuine power that we must seriously ask ourselves whether we should use them at all, or whether we should discard them as useless tools. But there is a mysterious fact about the great words of our religious tradition: they cannot be replaced. All attempts to make substitutions, including those I have tried myself, have failed to convey the reality that was to be expressed; they have led to shallow and impotent talk. There are no substitutes for words like "sin" and "grace". But there *is* a way of rediscovering their meaning, the same way that leads us down into the depth of our human existence. In that depth these words were conceived; and *there* they gained power for all ages; *there* they must be found again by each generation, and by each of us for himself. Let us therefore try to penetrate the deeper levels of our life, in order to see whether we can discover in them the realities of which our text speaks.

Have the men of our time still a feeling of the meaning of sin? Do they, and do we, still realize that sin does *not* mean an immoral act, that "sin" should never be used in the plural, and that not our sins, but rather our *sin* is the great, all-pervading problem of our life? Do we still know that it is arrogant and erroneous to divide men by calling some "sinners" and others "righteous"? For by way of such a division, we can usually discover that we ourselves do not *quite* belong to the "sinners", since we have avoided heavy sins, have made some progress in the control of this or that sin, and have been even humble enough not to call ourselves "righteous". Are we still able to realize that this kind of thinking and feeling about sin is far removed from what the great religious tradition, both within and outside the Bible, has meant when it speaks of sin?

I should like to suggest another word to you, not as a substitute for the word "sin", but as a useful clue in the interpretation of the word "sin": "separation". Separation is an aspect of the experience of everyone. Perhaps the word "sin" has the same root as the word "asunder". In any case, *sin is separation.* To be in the state of sin is to be in the state of separation. And separation is threefold: there is separation among individual lives, separation of a man from himself, and separation of all men from the Ground of Being. This three-fold separation constitutes the state of everything that exists; it is a universal fact; it is the fate of every life. And it is our human fate in a very special sense. For *we* as men know that we are separated. We not only suffer with all other creatures because of the self-destructive consequences of our separation, but also know *why* we suffer. We know that we are estranged from something to which we really belong, and with which we *should* be united. We know that the fate of separation is not merely a natural event like a flash of sudden lightning, but that it is an experience in which we actively participate, in which our whole personality is involved, and that, as fate, it is also *guilt.* Separation which is fate *and* guilt constitutes the meaning of the word "sin". It is *this* which is the state of our entire existence, from its very beginning to its very end. Such separation is prepared in the mother's womb, and before that time, in every preceding generation. It is manifest in the special actions of our conscious life. It reaches beyond our graves into all the succeeding generations. It is our existence itself. *Existence is separation!* Before sin is an act, it is a state.

We can say the same things about grace. For sin and grace are bound to each other. We do not even have a knowledge of sin unless we have already experienced the unity of life, which is grace. And conversely, we could not grasp the meaning of grace without having experienced the separation of life, which is sin. Grace is just as difficult to describe as sin. For some people, grace is the willingness of a divine king and father to forgive over and again the foolishness and weakness of his subjects and children. We must reject such a concept of grace; for it is a merely childish destruction of a human dignity. For others, grace is a magic power in the dark places of the soul, but a power without any significance for practical life, a quickly vanishing and useless idea. For others, grace is the benevolence that we may find beside the cruelty and destructiveness in life. But then, it does not matter whether we say "life goes on", or whether we say "there is grace in life"; if grace means no more than this, the word should, and will, disappear. For other people, grace indicates the gifts that one has received from nature or society, and the power to do good things with the help of those gifts. But grace is more than gifts. In grace something is overcome; grace occurs "in spite of" something; grace occurs in spite of separation and estrangement. Grace is the *re*union of life with life, the *re*conciliation of the self with itself. Grace is the acceptance of that which is rejected. Grace transforms fate into a meaningful destiny; it changes guilt into confidence and courage. There is something triumphant in the word "grace": in spite of the abounding of sin grace abounds much more.

And now let us look down into ourselves to discover there the struggle between separation and reunion, between sin and grace, in our relation to others, in our relation to ourselves, and in our relation to the Ground and aim of our being. If our souls respond to the description that I intend to give, words like "sin" and "separation," "grace" and "reunion," may have a new meaning for us. But the words themselves are not important. It is the response of the deepest levels of our being that is important. If such a response were to occur among us this moment, we could say that we have known grace.

Who has not, at some time, been lonely in the midst of a social event? The feeling of our separation from the rest of life is most acute when we are surrounded by it in noise and talk. We realize then much more than in moments of solitude how strange we are to each other, how estranged life is from life. Each one of us draws back into himself. We cannot penetrate the hidden centre of another individual; nor can that individual pass beyond the shroud that covers our own being. Even the greatest love cannot break through the walls of the self. Who has not experienced that disillusionment of all great love? If one were to hurl away his self in complete self-surrender, he would become a nothing, without form or strength, a self without self, merely an object of contempt and abuse. Our generation knows more than the generation of our fathers about the hidden hostility in the ground of our souls. Today we know much about the profusive aggressiveness in every being. Today we can confirm what Immanuel Kant, the prophet of human reason and dignity, was honest enough to say: there is something in the misfortune of our best friends which does not displease us. Who amongst us is dishonest enough to deny that this is true also of him? Are we not almost always ready to abuse everybody and everything, although often in a very refined way, for the pleasure of self-elevation, for an occasion for boasting, for a moment of lust? To know that we are ready is to know the meaning of the separation of life from life, and of "sin abounding".

The most irrevocable expression of the separation of life from life today is the attitude of social groups within nations towards each other, and the attitude of nations themselves towards other nations. The walls of distance, in time and space, have been removed by technical progress; but the walls of estrangement between heart and heart have been incredibly strengthened. The madness of the German Nazis and the cruelty of the lynching mobs in the South provide too easy an excuse for us to turn our thoughts from our own selves. But let us just consider ourselves and what we feel, when we read, this morning and tonight, that in some sections of Europe all children under the age of three are sick and dying, or that in some sections of Asia millions without homes are freezing and starving to death. The strangeness of life to life is evident in the strange fact that we can know all this, and yet can live today, this morning, tonight, as though we were completely ignorant. And I refer to the most sensitive people amongst us. In both mankind and nature, life is separated from life. Estrangement prevails among all things that live. Sin abounds.

It is important to remember that we are not merely separated from each other. For we are also separated from ourselves. *Man Against Himself* is not merely the title of a book, but rather also indicates the rediscovery of an age-old insight. Man is split within himself. Life moves against itself through aggression, hate, and despair. We are wont to condemn self-love; but what we really mean to condemn is contrary to self-love. It is that mixture of selfishness and self-hate that permanently pursues us, that prevents us from loving others, and that prohibits us from losing ourselves in the love with which we are loved eternally. He who is able to love himself is able to love others also; he who has learned to overcome self-contempt has overcome his contempt for others. But the depth of our separation lies in just the fact that we are not capable of a great and merciful divine love towards ourselves. On the contrary, in each of us there is an instinct of self-destruction, which is as strong as our instinct of self-preservation. In our tendency to abuse and destroy others, there is an open or hidden tendency to abuse and to destroy ourselves. Cruelty towards others is always also cruelty towards ourselves. Nothing is more obvious than the split in both our unconscious life and conscious personality. Without the help of modern psychology, Paul expressed the fact in his famous words, "For I do not do the good I desire, but rather the evil that I do not desire." And then he continued in words that might well be the motto of all depth psychology: "Now if I should do what I do not wish to do, it is not I that do it, but rather sin which dwells within me." The apostle sensed a split between his conscious will and his real will, between himself and something strange within and alien to him. He was estranged from himself; and that estrangement he called "sin". He also called it a strange "law in his limbs", an irresistible compulsion. How often we commit certain acts in perfect consciousness, yet with the shocking sense that we are being controlled by an alien power! That is the experience of the separation of ourselves from ourselves, which is to say "sin," whether or not we like to use that word.

Thus, the state of our whole life is estrangement from others and ourselves, because we are estranged from the Ground of our being, because we are estranged from the origin and aim of our life. And we do not know where we have come from, or where we are going. We are separated from the mystery, the depth, and the greatness of our existence. We hear the voice of that depth; but our ears are closed. We feel that something radical, total, and unconditioned is demanded of us; but we rebel against it, try to escape its urgency, and will not accept its promise.

We cannot escape, however. If that something is the Ground of our being, we are bound to it for all eternity, just as we are bound to ourselves and to all other life. We always remain in the power of that from which we are estranged. That fact brings us to the ultimate depth of sin: separated and yet bound, estranged and yet belonging, destroyed and yet preserved, the state which is called despair. Despair means that there is no escape. Despair is "the sickness unto death." But the terrible thing about the sickness of despair is that we cannot be released, not even through open or hidden suicide. For we all know that we are bound eternally and inescapably to the Ground of our being. The abyss of separation is not always visible. But it has become more visible to our generation than to the preceding generations, because of our feeling of meaninglessness, emptiness, doubt, and cynicism—all expressions of despair, of our separation from the roots and the meaning of our life. Sin in its most profound sense, sin, as despair, abounds amongst us.

"Where sin abounded, grace did much more abound", says Paul in the same letter in which he describes the unimaginable power of separation and self-destruction within society and the individual soul. He does not say these words because sentimental interests demand a happy ending for everything tragic. He says them because they describe the most overwhelming and determining experience of his life. In the picture of Jesus as the Christ, which appeared to him at the moment of his greatest separation from other men, from himself and God, he found himself accepted in spite of his being rejected. And when he found that he was accepted, he was able to accept himself and to be reconciled to others. The moment in which grace struck him and overwhelmed him, he was reunited with that to which he belonged, and from which he was estranged in utter strangeness. Do we know what it means to be struck by grace? It does *not* mean that we suddenly believe that God exists, or that Jesus is the Saviour, or that the Bible contains the truth. To believe that something *is,* is almost contrary to the meaning of grace. Furthermore, grace does not mean simply that we are making progress in our moral self-control, in our fight against special faults, and in our relationships to men and to society. Moral progress may be a fruit of grace; but it is not grace itself, and it can even prevent us from receiving grace. For there is too often a graceless acceptance of Christian doctrines and a graceless battle against the structures of evil in our personalities. Such a graceless relation to God may lead us by necessity either to arrogance or to despair. It would be better to refuse God and the Christ and the Bible than to accept Them without grace. For if we accept without grace, we do so in the state of separation, and can only succeed in deepening the separation. We cannot transform our lives, unless we allow them to be transformed by that stroke of grace. It happens; or it does not happen. And certainly it does *not* happen if we try to force it upon ourselves, just as it shall not happen so long as we think, in our self-complacency, that we have no need of it. Grace strikes us when we are in great pain and restlessness. It strikes us when we walk through the dark valley of a meaningless and empty life. It strikes us when we feel that our separation is deeper than usual, because we have violated another life, a life which we loved, or from which we were estranged. It strikes us when our disgust for our own being, our indifference, our weakness, our hostility, and our lack of direction and composure have become intolerable to us. It strikes us when, year after year, the longed-for perfection of life does not appear, when the old compulsions reign within us as they have for decades, when despair destroys all joy and courage. Sometimes at that moment a wave of light breaks into our darkness, and it is as though a voice were saying: "You are accepted. *You are accepted,* accepted by that which is greater than you, and the name of which you do not know. Do not ask for the name now; perhaps you will find it later. Do not try to do anything now; perhaps later you will do much. Do not seek for anything; do not perform anything; do not intend anything. *Simply accept the fact that you are accepted!*" If that happens to us, we experience grace After such an experience we may not be better than before, and we may not believe more than before. But everything is transformed. In that moment, grace conquers sin, and reconciliation bridges the gulf of estrangement. And nothing is demanded of this experience, no religious or moral or intellectual presupposition, nothing but *acceptance.*

In the light of this grace we perceive the power of grace in our relation to others and to ourselves. We experience the grace of being able to look frankly into the eyes of another, the miraculous grace of reunion of life with life. We experience the grace of understanding each other's words. We understand not merely the literal meaning of the words, but also that which lies behind them, even when they are harsh or angry. For even then there is a longing to break through the walls of separation. We experience the grace of being able to accept the life of another, even if it be hostile and harmful to us, for, through grace, we know that it belongs to the same Ground to which we belong, and by which we have been accepted. We experience the grace which is able to overcome the tragic separation of the sexes, of the generations, of the nations, of the races, and even the utter strangeness between man and nature. Sometimes grace appears in all these separations to reunite us with those to whom we belong. For life belongs to life.

And in the light of this grace we perceive the power of grace in our relation to ourselves. We experience moments in which we accept ourselves, because we feel that we have been accepted by that which is greater than we. If only more such moments were given to us! For it is such moments that make us love our life, that make us accept ourselves, not in our goodness and self-complacency, but in our certainty of the eternal meaning of our life. We cannot force ourselves to accept ourselves. We cannot compel anyone to accept himself. But sometimes it happens that we receive the power to say "yes" to ourselves, that peace enters into us and makes us whole, that self-hate and self-contempt disappear, and that our self is reunited with itself. Then we can say that grace has come upon us.

"Sin" and "grace" are strange words; but they are not strange things. We find them whenever we look into ourselves with searching eyes and longing hearts. They determine our life. They abound within us and in all of life. May grace more abound within us!

SOURCE. Paul Tillich, *The Shaking of the Foundations,* New York, Charles Scribner's Sons, 1948, pp. 153–163. Copyright 1948 Charles Scribner's Sons. Reprinted by permission of Charles Scribner's Sons and SCM Press Ltd., London.

e. LOVE OF MAN AND PRAISE OF GOD: DYLAN THOMAS, "POEM IN OCTOBER"

MANY PEOPLE REGARD Dylan Thomas (1914–1953) as the most exciting poet of the century. Thomas described himself in these words: "One: I am a Welshman; two: I am a drunkard; three: I am a lover of the human race, especially of women." All these things were true. But Dylan Thomas was also an intensely sensitive and self-aware individual, a consummate artist of the English language whose poems, although sometimes superficially obscure, are tightly packed with ideas and images. Like C. S. Lewis, Dylan Thomas was obsessed by the notion of man's fall from grace, and he was fond of evoking the innocence of childhood. The boundless imagination and remarkable descriptive powers of this inventive poet find full expression in his "Poem in October." Dylan Thomas' description of his own works captures an important element in the spirit of twentieth-century man: "These poems, with all their crudities, doubts, and confusions, are written for the love of Man and in praise of God, and I'd be a damn' fool if they weren't."

It was my thirtieth year to heaven
Woke to my hearing from harbour and neighbour wood
　　And the mussel pooled and the heron
　　　　Priested shore
　　　　The morning beckon
With water praying and call of seagull and rook
And the knock of sailing boats on the net webbed wall
　　　　Myself to set foot
　　　　That second
　　In the still sleeping town and set forth.

My birthday began with the water-
Birds and the birds of the winged trees flying my name
　　Above the farms and the white horses
　　　　And I rose
　　　　In rainy autumn
And walked abroad in a shower of all my days.
High tide and the heron dived when I took the road
　　　　Over the border
　　　　And the gates
　　Of the town closed as the town awoke.

A springful of larks in a rolling
Cloud and the roadside bushes brimming with whistling
    Blackbirds and the sun of October
            Summery
        On the hill's shoulder,
Here were fond climates and sweet singers suddenly
Come in the morning where I wandered and listened
        To the rain wringing
            Wind blow cold
    In the wood faraway under me.

    Pale rain over the dwindling harbour
And over the sea wet church the size of a snail
    With its horns through mist and the castle
            Brown as owls
        But all the gardens
Of spring and summer were blooming in the tall tales
Beyond the border and under the lark full cloud.
        There could I marvel
            My birthday
Away but the weather turned around.

    It turned away from the blithe country
And down the other air and the blue altered sky
    Streamed again a wonder of summer
            With apples
        Pears and red currants
And I saw in the turning so clearly a child's
Forgotten mornings when he walked with his mother
        Through the parables
            Of sun light
    And the legends of the green chapels

    And the twice told fields of infancy
That his tears burned my cheeks and his heart moved in mine.
    These were the woods the river and sea
            Where a boy
        In the listening
Summertime of the dead whispered the truth of his joy
To the trees and the stones and the fish in the tide.
        And the mystery
            Sang alive
    Still in the water and singingbirds.

And there could I marvel my birthday
Away but the weather turned around. And the true
   Joy of the long dead child sang burning
         In the sun.
      It was my thirtieth
Year to heaven stood there then in the summer noon
Though the town below lay leaved with October blood.
      O may my heart's truth
         Still be sung
On this high hill in a year's turning.

SOURCE. Dylan Thomas, *Collected Poems,* Norwalk, Conn.: New Directions, 1957, pp. 113–115. Copyright 1946 by New Directions. Reprinted by permission of New Directions Publishing Corp., J. M. Dent & Sons Ltd., and the Trustees for the Copyrights of the late Dylan Thomas.

ILLUSTRATION CREDITS

PART ONE

CHAPTER 3. a. Marburg—Art Reference Bureau; Alinari—Art Reference Bureau *Vatican Museum).* b. Cliché des Musées Nationaux, Louvre; Cliché des Musées Nationaux, Louvre.

PART TWO

CHAPTER 5. e. Art Reference Bureau *(By kind permission of National Monuments Record)*; Art Reference Bureau *(By kind permission of National Monuments Record; Copyright Warburg Institute).* f. Cliché des Musées Nationaux, Bordeaux; Courtesy, Museum of Fine Arts, Boston, S. A. Denio Collection; Courtesy, Museum of Fine Arts, Boston, Henry Lillie Pierce Collection.

PART THREE

CHAPTER 7. d. Courtesy of The University of Guadalajara.

PART FOUR

CHAPTER 8. b. The Bettmann Archive *(Louvre).*

PART FIVE

CHAPTER 11. a. Gamäldegalerie Neue Meister, Dresden. b. Kunsthistorische Museum, Vienna; National Gallery of Art, Washington, D. C., Chester Dale Collection. c. Philadelphia Museum of Art, W. P. Wilstach Collection; Courtauld Institute Galleries, London *(Lee Collection)*; Reproduced by Courtesy of the Trustees, The National Gallery, London; Collection, The Museum of Modern Art, New York, Acquired through the Lillie P. Bliss Bequest.

PART SIX

CHAPTER 13. c. Collection, The Museum of Modern Art, New York, A. Conger Goodyear Fund.

PART SEVEN

CHAPTER 21. a. Collection, The Museum of Modern Art, New York, Mrs. Simon Guggenheim Fund; Collection, The Museum of Modern Art, New York, Mrs. Simon Guggenheim Fund; Collection, The Museum of Modern Art, New York; Collection of Harry Torczyner, New York; Photo, The Museum of Modern Art, New York; Collection, The Museum of Modern Art, New York, Purchase; Collection, The Museum of Modern Art, New York, Advisory Committee Fund. b. From the Joseph H. Hirshhorn Collection; Collection, The Museum of Modern Art, New York, Von Gogh Purchase Fund. c. Hedrich—Blessing; French Government Tourist Office; Photograph by Rondal Partridge.